TEMPORARY WORKERS OR FUTURE CITIZENS?

Also by Myron Weiner

CRISES AND SEQUENCES IN POLITICAL DEVELOPMENT
(*co-author with L. Binder, J. Coleman, J. La Palombara, L. Pye and S. Verba*)
INDIA AT THE POLLS: The Parliamentary Elections of 1977
INDIA'S PREFERENTIAL POLICIES: Migrants, the Middle Classes and
Ethnic Equality
INTERNATIONAL MIGRATION AND SECURITY
PARTY BUILDING IN A NEW NATION: The Indian National Congress
PARTY POLITICS IN INDIA: The Development of a Multi-Party System
POLITICAL CHANGE IN SOUTH ASIA
POLITICS OF SCARCITY: Public Pressure and Political Response in India
SONS OF THE SOIL: Migration and Ethnic Conflict in India
THE CHILD AND THE STATE IN INDIA: Child Labor and Education Policy in
Comparative Perspective
THE GLOBAL MIGRATION CRISIS: Challenge to States and to Human Rights
THE INDIAN PARADOX: Essays in Indian Politics
THE NEW GEOPOLITICS OF CENTRAL ASIA AND ITS BORDERLANDS
THE POLITICS OF DEVELOPING AREAS (*co-author with Gabriel A. Almond
et al.*)
THREATENED PEOPLES, THREATENED BORDERS: World Migration and
US Policy

Also by Tadashi Hanami

EMPLOYMENT SECURITY: Law and Practice in Belgium, Bulgaria, France,
Germany, Great Britain, Italy, Japan and the European Community
INDUSTRIAL CONFLICT RESOLUTION IN MARKET ECONOMIES: A
Study of Australia, the Federal Republic of Germany, Italy, Japan and the USA
INDUSTRIAL RELATIONS AND HUMAN RESOURCE MANAGEMENT IN
JAPANESE ENTERPRISES IN EUROPE
LABOR LAW AND INDUSTRIAL RELATIONS IN JAPAN
LABOR LAW AND SOCIAL SECURITY
LABOR RELATIONS IN JAPAN TODAY
MANAGING JAPANESE WORKERS

Temporary Workers or Future Citizens?

Japanese and U.S. Migration Policies

Edited by

Myron Weiner
Ford International Professor of Political Science
Massachusetts Institute of Technology

and

Tadashi Hanami
Professor of Labour Law
Sophia University

NEW YORK UNIVERSITY PRESS
Washington Square, New York

First published in the U.S.A. in 1998 by
NEW YORK UNIVERSITY PRESS
Washington Square
New York, N.Y. 10003

This book is printed on paper suitable for recycling and
made from fully managed and sustained forest sources.

Library of Congress Cataloging-in-Publication Data
Temporary workers or future citizens? : Japanese and US migration
policies / edited by Myron Weiner and Tadashi Hanami.
p. cm.
Includes index.
ISBN 0–8147–9326–6
1. United States—Emigration and immigration—Government policy.
2. Alien labor—Government policy—United States.   3. Japan–
–Emigration and immigration—Government policy.   4. Alien labor–
–Government policy—Japan.   I. Weiner, Myron.   II. Hanami, Tadashi.
JV6483.T47 1997
331.6'2'0952—dc21   97–12526
                                                      CIP

Printed in Great Britain

Contents

List of Tables

List of Figures

Acknowledgments

The editors wish to express their appreciation to the Japan Foundation Center for Global Partnership whose grant to the MIT Center for International Studies made this project possible. We are also grateful to the Japan Institute of Labour for co-sponsoring the project and providing supplementary financial support. We wish to acknowledge the assistance provided by the members of the MIT Inter-University Committee on International Migration, William Alonso (Harvard), John Harris (Boston University), Robert Lucas (Boston University), Rosemarie Rogers (Fletcher School of Law and Diplomacy), Reed Ueda (Tufts), and at MIT Nazli Choucri, Karen Jacobsen, Elizabeth Leeds, Melissa Nobles, Jerome Rothenberg, and Sharon Stanton Russell. At the Japan Institute of Labour we are grateful to Osamu Hirota, Counsellor for Foreign Affairs who served as liaison, and to his assistant, Kumiko Ogino, who helped organize our workshop in Tokyo.

We wish to thank the scholars who commented on the papers presented at the workshop held at MIT in November 1994, John Harris (Boston University) and Rosemarie Rogers (Fletcher School of Law and Diplomacy), and at the workshop held in Tokyo in June 1995, Keisuke Nakamura (Musashi University), Hiroshi Honma (Surugadai University), Kazuo Koike (Hosei University), Hiroshi Komai (Tsukuba University), Akira Takanashi (Japan Institute of Labour), Yoko Tanaka (UN Center for Regional Development), and Manabu Hatakeyama (Ministry of Justice).

For other assistance we are grateful to Haruo Shimada (Keio University), Sadako Ogata (UNHCR), Susumu Yamagami (Ministry of Justice), Sisters Nobuko Morimura and Mary Blish (University of the Sacred Heart), Sisters Machiko Yamashita and Setsuko Miyoshi (Sacred Heart School, Obayashi), Yuri Oiwa (*Asahi Shimbun*), Mary Lea Cox and Makoto Segi (Japan Foundation Center for Global Partnership in Tokyo), Ray K. Tsuchiyama (MIT Office of Corporate Relations in Tokyo), and at MIT Ronald Dore, Richard Samuels, my research assistants Cathy Scholz and Linda Kato, and Leah Anderson and Robert Davine at the Center for International Studies.

Our very special thanks to Lois Malone in the Department of Political Science at MIT who served as the overall coordinator of the project and as editorial assistant.

MYRON WEINER
TADASHI HANAMI

List of Contributors

Professor Thomas U. Berger, Department of Political Science, The Johns Hopkins University, Baltimore, Maryland

Professor Barry R. Chiswick, Department of Economics, University of Illinois at Chicago, Illinois

Professor Wayne A. Cornelius, University of California at San Diego, San Diego, California

Professor Nathan Glazer, Department of Sociology, Harvard University, Cambridge, Massachusetts

Professor Tadashi Hanami, School of Law, Sophia University, Tokyo

Professor Yasushi Iguchi, Faculty of Economics, Kwansei Gakuin University, Nishinomiya

Professor Takamichi Kajita, Hitotsubashi University, Faculty of Social Sciences, Tokyo

Professor Kazutoshi Koshiro, Faculty of Economics, Yokohama National University, Yokohama

Professor Yasuo Kuwahara, Department of Economics, Dokkyo University, Tokyo

Professor Peter H. Schuck, Yale University Law School, New Haven, Connecticut

Professor Isami Takeda, Dokkyo University, Faculty of Foreign Studies, Tokyo

Michael S. Teitelbaum, Alfred P. Sloan Foundation, New York City

Professor Motoko Tsuchida, Department of Political Science, Sophia University, Tokyo

Professor Reed Ueda, Tufts University, Department of History, Medford, Massachusetts

Professor Myron Weiner, Department of Political Science, Massachusetts Institute of Technology, Cambridge, Massachusetts

Part I
Introduction

1 Opposing Visions: Migration and Citizenship Policies in Japan and the United States

Myron Weiner

In the mid-1980s Japanese bureaucrats, politicians, the media and the public took notice of an increasing number of foreigners illegally living and working in Japan. The number was not particularly large – only about 300 000 persons – but their very presence was an occasion for much public discussion. Why had they come? Did Japan need foreign workers for jobs that Japanese did not want? Why had the demand for foreign workers arisen and what was different now from earlier? But to many Japanese the central question was, could Japanese learn to live with foreigners in their midst? Japan was, of course, experiencing a "crisis" – if one can call it that – familiar to other advanced industrial countries experiencing an influx of migrants. In the mid-1980s there was also a growing public concern over illegal migration to the United States and by the early 1990s there was a public debate over the impact of migrants, both legal and illegal, upon employment and social services. Similarly, European governments and publics have been concerned over the influx of asylum seekers and there has been much uncertainty as to how best to deal with guest workers and their families who have permanently settled.

In at least two respects, the situation in Japan is different from that in the United States and other advanced industrial societies. The first is that Japan has the lowest proportion of foreigners of any major industrial country, 1.3 million in a population of 123 million, or 1.1 percent. In virtually every industrial society the percentage of foreign-born or non-nationals is between 3 and 8 percent, in some cases substantially more. It is 8.6 percent in the United States, the same in Germany, 6.4 percent in France, 9.5 percent in Sweden, 3.3 percent in the UK, 4.6 percent in the Netherlands, 6.6 percent in Austria, 9.1 percent in Belgium, 18 percent in Switzerland, 23.4 percent in Australia and 15.1 percent in Canada. While there has been a movement against migration in most of these countries, opposition did not arise until economic growth slowed in the 1980s, unemployment increased, and, in several countries, claims for asylum accelerated. In contrast, Japanese anxieties grew in the midst of an economic boom, low unemployment, and, compared with Western Europe and North America, a low migration rate.

The second difference between Japan and other industrial countries is in the history of absorption of migrants. Japan may be expected to differ from traditional countries of immigration such as the United States, Canada and Australia, but Japan also differs from the so-called non-immigrant countries of Western Europe, several of which are, like Japan, regarded as homogeneous nation-states. European countries have in fact been host to migrants, many of whom subsequently became citizens. In the mid-nineteenth century, for example, migrant workers from Belgium, Italy and Poland staffed the mines and factories in which French peasants were reluctant to work and during the inter-war periods Czechs, Ukrainians and more Poles came to France. Many of these migrants stayed on to become French citizens. Indeed, many French have one or more foreign-born grandparents. Even Germany, with its concept of *jus sanguinis* citizenship and restrictive naturalization laws, incorporated Poles and other Central and East European migrant workers who settled in the early part of this century. Though the process of absorption and naturalization in Western Europe is now more complex and contentious, the locally born children of migrants have been incorporated into citizenship in France, the United Kingdom and in several other European countries – although not in Germany.

In its attitude toward the incorporation of foreigners, Japan remains an outlier. From the Meiji restoration until the onset of the Second World War, Japan was a labor-exporting country, as were most European countries. Japanese migrated to the west coast of the United States, to Hawaii, Brazil, Argentina, Bolivia, Uruguay and Peru, and to the Japanese colonies of Manchuria, Korea and Taiwan. In the 1930s, however, Japan began to import workers from Korea to meet labor shortages as its own young men were drawn into the military. For the first time in its modern history Japan had a significant non-indigenous minority. Koreans were guest workers – "corvée labor" may be a more accurate description – imported to meet short-term labor needs. When the war ended many of the Koreans went home, but many decided to remain rather than return to their own war-torn and divided country. Under a 1965 agreement with the government of South Korea, the Japanese government granted permanent residence status to the Koreans in Japan, who were to retain their Korean citizenship. Of the 700 000 Koreans in Japan in the 1980s, approximately 75 percent were born in Japan. Except for those who married Japanese, few Koreans have become Japanese citizens.

Thus, Japan has a history of non-incorporation of foreigners and a level of anxiety toward the presence of a small number of foreign workers that is unusual even for a country that is not a traditional country of immigration. Japan clearly approaches the issues of migration and citizenship in a historic and cultural context that is different from that of other industrial democracies. Japan remains ill at ease with the notion that individuals not of Japanese origin can become Japanese. At the same time, Japan also remains uncertain as to how to deal with the demand by its employers for unskilled manpower, how to cope with an increase in illegal migrants, whether to liberalize naturalization laws, and what Japan's responsibilities are with respect to the global increase in refugees. In the most general sense, the issue for Japan is whether and how it can reconcile employer demands for labor and its own notion of collective identity.

To address these issues, the Massachusetts Institute of Technology (MIT) Center for International Studies, in conjunction with the Japan Institute of Labour (JIL), organized two symposia of Japanese and American scholars to consider the ways in which Japan and the United States deal with immigration, refugees, illegal migration and citizenship policies. Japan has given a higher priority to cultural and social than to economic considerations in determining how best to satisfy a structural economic need and has, therefore, stood virtually alone among the industrial countries outside any of the global international migration systems. In contrast, the United States, whose cultural and social system has a high capacity to absorb peoples of other societies, continues to admit a larger number of migrants than any other industrial society (though it is average in percentage terms) and to admit significant numbers of refugees. In their approach to issues of migration, therefore, Japan and the United States represent polar cases. The object of the MIT/JIL symposia was to explore these differences and to understand how each country is responding to global and domestic pressures to expand migration.

With financial support from the Japan Foundation Center for Global Partnership, the Japanese and American participants met in Cambridge, Massachusetts, in December 1994 and again in Tokyo in June 1995. At these symposia the papers included in this volume were presented and discussed. The discussion often went beyond the papers, not only drawing comparisons but revealing the views, conjectures and concerns of the American and Japanese participants that cautious academics do not readily incorporate into their scholarly writings. In this introductory chapter I shall recapitulate some of the themes of the papers and of the discussions that followed their presentation.

COLLECTIVE IDENTITY

In choosing migrants, the United States is choosing its future citizens. The widely held American view is that individuals admitted as immigrants ought to be and can be incorporated into the American society, economy and polity. This is an assumption of human pliability, that foreigners can become American by living in the United States, and that their children, through the impact of the educational system and popular culture, can become Americanized. The traditional American conception of incorporation into the collective identity is that newcomers should adopt the American civic code with its notions of egalitarianism (equality of opportunity and personal respect as distinct from equality of condition), individualism, liberty, and populism or the rule of the people. The traditional widely held American self-image is of a society that emphasizes nonconformism, individual and group variations, and an acceptance of conflict and adversarial relations as part of the country's pluralism.

The Japanese collective identity, on the other hand, emphasizes the importance of the group, an ethic of harmony and primordialism. The Japanese, like the Americans, emphasize their uniqueness (*Nihonron*), but while the American conception of uniqueness is a principled universalism (others can be like us), the Japanese sense of uniqueness is a principled denial of any universal mission (no one can be like us). The comparative sociologist, Shmuel Eisenstadt, writes of the Japanese collective identity as being characterized by principled primordiality: the Japanese view of immigration rests on their self-image as a country whose members can trace their lineage to an antique past, with "Japaneseness" more than a matter of race (though it is clearly that), residing in qualities that are inbred, inherent, even divine, and that therefore cannot be acquired by others no matter how long they reside on the Japanese islands. Until the middle of the nineteenth century, when Perry's black ships arrived, Japan regarded itself as an insular society, prepared to borrow from others, but without a vision of itself as part of a larger world. Even after the Meiji restoration when Japan set out to internationalize itself, borrowing from Europe and the United States in an effort to create a modern society and economy capable of sustaining its independence and competing in world markets, the Japanese continued to maintain an insular view of themselves as a unique culture and society that others might not fully understand and into which others could certainly never be incorporated.

In contrast with the American view that anyone can become an American, the Japanese view is that no one not born Japanese can become Japanese. One can become American by conversion, so to speak, but one cannot become Japanese by conversion. Thus, with respect to immigrants, the Japanese exclude the possibility of assimilation, while Americans regard assimilation into an American creed (if not culture) as both desirable and possible. These notions of collective identity – inclusiveness, universalistic, assimilative on the one hand, and

exclusiveness, particularistic, primordialist on the other –
shape how the two cultures deal with the issues of migration.
To these generalizations there are important qualifications
that we shall subsequently provide, but it is important to
recognize these fundamental differences.

THE HISTORICAL EXPERIENCES

Historically, the United States recruited migrants to fill its vast
western territories and to serve as the labor force for its expanding industries. Migration policies were underlined by a
widely shared ideology that believed diversity could be a
source of creativity. Nonetheless, as Reed Ueda points out,
migration was never fully open, for there were always political
and cultural concerns by both elites and the masses over its
implications for American national identity. The harshest restrictions were directed against Japanese and Chinese workers,
who were prevented from bringing their spouses and were
denied the opportunity to become naturalized citizens. These
and other restrictions limiting the entrance of Asians were not
eliminated until the 1952 Immigration and Nationality
Act ended racial barriers to immigration and the 1965
Immigration Act allocated 20 000 immigration visas annually
to every country. Today, many if not most Americans look
upon immigration as an important element in the United
States' capacity to innovate and to compete globally. It is
widely noted that a high proportion of American Nobel prize
winners are migrants or the children of migrants and that very
many of the country's engineers, scientists and professionals
are of foreign origin. At MIT, a quarter of the freshman class,
and at the University of California, Berkeley half the entering
class, are Asian-Americans. Ueda reminds us that migrants
have not only made an enormous contribution to the American
economic growth and to technological innovation, but have
also helped to define a distinctive American nationality that
incorporates ethnic pluralism.

In contrast, Japanese regard their ethnic homogeneity as a
major contributing factor to their post-war economic miracle
and are fearful of any immigration policy that would dilute
their homogeneity and its accompanying collective spirit and

group harmony. It is for this reason, as we shall see, that virtually all discussions of migration to Japan assume that migrants should be temporary residents, that some kind of rotation system should be in place, and that whoever is allowed to enter to work, skilled or unskilled, should remain only for a brief period and then return home.

Nathan Glazer, a distinguished contributor to the analysis of ethnic pluralism, notes that since the mid-1980s there has been a reconceptualization of migrant incorporation in the United States as a result of the rise of the notion of multiculturalism. It is, says Glazer, no longer clear what migrant absorption means in a society that has become uncertain of what it means to be an American. Paradoxically, he suggests, the growth of multiculturalism has alarmed many Americans who fear that the new migrants will not be assimilated and that American society will become ever more fragmented. The concern may be misplaced (the children of migrants learn English quickly and become absorbed by American popular culture), but it may be an important element in the growing public anxieties over migration and the call for designating English as the "official" language apart from a concern about the impact of migration on employment and social services.

Motoko Tsuchida describes how Japan made the transition from being a country of emigration to one having immigrants. In the latter part of the nineteenth century, economic distress led many Japanese farmers to respond to offers from labor recruiters from Guam and Hawaii seeking workers for the sugar cane plantations. Many Japanese also emigrated to California where they encountered fierce resistance; this anti-Japanese sentiment led to national legislation restricting the admission of Asians. As entrance into the United States became more difficult, Japanese migrated to Peru, Brazil and subsequently to Manchuria, this last migration being promoted by the Japanese government which hoped to settled 5 million Japanese over a period of 20 years in order to solidify its political and military control of the colony.

Japan's economic boom after the Second World War did not lead to the recruitment of foreign workers, as it did in Western Europe. Japanese who lived in the colonies returned home, where they resupplied the labor force and Japanese employers were still able to turn to the agricultural sector to recruit low-skilled workers. Companies that required unskilled and semi-skilled labor unavailable within Japan were encouraged to move their plants abroad. Japan's automobile industry created platforms in South Korea for the production of components; in the 1980s Japanese firms expanded into Indonesia, Thailand, Singapore and Malaysia; foreign investment and the employment of labor abroad became, in effect, a substitute for the importation of labor. The Japanese government, working with Japanese industries, encouraged the development of technologies to reduce the demand for unskilled workers in manufacturing, thus removing the need for immigrants. Alone among the advanced industrial countries, Japan entered the 1980s with a nearly homogeneous population, no large number of foreign workers, and no significant ethnic cleavages.

The term internationalization (*kokusaika*) became widely used in the 1970s and 1980s. For many Japanese it meant learning English, traveling abroad, keeping up with advanced industrial societies, acquiring the latest state-of-the-art technology, and fully participating in the global economy and in international institutions. What it did not mean was the incorporation of foreigners into Japanese society and becoming ethnically diverse.

THE NEW DEMAND FOR MIGRANT WORKERS

Why some Japanese employers sought foreign workers in the economic boom of the mid-80s is clear. One factor is the virtual disappearance of the labor reserve in agriculture. The traditional source of labor for work widely regarded in Japan as "dirty, dangerous and demanding" – the "3D" jobs or in Japanese the "3K" jobs, *kitanai, kiken* and *kitsui* – was farmers made idle by winter, but this source was no longer available as agriculture dwindled to a small share of the Japanese economy. Japan had become an urban, middle-class society and few of its young people were willing to take low-skilled, low-wage jobs. The result was an increase in the cost of low-skilled labor. A second factor is a change in the country's age structure: as a result of declining fertility rates Japan has proportionately fewer young people and more elderly. The rising dependency ratio has meant a tightened labor market and higher wages. A third factor is the continued demand for low-skilled labor in selected areas of the Japanese economy – in construction, the low-productivity service sector and in small-scale industries. Many small firms that supply components to larger industries have been in danger of failure unless they can keep wages down and compete with firms abroad. In spite of a government ban on the employment of unskilled guest workers, small manufacturing companies and the construction industry began to recruit foreign labor.

In 1990 the New Immigration Control and Refugee Act was passed, imposing penalties on employers who recruited illegal workers, a fine of up to 2 million yen and 3 years' imprisonment. It permitted the employment of professional and skilled workers from abroad, but excluded hiring workers for restaurants, pubs, hotels, motels and, more generally, any unskilled workers. The legislation failed to halt the influx of illegal workers. Since construction firms often employed illegal migrants in remote areas of the country, they were not easily detected by the police; for many companies it was easier to employ low-paid illegal migrants than to invest in high-technology equipment. The media reported a growing number of foreign disco dancers, waitresses, hostesses and massage parlor prostitutes. Many of the migrant workers, who came from Thailand, the Philippines, Pakistan, China and Iran, entered legally on entertainment visas, as tourists and as students, then stayed on illegally. As in the United States, illegal workers live in the shadow of the law but with fewer public benefits or opportunities for mobility.

According to economist Kazutoshi Koshiro, Japan's labor force (those between the ages of 15 and 59) in the next decade will increase by 4.1 million, or 7 percent, while those over the age of 65 will increase by 2.3 million, or 25 percent. Labor shortages are expected in the service sector, including the care of the aged, and in construction. As the labor market grows tighter, says Koshiro, employers will continue to seek workers from abroad, although the employment of the elderly, increased labor force participation by women, and the application of technology to the service sector are expected to reduce the need for foreign workers. Still, concludes Koshiro, the Japanese economy may need a half-million additional workers each year after 2000. The Ministry of Labour has opposed the importation of immigrant workers and called instead for increasing automation, the extension of the mandatory retirement age, the greater use of female labor, a more efficient use of labor in the service sector, and the export of some production facilities to other Asian countries. The Ministry is particularly concerned with the political and social consequences of a more heterogeneous labor force and the pressures that would arise for admitting spouses and children were foreign workers permitted to stay in Japan for any extended period. The Ministry of Justice is similarly opposed to admitting foreign workers, arguing that immigrants have a higher crime rate than Japanese.

Economist Barry Chiswick rejects the notion that the Japanese and the US economies "need" foreign workers for jobs that natives do not want. He argues that with higher real wages and better working conditions more native labor would be forthcoming, that there are substitutes for the use of labor, that some production facilities could be moved abroad, and that technologies could make jobs more attractive. Chiswick offers a three-factor model incorporating capital, less-skilled labor (engaged in "3D" jobs) and more-skilled labor (white collar professionals, technical and managerial workers, etc.). He concludes that "in terms of maximizing the income of the native population, the optimal level of immigration would be highest if the immigrants are skilled workers, lower if they are unskilled workers but do not receive income transfers (such as welfare benefits), and lowest (possibly negative) if the immigrants were unskilled and receive income transfers on the same basis as the native population." Applying this analysis to economies with high levels of inequality (such as the United States) or of crowding (such as Japan), he argues that the United States should focus on high-skilled permanent immigrants and avoid low-skilled migrants, while Japan would benefit most from guest worker policies in both low- and high-skilled labor markets, notwithstanding leakage as some temporary workers become permanent residents.

It should be noted that US legal immigration is largely independent of the demands of the labor market. American migration policy is based on the principle of family unification: parents, minor children and (until recently) siblings were given preference, and these categories consumed an overwhelming proportion of the annual quota. (Barely 15 percent of migrants enter the United States under the skill categories.) Family unification is discouraged by Japanese policy makers precisely because it induces permanent settlement.

RIGHTS AND BENEFITS

Sociologist Takamichi Kajita distinguishes among three groups of immigrants in Japan: Koreans numbering nearly 700 000, most of whom were brought to Japan before the Second World War; *Nikkeijin* – overseas migrants and their descendants who were actively recruited to return to Japan mainly from Peru and Brazil – numbering about 190 000; and the more recent migrants from Asia, about 300 000, most of whom are in Japan illegally. Koreans residing in Japan have permanent residence status and *Nikkeijin* may also remain as "long-term residents" with the right work. Tadashi Hanami notes that foreigners with work permits are covered by most of Japan's protective labor laws, including medical insurance, survivor's benefits and the like. Except for those who are permanent residents, foreigners with temporary work permits are not entitled to pensions, although they are required to pay into the pension fund. (They can, however, receive a lump-sum payment after they leave Japan.) Nor are foreigners with work permits entitled to unemployment benefits.

Japanese participants in the symposia agreed that discrimination against foreigners is a fact of life in Japan. Landlords often will not rent to foreigners, including long-term Korean residents and Japanese-born Koreans, and foreigners are generally excluded from employment in local government offices and complain of discrimination in employment. Hanami notes that there are no laws in Japan that effectively deal with discrimination against foreigners in employment and that the courts lack the means to protect foreigners in housing, employment and education. Illegal migrants are excluded from all benefits and have difficulty obtaining medical care; employers may dismiss workers who become ill, or at best, arrange for their return to their home country. Working conditions are also often unsatisfactory for illegal workers.

While 1.1 percent of Japan's population is foreign born, 8.6 percent of the US population, more than 20 million people, is foreign born and approximately 800 000 migrants legally enter the United States yearly. The continued influx of immigrants, writes Peter Schuck, is changing the ethnic and racial composition of the United States, so that by the year 2020 people of Hispanic descent will rise to 15.7 percent, blacks will constitute 13.9 percent, and Asians and Pacific islanders 6.9 percent. Schuck reviews the evolution of migrant laws since the latter part of the nineteenth century, the sweeping changes in admissions and migration enforcement with the passage of the Immigration Reform and Control Act of 1986, and the Immigration Act of 1990.

The principle difference, writes Schuck, between Japan and the United States with respect to the rights of migrants is in the conditions under which citizenship is granted. Though Japan does have procedures for naturalization, relatively few foreigners (221 000 between 1952 and 1992) out of 1 320 000 foreigners in the country have been naturalized; the children of noncitizens do not acquire citizenship by being born in Japan. In the United States, citizenship is based upon birth in the United States, through descent from one or more American parents, or through naturalization. There are differences in the legal rights and benefits between legal permanent resident aliens and American citizens. Legal permanent resident aliens may not vote, run for high office, or be appointed to some government positions, nor can they sponsor family members for immigration as easily as can American citizens. There are also restrictions on their use of state and federal benefit programs, but given the relative ease with which citizenship can be obtained in the US, these limitations, writes Schuck, need only be temporary. Moreover, asylum seekers can have access to many government benefits as they wait for their asylum review and they are free to seek employment. The United States also provides temporary protected status to aliens who cannot obtain refugee status under the terms of the UN Convention on Refugees. Even illegal migrants receive some benefits, for the Supreme Court has ruled that illegal alien children cannot be barred from attending public schools. Whether the Court's reasoning on this case is applicable to other efforts to restrict benefits provided illegal migrants remains to be determined. It should be noted that children born in the United States of illegal aliens are citizens at birth. It should also be noted that legislation passed in 1986 granted amnesty to a large number (about 3 million) of illegal migrants. Many features of immigrant policy are now contested, some by state legislatures, others by the federal government – particularly the right of illegal migrants and resident aliens to public benefits and the distribution of immigrant-related costs between federal, state and local governments. It is clear, however, that, overall, aliens in the United States, including asylum seekers and even illegal migrants, have greater access to naturalized citizenship, to social benefits and to protection against discrimination than is the case for aliens in Japan, notwithstanding that some of these benefits are now politically contested.

THE RELEVANCE OF THE GERMAN EXPERIENCE

Japanese officials and scholars have been particularly interested in the German approach to migration and to citizenship, since on these issues Japan appears to be more like Germany than the United States. The papers by Thomas Berger and Yasushi Iguchi explore this comparison. In both countries citizenship is based on ties of blood, and both countries have had difficulties accepting foreigners. The principal difference is that Germany has had considerable experience with foreign workers in the post-war era, while Japan has not. Many of the issues raised in Germany resonate in Japanese discussions: whether the presence of foreign workers increases unemployment for German workers or helps to overcome bottlenecks in the labor market and thereby increase employment; whether foreign workers contribute to economic growth or slow the structural evolution of the German economy; whether foreign workers burden the German welfare system; whether there are high social costs as a result of the social divisions between Germans and foreign workers; whether foreigners commit a disproportionate number of crimes; whether the presence of foreigners has generated social tensions in German society and stimulated the growth of right-wing xenophobic political groups; and, finally, whether a system of temporary guest-worker migration will result in a substantial permanent foreign population. Berger points out that many Japanese look upon the German experience as a warning that Japan ought not to follow a similar route.

Professor Yasushi Iguchi, himself a former official of the Japanese Labour Ministry concerned with migration policy, describes the disagreement between the Ministry of Labour and Ministry of Justice in the late 1980s, when the demand was growing to admit unskilled foreign workers. The Labour Ministry supported an institutionalization of a limited employment permit scheme while the Ministry of Justice was eager to take more forceful measures to deal with illegal employment. Many influential members of the Liberal Democratic Party (LDP), the Tokyo Chamber of Commerce, and the Ministry of Labour supported proposals for a system that would permit foreign workers to enter for short-term periods to acquire skills while they work. Iguchi's own view, drawing from the German experience, is that Japan should severely restrict the number of foreign workers admitted, that they be limited to skilled personnel and not simply be responsive to labor market tests, and that one must consider the country's capacity to integrate, "either in the labor market or in society."

Though there is support in Japan from sections of the business community for a variety of temporary guest-worker programs – usually described as "training programs" that combine training and employment – opponents of guest-worker programs have pointed to the experiences of West Germany, France and Switzerland who found that the programs left a legacy of permanent settlers because the governments lacked the procedures and political will to make them temporary. They point to the social costs, the problems of integrating minorities, the costs of housing, education and social services, and to the potential for ethnic conflict as reasons for not following the European model. They also argue that migrants are not needed, that the use of robots, highly mechanized equipment, and factory and office automation can reduce the need for unskilled labor in both the manufacturing and construction industries, while labor intensive industries can be transferred to developing countries where low-wage unskilled workers are readily available. Most trade union officials also oppose the use of guest workers on the grounds that it will result in a secondary labor market whose workers would be outside the trade union movement, and that a dual labor market would result in a general depression of wage levels for all workers.

MIGRATION CONTROLS

The question for many Japanese is whether the government can actually prevent the entry of illegal immigrants looking for unskilled jobs. Although the number of foreigners illegally residing in Japan is still small, it is for the Japanese an indicator of future flows. Even the slowdown in the economy and a rise in unemployment after 1990 failed to reduce the number of visa overstayers, though, as Yasuo Kuwahara pointed out, the effect of the recession was to silence those Japanese who called for a wider opening to foreign workers. Kuwahara reports that illegal migrants are largely employed in small companies in manufacturing, construction and services at wages below those that most Japanese are prepared to accept. He does not believe that a policy of legalization or the use of training programs for semi-skilled labor would reduce the number of illegal migrants. He is also concerned that by permitting significant numbers of foreign workers to enter the country many small companies will become dependent upon them. Although the Japanese government hopes to reduce the flow of illegal migrants by promoting the greater use of labor-saving machinery (i.e. the replacement of labor with capital), Kuwahara argues that without government assistance small firms cannot afford the use of new technologies. He is also doubtful that more effective border controls would reduce the number of illegal migrants or whether employer sanctions will work unless there is far more rigorous enforcement of labor standards.

Wayne Cornelius, drawing from his own research on the control of illegal immigration in the United States, describes what he calls the "get-tough" approach to immigration control, including increased border enforcement and proposals for creating a new employment eligibility verification system. After reviewing the experiences of recent efforts at border enforcement – albeit at limited points along the US/Mexican border – Cornelius concludes that if borders are controlled at one point, illegal migrants will move elsewhere along the borders. "Every time we do something, they do something," he reports as the comment of one Immigration and Naturalization Service official, who noted (with some admiration!) the skill with which Mexicans succeeded in crossing the border. Cornelius suggests that border enforcement serves to increase the propensity of some temporary illegal migrants to remain permanently in the United States rather than risk apprehension at the border.

Cornelius is similarly skeptical that denying illegal immigrants access to social services would deter migrants. Illegal residents are already denied access to many social services and few take advantage of those that are available, except for free schooling and access to emergency medical facilities; more significantly, he notes, most surveys conducted in migrants' communities of origin reveal that access to social services plays a very minor role in decisions to cross the border. Jobs, higher wages and family ties are the principal reasons for the move. However, access to social services may play a role in decisions not to return.

Worksite enforcement, suggests Cornelius, is the alternative possibility, much underutilized in the United States. He argues that it can be more effective in reducing illegal migration were labor standards better enforced, including occupational safety and minimum wage laws. Cornelius notes that illegal migrants are now dispersed throughout the economy, geographically and sectorially, that they are employed in sectors of the economy where it is difficult to enforce any labor laws (landscape maintenance, domestic services, messenger and package delivery services, small industrial sweat shops, etc.). The public is also hostile to rounding up and deporting individual illegal migrants – "valued employees, co-workers, neighbors, classmates, fellow church members."

Cornelius reviews alternative proposals. These include the creation of a new temporary guest-worker program (politically unacceptable and probably unworkable), and an expansion of trade and investment in Mexico as a means of reducing the pressure to emigrate for employment (a policy with long-term rather than short-term benefits). Cornelius concludes that "any policy option now being touted in the United States as both a politically realistic and efficacious instrument for controlling illegal immigration, especially from Mexico, must be greeted with a strong dose of skepticism." It is, he argues, "fundamental market forces, demographic pressures and transborder family networks that drive most illegal migration to the United States today."

Not all the US participants in the symposia agreed with Cornelius that illegal migration could not be significantly controlled, though no one argued that it could ever be ended. The question is whether illegal migration can be significantly reduced through a higher level of enforcement. Several participants supported the position taken by the recent government Commission on Immigration Reform, which called for the establishment of a national work registry to which employers could turn for information on whether individuals were legal residents or citizens; and there was considerable support for greater border enforcement. While some experts on migration advocate the adoption of a counterfeit-resistant identification card for citizens and legal residents, there is considerable opposition from human rights groups.

The larger question, both for the United States and Japan, is whether there is now a global labor market that largely determines the flow of people, so that attempts by government to restrict entry result in the growth of an illegal migrant population. The factors at work in Japan are also present in the United States: low fertility, an aging population, and a preference by employers for low-wage workers who can no longer be recruited from the rural hinterland or, in the United States, from some urban poor who reject low-wage employment when they can do better on welfare entitlements. Facing a tight labor market for low-wage labor, employers turn to the global market to meet their needs. US employers have found low-wage workers in Mexico and the Caribbean; German employers in Turkey, Yugoslavia, Greece and now Eastern Europe; French, Italian and Spanish employers find their workers in North Africa; and Japanese employers turn to Southeast Asia. Even when employers can find workers on the local market, they often prefer foreign workers who are pliable, unlikely to join unions, willing to work long hours, tolerant of conditions that local labor finds unacceptable, and readily disposable when no longer needed. Cultural factors can also condition how great the demand is for foreign labor: norms that discourage married women from remaining in the labor force; a preference by workers for more leisure time (shorter working hours, more vacations); an early age of retirement; and a young population schooled to the idea that middle-class occupations are preferable to manual labor.

According to this argument, migration is so employer-driven that policy instruments to reduce the flow – including employer sanctions, border controls and denial of social benefits to illegal residents – are not likely to work. Moreover, temporary migrants are likely to become permanent settlers, in part because employers will be reluctant to dismiss them after a year or two, and in part because legal temporary residents will soon bring (often by illegal means) members of their own family. Indeed, as many scholars have pointed out, not only do guest workers often become permanent residents, but guest-worker programs are not effective tools for reducing illegal immigration. The historical and comparative experience is that guest-worker programs increase the number of illegal entries by workers who hope to become part of the program or who come to take advantage of employment possibilities in the illegal labor market.

Liberal democratic societies, it is further argued, are constrained from adopting policies that tightly control immigration. They provide entitlements to legal and even illegal migrants, are reluctant to introduce counterfeit-proof identity cards, do not take employer penalties seriously, and hesitate to engage in deportations. Indeed, as the number of illegal migrants increases, the United States and some other countries (though not Japan) have granted them a one-time amnesty to avoid creating a permanent underclass that lacks legal protection.

Other scholars argue that governments can control entry, and that broader national interests should be taken into account, not simply the demands of employers or, for that matter, the claims of ethnic groups. They argue that controls do work, not perfectly – but then laws against crime are not perfect either. Governments have been able to limit the number of illegal migrants by the use of counterfeit-proof national identification cards and work authorization procedures, as in Sweden; governments can restrict family unification and thereby keep down the number of permanent settlers, as has Japan; and governments have tightened visa procedures to make entry difficult for unskilled individuals who might over-stay their visas in order to seek employment, as has Australia.

MIGRANT INCORPORATION

The difficulties in incorporating foreigners into Japanese society was a central theme of the symposia. The scale of these difficulties is demonstrated by the problems encountered by the *Nikkeijin*, Japanese emigrants and their descendants, many of whom "returned" to Japan in the late 1980s and early 1990s. In 1986 there were about 1.6 million Japanese emigrants and their descendants living outside of Japan (a number, inciden-tally, higher than the total number of foreigners then or now living in Japan). In an effort to meet the demand for labor in ways that the government regarded as socially acceptable, companies were permitted to recruit from among the overseas migrants and their descendants. Although welcomed by the Japanese government, the *Nikkeijin* experienced difficulty in becoming absorbed into Japanese society. Motoko Tsuchida writes: "Well educated, with Brazilian values, but hardly speak-ing Japanese, they have gradually come to realize that they can be neither Japanese nor completely Brazilian in the closed *Nikkeijin* society in Japan." The *Nikkeijin* encountered con-siderable discrimination in housing and in the workplace, and their children have had difficulties in school relating to their Japanese classmates. It is noteworthy that in this instance the barriers to absorption are not racial, but cultural.

The difficulties in the incorporation of migrants are further illustrated by the experiences of Koreans in Japan, many of whom are now third- or fourth-generation settlers. For reasons explained by Takamichi Kajita, Koreans retain strong ties to their country of origin, most especially those who possess North Korean citizenship (a majority of the Koreans in Japan). Since Koreans are often excluded from the primary labor market, they have created their own businesses, such as pinball parlors and ethnic-oriented enterprises. Children of North Korean ancestry attend Korean schools and only a few go on to the universities. Not many have become citizens. South Korean children are more likely to attend Japanese elementary schools, attend Japanese universities, intermarry with Japanese, and become naturalized. Still, notes Kajita, most Koreans remain denizens, or permanent residents, without citizenship. Again, it should be noted that race is not a barrier to absorption since Koreans and Japanese cannot readily be distinguished along racial lines.

REFUGEES

The first Vietnamese refugees arrived in Japan by boat in 1975. Although at the time Japan lacked a refugee policy, the Ministry of Justice granted a small number of refugees special permission to enter. In 1981 Japan signed the Geneva Convention Relating to the Status of Refugees and the following year promulgated an Immigration Control and Refugee Recognition Act. The government established a quota for Indo-Chinese refugees of 10 000. In June 1989 a new screening process was put in place to stop the flow of Indo-Chinese boat people. The Japanese were particularly alarmed at the arrival of "Vietnamese", many of whom proved to be mainland Chinese posing as Vietnamese. The Japanese regarded the Chinese "boat people" as economic migrants seeking higher wages than could be earned in China. Tougher screening procedures, introduced in September 1989, enabled the government to return Chinese from Fukien in agreement with the Chinese government. The policy also served as a warning to Indo-Chinese and other potential asylum seekers and refugees that resettlement in Japan would be difficult and that refugees ought to seek admission elsewhere.

The Japanese government took the position that Japan is too small and too densely populated to accommodate significant number of refugees, no matter how bona fide their claims. Instead, the Japanese government said it was prepared to provide financial support to the United Nations High Commissioner for Refugees (UNHCR) as an expression of its willingness to be internationally cooperative and to share the burden, at least financially. Japan's contributions for refugee assistance increased significantly: to the UNHCR, to other international agencies and to the governments of Thailand and the Philippines. By the 1990s Japan was providing more than $200 million annually for refugee relief, with substantial sums for the relief of displaced foreign workers from Kuwait. Japan was the third largest donor to UNHCR, after the United States and the European Community.

Isami Takeda notes that a few dramatic asylum cases – a Soviet defector who was deported by the Japanese government, a Chinese defector then sent to a third country, and a North Korean defector who was also deported – demonstrate the reluctance of the Japanese government to grant asylum. The difficulties in obtaining asylum are so great that few apply. Indeed, "the Japanese government" wrote one leading newspaper, "does not have a policy of accepting asylum seekers". A public opinion survey reported that 87 percent of the Japanese population favored financial assistance to international institutions or to other Asian countries or sending medical teams to refugee-receiving countries; only 3 percent said that Japan should receive refugees as settlers. Other surveys reported that Japanese were prepared to admit more refugees, but only if it were on a temporary basis. Takeda approvingly quotes another Japanese who wrote that "a deep rooted insularity appears to condition the Japanese ambivalent attitude toward refugees". Indeed, as we have seen, the same statement can be made with respect to all migrants and foreigners living in Japan.

The contrast with the United States on refugee policy is striking. The United States is a traditional country of immigration and refuge. Michael Teitelbaum reminds us that in Colonial times those who came were fleeing persecution in Europe. Teitelbaum also points out that public-opinion surveys reveal that while Americans are ambivalent on immigration they are generally positive toward refugees and their families. However, policies toward refugees and asylum seekers have been ambiguous, contradictory and often perverse. While the United States admits individuals who can demonstrate they have a well-founded fear of persecution (following the wording of the UN Refugee Convention), the government has also admitted individuals who have not been persecuted but came from Communist countries, a policy that led to easy admissions from Cuba, but not from Haiti. Legislation provides for temporary asylum for individuals fleeing from violence, but officials have been reluctant to deport individuals even when conditions in their country of origin have improved, with the result that the executive branch has become increasingly restrictive on admitting persons at risk. The US government also provides large sums of money to accommodate relatively small numbers of refugees and asylees in the United States, but much smaller sums for the millions of refugees and internally displaced persons abroad. Overall, the US, in its financial support for refugees within and outside its borders, may be among the highest in total per capita contribution to refugees. On a per-capita basis the US contribution to the UNHCR is 14th, well behind the Scandinavia countries, Switzerland, and the Netherlands, but only slightly behind Japan (the 13th largest contributor on a per-capita basis).

POLICY-MAKING

The American participants characterized the US immigration and refugee policy-making process as highly politicized and fragmented. A major role is played by the US Congress, which in turn is subjected to lobbying from constituencies, ethnic groups, the business community, trade unions and human rights activists. In the executive branch a variety of agencies are involved, including the Immigration and Naturalization Service within the Justice Department, the Labor Department, the Commerce Department, the State Department, the National Security Council and the White House. State governments influence what benefits are provided migrants, and the courts determine the constitutionality of government decisions. The process, as Teitelbaum notes, is more likely to result in unintended consequences than if policy were determined principally by the executive branch of government. On the positive side, however, one can say that the process is transparent.

The Japanese migration policy-making process is not as transparent. On the administrative side there are numerous ministries engaged in considerations of foreign worker policies, joined together in a special liaison group. The Justice Ministry, the Labour Ministry and the National Police Agency pay particular attention to the question of illegal workers, and policy making is hardly influenced by pressure groups. The Korean and Chinese communities play little role in considerations of migration policy; nor do agricultural employers as in the United States. The issue of illegal workers is of great concern to small industries (whose political voice is small), but not the large corporations. What role is played by the Construction Ministry (whose clients are major users of illegal migrants) or by the Chamber of Commerce (which promotes training programs for guest workers) is unclear. One Japanese participant with considerable experience within government concluded that there are no major players regarding these issues as in the United States. Policy outcomes are the result of discussions and bargaining among the ministries (and with officials in the governing LPD) with little public input.

LOOKING AHEAD

Migration issues are higher on the political agenda in the United States at present than in Japan. Several presidential candidates and many members of Congress have called for policy changes. Public perceptions of loss of control over borders, the high absolute level of annual migration, and public concern over the effects of migration on the employment of low-skilled, low-wage native labor and on the costs of social services, have made public officials conscious of the need to reformulate policies. The impact of migrants on the welfare system has been particularly contentious. At the time when federally funded health, education, and welfare services are under political assault and financial strain, the questions of whether migrants use these services more than native-born Americans do and whether they pay taxes to defray the attendant costs have been under public scrutiny. California's Proposition 187 was directed at the use of these services by illegal migrants, and the Welfare Reform Law of 1996 went even further, restricting use by legal permanent residents. Other proposals for overhauling the country's immigration policy are pending before Congress. An unusual coalition of interest groups are engaged by these issues.

Many pro-labor liberals, conservatives, environmentalists and population control advocates have joined together to call for cuts in levels of legal immigration, while prominent free market conservatives, and CEOs of hi-tech firms have joined pro-immigration internationalist liberals, civil rights advocates and ethnic groups. There are strong political pressures to pass legislation slowing immigration, especially from heavily impacted states such as California and Florida, but it seems unlikely that policy makers will halt family unification, cease to admit refugees, or prevent high-tech firms and universities from recruiting skilled individuals. Indeed, were unemployment levels to decline significantly, especially among minorities, the demand for skilled labor to increase, and the federal government to be more effective at reducing the level of illegal migration, one might expect a lowering of migration issues on the political agenda.

Migration is, for the moment, of less concern in Japan than in the United States since the demand for foreign workers has declined as a result of increased unemployment, but this may be only temporary. However, the Japanese are acutely concerned by the high emigration pressures from the Asian mainland. As a small and crowded country on the edge of a vast and populated continent where wages are low, many Japanese regard a small influx of illegal migrants as portending a larger and uncontrollable flow. The Japanese are also concerned that political turmoil in Korea could precipitate a refugee flow. Most of these concerns are exaggerated, though it is true that individuals are fleeing from oppressive regimes and violence, the global media increase awareness of opportunities for employment and higher wages in Japan, and word is spreading that it is possible to enter Japan legally, then to avoid detection and deportation. While some officials and scholars believe that steps can be taken to reduce these pressures by overseas assistance and foreign investment, most Japanese and American migration experts agree that economic growth and job creation in China and elsewhere in Asia will not significantly reduce the pressure for emigration in the visible future. For both the Japanese and the US governments, the management of illegal migration depends principally upon how effective they are in controlling entry and in exercising greater control over the workplace, rather than their economic policies toward the countries of origin. And for both countries the issue for government is whether the costs –

financial, administrative and political – of increasing controls are acceptable.

For Japan, so unaccustomed to foreigners, the most acceptable policy when labor demand increases is to fill niches in the labor market with temporary workers. A handful of scholars, social activists and journalists argue, however, that Japan would benefit if it were more accepting of people from other cultures, that Japan should open its doors to more foreigners and adopt a naturalization policy that would enable migrants and their locally born children to become Japanese citizens, and that permanently settled skilled migrants would be as valuable to Japan as they are to the United States. There is no sociological law that says that Japanese could not learn greater toleration for strangers. After all, the United States overcame its antipathy to Chinese and Japanese in its migration and naturalization policies, and Australia once recruited its migrants only from Europe but now a majority of new immigrants come from Asia.

However, given the near universal reluctance of Japanese officials, politicians and voters to want migrants who would settle in Japan, it seems unlikely that a change in attitudes would precede a change in policy. More likely, Japan would respond to a rise in employer demands for foreign workers through temporary work programs, or through an increase in the number of illegal workers. A reconsideration of Japanese policies on permanent migration and on citizenship policies is more likely to take place, if at all, only after there is a significant influx of workers and a *de facto* settled foreign population. Paradoxically, then, a tight labor market and an increasing demand for foreign workers would probably reduce the level of concern over migration in the United States, while in Japan a similar tightening of the labor market and a growth in the demand for foreign workers would sharply increase the level of anxiety and put migration and citizenship issues high on the policy and political agendas.

Part II
The Challenge of Migrant Incorporation in Japan and the United States

2 Historical Conditions in the United States for Assimilating Immigrants

Reed Ueda

IMMIGRATION PATTERNS AND POLICIES

To note that the greatest mass immigration in world history created the United States only begins the task of grasping the complex character of the population movement that placed ethnic diversity and its continual renewal at the center of American nationhood. From the nineteenth to the early twentieth century, more immigrants went to the United States than to all other countries in the world combined. From 1820 to 1900, an average of 240 000 newcomers a year arrived; from 1901 to 1990, an average of 420 000 immigrants came yearly. By 1990, the United States had received 56 million immigrants since its founding. They constituted the greatest variety of nationality groups in history to enter any single country. In 1990, the United States admitted immigrants from thirty Asian countries, twenty-two European countries, seventeen Central and South American countries, thirteen Caribbean countries, and thirteen African countries (Bernard, 1950: 204, 311; US Immigration and Naturalization Service, 1992: 47, 52–3).

The gradual expansion of immigration to a worldwide influx was the underlying factor that ensured the continuous restructuring of American national society and culture. The history of the relation between immigration and American nationhood resembled a kind of spiral; the evolution of American society turned on cumulative stages of national creation and recreation. A series of three cycles of immigration altered the character of society, its cultural life and its institutions of governance. The first, from the beginning of the eighteenth century to the American Revolution, arose out of the migration of non-English Protestant settlers, particularly from Northern Ireland, Scotland, France and Germany. The second cycle began in the middle decades of the nineteenth century, as the new republic received an expanding immigration from Catholic Ireland as well as Germany and Scandinavia. This wave formed the first great peak in the second cycle and by the turn of the century had come to be known as the "Old Immigration". A second and even larger immigration peak originating chiefly from southern and eastern Europe, but also from the direction of East Asia, Mexico and the Caribbean, grew from 1880 to the First World War and was labelled by contemporaneous observers the "New Immigration". This peak declined sharply in the late 1920s and the Depression Era, marking the close of the second cycle. The third cycle of immigration began after the 1960s as the circuit of immigration touched every region of the world and made the United States history's first global immigration country. It was, however, an imbalanced influx in which arrivals from Latin America and Asia composed a large majority. Historians of the future may someday argue that the most profound social changes in twentieth and twenty-first-century United States emanated from the third great cycle of American immigration, referred to as the "worldwide system of immigration" (Higham, 1975: 17–28; Bailyn, 1977: i; Glazer, 1985: 3).

From the first to the third cycle of immigration, immigrants by and large did not spring from the most deprived and stagnant orders of their homelands. They were rural and urban laborers who had already initiated adaptations to survive in the intersection of population pressure and limited resources. They were in the process of negotiating an unsettling transition and overcoming the insecurity it produced. Dislodged by an expulsive wave of "push" forces in homeland societies, they were attracted by the "pull" forces of material opportunities and political liberties in the new American lands. In spite of these external pressures, immigrants were not passive particles in a historical force field; their decision to migrate depended always on a capacity for individual risk-taking that was exceptional relative to their risk-averse countrymen who stayed behind (Taeuber and Taeuber, 1958: 55–8, 202–6; Habakkuk and Postan, 1965: 60–9, ch. 2; Easterlin, 1968: 30;

Thomas, 1973: ch. 3; Archdeacon, 1983: 37–56, 117, 120–7; Bodnar, 1985: 30–7; Daniels, 1991: 16–22).

The rise of worldwide immigration to the United States was shaped by three historical eras of admissions and naturalization policy. The first era unfolded from the founding of the United States as a political society based upon rational principles of self-government embodied in the federal and state constitutions of the 1780s. The establishment of voluntary citizenship and nationality permitted the accommodation of immigrants to assume a central place in the life of the new republic. In a time of political movements against the old regimes of Europe, the United States was envisiged as an asylum for those seeking freedom from feudal oppression. Confidence that new citizens could come from many backgrounds supported an admissions policy that avoided restrictions based on religion, national origin and social class. Moreover, the federal and state governments left admissions unlimited, responding to the demand for new settlers to populate a transcontinental country. Confidence in the openness and diversity of American national culture and the cosmopolitan qualities of human identity formed the ideological seedbed of the nation's earliest immigration policy (Wood, 1969: chs 1, 2; Kettner, 1974: 208–42; Rahe, 1994: 32–4).

Beginning in the 1880s, the federal government abandoned the historic tradition of unregulated and open immigration, initiating the second era in the history of immigration policy. This shift emerged out of spreading pessimism about the political, cultural and economic assimilability of immigrants from outside the states of northern and western Europe and culminated in the establishment in the 1920s of a severely restrictive and discriminatory admissions program for these immigrants.

The rise of restrictive policies hinged upon a historic transformation of the relationship of government to immigration. From 1880 to 1930, Congress took control of admissions policy from the states and built a complex body of law which prescribed the kinds of immigrants qualified and unqualified for admission. From this era forward, Congress would grow increasingly active in immigration policy in order to regulate its social impact. Its goal was to admit only those who theoretically could be assimilated into the host society and to exclude those deemed incompetent or dangerous to the nation's security (Bernard, 1980).

In the half-century after 1880, American lawmakers gradually redefined the place of immigration and that of the immigrant in the nation. Congress invented tests for admission on qualitative criteria such as health, sexual behavior, political orientation and literacy, and then attempted to regulate the influx by a radical shift from admission by individual qualification to qualification according to membership in a nationality group (Higham, 1975: 34–58).

Federal lawmakers installed *ad hoc* legislation that accumulated into an admissions system controlling and limiting the ethnic pluralism of the nation. Congress excluded Chinese laborers in 1882. After the Gentlemen's Agreement of 1907–8 produced a diplomatically negotiated exclusion of Japanese laborers, Congress created an Asiatic Barred Zone in 1917 from which no other Asian laborers could immigrate, and in 1921 passed the first Quota Act (the Johnson Act) which set up discriminatory quotas for immigrant admissions. The number of aliens of any admissible nationality could not exceed 3 percent of the foreign-born population of that nationality enumerated in the United States census of 1910. These quotas were limited to Europe, the Near East, Africa, Australia, New Zealand and Siberia and did not apply to nationalities excluded previously by the Chinese Exclusion Act, the Gentlemen's Agreement and the Asiatic Barred Zone. Nor did the quotas apply to countries in the western hemisphere. The 1921 act introduced an unprecedented annual ceiling on admissions of 355 000, 200 000 (56 percent) of which were available to immigrants from northern and western Europe and 155 000 (44 percent) reserved chiefly to those from southern and eastern Europe. Three years later, Congress passed the Second Quota Act (the Johnson–Reid Act), imposing even smaller quotas on southern and eastern European immigrants. The annual limit on total immigration dropped to 165 000, by reapportioning the quotas to 2 percent of the foreign-born population of a nationality in the United States in 1890, when even fewer immigrants from southern and eastern Europe were represented. Resetting the quotas reduced the southern and eastern European share of annual admissions to only 20 percent (Bernard, 1950: 25–6; Higham, 1955: 165–7, 203,

308–11, 319–24; Divine, 1957: 4–9, 17; Daniels, 1962: ch. 3; Hutchinson, 1981: 64–84, 430–2 478–91).

The installation of quotas keyed to census tabulations nearly two generations in the past reflected the desire of restrictionists to reverse the course of ethnic change in the population and to calibrate immigrant admissions to accord with the greater demographic dominance of the Anglo-Saxon stock of an earlier era. Using hyperbole, Representative Elton Watkins of Oregon bluntly expressed in 1924 the essence of this idea in a speech in favor of the Second Quota Act: "So far as I am concerned," he declared, "it would be all right to go back there [to 1790] and begin anew and let nobody in this country except those who have Anglo-Saxon or Nordic blood throbbing in their veins" (US Congress, 1924: Part 2, 5677).

The Second Quota Act marked the pinnacle of exclusionary policies against Asian immigrants. It dictated that "no alien ineligible for citizenship shall be admitted to the United States". The Chinese Exclusion Act of 1882 had rendered Chinese immigrants ineligible for citizenship, and court decisions put the Japanese and other Asians in the same position. The development of the status of aliens ineligible for citizenship in naturalization law served as the key to the complete exclusion of Asian immigrants (Gulick, 1918: 59, 71; Malcolm, 1921: 77–81; McGovney, 1923: 129–61, 211–44).

Restrictionists used the Second Quota Act as a temporary measure before more stringent regulations finally went into effect in 1929. The annual ceiling for immigration shrank once more, to 150 000. A formal "National Origins" plan was installed in which quotas were allocated to an eligible nationality in proportion to their representation by birth or ancestry in the population. Through statistical extrapolations based on the census and other population samplings, northern and western Europeans received 82 percent of the total annual quota; southern and eastern Europe 16 percent; and the rest of the world 2 percent. The United States became one of the few countries in the world to control immigration by ethnic quotas. In 1952, the United States, Brazil and the Philippines were the only countries regulating immigration through nationality quotas (US Congress, 1950: 27; Divine, 1957: 28–33; Higham, 1975: 55–6).

The emergence of an omnibus restrictionist admissions system was the result of a long, drawn-out contest between two sets of interest groups. Among the principal forces in favor of keeping admissions open and unregulated were large-scale employers in manufacturing industries, construction, and commercial agriculture, who depended upon cheap immigrant labor. Although capitalist magnates feared the unregulated foreign influx of the 1880s due to a rise in labor radicalism, after the depression of 1893–4 they united in favor of maintaining the *status quo* of open admissions. The National Association of Manufacturers and the Chamber of Commerce operated intensive lobbying efforts against restrictionist legislation. The industrial capitalist interests were joined by leaders of immigrant ethnic constituencies who wished to keep the gates open to their countrymen, and by social reformers who believed in America's role as an international haven for foreign seekers of new opportunities. The forces in favor of restricted admissions included the representatives of skilled workers, particularly the American Federation of Labor, who feared the depressing effects upon the labor market of unskilled newcomers. Another influential group consisted of scholars, intellectuals and progressive reformers, who argued that immigrants contributed to social and economic pathologies. The last of these, in particular, saw restriction as a key to implementing their goals of creating a more centrally organized social and political order. These two wings of restrictionists were backed up by the congressional delegations from the South and the Far West, whose constituents acutely feared the alien cultural influences and economic competition of immigrants from southern and eastern Europe and Asia. This anti-immigrant bloc grew increasingly opposed to immigration from the late nineteenth century to the 1920s. The pro-immigration constellation and the anti-immigration ensemble were closely matched in strength, but the former was narrowly able to keep the upper hand until 1917, when legislation enacting a literacy test and the Asiatic Barred Zone was passed over President Woodrow Wilson's veto (Jones, 1960: 260–1; Higham, 1975: 42–57; Goldin, 1993: 2–11).

The evolution of immigration policy from 1880 to 1930 deviated from the early republic's commitment to cosmopolitan views of membership in the American nation. Policies controlling the status of immigrant minorities gradually came to rest in a constrictionist ideology – derived from popular experience as well as intellectual speculations – holding that group cultures were enclosed in a fundamental way and that American society was organized in a rigid ethnic hierarchy. Constrictionists believed culture and race pre-determined boundary conditions between ethnic subpopulations, and thus served as boundary-keepers rather than boundary-crossers or changers. In the constrictionist view, social life was reduced to an extension of pre-existing ethnic and racial divisions, hierarchies, and separations. For constrictionists with nativist leanings, there was no historical assimilation and little possibility of its occurrence in the future. They tended to see immigrants as enclosed in groups that competed to dominate each other, rather than as individuals merging into a national life (Handlin, 1957: 71–3; Mann, 1979: 126–35).

The various advocates of restriction shared a fear that immigration tightened boundaries between groups, worsening social stratification and communal fragmentation. They argued that immigration caused social mobility to decline, enabled the rise of an unbridled and exploitative elite, and fostered the formation of ethnic and religious separatism. To many Americans, their country had become a society of myriad subcommunities isolated and alienated from each other. Many commentators beheld the spectre of a radically divided society. The urban reformer Jacob Riis, the son of Danish immigrants, entitled his book (1890) about New York's Lower East Side immigrant communities *"How the Other Half Lives"* implying that American society was divided into parts completely separate, out of touch, and ignorant of each other. The fear of a society polarized between plutocrats and the toiling and dehumanized masses on the verge of revolt was expressed in the prophetic visions of Ignatius Donnelly's *Caesar's Column* (1891) and Jack London's *The Iron Heel* (1908) (Boyer, 1978: ch. 8).

The social divisions and compartmentalization of industrial and urban growth, in which immigration played a large role, produced a deep anxiety and a sense of lost control. The forces of change seemed so vast and powerful as to overwhelm the rational capacity to preserve the foundations of liberal and republican government and evoked a sense that deterministic factors governed human behavior (Hays, 1967: chs 2, 4, 5; Wiebe, 1967: ch. 2; Higham, 1970: 73–102).

A new critique of the unity of mankind offered the possibilities for a racial explanation of cultural differences. Nativist intellectuals drew upon European scholars who posited a typology of physical differences separating "teutons", "goths", "nordics", "alpines", "mediterraneans", "orientals", "Africans" and "aboriginals". The economist William Z. Ripley published a corroboration of these speculations for an American audience in 1899. In *The Races of Europe*, Ripley argued that Europeans consisted of three neatly divided and separate races: the Teutons of the north, the Alpines of central Europe, and the Mediterraneans of the south. The races could be distinguished by measurable physical forms, in particular, the shape of the head. Ripley's demonstration of the existence of racial classes exerted a profound influence on the efforts of social scientists to analyze the behavior of immigrant populations. Two scholars at the University of Wisconsin, the economist John R. Commons and the sociologist Edward A. Ross, who were concerned with the social effects of mass immigration, treated the normative racial characteristics of immigrants as a causal factor for observed patterns of behavior. Commons concluded in *Races and Immigrants in America* (1907) that the newcomers could be divided into two classes corresponding to those who originated from modern advanced northern European societies, and those from southern and eastern Europe who constituted a "degraded peasantry". Ross analyzed the latter class of immigrants in terms of a hereditary inferiority predisposing them to primitive and dysfunctional forms of family life, cultural behavior and economic husbandry that, unlike the progressive Teutons, made them "beaten members of beaten breeds ... that ... lack the ancestral foundations of American character" (Ross, 1901: 16–22, 32–5, 439–49; Commons, 1907: 69–70; Ross, 1914: ch. 12; Higham, 1955: 109, 154; Jones, 1960: 267; Taylor, 1971: 249).

The assumption of the fixed and racially determined character of ethnicity was revealed in many important policy documents. In 1899, the US Bureau of Immigration adopted a classification of immigrant "races or peoples" to use for purposes of enumerating immigrants arriving each year. The US Immigration Commission submitted reports that interpreted the social data on immigration it gathered according to racial differences and categories. The federal report published in

1950 for lawmakers seeking to revise immigration policy, *The Immigration and Naturalization Systems of the United States*, also provided stereotypic and reified categories for classifying immigrants (US Commissioner-General of Immigration, 1899; US Congress, 1950: 7–14, 82–156; Handlin, 1957: ch. 5).

Restrictionists linked race to collective dysfunctional, antisocial and undemocratic behavior by manipulating ambiguous and even contrary data, a tactic by which they sought to give immigration the appearance of a destructive force that had to be stopped at all costs.

The Second World War marked the emergence of a new internationalism that would form a bridge toward a third pattern of immigration policy which would depart from discriminatory restrictionism. Seeing admissions and naturalization policy as tools for shaping international relations, lawmakers began to take a more pragmatic and flexible attitude toward the assumptions of restrictionism. To cement the wartime alliance between China and the United States, Congress in 1943 repealed the Chinese Exclusion Act (Riggs, 1950: 195–6; Reimers, 1985: 13–15).

With the onset of the Cold War, the United States sought to establish its leadership of the free, democratic world and to oppose national forces aligning with the Soviet Union by offering asylum to persons escaping from communist rule. The debate in the Eightieth Congress in 1948 over the passage of the first bill to admit displaced persons, or refugees, from war-torn Europe provided the occasion for rekindling the cosmopolitan ideal of American nationality. Lawmakers argued in favor of the measure by invoking the status of immigration in democratic ideology, redirecting the historic concept of the United States as an asylum into a new pragmatic role suited to cold war international politics (Divine, 1957: 118–29).[1]

The senators and congressmen who supported passage of this legislation used the strategy of appealing to patriotic traditions historically rooted in ideological as opposed to organic nationality. Imbedded in their arguments was the call to resurrect the national self-concept of immigrant nationhood, of America as the quintessential "immigration country" – a nation built by immigrants – and to focus on its role as a haven for the downtrodden. The Displaced Persons Act of 1948 was the first in a series of refugee laws that made the United States the world's leader in refugee admissions. One out of seven immigrants arriving from 1945 to 1990–2.5 million immigrants out of a total of 18.6 million – were refugees (Ueda, 1994: 50).

Lawmakers showed a proclivity to treat immigration from the western hemisphere as a special case from the inception of restrictionist policies. Immigration from Canada and Latin America was exempted from nationality quotas and yearly admissions ceilings; seeking to assist agricultural and industrial employers, Congress kept a "backdoor" open to cheap labor from these areas. Congress also introduced a guest-worker program with Mexico in which 4.7 million "braceros" (agricultural laborers) were admitted on temporary work contracts from 1943 to 1965 (Ueda, 1994: 31–3).

From the Second World War to the Great Society era, the United States dismantled the fortress of restrictive admissions and naturalization policies. By 1952, all exclusions against immigrants from Asia had been dropped; in 1965, the Hart–Celler Act abolished the discriminatory national-origins quota system. Immigration policy had demonstrated the ability of the nation to recover its founding ideological commitment to the eclectic sources of nationality and citizenship, despite the powerful xenophobia produced by the growth of immigration under the social stresses of the industrial and urban revolution. The deep historical roots of cosmopolitan national identity had implanted a residual capacity to repel and overcome national-origins discrimination in admissions and naturalization.

After 1965, the stage was set for the United States to become the first country in history to receive a worldwide mass immigration. Lawmakers had established an admissions policy with large and flexible annual ceilings that encouraged family reunion and occupational matching, and had removed all vestiges of exclusion in the naturalization system, making it universally accessible. Opinion makers had revived the democratic ideology of America's national destiny as an immigration country. Finally, the nation had launched a new movement in public policy to eradicate invidious discrimination based on ethnic origins. The Civil Rights revolution enlarged the possibilities for the assimilation of immigrants from Latin America, Asia, Africa and the Caribbean who were racial minorities. The United States had achieved the conjunction of the key conditions for a worldwide multiethnic and multiracial immigration based on permanent incorporation within a pluralist democracy.

THE SEEDS OF DEMOCRATIC PLURALISM

The pre-eminent historical problem of immigration was the formation of the relationship of the part to the whole, the ethnic fragment to the nation. For the custodians of the whole – the native legislators, opinion makers and educators – the key aspect of this nexus was whether national citizenship could unite the disparate and multitudinous subgroups settling in the country. The nation-building role of citizenship assumed the highest importance, as lawmakers sought to resolve what historian John Higham has described as the tension of the two national foundings.

The first founding occurred in the seventeenth century, as the English colonists sought to replicate a familiar community based on organic order, ethnic closure and homogeneity. The settlers involved in this first founding took for granted the expulsion of Indians and enslavement of blacks; their legacy was the vision of a nation whose institutions would serve the power of an exclusive Anglo-Saxon core. The second founding was the American Revolution. Drawing on the ideals of the Enlightenment, it institutionalized a republican form of self-government with the capacity to forge a nation out of eclectic sources. Voluntary citizenship became the axis of nationhood, resting on popular faith in a common humanity and confidence in the rational structure of history. During the era of the second founding, citizenship was conceived to apply centrally to individuals of European origin (Bailyn, 1967: 26–30; Wood, 1969: 4–9; Nash, 1974: chs 4–8; Morgan, 1975: chs 13, 16; Handlin and Handlin 1989: 170–3; Fuchs, 1990: ch. 1; Greenfeld, 1992: 422–3; Wood, 1992: 221–2; Higham, 1993; Foner, 1994: 436)

The tension between the two foundings in national history complicated the capacity of citizenship to unify the multiplying subpopulations of the nation. The first was a charter group formed of English colonizers who assumed they were the custodians and proprietors of the nation; this Anglo-Saxon core broadened into an umbrella category absorbing descendants of Protestant immigrants from the British Isles and various parts of Northern Europe; national expansion brought the core group into positions of dominance over various conquered and captured subpopulations: African blacks, Native Americans, Hawaiians, Puerto Ricans and Filipinos. In addition to these collective groupings, aliens arrived to join American society by a voluntary act of immigration (Higham, 1975: 3–8).

The American constitutional underpinnings of the revolutionary founding excluded artificial privileges and hereditary status distinctions in order to release the virtues of a populist and mixed society. The revolutionary founders claimed that the privileged orders of England – the crown and the nobility – had degenerated into tyranny because inherited privilege conferred the power to act without responsibility to the public good. Artificial distinctions spawned abuses and evils. Thus the new federal constitution provided that in America there could be but one status: indivisible citizenship; badges of rank and nobility were outlawed. Citizenship did not draw distinctions between individuals on the basis of class, nativity, ancestry or religion, but was inclusive because so many different European peoples – English, Dutch, Germans, French, Swedes, Scots and Scots Irish – had formed the colonies. This feature of citizenship reflected the voluntary spirit of forming new communities through colonization. Citizenship derived ultimately from legal consent and subscription, because birth and social origin could not determine the status of an individual (Handlin and Handlin, 1961: 26–30; Bailyn, 1967: ch. 4; Pocock, 1975: 507, 517, 521, Wood, 1969: ch. 7).

Although the Constitution remained ambivalent on race, it provided for the possibility of citizenship of freed African slaves and their descendants in the northern states. Moreover, the cosmopolitan principles of American constitutionalism possessed a potential for legalistic transcendence of race and other "accidental" factors. These principles endowed government with a capacity for self-reform and self-transformation that over time generated legal measures to increase the equal treatment of races.

Citizenship expanded to include all races after the Civil War. The Fourteenth Amendment to the Constitution, ratified

in 1868, included a proviso that "all persons born or naturalized in the United States and subject to the jurisdiction
thereof, are citizens of the United States". This "birthright citizenship" clause proved pivotal to the nation's capacity to
absorb immigrants. The political scientist Stephen Castles has
shown in a survey of immigrant populations in nations
throughout the world that the disposal of the status of
the second generation is the critical turning-point in determining their incorporation into the nation. The Fourteenth
Amendment, by providing that all descendants of immigrants
born within the territory of the United States would automatically gain citizenship, assured that barring naturalization any
disabilities of alien status would be limited only to the first
generation. This guarantee of birthright citizenship provided
the key to consolidating the integenerational process of political assimilation. The United States would be a country in
which no permanent immigrant community could be com-
partmentalized as a permanent alien community (Schuck and
Smith, 1985; Castles, 1993). Democratic individual naturalization procedures and universal birthright citizenship provided
the dual routes by which American nationality and American
citizenship became coterminous, while other societies that
eschewed becoming "immigration countries" maintained a
tradition of access to citizenship that reinforced an ethnic
sense of nationality. In countries such as Germany and Japan,
the naturalization procedure was complicated and demanding, foreclosing the mass social movement toward naturalization found in the United States. Furthermore, these countries
made the *jus sanguinis* tradition of citizenship–citizenship by
ancestry – the dominant means of acquiring citizenship and
rejected the *jus soli* principle of gaining citizenship through
native birth.

In the twentieth century, the United States became a
country in which citizenship and nationality were equivalent:
all citizens were members of the nation and all members of
the nation were citizens. This development was crucial for the
incorporation of the wave of non-European immigrants arriving since the 1960s. In the words of political scientist Donald
L. Horowitz, the convergence of American citizenship and
nationality reflected the "non-blood-based definition of
Americaness" (Wood, 1969: 606–15; Horowitz, 1992: 12).

The republican and liberal framework also expressed the need for a large and protected sphere of individual civil rights. It reflected a profound animus against centralized power and its intrusions, in favor of the liberty of individuals. The social development of colonies far removed from close imperial supervision had encouraged private, individual decision-making and local self-rule. Thus the federal constitution severely circumscribed the potency of government, especially the national government, by establishing separations and balances, limiting the radius of government power so that it could not reach into the civil sphere, and leaving people free to pursue their communal and individual ways of cultural life (Handlin and Handlin, 1961: 32–48; Lipset, 1963: chs 2,3; Greenfeld, 1992).

The fragment of ethnic group life was loosely embedded in the web of a national civil society, where the curtailing of centralized power produced a federal structure of government that would deeply affect American ethnic relations. Political federalism permitted the unregulated expression of ethnic pluralism, giving ethnic groups opportunities to fashion control over a variety of territorial subcommunities. The pursuit of group interests and recognition could occur through local and regional impulses toward power (Glazer, 1983: 274–92; Horowitz, 1992: 23–5).

The pattern of limited government inherent in American constitutionalism prevented the creation of a fundamental body of law that would prescribe the characteristic features of the national culture or the subcultures of ethnic groups, and opened up a public space in civil society where both accommodation and acculturation could occur. Unlike the multicultural constitutions of pluralistic societies in Asia, Africa and Latin America, the United States Constitution did not designate official languages, religions, subcommunities or other structures of group identity; without constitutional formulation, the national culture and subcultures remained legally unfixed and thus more open to influence from informal decisions and popular social processes. A legally undefined national culture modified by the addition and mixing of new ethnic ingredients could more freely adjust to the effects of the development of multiple subcultures (Glazer, 1975: 24–5; Horowitz, 1985: chs 7, 16).

In an analysis of American and European nationalization, Liah Greenfeld observed, "In contrast to the European nations, where the primacy of the nation over the individual imposed general uniformity," in the United States "the entity which took the place of a state in the heart of an American citizen, and which from then on, above any other factor, defined the identity of different *groups* of Americans and distinguished between them, was ancestral nationality, or, as it came to be defined, 'ethnicity'." Conversely, nation-building in Europe involved the development of homogeneous and centralized forms of nationality that facilitated state power. The ethnic fragment had to vanish in an assimilation within the national whole or it had to be relegated to separate, external, inferior compartments of status. Under these conditions, the absorption of immigrants could only take the form of complete assimilation or unequal minority status (Greenfeld, 1992: 482).

The aegis of American federalism produced possibilities for the blending of particular elements into local plural cultures. "Between assimilationism and radical multiculturalism," historian Sean Wilentz has pointed out, "there is a third conception of America as a miscegenated or Creole culture, born of oppression as well as opportunity – an America that is not something that must be assimilated to, but that is always (and often painfully) creating itself." In this way, the immigrants, who were culturally alien, poor and powerless, gradually but inexorably transformed the borders of American culture. Accelerated by generational change, local plural cultures grew more syncretic until they penetrated the mainstream. A pluralistic assimilation occurred that was additive and reciprocal, one in which even natives absorbed the new cultural influences brought by immigrants. Ethnic elements did not disappear, but became part of a metaculture in which the locally marginal and the nationally dominant assimilated each other. Thus the process of pluralistic assimilation was not linear or unidirectional, but was repetitive and cyclical. The ethnic parts constituted a new cultural whole which, in turn, had to absorb new and different ethnic parts carried into the arena of national history by successive waves of immigration (Wilentz, 1994: 46).

Although in the official spheres of American society Anglo-Saxon cultural power and forms were dominant, throughout national history there was a social level that accommodated an unregulated set of cultural exchanges that kept ethnic boundaries shifting and amorphous, creating a variety of possibilities for intergroup association. Such boundaries were open to variegated crisscrossing by countless individuals. This is evidenced in the recollections of Aiji Tashiro, a son of Japanese immigrants, in 1934:

[I]sat down to American breakfasts and Japanese lunches. My palate developed a fondness for rice along with corned beef and cabbage. I became equally adept with knife and fork and with chopsticks. I said grace at meal times in Japanese, and recited the Lord's Prayer at night in English. I hung my stocking over the fireplace at Christmas and toasted "mochi" at Japanese New Year. The stories of "Tongue-cut Sparrow" and "Momo-taro" were as well known to me as those of Red Riding Hood and Cinderella. ... On some nights I was told bedtime stories of how Admiral Togo sent a great Russian fleet down to destruction. Other nights I heard of King Arthur or from *Gulliver's Travels* and *Tom Sawyer*. I was spoken to by both parents in Japanese and English. I answered in whatever was convenient or in a curious mixture of both. (Tashiro, 1934: 99)

Historian Arthur Mann described the cultural mixing in the personal background of a much more well-known individual, Fiorello LaGuardia, Mayor of New York City during the Great Depression:

Tammany Hall may have been the first to exploit the vote-getting value of eating gefullte fish with Jews, goulash with Hungarians, sauerbraten with Germans, spaghetti with Italians, and so on indefinitely, but this unorthodox Republican not only dined every bit as shrewdly but also spoke, according to the occasion, in Yiddish, Hungarian, German, Italian, Serbian-Croatian, or plain New York English. Half Jewish and half Italian, born in Greenwich Village yet raised in Arizona, married first to a Catholic and then to a Lutheran but himself a Mason and an

Episcopalian, Fiorello LaGuardia was a Mr. Brotherhood Week all by himself. (Mann, 1959: 21)

As immigrants and their children improvised with inherited and borrowed cultural elements, they stimulated the pace of boundary crossing and straddling. A higher stage of hybridization was reached in the culture of the American-born generation. Culturally mixed identities, like the diversity that nourished them, were part of a deeply rooted pattern in national history. The French–American immigrant, J. Hector St. John de Crevecoeur, perceived in 1782 the blending and fusing forces at work in a famous existential soliloquy:

What, then, is the American, this new man? he is neither an European nor the descendant of an European; hence that strange mixture of blood, which you will find in no other country. I could point to you a family whose grandfather was an Englishman, whose wife was Dutch, whose son married a French woman, and whose present four sons have now four wives of different nations. *He* is an American, who, leaving behind him all his ancient prejudices and manners, receives new ones from the new mode of life he has embraced, the new government he obeys, and the new rank he holds. ... Here individuals of all nations are melted into a new race of men, whose labours and posterity will one day cause great changes in the world.   (Crevecoeur, 1981 (1782): 69–70)

Over 200 years after Crevecoeur, Leon Wieseltier described the America of the 1990s as a "multicultural society" of "multicultural individuals" "Many things are possible in America, but the singleness of identity is not one of them," Wieselter noted, because the "dream of liberalism was not the multicultural society, it was the multicultural individual; and in America the dream came true" (Wieseltier, 1994: 11).

To summarize, over the course of American national history loose and fluid interethnic boundaries came to define the situation of immigrant groups. A set of political and civic patterns generated inclusionary and integrative processes as Americans became less apprehensive of the fractiousness of immigration and grew to regard pluralism as a positive aspect of their nationhood. The most fundamental pattern remained the legalistic and cosmopolitan conception of national identity issuing from the constitutional tradition of the American Revolution. Its movement toward a universal national identity was articulated through the historical development of an immigration policy that culminated in a worldwide system for admissions under a uniform alien status; and a naturalization policy paralleling an inclusive immigration policy that formed a single community of citizenship. The federalism of American political society constituted a secondary pattern. Through its inherent decentralization it provided a wide sphere of civil society in which immigrant populations could develop a communal life, and institutions that reflected their needs for security and identity. Because the federal polity limited centralized governmental power and allowed ample space for local divergence and control, immigrants exercised extensive self-determination and self-maintenance of their cultural and social existence. Through the civil rights of citizenship, immigrants invested local politics and public life with their ethnic interests.

Faced with the largest and most variegated immigration in world history, a federal polity eschewing centralized management perforce developed a deregulated tradition of pluralism in which ethnic identity and national identity coexisted in a kind of dynamic balance. A Harvard social psychologist, Thomas F. Pettigrew, noted that in the United States, "We have neither complete assimilation nor pluralism." The cosmopolitan and federal constitutionalism inherited from the American Revolution accommodated this equilibrium in a social order of fluidity and voluntary integration (Franklin *et al.*, 1971: 34; Glazer, 1975: 26–7; Higham, 1975: 18–20).

The United States early in its history faced the challenge of multicultural pluralism which other nations in the old world such as Germany, France, England and Japan are facing only today. Moreover, the United States stood out among many historically plural societies such as India, the Soviet Union or Brazil in its ability to develop unity out of ethnic diversity. Due to the mixing of migrant subpopulations, the United States has experienced a long, continuous process in which cultural hierarchies and partitions have broken down. This process generated patterns of cultural transfer, combination and unification guided by the practical need to find points of accommodation among the many ethnic fragments and between the fragments and the national whole.

In most eras of American national history, the organization of the whole under its values, institutions, social negotiations and cultural processes was controlled by an Anglo-Saxon core group who sustained their power and ruling identity in ways that countenanced domination and coercion (Mann, 1979: 44). Because they were involved in a balanced coexistence with the forces of external merger, immigrant subcommunities provided a pluralism that integrated the total society. Immigrant ethnic groups never became isolated, and national life depended on openness toward them. It is important to understand that these processes took time. The enclaves formed by immigrants gradually decomposed as one generation succeeded the next. The liberal and democratic conditions of the United States permitted immigrant subpopulations to turn themselves into building blocks for a national community through a cumulative – though not uniformly linear – process of social mobility and acculturation. Over the long term of national history, immigration in the United States did not entail a loss of social cohesiveness, despite the cultural diversity of the immigrants.

Specific social and cultural changes prevented the isolation of groups and created possibilities for broader associations. The latter patterns were the intermediary structures constituting the basis for higher levels of social cohesion and nationalization. Immigrant subpopulations travelled various ascending pathways corresponding to their situational and internal differences, into a fluid social structure of dynamic inequalites. Some ethnic groups possessed more members who capitalized on educational opportunity and entrepreneurialism; in other groups, individuals climbed the job rungs of the industrial occupational ladder. Immigrant ethnic groups did not fall into a fixed economic hierarchy. Popular education integrated the descendants of immigrants into unitary cultural communities based on English monolingualism and a common core of scholastic and civic knowledge (Tyack, 1974: 229–55; Lieberson, 1980: 163–4; Handlin, 1982; Conklin and Lourie, 1983: 54, Libereson and Waters, 1988). The expansion through schooling of social intercommunication among individuals and communities helped to integrate a national community. Family formation and intermarriage blended immigrant subpopulations into the patterns of the wider population, thus encouraging social cohesion. Ethnic exogamy had far-reaching effects on recomposing immigrant groups into a super-category of mixed and multiple ancestry that supported a broader national identity detached from homeland identification (Kennedy, 1944: 331–9; Herberg, 1955: 32–4; Alba, 1990: 14–15, 310–13; Lieberson and Waters, 1988: 6–8). At first embedded in ethnic enclaves, popular culture merged with a national mass culture that provided a wider identity (Handlin, 1973: 152–65; Rosenzweig, 1983: chs 2, 5; Peiss, 1986: 17–21; Cohen, 1990: ch. 2).

In American history, national democracy and society were closely coordinated. On the one hand, there was a positive correlation: a national life based on democracy was made vigorous and creative when the social system was fluid and group boundaries were weak and loose; when opportunities for social mobility and acculturation expanded; when the public arena included a variety of interests and communities. On the other hand, there was a negative correlation: a national life based on democracy declined when social and cultural fluidity shrank; when individuals and groups competed under conditions constricted by material limitation and social ostracism. In the short term, immigration probably reinforced the latter correlation. In its immediate temporal wake, immigration probably increased cultural distances and social divisions, exacerbating xenophobia and intergroup tensions. Depending on period and place, immigrants strained institutions and increased competition for resources, to the disadvantage of natives. The immediate tasks of finding a job and a home and starting a family were harsh and punishing for newcomers who were poor, uneducated and mistrusted as strangers. Conflict and struggle with unfriendly majorities, powerful elites and rival groups marked their steps toward meagre improvements in their lives. For each one who pushed doggedly ahead, others fell back into stagnant and confining situations.

Over the long term of national history, however, immigrants made possible the transformation of a rural province of England into the world's largest modern democracy. This immense achievement could not have occurred without the inputs of immigration that enlarged the pool of producers, consumers, entrepreneurs and human capital. Through their ethic of work, savings, familism, self-education and practical consumerism, the immigrants injected new vigor into the national economic culture. The economic historians have verified that immigration consistently pushed the economy ahead, or followed economic growth to galvanize it further (Jerome, 1926: 208; Kuznets and Rubin, 1954: 4–5; Easterlin, 1968: 30–2; Thomas, 1973: ch. 7; Muller, 1993: ch. 3).

As they helped create new conditions for expansion, immigrants created the opportunities that would lift them and their descendants upward on the economic ladder. The dynamic economic effects of immigrants upon the wider society and on their own communities have also been evinced by the most recent immigrants from the third world (Winnick, 1990: 34, 35, 39, 42; Chavez, 1991: 110–16; Kasinitz, 1992: 68–70, 93–5, 185–86; Moore and Vigil, 1993: 35, 72–3, 144). Over the succession of generations, more descendants of immigrants would advance than fall behind their ancestors.

Furthermore, in the long term, immigrants also helped expand the dimensions of liberty in a democratic society. They sought conditions that allowed them the freedom to rebuild their lives through their families and communities. They wished to insure self-determination of social, cultural and political choices, and thus widened the range of freedom for individual action. Immigrants established their rights to maintain elements of their ethnic legacies, as well as to modify them or to depart from them. By strengthening conditions for voluntary association and achievement, immigration has been a historic force for bringing national life to rest increasingly upon the interdependence of groups. Over the total span of history, the ethnic diversity created by worldwide immigration to the United States has proved to be a social integrator and a catalyst of nationhood.

NOTE

1. See the debates and discussion in the *Congressional Record* of the Eightieth Congress on the bills that produced the Displaced Persons Act of June 25, 1948 (62 Stat. 1009).

REFERENCES

Alba, Richard D. (1990), *Ethnic Identity: The Transformation of White America* (New Haven, CT: Yale University Press).

Archdeacon, Thomas (1983), *Becoming American: An Ethnic History* (New York: Free Press).

Bailyn, Bernard (1967), *The Ideological Origins of the American Revolution* (Cambridge, MA: Harvard University Press).

―― (1977), *The Peopling of British North America* (New York: Alfred A. Knopf).

Bernard, William S. (1950), *American Immigration Policy* (New York: Harper & Bros).

―― (1980), "Immigration: History of US Policy," in Stephan Thernstrom (ed.), *Harvard Encyclopedia of American Ethnic Groups* (Cambridge, MA: Harvard University Press).

Bodnar, John (1985), *The Transplanted: A History of Immigrants in Urban America* (Bloomington, IN: Indiana University Press).

Boyer, Paul (1978), *Urban Masses and Moral Order in America, 1820–1920* (Cambridge, MA: Harvard University Press).

Castles, Stephen (1993), "Immigration, Citizenship and the Nation State: An International Comparison," Thirty-first Congress of the International Institute of Sociology, University of Paris.

Chavez, Linda (1991), *Out of the Barrio: Toward a New Politics of Hispanic Assimilation* (New York: Basic Books).

Cohen, Lizabeth (1990), *Making a New Deal: Industrial Workers in Chicago, 1919–1939* (Cambridge: Cambridge University Press).

Commons, John R. (1907), *Races and Immigrants in America* (New York: Macmillan).

Conklin, Nancy Faires and Lourie, Margaret A. (1983), *A Host of Tongues: Language Communities in the United States* (New York: Free Press).

Crevecoeur, J. Hector St. John de (1981), *Letters from an American Farmer* (New York: Viking Penguin; originally published in 1782).

Daniels, Roger (1962), *The Politics of Prejudice: The Anti-Japanese Movement in California and the Struggle for Exclusion* (Berkeley, CA: University of California Press).

―― (1991), *Coming to America: A History of Immigration and Ethnicity in American Life* (New York: HarperPerennial).

Divine, Robert (1957), *American Immigration Policy, 1924–1952* (New Haven, CT: Yale University Press).

Donnelly, Ignatius (1891), *Caesar's Column: A Story of the Twentieth Century* (Chicago, IL: F. J. Schulte).

Easterlin, Richard (1968), *Population, Labor Force, and Long Swings in Economic Growth: The American Experience* (New York: National Bureau of Economic Research).

Foner, Eric (1994), "The Meaning of Freedom in the Age of Emancipation," *Journal of American History*, 81 (2), pp. 435–60.

Franklin, John Hope, Pettigrew, Thomas F. and Mack, Raymond W. (1971), *Ethnicity in American Life* (New York: Anti-Defamation League of B'nai B'rith).

Fuchs, Lawrence H. (1990), *The American Kaleidoscope: Race, Ethnicity, and the Civic Culture* (Hanover, NH: University Press of New England; Wesleyan).

Glazer, Nathan (1975), *Affirmative Discrimination: Ethnic Inequality and Public Policy* (New York: Basic Books).

—— (1983), *Ethnic Dilemmas, 1964–1982* (Cambridge, MA: Harvard University Press).

—— (ed.) (1985), *Clamor at the Gates: The New American Immigration* (San Francisco, CA: Institute for Contemporary Studies).

Goldin, Claudia (1993), "The Political Economy of Immigration Restriction in the United States, 1890 to 1921," Working Paper no. 4345 (Cambridge, MA: National Bureau of Economic Research).

Greenfeld, Liah (1992), *Nationalism: Five Roads to Modernity* (Cambridge, MA: Harvard University Press).

Gulick, Sidney L. (1918), *American Democracy and Asiatic Citizenship* (New York: Charles Scribner's Sons).

Habakkuk, H. J. and Postan, M. (1965), *The Cambridge Economic History of Europe, The Industrial Revolutions and After: Incomes, Population and Technological Change*, vol. VI (Cambridge: Cambridge University Press).

Handlin, Oscar (1957), *Race and Nationality in American Life* (Boston, MA: Little, Brown).

—— (1973), *The Uprooted*, 2nd edn (Boston, MA: Little, Brown).

—— (1982), "Education and the European Immigrant, 1820–1920," Bernard J. Weiss (ed.), *American Education and the European Immigrant, 1840–1940* (Urbana, IL: University of Illinois Press).

Handlin, Oscar and Handlin, Lilian (1989), *Liberty in Expansion, 1760–1850* (New York: Harper & Row).

Handlin, Oscar and Handlin, Mary (1961), *The Dimensions of Liberty* (Cambridge, MA: Harvard University Press).

Hays, Samuel P. (1967), *The Response to Industrialism: 1885–1914* (Chicago, IL: University of Chicago Press).

Herberg, Will (1955), *Protestant–Catholic–Jew* (New York: Doubleday).

Higham, John (1955), *Strangers in the Land: American Nativism, 1860–1925* (New Brunswick, NJ: Rutgers University Press).

—— (1970), "The Reorientation of American Culture in the 1890's," John Higham, *Writing American History: Essays on Modern Scholarship* (Bloomington, IN: Indiana University Press).

—— (1975), *Send These to Me: Jews and Other Immigrants in Urban America* (New York: Atheneum).

—— (1993), "History of American Immigration: An Overview," presented at "U. S. Immigration: The Land of Promise," Smithsonian Institution and Federal Judicial Center Seminar, Washington, DC, 2 November.

Horowitz, Donald L. (1985), *Ethnic Groups in Conflict* (Berkeley, CA: University of California Press).

—— (1992), "Immigration and Group Relations," in Donald L. Horowitz and Gerard Noiriel (eds), *Immigration and Group Relations in France and America* (New York: New York University Press).

Hutchinson, E. P. (1981), *Legislative History of American Immigration Policy, 1798–1965* (Philadelphia, PA: University of Pennsylvania Press).

Jerome, Harry (1926), *Migration and Business Cycles* (New York: National Bureau of Economic Research).

Jones, Maldwyn Allen (1960), *American Immigration* (Chicago, IL: University of Chicago Press).

Kasinitz, Philip (1992), *Caribbean New York: Black Immigrants and the Politics of Race* (Ithaca: Cornell University Press).

Kennedy, Ruby Jo Reeves (1944), "Single or Triple Melting Pot? Intermarriage Trends in the New Haven, 1870–1940," *American Journal of Sociology*, 49, pp. 331–9.

Kettner, James H (1974), "The Development of American Citizenship in the Revolutionary Era: The Idea of Volitional Allegiance," *American Journal of Legal History*, 18, pp. 208–42.

Kuznets, Simon and Rubin, Ernest (1954), *Immigration and the Foreign Born*, Occasional Paper 46 (New York: National Bureau of Economic Research).

Lieberson, Stanley (1980), *A Piece of the Pie: Blacks and White Immigrants since 1880* (Berkeley, CA: University of California Press).

Lieberson, Stanley and Waters, Mary (1988), *From Many Strands: Ethnic and Racial Groups in Contemporary America* (New York: Russell Sage).

Lipset, Seymour Martin (1963), *The First New Nation* (New York: Basic Books).

London, Jack (1908), *The Iron Heel* (New York: Macmillan).

Malcolm, Ray (1921), "American Citizenship and the Japanese," *Annals of the American Academy*, 93, pp. 77–81.

Mann, Arthur (1959), *La Guardia: A Fighter against his Times* (Chicago, IL: University of Chicago Press).

—— (1979), *The One and the Many: Reflections on the American Identity* (Chicago, IL: University of Chicago Press).

McGovney, D. O. (1923), "Race Discrimination in Naturalization," *Iowa Law Bulletin*, 8, pp. 129–61, 211–44.

Moore, Joan and Vigil, James Diego (1993), "Barrios in Transition," in Joan Moore and Raquel Pinderhughes (eds), *In the Barrios: Latinos and the Underclass Debate* (New York: Russell Sage Foundation).

Morgan, Edmund S. (1975), *American Slavery – American Freedom: The Ordeal of Colonial Virginia.* (New York: W. W. Norton).

Muller, Thomas (1993), *Immigrants and the American City* (New York: New York University Press).

Nash, Gary (1974), *Red, White, and Black: The Peoples of Early America* (Englewood Cliffs, NJ: Prentice Hall).

Peiss, Kathy (1986), *Cheap Amusements: Working Women and Leisure in Turn-of-the-Century New York* (Philadelphia, PA: Temple University Press).

Pocock, J. G. A. (1975), *The Machiavellian Moment: Florentine Political Thought and the Atlantic Republican Tradition* (Princeton, NJ: Princeton University Press).

Rahe, Paul A. (1994), *Republics Ancient and Modern*, vol. 3 (Chapel Hill, NC: University of North Carolina Press).

Reimers, David M. (1985), *Still the Golden Door: The Third World Comes to America* (New York: Columbia University Press).

Riggs, Fred W. (1950), *Pressures on Congress: A Study of the Repeal of Chinese Exclusion* (New York: Columbia University Press).

Riis, Jacob A. (1890), *How the Other Half Lives* (New York: Charles Scribner's).

Rosenzweig, Roy (1983), *Eight Hours for What We Will: Workers and Leisure in an Industrial City, 1870–1920* (Cambridge: Cambridge University Press).

Ross, Edward A. (1901), *Social Control: A Survey of the Foundations of Order* (New York: Macmillan).

—— (1914), *The Old World in the New: The Significance of Past and Present Immigration to the American People* (New York: Century).

Schuck, Peter H. and Smith, Rogers M. (1985), *Citizenship without Consent: Illegal Aliens in the American Polity* (New Haven, CT: Yale University Press).

Taeuber, Conrad and Taeuber, Irene B. (1958), *The Changing Population of the United States* (New York: John Wiley & Sons).

Taylor, Philip (1971), *The Distant Magnet: European Emigration to the USA* (New York: Harper & Row).

Thomas, Brinley (1973), *Migration and Economic Growth: A Study of Great Britain and the Atlantic Economy* (Cambridge: Cambridge University Press).

Tyack, David B. (1974), *The One Best System: A History of American Urban Education* (Cambridge, MA: Harvard University Press).

Ueda, Reed (1994), *Postwar Immigrant America: A Social History* (New York: St Martin's Press).

US Commissioner-General of Immigration (1899), *Annual Report* (Washington, DC: US Government Printing Office).

US Congress (1924), Sixty-Eighth, First Session, *Congressional Record – House*, Part 2 (Washington, DC: US Government Printing Office).

US Congress (1950), Senate, Committee on the Judiciary, *The Immigration and Naturalization Systems of the United States* (Washington, DC: US Government Printing Office).

US Immigration and Naturalization Service (1992), *1990 Statistical Yearbook of the Immigration and Naturalization Service* (Washington, DC: US Government Printing Office).

Wiebe, Robert (1967), *The Search for Order, 1877–1920* (New York: Hill & Wang).

Wieseltier, Leon (1994), "The Trouble with Multiculturalism," *New York Times Book Review*, 23 (October), p. 11.

Wilentz, Sean (1994), "Sense and Sensitivity," *The New Republic*, 211 (31 October), pp. 43–8.

Winnick, Louis (1990), *New People in Old Neighborhoods: The Role of New Immigrants in Rejuvenating New York's Communities* (New York: Russell Sage Foundation).

Wood, Gordon S. (1969), *The Creation of the American Republic, 1776–1787* (Chapel Hill, NC: University of North Carolina Press).

—— (1992), *The Radicalism of the American Revolution* (New York: Alfred A. Knopf).

3 The Incorporation of Immigrants in the United States

Nathan Glazer

Many terms have been used to describe the process by which immigrants become part of the American population: they are "incorporated", or "absorbed", or "integrated", or "assimilated". Each of these terms has a somewhat different meaning, a somewhat different set of implications. "Assimilation" is perhaps the most widely used, and it is also the term that has become, in recent years, the most objectionable to many elements in the United States. It implies the almost complete disappearance of the original ethnic traits that characterize immigrants from a given nation. We also use the term "Americanization" to describe the process by which assimilation occurs. That also has become objectionable. The popular term that has been widely used to characterize the process and end-product of assimilation and Americanization, the "melting pot", has equally become objectionable to many (Glazer, 1993). Terms such as "salad bowl" or "glorious mosaic" (in which the individual ethnic and racial elements that make up the American population would still be identifiable) have replaced these earlier terms.

We are in an age, to use another term that has only recently come to prominence, of "identity politics", and "identity" is threatened by "assimilation" and the "melting pot", which both refer to the reduction of only one kind of identity, ethnic or racial or national. "Identity", as in "identity politics", also refers to other identities, as a male or female (or homosexual or lesbian), as an adolescent or aged person, as someone handicapped or distinctively gifted, and these identities are not in question when we speak of assimilation or the melting pot, although all these other non-ethnic and nonracial identities play a role in identity politics.

56

This chapter will examine some contemporary and to my mind relatively new issues that have emerged around this question of absorption, integration, or incorporation, of immigrants into American society. It will complement Reed Ueda's treatment (see Chapter 2) of major themes in the history of the absorption of immigrants in the United States by providing a discussion of the contemporary disputes around the issue of the incorporation of immigrants into American life.

Thirty years ago one could have argued that a common understanding pervaded the treatment of this issue, among politicians, in the general public, among scholars. It was the era of John F. Kennedy's *A Nation of Immigrants*, a time when the quota restrictions, by race and ethnicity, that had characterized American immigration policy for 40 years were being swept away by the historic reforms of 1965. That era of good feeling in regard to immigration lasted for perhaps 20 years. It climaxed in the celebrations around the 1986 rededication of the Statue of Liberty, which had become reinterpreted through a series of historical accidents as an emblem of America welcoming immigrants. The historical accidents included its adjacency to the major immigrant stations that processed the vast stream of immigrants from Europe – first Castle Garden, then Ellis Island, which is now a museum to immigration – and the affixing to the statue's base of Emma Lazarus' famous poem, in which the Statue welcomes the unfortunates of the world.

The Statue's original theme and title, "Liberty *Enlightening* the World", whose point was that America was sending throughout the world the beneficent rays of freedom, was thus reinterpreted into the somewhat different theme of America *welcoming* the world. But even as the Statue was being rededicated after a very expensive restoration, and the new national museum of immigration was preparing to open on Ellis Island, there were harbingers of a new mood toward immigration developing in the country. In 1978, Congress had set up the Select Commission on Immigration and Refugee Policy; in 1981 the commission issued its report and in 1986, in the very year of the high point of the celebration of American immigration, after years of discussion and argument, Congress passed the Immigration Restriction and Control Act (IRCA), embodying the major thrust of the Commission's proposals.

IRCA was expected to address decisively the issues that had developed in the wake of the landmark legislation of 1965, in particular the flow of illegal immigrants and the buildup of a large number of illegal immigrants living permanently in the country.[1] The legislation incorporated penalties on the employers of illegal immigrants which were expected to cut the flow of illegal immigrants, because they would no longer easily find work, and an amnesty for those in the country for some years, which was expected to eliminate the problem of a large population that remained in illegal status. As it has turned out, it has been far more difficult than expected to deal with these issues. After a brief drop, illegal immigration resumed its old rate of 200 000–300 000 a year, and another backlog of illegal immigrants began to build up, after the reduction in the old backlog by 3 million applications for permanent residency as provided for in the 1986 act. Immigration was addressed again in major legislation in 1990, whose major effect was to increase legal immigration, and by 1994 immigration, once of interest only to specialists and advocates, had become an important national issue. The new mood of discontent with the scale and character of immigration, evident since the middle 1980s, had flowered by 1994 and 1995 into a full debate on immigration, with a new commission holding hearings and conducting studies, and new legislation expected.

One major concern in the new debate is indeed over the "absorbability" of new immigrants, or, to use the older and more widely used term, their "assimilability". These concerns are not simple, nor simply presented. In the historic action taken by the citizens of California in a referendum in 1994, to deny illegal immigrants access to most public services and benefits paid for or administered by the state, the major issue seemed to be the costs of immigration, and the degree to which these costs were imposed on the state by illegal immigrants. The voting public seemed to be primarily concerned with the public burden of immigration. This was also the issue raised by the Governor of California and by the governors of other states seriously affected by immigration, such as Florida, who called upon the federal government to reimburse them for some of the costs of illegal immigration, such as the cost of maintaining illegal immigrants convicted of crimes in state prisons, of educating the children of illegal immigrants, and of providing health care to them.

This seems on the face of it a very different issue from that of absorption or assimilation. But it is closely connected with it. For if new immigrants can adapt to American life in the way it is popularly believed that earlier, predominantly European, immigrants did, then there would be less concern over the new immigrants and their costs to government. It is commonly believed that new immigrants are not adapting as well as old. Whatever history may tell us about this, the belief that something has changed plays a key role in popular thinking about immigration. The public debate is over public costs, which seems a far cry from the ethnic, religious and racial prejudice that led to sharp restriction of immigration in the 1920s. But behind the public debate, I would argue, is a concern about absorbability or assimilability, in large part driven by the striking asymmetry between the racial and ethnic character of contemporary immigration, which is about 85 percent non-European, and the racial and ethnic character of the existing population of the United States, which is about 75 percent European in origin. (Of course that percentage is declining under the impact of immigration. That is part of the reason for concern.)

The easiest way to talk about immigrant problems in the United States, a way that does not apparently threaten to raise the disruptive specters of racial, ethnic and religious prejudice, is economic. The public debate – as in the case of the debate over Proposition 187 in California, which banned public benefits to illegal immigrants (this matter is now in the courts, where its constitutionality is being tested), or the demands for financial relief from the national government by governors of immigrant-impacted states, or the current (spring 1995) debates in the new Republican-controlled Congress over the eligibility of immigrants, legal as well as illegal, to receive various government benefits – is about costs, an economic matter. But it will not be long before concern over the racial and religious and cultural characteristics of the new immigrants also becomes part of the public debate (see, for example, Brimelow, 1995). Costs are in part dependent on the educational and economic capacity of immigrants, how they manage economically in the new environment. Managing well means that public costs will be low, and indeed costs may be covered or more than covered by revenue raised in taxes from the working immigrants.

Much of the debate centers on the economic fate of the new immigrants, and here there is a range of opinion among competent economists, from those who see immigrants as fairly rapidly equalling the occupational and taxpaying level of natives (for example, Simon, 1989) to those who emphasize the decline in the educational level and occupational skills of immigrants (Borjas, 1990). Many issues ancillary to this central one of costs come up in this debate. Do new immigrants create jobs – either as entrepreneurs, redevelopers of derelict city areas [an important role emphasized by Muller (1993)], or as expanders of a market for goods and services provided by others? [The ironic result of one econometric analysis was that immigration in California was good for the job prospects and income of black women, probably because these were concentrated in the public sector, providing the services that grew as a result of immigrant needs! (Muller and Espenshade 1985: 97).]

The debate is complicated by the fact that the immigrants are diverse – more diverse in some key respects than those of the mass immigrations of the nineteenth and early twentieth centuries – and thus provide evidence for contradictory and conflicting positions. This diversity is one of nation of origin, of race and of religion (there were very few if any Buddhist, Hindu or Muslim immigrants during the earlier period of mass immigration), but the key issue as far as costs are considered is the capacity to participate in the labor market, best measured by education.

Here we find the most distinctive aspect of the diversity of the new immigrants: they are polarized between those who come in with less education than the "average" American, and thus can be seen as a potential burden (or as a source of low-cost labor, depending upon the economic position of the observer, and his attitude to the maintenance of low-labor-cost industries in the United States), and those who come in with more education than the average American, and thus may be seen as potentially high earners and substantial taxpayers. The first may be disproportionately liable to becoming public charges; the latter will disproportionately contribute through taxation to the public resources necessary to maintain public charges. Asian immigrant groups on the whole come in with high educational and occupational qualifications, equalling or surpassing the mean of the native American population. Among the Latin American and Caribbean immigrants, a very substantial number enter with educational and occupational qualifications less than the average in the American population. The former group may take jobs as doctors, engineers, nurses, etc. and indeed may create jobs for the less qualified, the way a doctor's practice does.[2] The latter may compete with the less qualified native American, principally black Americans and earlier immigrant and longtime-resident Latin Americans, taking jobs away from them and thus adding to public costs, even if the immigrants themselves do not become public charges.

The economic argument, which gets more and more sophisticated, is in the end inconclusive, perhaps not scientifically, but certainly politically: people will act on anecdotal evidence, out of concern over their own economic condition. In economically hard-pressed California, they won't wait for, or be affected by, the latest economic analyses; in Miami and Dade County, where it is impossible to build schools fast enough to accommodate new immigrant children, they won't be much persuaded by an economic analysis showing that building these schools and educating these children will more than pay for itself when the children enter the labor force. (I am not suggesting that this case can be made, only that it will not be on the basis of such analyses that decisions on immigration are taken.)

Three new features, none of them purely economic, deeply affect American thinking about immigration, and all of them relate to this issue of absorbability or assimilability. The first is a concern over the American future in general, which takes its clearest form in worries over the economic future. We have had periods of uneasiness and uncertainty over the economic future of the United States before and, indeed, one period of deep pessimism, the Great Depression. Immigration was not an issue at the time: it had been sharply reduced by the immigration legislation of the 1920s, and would in any case have been reduced by the impact of the Great Depression itself. During the 1930s, more people probably left the United States than entered it.³ Today, Americans are worried about the economic future of the country, and don't see it as a short-term crisis. They see ever more effective economic competition from abroad, taking away American markets abroad and American jobs at home; they are shaken by the troubles of such American giants as IBM and General Motors (other American giants which once attested to American predominance, such as US Steel, no longer exist, and US Steel has been swallowed by the anonymity of USX). They are shaken by the reduction in so many good white-collar jobs as American corporations "downsize", "rightsize", merge or go under. If native Americans are having a hard time, the thinking goes, will new immigrants make it harder or easier for them? Economic analyses may demonstrate that new immigrants create new markets, creating new jobs, but these are less persuasive than the reality of Asian computer programmers and financial analysts, nurses and doctors, who have become so visible in some of the few areas of the American economy that are still expanding.⁴

The concern about the American future, the shift from a prevailing optimism to a prevailing uncertainty, if not yet pessimism, is more than simply economic, and is evoked by other than purely economic concerns. For example, there is concern over the future of the American family, with its high divorce rates and high rates of birth out of wedlock. There is concern over crime. There is concern over the American environment. If one is worried about the environment, immigration may appear as exacerbating rather than neutral or helpful. If one is worried about crime, it can be argued that there is no good evidence of greater criminality among immigrants than native Americans, but that may not affect public perceptions, which focus on Colombian and Dominican drug dealers, presented in the mass media as particularly vicious and brutal. If one is worried about the family and illegitimacy, the argument can be made – and is made by some immigration advocates – that immigrant families hardly contribute to the crisis, for they are more stable and more solid than native American families, white or black, but that does seem to be a counsel of despair in dealing with our own family problems.

Clearly these concerns will rise and fall, depending on economic circumstances primarily, and we can argue over whether there is a long-range trend toward pessimism. Yet it seems clear that the factors that encouraged a positive attitude toward immigration until the 1920s, and again for the first three decades after the Second World War, no longer prevail: on the whole, people do not think the United States needs more people to fill up empty lands. They do not think the American economy will ever again be as blessed by good fortune (plentiful raw materials, unsettled land, advantage over competitors owing to widespread public education, etc.) as it was during the nineteenth century, or in the decades of the brief "American Century" following the Second World War. They do not believe the American economy can ever be as predominant as it was in the first few postwar decades (Glazer, 1995).

Are these concerns over what may be conceived of as a new "closing of the frontier" valid? Are the economic circumstances that face today's immigrants so different from those that faced immigrants in the decades before the sharp reduction of immigration by law in the 1920s, and do they warrant these fears over their economic assimilability? I believe the circumstances are vastly different, but not in ways that support the argument that assimilation was easy then based on the availability of work, now it is hard because of the scarcity of jobs; or that entry into the economy for the unskilled was easy then because of the great demand for unskilled labor to build railroads, expand cities, and the like, but now it is harder because there are fewer jobs for the unskilled.

This point of view, focusing on differences in job opportunities for immigrants, is common and widely expressed. But the change in the economy does not mean there are fewer jobs for the unskilled: there are, rather, different jobs, in particular a shift from construction and manufacturing to services. Nor is it the case that the former jobs paid "better" than the unskilled jobs now available. When new immigrants went into the steel mills or coal mines, or the textile and automobile and clothing industries, these were not unionized, did not pay high wages, and were far from offering a platform for economic mobility, for the immigrants themselves or for their children. Yet it seems to be taken as self-evident in many contrasts between then and now that conditions were better from the point of view of economic opportunity for earlier immigrants than for current immigrants.

A similar argument has been made to explain the difficulties of American blacks, who moved north into the cities in great numbers during and after the Second World War, and whose condition has been a permanent subject of national concern since the civil rights movement and the urban riots of the 1960s. This black migration occurred before the great expansion of immigration in the 1970s and 1980s. Many asked, why are the blacks having a harder time in moving upward economically than European immigrants did? This was a question asked by the public generally and by social scientists.[5] Of course, one answer was that those asking the question had forgotten what great difficulties immigrants had faced, despite the abundant literature describing their trials. Immigrants had not had it so much easier. Another answer that sadly had to be given a large place was that blacks faced a much greater degree of prejudice and discrimination. But one answer that was commonly given – that immigrants had entered an expanding economy with plentiful jobs for the un-skilled and uneducated, while blacks were entering an economy in which such jobs were declining – did not stand up under analysis. It is true that the number of jobs based only on simple muscle power were declining. But these were never good jobs, from the point of view of earnings or opportunity to advance. Further, while it is true that jobs increasingly demanded more in the way of literacy and education, it was also the case that opportunities to acquire the necessary liter-acy and skills had greatly expanded. In the post-war period there was a huge expansion in community colleges, which were mostly oriented to providing education for the kinds of jobs that were expanding and that were based on a higher level of literacy and some specialized education. The notion does not seem convincing that the great opportunity offered the earlier immigrants was the availability of unskilled jobs, and that the decline in such jobs was the problem faced by blacks migrating north in the 1940s, 1950s and 1960s, and by immigrants coming in on the basis of more liberal legislation in the 1970s and 1980s.

Immigrants came here to work, then and now, and over-whelmingly they found work. The change in the kinds of jobs made available by the rapidly changing American economy did not mean that they disproportionately contributed to the numbers of unemployed. Further, as was pointed out above, many immigrants came with the higher education and higher skills that the expanding sectors of the economy demanded. Some, because of language difficulties, could not make use of their higher education and specialized skills: it was common to find college-educated Koreans operating stores in ghetto areas. But many came with English (Indians, Filipinos) and were able to enter the expanding sectors of the economy that offered better-paying work and generally required knowledge of English. A higher proportion of immigrants today are liter-ate and educated, compared to the immigrants of the earlier third of the century, and the opportunities for more educa-tion to qualify for jobs that demand it has also greatly expanded, in our hugely expanded system of community and state colleges.

WELFARE

A second troubling theme that is new on the American scene, and new in relation to mass immigration, is that of "welfare" narrowly conceived, or the "welfare state" generally. This also raises concerns about assimilability, as well as the more obvious concerns about the costs of new immigrants (see Schuck and Smith, 1985). Welfare has become a major issue in the middle 1990s, with Democrats and Republicans, governors and congressmen, seemingly competing to see who can be more harsh in cutting back benefits. In previous waves of mass immigration, the provision of public welfare was not an issue because such provision was very limited indeed: immigrants sank or swam, with no public assistance, and at little cost to the public finances. That helps explain the pattern by which in the past immigrant flows rose and fell depending on econ-omic circumstances in the United States. This pattern it seems has ended: the jagged shape of the immigrant curve, with sharp rises and falls, characteristic of immigration until the Second World War, has been replaced by a steady upward curve, impervious to economic conditions and affected only by the regulations governing the number and type of immigrants: if they can come, they do. Immigrants now come at a steady rate, regardless of economic opportunity. The troubles of New York City in the 1970s and 1990s, in which hundred of thousands of jobs were lost, did nothing to reduce its flow of immigrants: indeed the flow has increased.[6] The economic troubles of California in the 1990s seem to have done very little to reduce the flow of immigrants, legal and illegal, into California. One reason for this must be the safety net of social and income support programs, which, inadequate as they appear compared to those of Sweden or Germany, look very good compared to those of Mexico or the Dominican Republic or the Philippines.

There must be other reasons, of course, for this new factor of relative unresponsiveness of immigration from underdeveloped into developed countries, to economic conditions in the developed countries: the differences between wages and opportunities in the sending country (or the country from which people are fleeing) and the advanced industrial countries they seek to enter are so great that temporary declines in economic activity in the economically developed world do not seem to matter much to the intending migrant. Immigrants take the opportunity to enter, regardless of economic conditions, and wait for the next upturn. The intensity of civil conflicts, the degree of misery, the amount of poverty, in many of the sending countries (El Salvador, Nicaragua, Haiti, Cuba, Mexico, Vietnam, Cambodia and others) has increased. And there are all the other factors encouraging greater mobility, such as more vivid communication through new media, better conditions of life in economically developed nations, easier transportation and the like. But the welfare safety net may be one factor, and even if it is not, the public believes it is, and in any case does not want to extend its benefits to illegal immigrants. The trend of public policy in the United States, at both the state and federal levels, is now in favor of cutting public benefits for illegal immigrants, and some benefits also for legal immigrants, which certainly suggests that whatever conclusion sound analysis may reach as to the effect of welfare benefits on immigration, the public believes it does have some effect, and this becomes an important factor in the turn against high levels of immigration.[7]

It is in fact the case that some groups of legal immigrants (Vietnamese, Hmong from Laos) have a high proportion on welfare. Some of the groups with the highest proportion on welfare are refugees rather than purely voluntary immigrants, and the fact that they come for political reasons to escape persecution, rather than primarily for calculated economic advantage, may in part explain this phenomenon. Another reason may be the automatic availability to refugees of federal income support, which may habituate them to the view that income support from the state, replacing federal refugee support, is natural and their due, rather than a stigmatized last resort, which is what welfare support is supposed to be. Nor are all the groups with high levels of welfare use refugees: the Dominicans stand out (Borjas, 1990: 236).[8]

Welfare may also mean different things and have different implications for different groups. In the American mind, it means family breakup and families headed by women, but this is not the case for the Vietnamese and the Hmong. The immigrants' disproportionate use of welfare for the aged may itself be a sign of family strength. There seems to be a pattern in which immigrant families bring over aged parents under the family reunification provisions of immigration law, and since these have neither income of their own nor Social Security benefits on the basis of work in the United States covered by social security contributions, they are eligible for payments under Supplemental Security Income, a federal program. Here the admirable strong family commitments of some immigrant groups – which have been presented by some advocates of higher immigration as a model that Americans, notorious for family break-up, might follow – interact with immigration and welfare law to create a substantial burden.[9]

In any case, just as "welfare" in general has become a major political issue in the United States, "immigrants on welfare", whether or not the proportions are greater than among other Americans, has become a major issue. The existence of the welfare state thus raises a new concern about assimilability: instead of returning home if they cannot make it in the United States, immigrants will stay and become part of the dependent class, which, whatever its size or cost, has become a major issue in the United States.

Does this new situation of an expanded safety net change the pattern of assimilation of new immigrants? One thing it does mean is that there is a reduced rate of return of immigrants to their native lands on the basis of poor economic prospects. Many immigrants, in particular refugees, would not return under any circumstances. The safety net – now being modified so that its meshes will be much larger – does create the risk that immigrants can adapt to welfare and become a dependent class, and this would certainly affect their assimilability. This seems to be the case with the small group of Hmong. But the danger of new immigrants forming a large new underclass of persons disproportionately on welfare does not at present seem to be great. The American underclass is primarily made up of native blacks, and the contribution of new immigrants to it is minor. Nevertheless, the relationship of new immigrants to welfare is not something that can be summarily dismissed: welfare undoubtedly contributes to the propensity to immigrate owing to the protection it provides, and whether it goes further to help create a substantial number of the permanently dependent is something that will have to be monitored.

MULTICULTURALISM

A third new element in the equation affecting assimilability is the impact of the growing acceptance of American multiculturalism and diversity, in public schools, in the mass media, in industry, in American social life. This has an ambiguous and complex relation to immigrant absorbability and assimilability. On the one hand, the fact that nativist resistance to non-white, non-Christian and non-Protestant immigration has never been weaker means that no significant public objection is raised to the present religious, ethnic and racial character of immigration (which is overwhelmingly non-white, prevailingly non-Protestant and in large measure non-Christian). The low level of prejudice should foster the conditions that make settlement and success in this country easier. On the other hand, the fact that multiculturalism and diversity are so widely accepted, particularly in the public schools, once leading agents of "Americanization", leads to alarm among many, that under these conditions the new immigrants will not be successfully assimilated or absorbed, particularly from a cultural point of view.[10]

Once again, how valid are these fears? That there has been a change in the culture, expectations and ambitions of the public schools since the age of mass European immigration is undeniable. The Superintendent of Schools of New York City at that time, William H. Maxwell, said the school "is the melting pot which converts the children of the immigrants ... into sturdy, independent American citizens".[11] No head of the New York City public schools would dream of speaking up for assimilation this boldly today.

How much does it matter? What were the effects of this emphasis on assimilation in American public schools, an emphasis that was dominant until the 1960s? Did it matter that the portraits of Washington and Lincoln left the walls to be replaced by Martin Luther King and Cesar Chavez? That bilingual education, much of it aimed at maintaining the home language, replaced the sink-and-swim, English-language-only classrooms? Of course it must have had some effects, but probably not as great as is commonly feared. There is no good evidence that today's immigrant children on the whole learn English at a slower rate than in the past. Their attitudes may be less patriotic – but so are the attitudes of most Americans in a post-Vietnam and post-Cold-War world. One would not be surprised if Mexican children were learning English at a slower rate, both because of the prevalence of bilingual classrooms (argued for because this would facilitate entry into English-language classes, but there is no evidence that it does so) and because of the Mexican and Spanish-language dominance of huge neighborhoods. But the power of American popular culture, operating through television, movies, sports and the like, is such that I think assimilation, if measured by English-language ability and use, and adoption of some elements of American culture, proceeds at a rate no slower than in the age of mass European immigration.

Students of the assimilation process among new immigrants have recently noted another basis of concern regarding assimilation. Into what are new immigrant children assimilated?

The conditions of life in big-city schools are so disordered, the prevalence of violence so marked, the degree of failure and the resistance to authority so great, that one can well fear that assimilation of new immigrants may be to a dysfunctional America, the America of the lower-depths of the large urban centers. This concern emerges in the research of Alejandro Portes and Min Zhou (1993) on adolescents in Miami and San Diego, and that of Mary Waters (1994) on Caribbean youths in New York City. This is a fear that simply did not exist in the age of mass European immigration: becoming more like native Americans, more like the children of earlier immigrants, was considered uniformly a good thing. But it is ironic that one legitimate fear concerning new immigrants compared with old is created not by anything in the new immigrants but by what has happened to American society. In the disordered life in the poor sections of the large American cities, the nation provides an unhealthy environment for the new immigrant.

Of course, this sweeping judgment does not characterize all low-income section of large cities, or all immigrants. Immigrants have also been able to impose their stamp on declining central-city areas, reviving them economically, as we see in many accounts (for example, Winnick, 1990), and perhaps improving their schools, but there is less evidence of that.

Most Americans still feel that assimilation and "Americanization" are the right objectives in immigrant policy, and still find it desirable that immigrants be absorbed and assimilated. For this reason, the general view regarding how well assimilation is proceeding will affect how Americans respond to immigration. They will be friendly if the prospects for absorption are good, hostile if they are not. These issues are now hotly contested. The advocates of multiculturalism are perhaps strongest in the field of education and schooling, and resist the notion that immigrants, from a cultural point of view, should be absorbed or assimilated. They argue that original cultures should be maintained, and that the assimilationist and "Americanizing" policies dominant during and after the period of the last mass immigration, in the 1920s through the 1950s, were wrong morally and psychologically, imposing great damage on immigrants, adult and children, who were deprived of their identity.

In view of the strength of these trends, expressed in the new curricula in the schools emphasizing multiculturalism and diversity, and in bilingual education for children from non-English speaking families, those who believe immigrants should be Americanized, should be assimilated, that a common American identity has been created and should be maintained, see present levels of immigration as alarming. This alarm, we should emphasize, is cultural, not economic (though one may be alarmed on both grounds). It is activated by the fear that immigrants can no longer be successfully assimilated and absorbed, that they will remain as distinct sub-cultures, raising possibilities of conflict of the kind we have recently seen in Quebec and elsewhere.

I have been speaking in this chapter more about fears and concerns than about actualities, more about what people think is happening in regard to the absorption or assimilation of immigrants than about what is really happening. I have given my own views and some evidence from current research. But the extent of our knowledge is not very satisfactory. There are various measures that are, in one respect or another, suitable for making a judgment about assimilation – for example: the learning of English; the rate at which immigrants become citizens; their economic position, and to what degree they lag behind or move ahead of native Americans; their level of achievement in school and in higher education; the immigrant role in politics; the degree of intermarriage between immigrants and natives, or between immigrant groups; the degree to which there is a strong commitment to the maintenance of an original identity. I do not think, if we accumulated all these figures and estimated the situation in these and other respects, we would find evidence that supports the considerable alarm about these matters. I believe we would find that, overall, present-day immigrants probably show rates of English acquisition, naturalization, acceptance of a new American identity and so on, not markedly different from those of older immigrants (Glazer, 1997).

The issue that confuses judgment in these matters is the great diversity among immigrant groups themselves. For example, Asian groups with high proportions of professionals learn English faster, naturalize at a higher rate, attain more satisfactory economic positions and become more active in politics, than Mexican or Dominican immigrants. And so the question becomes: to what extent should we try to limit the immigration of the latter, foster the immigration of the former? We also know that legal immigrants score better on all these measures than illegal – it is almost tautologous to say so. So almost everyone agrees on limiting illegal immigration. Yet the matter is not so simple, even leaving aside the great difficulty of actually controlling illegal immigration. Whenever we make a broad statement, we cover a host of difficulties and contradictions. Thus, illegal immigrants include not only the relatively poorly educated Mexicans, but the relatively well-educated and English-speaking Irish, a good number of well-educated Israelis, and other who do not necessarily do poorly in the US labor market. It is because of these differences among groups that in the next steps in immigration reform we will undoubtedly see further effort to raise the educational and occupational quality of immigrants.

This entire discussion, it should be realized, should be placed in the larger historical context that has been set out in chapter 2 by Reed Ueda. That context is one in which racial, religious and ethnic limits on immigration have been consistently reduced; in which the American people have increasingly seen immigration as one of the fundamental commitments of American polity and society; in which their popular leaders, whether John F. Kennedy or Ronald Reagan, have in the last half-century been consistent supporters of the worth and value of immigration for American society; in which immigrants, whatever the degree of prejudice and discrimination they have met, have, at a public level, been welcomed into American society – indeed, as some now argue, have been forced into it by vigorous policies of assimilation, Americanization, naturalization and Anglicization. Within this prevailingly positive attitude to immigration, however, changes in American life and institutions do raise questions as to how strong these forces for absorption will be in the future.

The shift from a generally approving attitude toward the process of assimilation and the working of the melting pot, to one in which these terms take on, for many, a pejorative meaning, must also affect popular attitudes toward immigration. In a word, Americans ask, will these new immigrants become Americans, in the same way and at the same rate as others in earlier decades became Americans? These fears can be dismissed as ethnocentric, ahistorical, narrow-minded, even racist, but they certainly exist and affect public attitudes toward immigration policy and toward many other policies that affect immigrants and minority groups.

NOTES

1. For the work of the Commission and the conflicts over the subsequent legislation see Fuchs (1985) and Harris N Miller (1985).
2. See Fix and Zimmermann (1944:257). Almost a quarter of immigrant male workers have less than 9 years of education, compared with only a few percent of native male workers. As many immigrant as native male workers have 16 years of education or more. The higher-educated are found among the Asian immigrants, the more poorly educated among the Hispanic. The mean years of education of male native workers is 13.2, of Asian immigrants 14.2, of Hispanic immigrants 9.7 (see also Sorensen and Enchautegui, 1994). But all these categories are actually too crude, and a finer breakdown would show that some Asian groups such as Laotians, Hmong and Cambodians, have very little education, and some Hispanic groups, for example Cubans, have substantially higher levels of education than the mean among Hispanics. Further, the immigrant categories must be broken down by time of immigration, since their composition does change over time, a point emphasized in the study by Borjas (1990).
3. See Passel and Edmonston (1994), table on p. 35: during that decade, they estimate a net loss to population through emigration.
4. It is not only the less educated who are influenced by anecdotal evidence. In some cases, the anecdote may simply sum up the reality. A distinguished American expert in higher education told me not long ago that native Americans had little chance to get good jobs today in mathematics departments in colleges and universities – there were, he said, too many very able Russian immigrants available.
5. The fullest study comparing the economic mobility of immigrants and native American blacks is Lieberson (1980). The Report of the National Commission on Civil Disorders (commonly known as the Kerner Commission) included an influential chapter taking up the question, so commonly asked, as to why blacks had not done as well as European immigrants.
6. "Immigration Rises by 30% since 1980's" (*New York Times*, 20 November 1994): "About 111,500 legal immigrants are settling in New York City each year, up nearly a third since the 1980s, and more than 40 percent since the 1970s, according to [statistics compiled by the Population Division of the Department of City Planning]."

7. Fix and Passel (1994) give a good summary of the situation: "Among non-refugee immigrants of working age who entered during the 1980s, 2.0 [percent] report welfare income versus 3.7 percent of working-age natives. The difference is quite substantial, particularly in light of the relatively low income of these recent immigrants. Among longer-term immigrants of working age, 3.2 [percent] are on welfare, still below the proportion of working-age natives on welfare. The two immigrant groups whose welfare use is high are refugees, as expected given their explicit eligibility and the circumstances of their arrival, and elderly immigrants who have arrived since 1980. More than 25 percent of post-1980 elderly immigrants receive welfare, compared to 7 percent of elderly natives."

8. Dominicans, a group that includes neither refugees nor a disproportionate number of aged people – disproportionately to be found on welfare – showed the highest rate of welfare use, even higher than Vietnamese. This is probably related to the fact that they are concentrated in New York City, where welfare benefits and use have been traditionally high, and to the presence of a very large Puerto Rican population, which is not an immigrant population since Puerto Ricans come from a possession of the United States. Puerto Ricans have a very high use of welfare, and this may affect Dominicans, who often settle in the same neighborhoods and who are linked by language and culture to the Puerto Ricans.

9. "Between 1982 and 1993, the number of illegal immigrants receiving SSI increased an average of 16.5 percent a year … [T] he portion of immigrant recipients grew from 3 percent of all SSI recipients to over 11 percent. In 1993, an estimated 683,000 legal immigrants received SSI benefits at a cost of about $3.3 billion. … Slightly more than 60 percent of these immigrants received aged benefits and the remainder received disabled benefits" (Ross, 1995: 7).

10. The literature on multiculturalism is vast. As to the concern on how it affects assimilation, once a major object of the public schools: note the alarmed response of the United States Senate to new standards proposed for American history by a committee of educators and historians which emphasized multicultural contributions and reduced the emphasis on traditional American heroes. It voted 99 to one that these standards were unacceptable, and that any further recipient of federal funds to develop national standards "should have a decent respect for the contributions of Western civilization and United States history, ideas and institutions" (*Wall Street Journal*, 19 January 1995, editorial page, "Asides").

11. Brumberg (1986: 55), quoted in Binder and Reimers (1995: 129).

REFERENCES

Binder, Frederick M. and David M. Reimers (1995), *All the Nations under Heaven: An Ethnic and Racial History of New York City* (New York: Columbia University Press).

Borjas, George (1990) *Friends or Strangers* (New York: Basic Books).

Brimelow, Peter (1995), *Alien Nation* (New York: Random House).

Brumberg, Stephan F. (1986), *Going to America, Going to School: The Jewish Immigrant Public School Encounter in Turn-of-the-Century New York City* (New York: Praeger).

Edmonston, Barry, and Passel, Jeffrey S. (1994), *Immigration and Ethnicity* (Washington, DC: The Urban institute Press).

Fix, Michael and Passel, Jeffrey S. (1994), *Immigration and Immigrants: Setting the Record Straight* (Washington, DC: The Urban Institute Press).

Fix, Michael and Zimmermann, Wendy (1994), "After Arrival: An Overview of Federal Immigrant Policy in the United States", in Barry Edmonston and Jeffrey S. Passel (eds), *Immigration and Ethnicity: The Integration of America's Newest Arrivals* (Washington, DC: The Urban Institute Press).

Fuchs, Lawrence S. (1985), "The Search for a Sound Immigration Policy: A Personal View," in Glazer, Nathan (ed.), *Clamor at the Gates* (San Francisco, CA: Institute for Contemporary studies Press).

Glazer, Nathan (1997), "Governmental and Nongovernmental roles in the Absorption of Immigrants in the United States," in Schuck, Peter, and Munz, Rainer (eds), *Paths to Inclusion: The Integration of Migrants in the United States and Germany* (Oxford: Berghahn).

—— (1995), "Immigration and the American Future," *The Public Interest*, Winter, pp. 45–60.

—— (1993), "Is Assimilation Dead?," *The Annals*, 530 (November), pp. 122–36.

Kerner Commission (1968), *Report* (Washington, DC: US Government Printing Office).

Lieberson, Stanley (1980), *A Piece of the Pie: Blacks and White Immigrants since 1880* (Berkeley, CA: University of California Press).

Miller, Harris N. (1985) "The Right Thing to Do: A History of Simpson-Mazzoli," in Glazer, Nathan (ed.), *Clamor at the Gates* (San Francisco, CA: Institute for Contemporary Studies Press).

Muller, Thomas (1993), *Immigrants and the American City* (New York: New York University Press).

Muller, Thomas and Espenshade, Thomas J. (1985), *The Fourth Wave: California's Newest Immigrants* (Washington, DC: The Urban Institute Press).

Passel, Jeffrey S. and Barry Edmonston (1994), "Immigration and Race: Recent Trends in Immigration to the United States", in B. Edmonston and J. S. Passel, *Immigration and Ethnicity*.

Portes, Alejandro and Min Zhou (1993), "The New Second Generation: Segmented Assimilation and its Variants", *The Annals*, 530 (November), pp. 74–96.

Ross, Jane L. (1995), "Supplemental Security Income: Recent Growth in the Rolls Raises Fundamental Program Concerns", testimony before the Subcommittee on Human Resources, Committee on Ways and Means, House of Representatives, 27 January 1995.

Schuck, Peter H. and Smith, Rogers M. (1985), *Citizenship without Consent: Illegal Aliens in the American Polity* (New Haven, CT: Yale University Press).

Simon, Julian (1989), *The Economic Consequences of Immigration* (Cambridge, MA: Blackwell).

Sorenson, Elaine and Enchautegui, Maria E. (1994), "Immigrant Male Earnings in the 1980s: Divergent Patterns by Race and Ethnicity," in Edmonston and Passel, *Immigration and Ethnicity.*

Waters, Mary (1994), "Ethnic and Racial Identities of Second-generation Black Immigrants in New York City," *International Migration Review*, 28(4), pp. 795–820.

Winnick, Louis (1990), *New People in Old Communities: The Role of New Immigrants in Rejuvenating New York's Communities* (New York: Russell Sage Foundation).

4 A History of Japanese Emigration from the 1860s to the 1990s

Motoko Tsuchida

INTRODUCTION

Modern Japanese emigration began in 1868 with the Meiji Restoration of 1868–1912. From the outset, the emigrants were migrant workers and were regarded as such by the Japanese government; those who sought permanent residency at their destinations were an exceptional few. As of October 1986, the total number of *Nikkeijin* exceeded 1 640 000, with the large majority residing in the United States (740 000) and Brazil (630 000). By *Nikkeijin* is meant two categories of Japanese emigrants – first-, second- and third-generation Japanese who are naturalized citizens of their host countries, and Japanese citizens who are permanent residents in those countries (see Table 4.1 and 4.2).[1]

The flow of emigration changed with the times. Starting with Hawaii, it gradually turned to the Pacific coast of North America. Then came other streams which made their way to Peru and Brazil in South America. From the end of the Taisho period (1912–26) and into the Showa (1926–89), the main current ran to Brazil, with some other tides running to the South Seas, including the Philippines. The 1930s saw the flow shift to Manchuria. Emigration changed its course depending upon the ruling government's policy in the countries involved.

Post-war emigration resumed in 1952, the year of the San Francisco Peace Treaty, with the tide headed for the United States and Brazil again. Together these countries absorbed the overwhelming majority of post-war Japanese emigrants, who totaled some 262 000 (135 000 to the United States and 71 000 to Brazil). From the mid-1980s on, a new phenomenon set in among the *Nikkeijin* in South America. This was the

Table 4.1 *Japanese emigrants and Japanese nationals abroad before the Second World War*

Country	Number of emigrants (1868–1941)	Number of Japanese nationals abroad		
		1909	1924	1936
United States (mainland)	107,253	76,709	131,357	111,184
United States (Hawaii)	231,206	65,760	123,036	152,199
Canada	35,777	8,850	19,160	20,593
Mexico	14,667	2,465	3,310	4,691
Peru	33,070	4,560	9,864	22,570
Bolivia	249	–	716	791
Chile	538	145	581	668
Brazil	188,985	605	41,774	193,057
Argentina	5,398	27	2,383	5,904
Paraguay	709	–	–	308
Dominica	–	–	–	–
Philippines	53,115	2,156	8,390	21,241
Australia	3,773	3,960	3,879	3,205
New Caledonia	5,074	(Unknown)	(Unknown)	Approx. 1,000
Borneo	2,829	2,611	5,424	7,185
Manchuria	270,007[a]	31,427	93,223	376,036
Others	93,661	23,910	60,290	75,638
Total I	**1,046,311**	**223,185**	**503,393**	**996,270**
Total II[b]		278,672	594,611	1,219,272

[a] Number of agricultural emigrants, 1932–45.
[b] Total number of Japanese nationals, including the Kwantung province and South Sea areas under mandate.

SOURCE: Haraguchi (1991: 21).

Table 4.2 *Number of Japanese emigrants and number of* Nikkeijin *abroad following the Second World War*

Country	Number of post-war emigrants[a]		Number of Nikkeijin[b]	
	Total number	Number with travel loans	Total number	Number with travel loans
United States	134,842	388	745,194	73,533
Canada	11,226	0	54,016	12,981
Mexico	671	20	11,936	1,456
Peru	2,615	6	55,335	3,035
Bolivia	6,357	1,894	8,123	2,401
Brazil	71,372	53,235	634,356	105,046[c]
Argentina	12,066	2,692	32,327	14,527
Paraguay	9,612	7,089	6,472	4,156
Dominica	1,390	1,330	614	501
Australia	1,525	0	7,568	4,561
China	–		31,276	2,338
Others	10,402	161	52,903	20,681
Total	**262,078**	**66,815**	**1,641,452**	**246,043**

[a] As of the end of March 1990. The figure for the number with travel loans is as of the end of 1989, and includes those with travel grants.

[b] Number of naturalized *issei, nisei* and *sansei* generations and permanent residents (with Japanese citizenship) as of October 1986.

[c] According to the surveys (1987–88) conducted by the São Paulo Institute of Cultural Sciences, the number of *Nikkeijin* in Brazil was approximately 1 230 000.

This table was drawn from *Waga Kokumin no Kaigai Hatten* (Shiryohen) (Our People's Development Abroad: Materials) published by the Foreign Ministry Consular and Emigration Affairs Department, and also from *Kaigai Iju Tokei (Emigration Statistics), 1952–1989,* complied by Kokusai Kyoryoku Jigyodan (Japan International Cooperation Agency/JICA).

SOURCE: Haraguchi (1991: 21).

return migration of *Nikkeijin*, flowing back to Japan to find employment. They came from Brazil, Peru, Argentina, Paraguay and Bolivia, with the total number reaching 120 000 by early 1991 and rapidly increasing thereafter. Alien Registration statistics indicate that, as of the end of 1993, approximately 200 000 *Nikkeijin* had entered Japan from South America, of whom 154 650 were from Brazil alone (see Tables 4.3 and 4.4). Since the number of *Nikkeijin* in Brazil is estimated at 1 300 000, this means that more than 10 percent of them are living in Japan as migrant workers (Ninomiya and the Ministry of Labor, 1994:1). This makes an interesting comparison to the Japanese emigrants to Brazil in and after 1908, who have thus far totaled 260 000. Between 1985 and 1988, Japan was still sending emigrants abroad at the rate of 2500–3000 per year, but the JICA (Japan International Cooperation Agency) supply of travel expenses diminished sharply year by year: from 67 cases in 1985 to 14 in 1990. While the total number of Japanese emigrants between 1945 and 1988 was 258 475, the total of registered aliens immigrating into Japan was 941 005 in 1988 and 1 320 748 in 1993 (see Tables 4.5, 4.6 and 4.7). Thus Japan changed from a country of emigration to one of immigration.

EARLY EMIGRANTS TO HAWAII

The Tokugawa shogunate, having been forced to open the country in 1854 following American Commodore Matthew C. Perry's arrival the year before, recognized visits by foreigners to Japan under the 1858 Treaty of Amity and Commerce with the United States. The Japanese people, however, had to wait until 1866 for the official end of the closed-door policy. The shogunate that year gave them permission to go abroad either for study or for commercial purposes, upon application, and began to issue passports. Of the 103 passports issued in 1867, 90 went to domestic servants employed by foreigners in Japan who were to leave Japan in the company of their employers.[2] This formula was gradually extended to cover the case of servants leaving alone first, while their employers remained in Japan. Then an American businessman who was the Kingdom of Hawaii's consul in Japan, Eugene M. Van Reed,

Table 4.3 Changes in the number of registered aliens by area (year-end)

Area	1988	%	1990	%	1992	%	1993	%	Ratio to previous year-end (%)
Asia	868,091	92.2	924,560	86.0	1,000,673	78.1	1,027,304	77.8	2.7
South America	6,872	0.7	71,495	6.6	187,140	14.6	196,491	14.9	5.0
North America	37,264	4.0	44,643	4.2	50,421	4.0	51,057	3.9	1.3
Europe	22,027	2.3	25,563	2.4	29,899	2.3	31,046	2.3	3.8
Oceania	3,462	0.4	5,440	0.5	7,982	0.6	8,601	0.6	7.8
Africa	1,631	0.2	2,140	0.2	4,027	0.3	4,749	0.4	17.9
Others (stateless persons)	1,658	0.2	1,476	0.1	1,502	0.1	1,500	0.1	−0.1
Total number	**941,005**	**100.0**	**1,075,317**	**100.0**	**1,281,644**	**100.00**	**1,320,748**	**100.0**	**3.1**

NOTE: The classification by area follows the classification in the *United Nations Statistical Yearbook*.

SOURCE: Immigration Bureau statistics in *Kokusai Jinryu* (1994, no. 89 (October), p. 37).

Table 4.4 *Changes in the number of registered aliens by nationality/area of origin (year-end)*

Area	1988	%	1990	%	1992	%	1993	%	Ratio to previous year-end (%)
ROK, Korea	677,140	72.0	687,940	64.0	688,144	53.7	682,276	51.7	-0.9
China	129,269	13.7	150,339	14.0	195,334	15.2	210,138	15.9	7.6
Brazil	4,159	0.4	56,429	5.2	147,803	11.5	154,650	11.7	4.6
Philippines	32,185	3.4	49,092	4.6	62,218	4.9	73,057	5.5	17.4
United States	32,766	3.5	38,364	3.6	42,482	3.3	42,639	3.2	0.4
Peru	864	0.1	10,279	0.9	31,051	2.4	33,169	2.5	6.8
Others	64,622	6.9	82,874	7.7	114,612	9.0	124,819	9.5	8.9
Total number	**941,005**	**100.0**	**1,075,317**	**100.0**	**1,281,644**	**100.0**	**1,320,748**	**100.0**	**3.1**

NOTE: The total number of registered aliens in 1970 was approximately 700 000, most of whom were Korean [Republic of Korea (ROK); Korea] and Taiwanese residents in Japan. The registered aliens as of the end of 1993 totaled approximately 1 320 000, of whom 650 000 were people other than Korean and Taiwanese residents in Japan (Katayama, 1995: 5–6).

SOURCE: Immigration Bureau statistics in *Kokusai Jinryu* (1994, no. 89 (October), p. 37).

Table 4.5 *Number of emigrants with JICA supply of travel expenses, by destination*

Country	1985	1986	1987	1988	1989	1990
Argentina	29	25	14	4	3	0
Bolivia	3	2	3	0	1	1
Brazil	30	41	32	20	9	9
Dominica	0	0	0	2	0	0
Paraguay	5	3	3	9	0	4
Total	**67**	**71**	**52**	**35**	**13**	**14**

Kokusai Kyoryoku Jigyodan Jigyo Jisseki Hyo (JICA Record of Performance) as of March 1991.

SOURCE: J. Suzuki (1992: 268).

Table 4.6 *Total number of emigrants in most recent years by destination*

Country	1985	1986	1987	1988	Total 1945–88
United States	1,441	1,528	1,603	1,554	133,326
Canada	119	100	102	103	11,136
Brazil	258	363	359	416	70,628
Paraguay	68	51	71	79	9,503
Argentina	269	330	357	319	11,367
Dominica	3	2	2	1	1,388
Bolivia	95	68	91	60	6,266
Mexico	14	16	14	14	653
Peru	22	29	18	18	2,594
Australia	24	61	65	107	1,440
Others	210	270	271	215	10,174
Total	**2,523**	**2,818**	**2,953**	**2,886**	**258,475**

This table is based on *Kaigai Iju Tokei* (Emigration Statistics, October 1989), complied by Kokusai Kyoryoku Jigyodan (Japan International Cooperation Agency/JICA).

SOURCE: J. Suzuki (1992: 268).

Table 4.7 *Changes in the total number of alien registrations (year-end)*

Year	Total number	Ratio to previous year (%)	Index	Ratio to Japan's total population (%)
1973	738,410		100	0.68
1978	766,894	3.9	104	0.67
1983	817,129	6.6	111	0.68
1986	867,237	6.1	117	0.71
1987	884 025	1.9	120	0.72
1988	941,005	6.4	127	0.77
1989	984,455	4.6	133	0.80
1990	1,075,317	9.2	146	0.87
1991	1,218,891	13.4	165	0.98
1992	1 281 644	5.1	174	1.03
1993	1,320,748	3.1	179	1.06
1994[a]	1,354,011			1.08

[a] *Asahi Shimbun,* 17 August 1995, p. 3.

SOURCE: Immigration Bureau statistics *Kokusai Jinryu* (1994: no. 89 October), p. 36).

began to act as an emigration agent. In his newspaper *Moshiogusa,* Van Reed advertised the recruitment of emigrants to Hawaii and Guam. In March 1868 he gathered 350 applicants for emigration to Hawaii and 42 to Guam and obtained passports for them from the Kanagawa Magistrate's Office. This would be the first group of migrant workers ever to leave Japan.

While these arrangements were in progress, however, a *coup d'état* deposed the reigning Shogun, Yoshinobu Tokugawa, and almost immediately a civil war broke out between the forces for and against the Tokugawa regime. The Restoration set the Emperor at the center of the new Meiji government and put an end to the centuries of Tokugawa feudalism. Van Reed negotiated with the new government and repeatedly applied for new passports, as the emigrants' departure was drawing near. The government, however, refused to sanction their departure on the grounds that they could hardly be protected if problems should arise, because Japan had no diplomatic relations with Hawaii. The government officials were also aware that emigrants would be no better than slaves, in the light of the situation in Ch'ing China and other Asian countries. In fact, semi-slavery, injustice and racial discrimination were prevalent in Hawaii and elsewhere when Japan started emigration, and continued into the first decade of the twentieth century. After fruitless efforts, Van Reed insisted on the validity of the old passports and, without authority, sent a final total of 153 Japanese workers to Hawaii aboard a British ship. Known as *Gannen mono,* or "first-year Meiji people," they were to work under a 3-year contract with a monthly salary of four dollars, and the expenses for their meals and medical treatment were to be borne by their employers.

What they found upon their arrival in Hawaii was that the prices were 40 percent higher than in Japan, and with four dollars a month for living expenses, it was simply impossible to make ends meet; that the hot climate seriously affected their health, causing four to die on the voyage alone; and that the employers would not help them with medical and other expenses as guaranteed by Van Reed in their contracts. These appeals finally reached the home government, and in November 1869 a government envoy, Kagenori Ueno, was dispatched to Hawaii to conduct talks with the Hawaiian government. Through his efforts, wages were raised to 15 dollars for many of the emigrants and even to 20 or 30 dollars for some of them. It was confirmed that the Hawaiian government would pay for the return trip upon the termination of their contracts. Forty workers sought to return to Japan with Ueno; all the others remained in Hawaii and worked until their contracts expired. After that, 12 wanted to return home, 46 sought to migrate to the American mainland, and 37 wanted to continue as migratory workers overseas. This last group seems to have remained in Hawaii, pursuing professions as stagecoach drivers, barbers, photographers, innkeepers, independent businessmen, and interpreters. The Japanese government, on the other hand, persistently questioned the responsibility of Van Reed, who had sent the emigrants out without permission, and pressed the American Minister to

Japan for his punishment and deportation. Thus the first emigration resulted in failure. The emigration of 42 workers to Guam was a failure, too: ten died of illness, one killed himself, two drowned, one disappeared, and only 28 were able to return to Japan. These cases were enough to convince the government that "emigrants are made slaves, after all". The government turned extremely negative toward emigration and refused successive offers from Hawaii and other countries of the world to invite Japanese emigrants. Among these were offers from the Southern Australian government (1877), the Hawaiian government proposing a 5-year contract (1879), the Spanish government proposing a treaty of immigration to Cuba (1880), the Dutch West Indies for work on sugar and coffee plantations (1883), the United States for 250 tracklayers, Russia for 200 construction workers, the Netherlands for 500 colony soldiers to Indonesia, California for coal miners, Oregon for 2 000 tracklayers, and so forth. All these offers were rejected by the Meiji Government (J. Suzuki, 1992: 21–7).

Yuji Ichioka, in his book *The Issei*, says that the history of Japanese immigration can be divided into two broad periods: 1885–1907, and 1908–24. The first was the period of *dekasegi* immigration in which Japanese workers left their native place temporarily to work elsewhere and returned home wealthy. In the second period, many workers started to settle on agricultural land to take up farming. This was the time of the anti-Japanese exclusion movement, and immigrant leaders encouraged permanent residency instead of itinerant labor for immediate wealth; hence the transition from laborer to farmer. Permanent residency induced many women to come and join the immigrant society and begin family lives (Ichioka, 1988: 3–5). A typical case of the first period was an organized emigration to Hawaii in 1885 under the treaty of passage between the two governments, in which 944 "government-contract emigrants" to Hawaii were sent to engage in sugar-cane plantation work and raw-sugar manufacturing for 3 years. Approximately 30 000 such workers migrated to Hawaii between 1885 and 1894. They were overwhelmingly from Hiroshima and Yamaguchi prefectures and less from Kumamoto and Fukuoka.[3] "Government-contract emigration" was abolished in 1894, to be replaced by private contracts through the mediation of emigration companies. By the time Hawaii became an American possession to which the United States Immigration Act applied, including a ban on contract labor in 1900, approximately 40 000 "private-contract emigrants" had been sent to Hawaii by emigration companies. They were from prefectures in the southwestern part of Japan, such as Hiroshima, Yamaguchi, Okinawa, Kumamoto and Fukuoka, and also from Niigata and Fukushima prefectures.

The first of these emigration companies was the Nihon Yoshisa Emigration Company, established in 1891. The company shipped 600 emigrants to New Caledonia in 1892 to engage in contract labor for nickel mining. In 1894, the company sent 305 emigrants to the Fiji Islands for contract labor on sugar-cane plantations and 490 to Guadeloupe, the West Indies, for the same type of contract labor. It also sent contract laborers to work in the sugar-cane fields of Queensland, Australia. Without exception, all these were failures due to the employers' disregard of contracts and to sweat labor in semi-slavery, resulting in great misery with a heavy toll of dead and sick. In the world of the late nineteenth century, where slavery still remained firmly rooted, the first Japanese emigrants were used as slave labor like the Indian and Chinese coolies. The number of emigration companies increased to about 30 before 1907. They are said to have shipped 75 percent of the Japanese emigrants during the Meiji period (Haraguchi, 1991: 22).

To drive out the unscrupulous emigration agents, the Meiji Government in 1894 established a set of regulations known as the Regulations to Protect Emigrants, which in 1896 became the Emigrants Protection Law. The regulations were intended to control emigration companies by putting them under the authority of the Minister of Home Affairs, rather than to protect emigrants. An emigrant was there defined as "any person who goes abroad to engage in labor," and emigration was limited to such persons and their families. By labor, the regulations meant agriculture, fishing, mining, construction, transportation, manufacturing and domestic service (Ichioka, 1988: 47). Government control was tightened further in 1898 to prohibit the emigration companies from entering into agreements with free emigrants whose destination was the United States, because such agreements were often misconstrued by the American immigration officials as employment contracts, and on that basis, the free emigrants were considered contract laborers and were denied landing permission. The Foreign Ministry took a more radical step in March 1898 and banned the companies from shipping any emigrants to the United States. Although the ban was lifted in June, the Ministry adhered strictly to its policy of not allowing any company to ship emigrants of classes defined by American immigration statutes as excluded. The companies then started to ship emigrants by way of Canada. Including migrants from Hawaii into the continental United States, Japanese laborers increased markedly, with a yearly number of 1 000–3 000 people in the 1890s. This gave rise to sharp agitation on the West Coast against Japanese immigration (Haraguchi, 1991: 23).

THE ECONOMIC BACKGROUND OF EMIGRATION

In commenting on the disparity in economic development between Japan and the Western powers, Nobutaka Ike cited John E. Orchard as saying that the Japan of the Tokugawa era should be compared with sixteenth-century Tudor England rather than with England on the eve of the Industrial Revolution (Ike, 1969: 72). The Japanese were painfully aware of the backwardness of their economy after foreign trade was resumed in 1859. There was, in fact, a century-wide gap between Japanese history and world history, and Japan's modernization at its starting point in 1868 was already about a century behind the French Revolution and the British Industrial Revolution.

Under the slogans *"Fukoku Kyohei"* (rich country, strong army) and *"Bunmei Kaika"* (civilization and enlightenment), the Meiji government launched capitalist industrialization and cultural Westernization in a society that was largely agrarian and unprepared to produce free citizens. The leaders, faced by the threat of colonialism, made concentrated efforts to preserve Japan's independence, while strengthening national unity, and to stand up to the Great Powers. Their objective was to "catch up", to go at one bound from feudalism to imperialism, rather than to build up a modern democratic society

(Fukutake, 1989: 14). The financial basis for the promotion of industrialization was provided by the heavy tax paid by farmers, who made up as much as 80 percent of the working population.[4] Nation-wide taxation reforms were carried out over a period of 7 years starting in 1873, and the farmers were required to pay the land tax, fixed at 3 percent of the "legal value" of the land, with no allowance for the cost of labor or for a reasonable profit, and without regard to the vicissitudes of nature. When the local tax of 1 percent was added, 30–40 percent of the annual yield went for taxes.

The crop failures of 1881, which extended over several years due to floods, insects, rain and hailstorms, severely affected the peasants throughout the land. Furthermore, the drastic deflationary measures taken by Finance Minister Masayoshi Matsukata during the depression years (1882–5), with a steep decline in the price of rice and other agricultural commodities, dealt a devastating blow to the rural economy. Impoverishment of the peasantry and peasant revolts were widespread. The Home Ministry officials who investigated conditions in the northern prefectures reported that "seven or eight out of ten people are living almost like horses and cattle" and that many of the poor were sleeping on straw, since they possessed no blankets. The officials also reported that beggars were found everywhere and that farm laborers were more than willing to work for just three meals a day. Newspaper accounts of the situation in the southern prefectures ran in a similar vein. In Fukuoka prefecture, some of the poor were eating bark stripped from pine trees; in Naka county, Wakayama prefecture, more than 10 000 people out of a population of 80 000 barely survived by eating a little gruel, and more than 3 000 were on the verge of starvation; in Kaga, 800 persons asked to be imprisoned rather than starve and suffer in the cold (Ike, 1969: 146–7). Unable to pay the land tax, many small farmers were forced into debt and eventually reduced to the status of tenants. It is said that 600 000 small farmer households and a million peasant households were crushed to dissolution under the Matsukata policy (J. Suzuki, 1992: 28).

The farmers, deprived of land to till, would go anywhere, even overseas, to find jobs. Japanese emigration in the 1880s and 1890s was spurred on by the sheer necessity of liberation from economic distress. The government, reluctant as it was, finally realized the need for emigration.

EMIGRATION TO AUSTRALIA

The resumption of government-approved contract labor was triggered in 1883 by an offer from Australia to hire skilled Japanese divers for the Thursday Island pearl fishery. The wage offered under the 2-year contract was exceptionally favorable: 530–1 600 dollars a year or 55 yen a month, which was seven to ten times as much as the pay in Japan, where a farm worker or a day laborer was paid five to six yen a month and a carpenter eight yen. Despite the Australian government's efforts to hire European divers, the technically superior Japanese were unrivaled. In consequence, Thursday Island pearling became a monopoly of the Wakayama divers, whose employment was extended for a virtually indefinite period in spite of the White Australia Policy of 1901, which was implemented along with the establishment of the federal system in Australia. As of July 1919, the number of Japanese workers was about 1800. Their average remittance home was about 570 yen a year, and the amount of money the returnees carried home with them ranged from one thousand yen to several thousand per person (J. Suzuki, 1992: 30–9).

The White Australia Policy emerged from Japanese emigration to the Australian mainland, first requested in 1887. Farm workers were wanted as a test case for work on sugar plantations in Queensland. The request was approved by the Japanese government the following year. Racial prejudice and anti-Japanese sentiments were deep-rooted in Australia, especially among working men, who accounted for 70 percent of the entire population. Whereas the employers were looking for cheap, stable labor, the local workers were understandably hostile to the immigrants, whose acceptance of low pay, longer hours of work and a lower standard of living would be a potential threat. Under the 3-year contract, more than 2000 Japanese immigrants were working in Australia in 1897, with wages at nearly half the local level, which was enough to cause intensified anti-Japanese agitation. The resulting White Australia Policy persisted until 1973.

EMIGRATION TO THE UNITED STATES

The earliest Japanese emigrants to the United States were students from the elite classes. They were generally favorably received in American society, which excluded the Chinese. The most elite among these students were government-scholarship holders, who studied in New England and assumed high posts upon their return to Japan. There were also private students, who were divided into two categories: those with and those without financial means. The latter were indigent students with high ambitions, who were prepared to endure hardships. These poor students landed in San Francisco in and after the mid-1880s. Of the 3475 passports issued by the Japanese government to persons leaving for the United States between 1882 and 1890, 1 519 went to private students, the majority of whom were student-laborers. They were heavily concentrated in San Francisco, and indigent students continued to arrive in the 1890s and after. Their arrival heralded that of large numbers of laborers (Ichioka, 1988: 8–9).

The American dream was a great attraction to the student emigrants. Yukichi Fukuzawa, the founder of Keio Gijuku, served as a guide to them with his books. In Wakayama prefecture, a Keio graduate, Honda Waichiro, opened a private school and taught his students Chinese literature, English, history, mathematics and Christianity, thereby preparing them for studies abroad. Most of the students had become Christians before they left for the United States. They were successful emigrants who held fast to the lofty ideals of their youth with a progressive spirit, the sons of wealthy farmers and village leaders (Tsuchida, 1997: 98–108). These private students, as well as the student-laborers and political exiles, arrived in San Francisco and joined a Japanese immigrant society centering around the Gospel Society. This was the first Japanese immigrant organization, composed of early student converts to Methodism and Congregationalism, including Kan'ichi Miyama, who had arrived in 1875 and had been baptized in 1877 by the Reverend Otis Gibson, superintendent of the Chinese Methodist Episcopal Mission in Chinatown. The Society later became a Japanese YMCA and grew into the Methodist, Congregational and Presbyterian Missions. These and other Christian institutions helped the indigent students from Japan to survive, by teaching them English, providing room and board, and providing employment and other assistance. The students, while attending school, worked as domestic servants. Some other job categories were: dishwashers, window-cleaners, janitors, waiters and cooks. The latter jobs required experience and a knowledge of English (Ichioka, 1988: 16, 23, 27). The arrival of Japanese immigrant labor in the United States occurred in two phases. The first phase, 1891–1900, brought in 27 440 persons, mostly laborers.[5] In the second phase, 1901–7, 42 457 persons were admitted. There were also Japanese migrant laborers from Hawaii, who totaled 38 000 by 1908 (Ichioka, 1988: 51–2). The result was a sharp rise in the number of Japanese residents in the United States: from 2038 in 1890 to 103 683 in 1908 (Haraguchi, 1991: 23). Early Japanese immigrants found employment as trackmen, miners, farm and home workers, taking the place of the Chinese, who had been banned from entry in 1882. Japanese workers were diligent, persevering and cheap. This gave rise to anti-Japanese sentiments among white workers.

Meanwhile, US immigration laws were gradually becoming more stringent. The United States, which had barred contract labor in 1885 and 1887, introduced regulations for the deportation of undesirable aliens in 1888. In 1891, the prohibited classes were enlarged to include "paupers, polygamists, and persons suffering from loathsome and contagious diseases". In 1903, "epileptics, prostitutes, professional beggars, and ... anarchists" were added to the excluded classes, in the aftermath of the assassination of President William McKinley by an alien anarchist. The Act of 1903 for the first time declared inadmissible "persons who believe in, or advocate, the overthrow by force or violence of the Government of the United States, or of all government, or of all forms of law, or the assassination of public officials" (Tsuchida, 1989: 93). Still, despite the gradual tightening of immigration regulations, vigorous protests against Japanese immigrants were yet to arise.

It was not until 1905 and 1906 that organized agitation against the Japanese attempted to involve the government authorities in anti-Japanese exclusion. Moritoshi Fukuda gives four major areas of complaint which were the causes of the intense American protests. First, the Japanese government's self-limiting step taken in 1900 not only failed to have long-lasting effects on Japanese immigration to the United States, but it did not apply to Japanese going to join the Hawaiian labor market. Emigration companies continued to bring Japanese laborers to work on the sugar plantations in Hawaii, and many of them found their way to the Pacific coast because of the higher wages paid on the mainland. Second, the white working class was beginning to fear the competition of Japanese labor, which was cheap and plentiful; the Japanese, moreover, were not content, as the Chinese had been, to remain a part of the working class. By 1909 the Immigration Commission, which was set up by the Act of 1907, estimated that there were 3 000–3 500 Japanese establishments employing some 10 000 individuals. This initiative and success on the part of the Japanese was frightening to the Caucasians in California, who had thought themselves to be the only class capable of managing independent businesses. Third, the Japanese bore the brunt of all the conventional misconceptions Americans entertained about Orientals. They were criticized for likening their emperor to a god, and they were accused of crowding American children out of schools. This type of racial prejudice was inescapable. Finally, the Russo-Japanese War, resulting in Japan's victory over a major European power, had a profound psychological impact on Americans. Even President Theodore Roosevelt expressed fears that "Japan might get a 'big head' and enter into a general career of insolence and aggression" (Fukuda, 1980: 31–6).

On 23 February 1905, the San Francisco Chronicle published an appeal against the dangers of Japanese immigration. On 7 May 1905, the Japanese and Korean Exclusion League was launched, with its platform carrying the following demands: (1) that the Chinese exclusion laws be extended to include all classes of Japanese and Koreans; (2) that members of the League should pledge not to employ or patronize Japanese or persons employing Japanese, or the products coming from such firms; (3) that a propaganda campaign calling the attention of the President and Congress to this "menace" be undertaken; and (4) that all labor and civic organizations in California be asked to contribute a fixed assessment to the cause (Fukuda, 1980: 38).

On 11 October 1906, the School Board of San Francisco resolved to establish separate schools for Orientals, on the basis of a school law which authorized school boards to establish separate schools for Indian, Chinese and Mongolian children at their discretion. Although the law did not mention the Japanese specifically, they were assumed to fall in the Mongolian category. This was the first case in which the immigration problem became a diplomatic issue between Japan and the United States. President Roosevelt denounced the School Board's actions in his annual message to Congress on 3 December 1906, saying that to shut the Japanese out of the common school was a "wicked absurdity" and that the Americans had "as much to learn from Japan as Japan has to learn from us; and no nation is fit to teach unless it is also willing to learn" (Fukuda, 1980: 40–2). The result of this incident was twofold: (1) The Presidential proclamation of 14 March 1907, which ordered that "Japanese or Korean laborers, skilled or unskilled, who have received passports to go to Mexico, Canada and Hawaii, and come therefrom, be refused permission to enter the continental territory of the United States;" and (2) the "Gentlemen's Agreement" of March 1908, in which it was agreed that Japan would not issue passports to laborers, skilled or unskilled, but could issue passports to laborers resuming residence in the United States, or persons who were parents, wives and children of laborers already resident in the United States (Wilson and Hosokawa, 1980: 125).

The above-mentioned actions were legally endorsed by the Act of 1907 which, besides establishing the Immigration Commission, authorized the President to exclude from admission persons who would adversely affect labor conditions in the United States. This was aimed at Japanese and Korean laborers who entered the United States from Hawaii, Mexico or Canada and who were willing to accept low wages and substandard working conditions. The Act also further extended the excluded classes to include "imbeciles, sufferers from tuberculosis, and persons who had committed a crime involving moral turpitude" (Tsuchida, 1989: 93). The Gentlemen's Agreement was in effect until 1924, when it was unilaterally abandoned and replaced by the Immigration Act of 1924, which limited the immigration of aliens found "ineligible for citizenship" in accordance with United States naturalization laws.

The Gentlemen's Agreement touched off the second period, 1908–24, in the history of Japanese immigration, in which workers began to settle on farm land (Ichioka, 1988). The focus was a shift from laborers to landowners and business owners. By 1913, 281 687 acres were being farmed by 6177 farmers. In 1918, there was a total of 7973 farmers, 4560 of whom had wives, with 6510 children. These farmers and their dependants comprised 27.5 percent of the Japanese population of 68 982 in California. There were still 15 794 farm laborers in 1918, 1666 of whom had wives with 1508 children. Thus, the total agricultural population was 38 011, or 55.1 percent of the total Japanese population. The Japanese agricultural landholdings dropped from the 1920 peak of 458 056 acres to 330 653 in 1922, and to 307 966 in 1925. By 1929 the number of farmers fell to 4591 (Ichioka, 1988: 151, 156, 234–5).

With the shift to permanent settlement, the so-called "Japanese Associations" were formed in California, Oregon, Washington and elsewhere, as the key political organizations of Japanese immigrants. They carried out education campaigns to disseminate the idea of permanent settlement among the immigrants, while educating Americans about Japan and the Japanese immigrants and informing the people in Japan of the real situation of Japanese immigrants in the United States. They invited Inazo Nitobe and Saburo Shimada from Japan in 1911 to engage in lecture tours; the lecturers advised the immigrants to settle down in the United States. The number of immigrant families increased between 1900 and 1920 as many men summoned wives from Japan. In 1900 there were only 410 married women in the immigrant society; by 1910 there were 5581 and by 1920, 22 193. Among them were the so-called "picture-brides" who were chosen through the Japanese practice of arranged marriages and entered the United States to join their legal husbands in the immigrant society. Americans attacked this practice, alleging that it violated the Gentlemen's Agreement. This caused the Japanese Foreign Ministry to cease issuing passports to picture-brides from 1 March 1920 (Ichioka, 1988: 164, 175, 186).

The immigrants' story cannot be concluded without mention of their struggle against exclusion. The landmark Ozawa case was brought before the Supreme Court to determine if the appellant, a native of Japan, would be eligible for naturalization. Takao Ozawa, a United States resident alien born in Japan, applied on 16 October 1914 to the United States District Court of Hawaii to be naturalized as a citizen of the United States. He had filed his petition of intent on 1 August 1902 in Alameda County, California. Ozawa had resided continuously in the United States for 20 years, was a graduate of Berkeley High School (California) and had studied at the University of California for 3 years. His children had been educated in American schools, his family had attended American churches, and he had maintained the use of English in his home. His petition was rejected. Classified as a member of the Mongolian race, Ozawa was excluded by the racial restrictions of section 2169, which limited the Naturalization Act of 1906. He filed an appeal, granted on 26 September 1916, and his case was passed on to the Ninth Circuit Court of Appeals in San Francisco. The appellate court then referred the case to the Supreme Court on 31 May 1917. The Supreme Court did not take up the case in 1918 or in 1919, when in the Paris Peace Conference Japan demanded insertion of a racial equality clause into the League of Nations Covenant. In 1921–2, when the Washington Conference took place, the Supreme Court postponed hearing the Ozawa case. Finally in 1922, the Supreme Court declared Ozawa "ineligible for citizenship", as he was judged to be neither a "free white person" nor an "African" by birth or descent. The Ozawa decision, which declared Japanese persons to be ineligible for naturalization, became the basis for all future exclusion of the Japanese (Fukuda, 1980: 11, 14, 18; Ichioka, 1988; 220–6).

The Act of 1924, which excluded aliens "not eligible for citizenship" from obtaining immigration visas, effective 1 July 1924, completely frustrated the immigrant struggle against exclusion.

EMIGRATION TO CANADA

For many Japanese who wanted to enter the United States, Canada offered easier access as a place of transit. Their migration to Canada began in 1877 and reached its peak in 1893–7. Chinese having also been excluded in Canada, Japanese immigration soon became the target of exclusion. Anti-Japanese sentiment flared up, particularly in British Columbia, where

98 percent of the total Japanese population of Canada resided. From 1898 to 1899, laws restricting occupations against Asians were passed one after another (Wakatsuki and Suzuki, 1975: 62). The Canadian exclusion of Japanese became critical in 1907 when large numbers of Japanese immigrants in Hawaii migrated to Canada as a result of the US ban on Japanese migration from Hawaii to the American mainland, pursuant to the Regulations of 26 March 1907, the "Regulations relating to the coming of Japanese and Korean laborers to the Continental Territory of the United States." From April to September of that year, some 2500 Japanese from Hawaii entered Canada, giving rise in June and September to massive assaults on Japanese immigrants by white workers and Vancouver citizens. In 1907, Japanese immigrants totaled 7601. In 1909, Japanese residents in Canada numbered 8850, most of whom lived in British Columbia. The consequence of all this was the conclusion in February 1908 of the "Lemieux Agreement", a gentlemen's agreement between Japanese Foreign Minister Tadasu Hayashi and Canadian Labor Minister Rodolph Lemieux, in which the Japanese government agreed to control Japanese emigration to Canada by limiting the number of emigrants to a yearly maximum of 400 (Haraguchi, 1991: 24). Thus, Canadian doors were closed not only to ordinary Japanese workers seeking to emigrate to Canada but also to the immigrant Japanese workers in Hawaii who wanted to enter the continental United States via Canada.

THE FLOW OF EMIGRATION SHIFTS TO SOUTH AMERICA: PERU AND BRAZIL

The US restrictions on immigration, including the ban on contract immigration to Hawaii and new immigration to the mainland, motivated Japanese migration overseas to change its course toward South America. The first mass emigration to South America was a group of 790 people aboard the *Sakuramaru*, who arrived in Peru in 1899. Among them were 369 people from Niigata prefecture, 187 from Yamaguchi, 176 from Hiroshima, 50 from Okayama, four from Tokyo, and one from Ibaraki. Upon their arrival, they were divided into eleven groups, each comprising 40–226 people, to work on the assigned sugar-cane plantations. The emigration was arranged by Morioka Emigration Company, which concluded "contracts" with the proprietors of the plantations, who showed strong interest in hiring Japanese workers. Since the Peruvian government was negative toward the introduction of contract labor, the proprietors and other agricultural delegates lobbied the President, who finally approved receiving Japanese workers in his Presidential Decree of 17 September 1898. On 6 October the Japanese government gave the company permission to handle emigration to Peru (J. Suzuki, 1992: 105–6).

Peru retained strong vestiges of slave labor, which had been forced upon Chinese coolies since 1872. Less than 2 months after Japanese immigrants started to work, trouble arose between the proprietors who were dissatisfied with Japanese labor's efficiency, which was at one-third of the Peruvian natives' level, and Japanese workers who complained about the drastic wage-cut and being prevented by their employers from buying more cheaply at the Chinese shops on the farms. Besides the bad housing and working conditions, the workers suffered from endemic diseases. On some farms, they were forced to work by threats of whipping. On one farm to which 226 immigrants were assigned, many fell victim to disease, and within a month or two after their settlement, 40 died and 30 were barely able to work. The immigrants petitioned the local agent of the emigration company to send them back to Japan, but without success. Many fled the farms and gathered in Callao, where they were involved in conflict with the natives and other Japanese immigrants. While anti-Japanese sentiments worsened to the extreme, neither the company nor the Japanese government would take remedial measures, and the immigrants were abandoned. During the year and eight months following their arrival in Peru, 124 died. Despite this situation, the Japanese government 3 years later approved resumption of emigration to Peru, and new immigrants flowed in. Not a few among the early immigrants had given up on Peru: they had crossed the Andes and moved into Bolivia or the Amazonian area of Brazil (Wakatsuki and Suzuki, 1975: 56–7).

In the whole history of Japanese migration overseas, the emigration to Peru proved to involve the most serious privations. A total of some 18 000 emigrants had been shipped by 1923, when the Peruvian government prohibited contract immigration (Haraguchi, 1991: 24).[6]

Brazil, as a Portuguese colony, developed products to meet the demands of the consumer market in Europe. Its exports, therefore, changed with the needs of the times and of the international market: sugar in the seventeenth century, gold in the eighteenth and coffee in the nineteenth. Slave labor for sugar and gold production was supplied by Africans, continuing for 350 years until the latter half of the nineteenth century, when coffee became the main export. Brazil, having abolished slave trading under British pressure in 1850 and slavery itself in 1888, needed to recruit labor for coffee plantations, and launched the full-scale introduction of European immigrants as contract workers, to whom the provincial government of São Paulo offered subsidies to cover their travel expenses, from 1886 to 1923. A total of 4 million immigrant workers entered Brazil between 1820 and 1930, 60 percent of whom were absorbed by São Paulo (Mita, 1990: 42). Among them were large numbers of Italians, who totaled 200 000 between 1880 and 1900 (Wakatsuki and Suzuki, 1975: 64). Asians and Africans were banned from entry into Brazil by the 1891 Constitution of the Republic. The labor situation experienced a turning point in 1906, when the Italian government banned its citizens from entering Brazil as contract workers, because of the deferred payment of salaries during a depression period in the coffee industry. Earlier, in 1859, the German government discontinued German immigration to Brazil, due to the harsh labor conditions, little different from slave labor. Brazil now turned to Japan.

Japanese emigration to Brazil thus began in 1908 with 781 people aboard the *Kasado-maru*, 60 percent of whom came from Kagoshima and Okinawa prefectures. Supplied with subsidies from the São Paulo provincial government, the immigrants were to work on coffee plantations in São Paulo for 3–4 years as contract workers in family units of more than three persons. Japanese immigrant workers totaled 33 000 by 1923, when the subsidies were cut off. The first *Kasado-maru* immigrants had a hard time, working under conditions of semi-slavery and low pay; many fled the plantations, were involved in farm trouble, and were dispersed in miserable conditions. The Japanese government regarded them as a test case and maintained a negative attitude, leaving recruitment and shipping of future emigrants up to the emigration companies. This marked the first phase (1908–23) in the history of Japanese emigration to Brazil (Haraguchi, 1991: 25).

STATE-POLICY EMIGRATION: BRAZIL AND MANCHURIA

The second phase (1924–41) of Japanese emigration to Brazil was supported and promoted by the Japanese government as a state policy. In October 1924, or 3 months after the United States' implementation of the Immigration Act of 1924, a group of 244 persons left Kobe Port for Brazil as the first government-subsidized emigrants. The Japanese government supplied the emigrants with subsidies to cover not only their travel expenses (200 yen per person) but also their commission (35 yen), thereby encouraging mass emigration to Brazil. Earlier, in 1921, the government had disbursed a subsidy of 100 000 yen to the Kaigai Kogyo Kaisha (Overseas Development Company), created in 1918 by amalgamating some existing emigration companies, and had it handle the encouragement, propaganda and recruitment of emigrants. The government, on the other hand, subsidized prefectural emigrant associations and private emigrant organizations and through them propagated the idea of "great ventures abroad".

This series of measures was initiated by the Social Affairs Bureau, created within the Ministry of Home Affairs in 1921 to establish a social administration under the Takashi Hara Cabinet. In 1922, the Social Affairs Bureau advocated a large-scale plan for the encouragement and protection of emigrants. From October 1924 on, the Bureau subsidized "state-policy emigration" by paying travel expenses and the commission, which had been the biggest burdens on the emigrants. During 1924, a total of 2000 government-subsidized, agricultural contract-emigrants were sent to São Paulo, in five successive groups. When the Ministry of Overseas Affairs (Takumusho) was created in 1929, the disbursement of subsidies was handled by that Ministry, instead of the Social Affairs Bureau. The second-phase emigration brought a total of 158 000 people to Brazil, while 20 000 more emigrants entered other countries in Central and South America (Haraguchi, 1991: 27).

A remarkable part of this national emigration enterprise was the Imperial Economic Conference of 1924. This was the first extensive economic conference ever to be held jointly by the government and the people to discuss solutions abroad for the serious social problems at home, such as increased population, unemployment during the chronic recessions following the First World War, and the relief of victims of the Great Kanto Earthquake of the previous year. With growing enthusiasm for migration overseas, the government and the conferees resolved to encourage emigration, and sought a provisional budget to supply 110 earthquake victims with funds needed for emigration to Brazil. In 1927, the Emigrant Union Law was passed to enable prefectural emigrant associations to send out emigrants. The annual number of emigrants for 1928 exceeded 10 000. In Kobe, temporary housing for departing emigrants was created, where they stayed free of charge and received orientation prior to their departure.

The government, from 1932 on, paid each emigrant 50 yen as an outfit allowance. In the peak years, 1933–4, the annual total of emigrants to Brazil exceeded 20 000. Besides agricultural emigration, the government planned and encouraged a new form of emigration called "business emigration"; 6000 such emigrants in 957 households were sent out by the Emigrant Union during 1929–35, but they failed to be a main current of emigration to Brazil (Haraguchi, 1991: 27–8).

Along with organized emigration planning and implementation, the government developed campaigns to disseminate information on emigration by sending its staff as speakers to public lectures, which increased in number from 27 in 1923 to 52 in 1925 and to 267 in 1930. In these lectures, government agencies and publicists urged Japanese to stay permanently overseas, instead of drifting back to Japan, and encouraged assimilation and acclimatization. An emigration official of the Foreign Ministry is quoted as saying "One defect of the Japanese is to seek quick success. This tendency has been destructive of any chance for Japanese expansion abroad. ... Once you go abroad you must be prepared to stay and die there. Be patient and do not hurry, but try slowly to build up your economic base, and only then will Japanese emigration succeed" (Iriye, 1974: 253–5). By the 1920s, a group of experts on emigration and colonization problems had emerged, and men such as Inazo Nitobe, Tadao Yanaibara, Kazan Kayahara, Minoru Togo and Kazutami Ukita, spoke and wrote extensively on the subject, encouraging agricultural settlement in Oceania, Southeast Asia and South America. At the same time, emigrants to the Philippines increased, riding on the wave of the government emigration enterprise. During 1925–38, the number of such emigrants exceeded 30 000. Early mass emigration to the Philippines resulted in failure: the Benguet road construction work in 1903–4 led to 700 deaths out of some 3000 workers sent as emigrants from Japan.[7] The government therefore did not particularly encourage emigration to the South Seas, including Australia and the Philippines (Haraguchi, 1991: 25).

Emigration to Manchuria or the northeastern part of China was another case of "state-policy emigration", and began in 1932. Although agricultural emigration to that area had been advocated as early as 1905, the number of such immigrants at the time of the Manchurian Incident (1931) was less than 1000, whereas the total Japanese population in Manchuria was 230 000. With the creation of the state of Manchukuo in 1932, the need for large-scale immigration from Japan was seriously studied by the Kwantung Army, the government and emigration publicists. The first test group of 492 armed emigrants, mainly reservists, was sent in October 1932 to a place where noisy protests were being organized by the Chinese against Manchukuo and Japan. The emigrants were also exposed to violent attacks by the local self-defense guerrillas. A total of 3106 households were sent to Manchuria in five test groups before 1936. Meanwhile, emigration to Brazil declined in and after 1935 due to the 1934 immigration restriction law confining the annual number of immigrants to 2 percent of the total number of those who had entered Brazil during the past 50 years. This stipulation became a part of the new 1934 Constitution of Brazil, under the Second Republic led by President Getulio Vargas (1930–45). Japan was virtually excluded from sending emigrants to Brazil; with the outbreak of the Pacific War in 1941, emigration to Brazil ended, and migration to Manchuria became the main current of Japanese agricultural emigration.

The Manchuria development plan adopted by the government was intended to send 5 million Japanese into Manchuria over a period of 20 years. This was based on the idea that Japanese immigrants would amount to 10 percent of the population of Manchukuo in 20 years. Between 1932 and 1940, some 145 000 emigrants were sent to Manchuria. With the addition of some 125 000 who were sent from 1941 to 1945, the grand total of emigrants dispatched was 277 000. This emigration was different in character from the previous ones. First and foremost, its objective was military and political. It was to maintain peace and security in Manchukuo, to defend it against the Soviet Union, and to establish Japanese order in Manchuria. For these purposes, approximately 86 000 youths and boys 15 years of age and above were organized into the "Youth Volunteer Corps for Developing Manchuria and Mongolia" with the purpose of fostering leading farmer-settlers (Haraguchi, 1991: 28–9).

THE WARTIME SITUATION

The China War and the Pacific War inflicted great distress and hardship upon the overseas Japanese. In the United States, approximately 110 000 Japanese nationals and *Nikkeijin* were confined in relocation camps as "enemy aliens" (Haraguchi, 1991: 29). The evacuation decision was made by Secretary of War Henry L. Stimson on 11 February 1942, 2 months after the Pearl Harbor attack, even though Attorney General Francis Biddle stated that "Under the Constitution 60 000 of these Japanese are American citizens" (Hosokawa, 1969: 277). In Canada, about 20 000 *Nikkeijin* were forced into concentration camps under the removal order issued by the federal government in February 1942 (Haraguchi, 1991: 29; Tsurumi, 1991: 47).[8]

Because of the secret nature of their work, the *Nikkeijin nisei's* wartime contributions as interpreters and translators for the US armed forces were not revealed to the nation at a time when they were most in need of publicity about their loyalty. While their accomplishments remained unknown, their brothers in the 442nd Regimental Combat Team stood in the publicity spotlight, praised for their valor and loyalty on the

European front (Hosokawa, 1969: 400). When on 28 January 1943 the Department of War announced its plan to recruit *nisei* volunteers for a special combat unit, it was greeted with enthusiasm in Hawaii, where no mass evacuation had been ordered. More than 10 000 volunteers responded to the recruitment call for some 1500. On the mainland, 2500 *nisei* left their parents and families behind the barbed wire to go out and fight for their country (Hosokawa, 1969: 402–3).[9]

Captain Dan Inouye, who would later become the first Congressman from Hawaii and in 1962 a Senator, was one of those young volunteers. In an assault he led against a German position on Mount Nebbione in Italy, he threw grenades into a machine gun nest and cut down the crew, suffering bullet wounds in the abdomen and in the right leg and losing his right arm. He received the Distinguished Service Cross. "But on his way home in 1945," Hosokawa writes, "Capt. Dan Inouye, his empty sleeve pinned to a beribboned tunic, was denied a hair cut in a San Francisco barbershop." "We don't serve Japs here," the barber said (Hosokawa, 1969: 416–17).

The men who served with the 442nd Regimental Combat Team won more than 18 000 individual decorations for valor, and as a unit the 442nd won many commendations, plaques and citations. In addition to these, the statement made by President Harry Truman in his reception in Washington of the *nisei* veterans of the 442nd upon their return home in 1946 would be widely repeated: "You fought for the free nations of the world along with the rest of us. I congratulate you on that, and I can't tell you how much I appreciate the privilege of being able to show you just how much the United States of America thinks of what you have done. You are now on your way home. You fought not only the enemy, but you fought prejudice – and you won. Keep up that fight, and we will continue to win ..." (Hosokawa, 1969: 410–11).

EMIGRATION AFTER 1945

The balance-sheet of Japanese overseas development by emigration (including China and Southeast Asia) for the 80 years from the Meiji era through the end of the Second World War shows that approximately one million people stayed abroad, which accounts for less than 2.5 percent of the natural increase in Japan's population during that period. Japanese emigration hardly contributed in a meaningful way to the solution of its population problem. According to Foreign Ministry statistics, the ratio of emigration to the natural growth in population, 2.5 percent in the Japanese case, makes an interesting comparison with Britain's 74.2 percent, Italy's 46.8 percent, Sweden's 34.8 percent, Germany's 14.6 percent, France's 9.1 percent, the Netherlands' 7.6 percent, and Belgium's 6.2 percent (see Table 4.8). Japan had no "new world" to absorb its population, nor relief from other countries or international organizations (Wakatsuki and Suzuki, 1975: 79). Postwar Japan began with a smaller territory and a swollen population.

Table 4.8   *Natural population growth and the number of emigrants (1851–1950) of major sending countries*

Country	Natural growth of population (A)	Number of emigrants (B)	Ratio of emigration (B/A) %
Britain	23,100,000	17,140,000	74.2
Sweden	3,500,000	1,218,000	34.8
France	4,300,000	393,000	9.1
Belgium	4,300,000	268,000	6.2
Netherlands	7,000,000	529,000	7.6
Germany	33,900,000	4,961,000	14.6
Italy	22,000,000	10,306,000	46.8
(Japan)[a]			(2.5)

[a] Insertion by Tsuchida.

Foreign Ministry Consular and Emigration Affairs Department, *Waga Kokumin no Kaigai Hatten* [Our People's Development Abroad], (1971, p. 320).

SOURCE: Wakatsuki and Suzuki (1975: 79).

Organized emigration started again in 1952 after the San Francisco Peace Treaty was signed. The first group to go abroad was composed of 54 people and 17 families, independent agricultural emigrants going to Brazil, with their travel expenses covered by a government loan. Argentina, Bolivia and Paraguay also concluded agreements for Japanese emigration. Large numbers of emigrants departed, encouraged by the government, between 1955 and 1965. By the 1960 peak, 46 016 emigrants had used government loans for their travel expenses (Haraguchi, 1991: 30).[10] In the United States, the passage of the Walter–McCarran Act of 1952 eliminated discrimination against Japanese–Americans and provided naturalization for persons regardless of race. The *issei*, or first-generation Japanese residents in the United States, became eligible for citizenship for the first time since their immigration in 1868. The Immigration and Nationality Act of 1965 finally eliminated the National Origins Quota Law of 1924. These legal measures significantly modified the American racial bias.

Post-war Japanese emigrants, who had numbered between 10 000 and 16 000 annually, started to decrease in 1962, to the 8000 level, and have continued to decrease thereafter. From about 1965, the type of emigration started to change: from mass emigration to personal-basis emigration and from agricultural emigration to technologist emigration. These changes reflect increased demands for labor, following Japan's high economic growth-rate after 1960, improved standards of living, easier travel abroad, and the receiving countries' selection policy of accepting technicians and other immigrants. About 67 000 emigrants, most headed for Central and South America, have thus far received government loans to cover their travel expenses. As of March 1990, the total number of emigrants was 262 573, of whom 135 000 were admitted into the United States and 71 000 into Brazil (Haraguchi, 1991: 30–1). Although there were still some 2500–3000 Japanese emigrating each year, "emigration" in the sense of "labor migration" has ceased to be meaningful. If this meaning of the word is still useful on the Japanese scene, such labor migration is now "into Japan", and not "out of Japan". This requires that the matter be looked at in a new light.

NIKKEIJIN AS MIGRATORY RETURNEES

The return migration of South American *Nikkeijin* as a labor force flowing back to Japan became a flood after about 1988. Dominant among them were the *Nikkeijin* from Brazil. Alien Registration statistics show that the number of such returnees from Brazil was 2135 in 1986, which nearly doubled to reach 4159 in 1988. In 1990, it rose sharply to 56 429, followed by 119 333 in 1991, 147 803 in 1992, 155 714 in June 1993, 154 650 in December 1993, and 154 762 in June 1994. Brazilians number about 12 percent of the total registered foreign migrants into Japan, while Peruvian *Nikkeijin* are fewer than one-fifth their number (Y. Suzuki, 1995).

The *Nikkeijin* return migration began in the late 1960s and 1970s with visits to Japan by first-generation Japanese, who came to visit Japan or to visit the graves of their ancestors and relatives to report to them about their decisions to "settle permanently" in Brazil. The 1970 Osaka Exposition gave them a good opportunity to visit their homeland. Such visitors numbered 3042 in 1968. The number increased 2.5 times in 1970, to 7949. A decrease after the Exposition was followed by a sudden increase in 1972. In 1973, the number was 8067, which exceeded that for 1970. This "return boom" was sustained by the high-rate economic growth in Brazil, which was called "the miracle of Brazil" and attracted the world's attention as a model of capitalist development in a developing country (Mita, 1990: 49).

Then came the "oil shocks" of 1973 and 1979, followed by the international recession. Brazilian economy and industry, which were largely dependent on imported oil, were seriously affected. Unbalanced finances, hyper-inflation, long-term recessions and unemployment: their adverse influence was widespread in the 1980s. From about 1980 on, the middle class began to leave Brazil, migrating to Portugal, Canada, the United States, France, Spain, Italy, Australia and New Zealand. In 1985, the number of Brazilian emigrants exceeded that of immigrants. Opinion polls taken in 1987 showed that 60 percent of the residents of São Paulo and two-thirds of the citizens of Rio de Janeiro wanted to leave Brazil, if possible, while about 30 percent of the citizens of São Paulo said they wished they had been born in a country other than Brazil. Brazilians had been restricted in their speech and movements during 21 years of military rule, but hardly anyone left Brazil, because its economy continued to grow by 10 percent even under military rule. The situation is now different (Mita, 1990: 51).

Post-war international migrations have grown in two phases. In the first, from 1945 to the early 1970s, the migratory movements were from less-developed to highly developed countries. There were mainly three patterns: workers migrating from the European periphery to Western Europe, often through "guestworker" systems; workers of former colonies migrating to the former colonial powers; and permanent migration to North America and Australia from Europe, Asia and South America. In the second phase, from the mid-1970s to the 1990s, the international migrations have affected both old and new receiving countries as a result of the restructuring of the world economy under the influence of the 1973–4 oil crisis and the ensuing recession. The patterns of migration in this phase are complex, as they involve "structural changes" caused by the population explosion and the North–South gap; the collapse of the Soviet–Eastern European bloc that triggered the intensification of ethnic conflicts; and the globalization of migrations to, from, and within Eastern European, Arab, African, Asian and South American countries as well as to Western Europe, Australia and North America, where the border controls have become tightened (Kuwahara, 1991: 205; Castles and Miller, 1993: 65–6, 124).

Through the irony of history, Japan was a latecomer to emigration to the New World and a latecomer to immigration as well. Thus it was able to cope successfully with the serious labor shortage in the 1960s and the economic recession following the oil shocks of the 1970s, without introducing a foreign labor force.[11] During its "bubble economy" of the 1980s, however, Japan experienced a labor shortage and began to admit highly educated, qualified and skilled workers from Asian countries, such as Bangladesh, China, Pakistan, the Philippines and Thailand, who would even accept the so-called "3 K" jobs – *kitanai* (dirty), *kiken* (dangerous) and *kitsui* (demanding) jobs.[12] The economic differential between Japan and Bangladesh was then 1 : 60 (Go, 1995: 21). These migrants became unauthorized workers.

Immigration Control statistics show that in 1993, illegal foreign workers came from 90 different countries, an increase of 14 over the previous year, and the number is continuously on the increase. By area, illegal workers from 25 Asian countries accounted for 94.6 percent of the total, followed by 11 South American countries, 27 African countries, 10 North American countries, nine European countries, three NIS countries,[13] four Pacific countries, and there were 11 stateless persons. By gender, the ratio was 70.2 percent of males to 29.8 percent of females. By age, those in their 20s and 30s accounted for 83.4 percent. By status of residence, 80.6 percent entered as temporary visitors (Japan Immigration Association, 1994: 89–93). Control of illegal workers was one of the two major objectives of the June 1990 amendments to the Immigration and Refugee Recognition Law; the other was to issue a Ministerial ordinance specifying the criteria for landing examinations.

The revised Immigration Law opened a new phase for the entry of the South American *Nikkeijin* into Japan. These people of Japanese ancestry, including *issei, nisei* and *sansei* generations, can now enjoy unrestricted access to the Japanese labor market; there is no ceiling on the number of immigrants of Japanese origin who can enter; the initial visa for them is for 3 years, but it can be renewed an unlimited number of times; and they can become permanent residents if they choose to (Cornelius, 1994: 395–6). The Japanese government is relatively lenient in admitting the South American *Nikkeijin* into Japan, particularly because they had emigrated "under the state policy" (Go, 1995: 21). On the other hand, there are growing gaps in awareness between the *issei* and their descendants (*nisei* and *sansei* generations). Whereas *dekasegi*, or going out to work, reminds the first-generation emigrants of their past full of sorrow, anguish and misery, the term holds only positive connotations to the second and third generations. The *nisei* and *sansei* Brazilians, for instance, define themselves as "Brazilians who go to Japan to improve their living." Well educated, with Brazilian values, but hardly speaking Japanese, they have gradually come to realize that they can be neither

Japanese nor completely Brazilian in the closed *Nikkeijin* society in Japan.[14] The 35th Convention of Japanese Abroad (*Kaigai Nikkeijin Taikai*) held in Tokyo on 11–13 May 1994 in the presence of the Crown Prince and Princess, was attended by 287 delegates from 13 countries including the Americas, Southeast Asia and Australia. The delegates appealed specifically for realization of the right to vote abroad and called for understanding toward the *Nikkeijin* workers in Japan (Kaigai Nikkeijin Kyokai, 1994: 6–66).

With 1995 marking the 50th anniversary of the end of the Second World War, special events and programs commemorating and reviewing the "war and 50 years after" were on the year's agenda. Noteworthy among them were publications and news dispatches uncovering the facts about the "remaining Japanese" (*zanryu nihonjin*) and their descendants in Asia, who had struggled in vain to obtain the Japanese government's recognition. "*Sokoku yo*" [Oh, my mother country!] is the cry of women whose love for their mother country sent them to Manchuria, and the title of a book about these women, who still remain in China (Ogawa, 1995).

According to a survey by the Foreign Ministry, approximately 1 550 000 Japanese lived in old Manchuria at the time of Japan's defeat in 1945, of whom some 270 000 were agricultural emigrants called the Manchuria Development Corps, including the Manchuria Construction Labor Service Corps and the Manchuria–Mongolia Development Youth Volunteer Corps. In the Soviet invasion of 9 August 1945 and in the ensuing confusion of defeat, some 176 000 Japanese died, of whom half, or 78 500 persons, were connected to the Development Corps: 11 520 killed themselves, 11 000 are missing with 6500 of these presumed dead, and possibly 4500 are alive (Ogawa, 1995: 28). The emigrants to Manchuria had been sent in family units under the state policy. Husbands were drafted just before the defeat, leaving their women and children to flee from place to place, trying to escape the attacks and assaults of Soviet soldiers and Chinese farmers. Some of the women were pregnant, children were sick and starving, and many died on their way to nowhere in the freezing cold, deserted by the Japanese military in the midst of the Soviet invasion. Those still alive were exhausted and taken by the native Chinese. For them, the war started on the day of Japan's defeat.

Even after normalization of Japan–China relations, the
Japanese government was not quick to come to the rescue of
these women and children who had narrowly escaped death.
The Welfare Ministry handled the "remaining orphans" separately from the "remaining women." "Orphans" were defined
as those who lost their Japanese parents by death or otherwise
and who were 12 years old or under before the Soviet Union
joined the war; the "women" included the children who were
13 years of age or over. They were judged to "have chosen not
to return home" and were excluded from candidacy for repatriation (Ogawa, 1995: 35–8). These victims of state-policy emigration are now in their late 70s. Their "mother country"
continues to live in their memories of childhood. The *Asahi
Shimbun* on 11 July 1995 reported that a Japanese national remaining in the Philippines since the war's end was recognized
by the Japanese government and granted a copy of his family
register. Daisuke Takezawa, 63, was visiting Japan with his
eldest and second sons, applying for his birth, as a Japanese, to
be entered in the family register. He was the first to obtain
such recognition among the remaining Japanese in the
Philippines. Another report by the *Asahi*, dated 13 July 1995,
said that the Foreign Ministry decided to issue Japanese passports to ten "remaining Japanese" in the Philippines who were
temporarily visiting Japan in a group of 32, calling for
confirmation and recovery of their Japanese citizenship. They
are the *nisei* of the "remaining Japanese" who lost the documents with which to prove their status or who went by their
Philippine names under the strong anti-Japanese situation.

On 22 August 1995 the *Asahi* noted that the Foreign
Ministry would carry out an "on-the-spot investigation" of the
Japanese nationals remaining in the Philippines, by means of
interviews at about 50 locations in 31 districts, starting on
23 August 1995. Many of these "remaining Japanese" are the
nisei and *sansei* of the Japanese immigrants who were engaged
in road construction and flax culture before the war, who cooperated with the Japanese military forces during the war, and
kept their status secret for fear of retaliation afterward. Many
of them lost their parents' marriage certificates and their birth
certificates in the war. These cases are only the very beginning
of the overseas Japanese nationals being officially recognized
as Japanese by the Japanese government.

CONCLUSION

A brief history of Japanese emigration for the past 130 years, from the 1860s to the 1990s, provides us with a valuable insight into the dynamic nature of human movement. The Japanese emigrants, migratory workers from the very beginning, were latecomers to emigration to the New World and elsewhere. To become settlers, they had to change from being workers to farmers. Under the state-policy emigration, numbers of families left their motherland for good, only to find themselves in a sad plight in the war-torn foreign lands. The return migrations of the *Nikkeijin* from South America were warmly accepted, like sprouting trees which herald the spring. First, they came for family reunion, and then for employment. The war made Japan smaller and over-populated, but the Japanese worked hard to develop technology in their limited space.

The post-war migrations have redrawn the map of the world. Hundreds of thousands of refugees and workers migrate, crossing national borders, yet the world still remains one of nation-states. The states are responsible for the protection of their nationals who have the right to stay in their motherlands if their peace and security are ensured. To keep them within their national borders, the governments should strive to close the gap between the rich and the poor both within and outside their countries. In the current migrations of workers, many countries have shifted from sending to receiving countries. Japan is one of them. As a latecomer to immigration, Japan established a latecomer model. Instead of introducing foreign labor, Japan made creative efforts to apply mechanized adjustment to productive capacity, while further intensifying technology.

What does Japan mean to the twentieth century? Japan's experience of the twentieth century had its beginning in the nineteenth century when the country was forced open to the outside world. Having been accustomed to using a foreign model for over a thousand years, the Japanese were now required to change the model from China to the West, for they realized that Japan was a latecomer far behind the Western imperialist powers which were competing for concessions in China at the height of their activities in East Asia. The

Japanese strove seriously to select their "teachers" in the different aspects of Western civilization, whether they be the British navy, German army, French police, or others. Above all, the British Empire remained the center of the model for a long time, as symbolized by the conclusion of the Anglo-Japanese Alliance in 1902, which ended in 1921 under American pressure.

The new situation in East Asia after 1919 combined together Chinese nationalism, American internationalism, and Soviet Communism, but Japan remained imperialist and "drifted through the 1930s with a basically pre-1914 mentality" (Hagihara, 1985: 21). The chain of events between the Manchurian Incident of 1931 and 1941 can hardly be called other than "a succession of imperialist aggressions". In the post-1945 world, completely "isolated from what was happening in the center of the twentieth century", the defeated and occupied Japan made its start over again as a latecomer among the democratic nations of the world.

Almost everything in modern Japan can be traced back to the Meiji Restoration of 1868. Emigration is not an exception. It started in 1868 when a group of 153 Japanese workers migrated to Hawaii, while 42 separately emigrated to Guam. As a latecomer to the global migration, the Japanese emigrants had to change their destinations from one place to another, faced with immigration control and restrictions on the part of the receiving countries. Despite their individual motivations and aspirations, they were destined to serve the states' purposes.

In his article "What Japan Means to the Twentieth Century," Hagihara tends to stress Japan's position as a latecomer *vis-à-vis* the advanced powers of the West and to say as if a latecomer could do nothing but "responding to history" rather than "making it" (Hagihara, 1985: 16 and 24). He means to criticize the passive, irresponsible attitude of the latecomer Japan.

Emigration resumed in 1952, with the conclusion of the San Francisco Peace Treaty. As Japan grew economically and technologically, the number of emigration to one of immigration, Japan was again a latecomer. Instead of passively imitating the other receiving countries, however, Japan creatively developed policies for adjusting the inflow of foreign workers. It gave a warm reception to the "return migration" of the overseas

Japanese emigrants and their descendants who are called *"Nikkeijin"*.

In dealing with these, other, and future immigrants and migratory workers from abroad, the Japanese Government and people could make meaningful contributions to enhancing the universal values of global human movement, on the basis of their experience of both sending and receiving migratory workers and their latecomer status during the past century.

NOTES

1. *Nikkeijin*, originally a Japanese expression, is used as it is in English sentences. In a broad sense, it denotes the "component members of an overseas Japanese immigrant society, including the Japan-born first generation (issei)" (Fuchigami, 1995: 3). Latin American *Nikkeijin* are defined as "Latin American immigrants of Japanese ancestry (the *Nikkeijin*)", the "descendants of Japanese emigrants to Latin America (the *Nikkeijin*)", or "Latin America-based persons of Japanese ancestry, including the first (issei), second (nisei), and third (sansei) generations" (Cornelius, 1994: 385n and 395). *Nikkeijin* is not a legal concept. It is an ethnicity-based "native concept or folk concept" which is given meaning by the *Nikkeijin* themselves (Maeyama, 1995: 60). The 1991–2 survey of the Brazilian *Nikkeijin* shows that *issei* are 19.0 percent of all, *nisei* of pure blood 46.5 percent, *nisei* of mixed blood 1.3 percent, *sansei* "pure" 24.7 percent, *sansei* "mixed" 5.6 percent, *yonsei* (fourth-generation) "pure" 0.5 percent, *yonsei* "mixed" 1.8 percent, and unknown 0.6 percent. When *issei* and the *nisei*, *sansei* and *yonsei* of pure blood are put together, they comprise 90.7 percent of the entire *Nikkeijin* population in Brazil, whereas 3 percent of *nisei* and 23 percent of *sansei* are of mixed blood (São Paulo Institute of Cultural Sciences, 1992: 13). These results endorse the meaning of *Nikkeijin* as ethnic immigrants.

2. Article 3 of the Japan–United States Treaty of Amity and Commerce (1858) specified that the "American residents in Japan shall be permitted to employ Japanese lowly people for various types of work" (J. Suzuki, 1992: 12).

3. Japan's diplomatic relations with Hawaii began with the conclusion of the 1871 Treaty of Amity and Commerce. Japanese emigration to Hawaii, which the Hawaiian government had repeatedly requested, was discussed between Hawaiian Consul-General Robert W. Irwin and the Japanese Foreign Ministry. With their negotiations concluded, the Foreign Ministry notified all the prefectures that it had permitted Japanese emigration to Hawaii and that the recruitment of emigrants

would be started in the name of the Hawaiian Immigration Bureau. Irwin opened his office in Yokohama and was about to start advertising for emigration, when Foreign Minister Kaoru Inoue advised him to focus recruitment on three prefectures – Yamaguchi, Kumamoto and Hiroshima. Inoue selected these prefectures with great expectations that their emigrants would contribute to Japan's modernization by acquiring Western-style agricultural techniques and orderly work habits (Doi, 1980: 13). As a matter of fact, the people from Hiroshima and Yamaguchi prefectures enjoyed an established reputation as the best of all emigrants, when inspected by the Consul-General in Hawaii, Taro Ando, in 1886, as they were moderate, industrious, thrifty, cleanly dressed and kept their houses neat and tidy, and the employers were most satisfied with them (T. Iriye, 1981: 70–1). It is to be noted that the Mitsui business firm was involved from the very beginning in the sending of emigrants from the four prefectures, including Fukuoka, and that behind the scenes were efforts by three persons closely interrelated with each other through the medium of the Mitsui. They were: Foreign Minister Inoue, Hawaiian Consul-General Irwin, and Mitsui Bussan President Takashi Masuda. Masuda, formerly in charge of the management of a company headed by Inoue, was recommended by Inoue to Mitsui Group leader Rizaemon Minomura, who was planning to open a trading sector and was looking for a person suitable for that business. Thus, Masuda, then 29 years old, became the President of Mitsui Bussan when it was established in July 1876. President Masuda found Irwin listed as an adviser to his firm. They had known each other before as colleagues working in an American business company in Yokohama. Irwin sought Mitsui Bussan's help in the recruitment of Japanese emigrants. Masuda sent his company employees to Fukuoka, Kumamoto, Yamaguchi and Hiroshima and had them take care of the emigrants from application to embarkation. This led Mitsui Bussan to open an export business to Hawaii, sending rice, medicine and daily necessities for emigrant use, and at the emigrants' request while handling their remittances and savings (Doi, 1980: 13–15).

4. In 1907, Japan was still an agricultural country, with the agricultural population estimated at 62 percent of the total. Manufacturing employed only 15 percent. The 1930 census showed the agricultural population still close to a half of the total work force, while the industrial population had barely reached 30 percent (Fukutake, 1989: 18–19).

5. In 1900, approximately 8000 Japanese entered the United States. Large-scale anti-Japanese rallies were held by labor unions, and bills calling for the exclusion of Japanese immigrants were submitted to the state legislatures (Haraguchi, 1991: 23).

6. People of Kumamoto prefecture joined in the mass emigration to Peru, from the second voyage in 1903, and the Amakusa Islanders from the third voyage in 1906. They totaled 2948 and 185, respectively, by 1923 (Kitano, 1985: 339–40).

7. The Benguet road construction work of 1903 was to link Manila with Baguio, about 130 miles to the north through dense jungles and along

precipitous cliffs. The construction work did not progress because of heavy casualties, many injuries and runaways due to epidemics and hazardous conditions. Desperate, the contractors came to Japan to recruit 1000 workers. Three thousand applied, and all were shipped to the Philippines. They worked for only 62 cents per diem, and 700 died (Wakatsuki and Suzuki, 1975: 73).

8. Tsurumi notes that this policy of "removal and segregation" of Japanese had been prepared by the William L. Mackenzie King Cabinet since 1938 (Tsurumi, 1991: 65n).

9. On 28 January 1943, when the War Department announced plans to accept *nisei* volunteers, Secretary Stimson said: "It is the inherent right of every faithful citizen, regardless of ancestry, to bear arms in the national defense ... Loyalty to country is a voice that must be heard, and I am glad that I am now able to give active proof that this basic American belief is not a casualty of war" (Hosokawa, 1969: 401). Up to the outbreak of the war, nearly 3500 *nisei* had been drafted.

10. The government hoped that the resumed emigration would help solve the serious problems of population increase and food shortages after the war. The approximately 6 million repatriates from former overseas colonies and other areas caused a sudden population increase from 72 147 000 in 1945 to 83 200 000 in 1950, or 15.3 percent (Yano, 1995: 68).

11. In the 1960s, the Japanese government and people discussed whether or not to introduce foreign workers to cover the labor shortage. The decision they reached was to cope with the shortage by means of mechanization and energy-saving. In 1968, the Cabinet decided that "foreign 'simple labor' would not be accepted". This decision was confirmed on three different occasions thereafter. In the business recession following the oil shocks of the 1970s, Japan was able to minimize its difficulties by mechanized adjustment of its productive capacity (Katayama, 1995: 3; Go, 1995: 20).

12. These foreign workers with high-level education and skills were inhabitants of major cities in their home countries, forced overseas when their cities became crowded with the jobless returnees from the Middle Eastern oil-producing countries where business declined, such as Bangladesh and the Philippines. The returnees, unable to find jobs in their home countries or abroad, gathered in the cities and started to work at lower wages than those paid to the earlier settlers. In Thailand, farm mechanization caused surplus labor to flow into cities, and the city dwellers were forced overseas. In China, the so-called "blind currents" of the people migrating from farm villages to cities pushed the inhabitants of Shanghai into Japan (Go, 1995: 20–1). Under these circumstances, the case of an illegal immigrant being informed by an immigration official upon his deportation that he "would be free to return to Japan, legally, in a year's time" (Cornelius, 1994: 393n) may be understandable.

13. NIS stands for New Independent States, consisting of the former Soviet countries, excluding the Baltic states.

14. Koichi Mori says that the *Nikkeijin* entertain effusive sentiments toward the Japanese and Japanese society, and expectations that they ought to be warmly accepted by the Japanese. However, they are Brazilians, not Japanese. When they are treated like foreigners, they feel discriminated against, and they have formulated a stereotype that the Japanese are discriminatory and cold (Mori, 1992: 159–64)

REFERENCES

Asahi Shimbun (1995), "Takezawa Daisuke-san ni Koseki Tohon wo Kofu" [Daisuke Takezawa Granted a Copy of Family Register], 11 July, p. 30.

—— (1995), "Kyo 10-Nin ni Ryoken Hakkyu" [Today, Passports Issued to Ten Japanese Remaining in the Philippines], 13 July, p. 1.

—— (1995), "Gaikokujin Toroku ga Kako Saiko Koshin" [Record-High Number of Registered Aliens Renewed], 17 August, p. 3.

—— (1995), "Gaimusho ga Genchi Chosa" [Foreign Ministry to Carry Out On-the-Spot Investigation], 22 August, p. 26.

Castles, Stephen and Miller, Mark J. (1993), *The Age of Migration* (London: Macmillan).

Cornelius, Wayne A. (1994), "Japan: The Illusion of Immigration Control," in Wayne A. Cornelius, Philip L. Martin, and James F. Hollifield (eds), *Controlling Immigration* (Stanford, CA: Stanford University Press), pp. 375–410.

Doi, Yataro (1980), *Yamaguchi-ken Oshima-gun Hawai Imin Shi* [A History of Emigration to Hawaii] (Tokushima: Matsuno Shoten).

Fuchigami, Eiji (1995), *Nikkeijin Shomei* [Identifying *Nikkeijin*] (Tokyo: Shin Hyoron).

Fukuda, Moritoshi (1980), *Legal Problems of Japanese–Americans* (Tokyo: Keio Tsushin).

Fukutake, Tadashi (1989), *The Japanese Social Structure*, trans. Ronald P. Dore (Tokyo: University of Tokyo Press).

Go, Munechika (1995), "Kigyo kara Mita Gaikokujin Kenshusei ya Rodosha no Ukeire" [Corporations' Views on Accepting Foreign Trainees and Workers] in *Kokusai Jinryu*, no. 92 (January) (Tokyo: Nyukan Kyokai), pp. 20–6.

Hagihara, Nobutoshi (1985), "What Japan Means to the Twentieth Century," in Nobutoshi Hagihara, Akira Iriye, Georges Nivat and Philip Windsor (eds), *Experiencing the Twentieth Century* (Tokyo: University of Tokyo Press), pp. 15–29.

Haraguchi, Kunihiro (1991), "Imin no Rekishi" [A History of Emigration], in *Rekishi to Chiri* [History and Geography], vol. 430 (June) (Tokyo: Yamakawa Shuppansha), pp. 20–31.

Hosokawa, William K. (1969), *Nisei* (New York: William Morrow).

Ichioka, Yuji (1988), *The Issei* (New York: Free Press).

Ike, Nobutaka (1969), *The Beginnings of Political Democracy in Japan* (Westport, CT: Greenwood Press).

Immigration Bureau, the Ministry of Justice (1994), "Heisei 5 Nen Matsu Genzai ni okeru Zairyu Shikaku (Zairyu Mokuteki) Betsu Gaikokujin Torokusha Tokei" [Statistics of Registered Aliens by Status/Objective as of the End of 1993], in *Kokusai Jinryu*, no. 89 (October) (Tokyo: Nyukan Kyokai), pp. 36–55.

Iriye, Akira (1974), "The Failure of Economic Expansionism: 1918–1931," in Bernard S. Silberman and Harry D. Harootunian (eds), *Japan in Crisis* (Princeton, NJ: Princeton University Press), pp. 237–69.

Iriye, Toraji (1981), *Hojin Kaigai Hatten Shi* [A History of Overseas Japanese Development], vols I and II (Tokyo: Hara Shobo; reprint of the 1942 edn).

Japan Immigration Association (1994), *1993 Statistics on Immigration Control* (Tokyo: Nyukan Kyokai).

Kaigai *Nikkeijin* Kyokai [*Nikkeijin* Association Abroad] (1994), "Dai 35 Kai Kaigai Nikkeijin Taikai" [The 35th Convention of Japanese Abroad Tokyo], in *Kikan: Kaigai Nikkeijin* [Quarterly: Japanese Abroad], no. 35 (October), pp. 6–66.

Katayama, Yoshitaka (1995), "Gaikokujin Rodosha no Ukeire no Genjo to Kongo no Tembo" [The Present Situation of the Acceptance of Foreign Workers, and Future Perspective] in *Kokusai Jinryu*, no. 92 (January) (Tokyo: Nyukan Kyokai), pp. 3–12.

Kitano, Norio (1985), *Amakusa Kaigai Hatten Shi* [A History of Amakusa Islanders' Development Abroad], vol. II (Fukuoka: Ashi Shobo).

Kuwahara, Yasuo (1991), *Kokkyo wo Koeru Rodosha* [Workers Crossing National Borders] (Tokyo: Iwanami Shoten).

Maeyama, Takashi (1995), "1930 Nendai San Pauro Shi ni okeru Nikkei Gakusei Kessha" [Nikkei-Student Associations in São Paulo City, 1930s], in Toshio Yanagida (ed.), *Amerika no Nikkeijin* (American *Nikkeijin*) (Tokyo: Dobunkan), pp. 57–86.

Mita, Chiyoko (1990), "Nihon to Burajiru wo Musubu *Nikkeijin* Ijusha no 80 Nen" [A History of 80 Years of Nikkei Immigrants Linking Japan with Brazil], in *Gaiko Jiho* (February), pp. 41–56.

Mori, Koichi (1992), "Burajiru kara no *Nikkeijin* 'Dekasegi' no Suii" [Changes in *Nikkeijin's "Dekasegi"* Emigration from Brazil] in *Iju Kenkyu* [Study on Emigration], No. 29 (March) (Tokyo: Kokusai Kyoryoku Jigyodan/JICA), pp. 144–64.

Ninomiya, Masato and the Ministry of Labor (1994), *Nihon Burajiru Ryokoku ni okeru Nikkeijin no Rodo to Seikatsu* [*Nikkeijin's* Work and Life in Both Japan and Brazil] (Tokyo: Nikkan Rodo Tsushinsha).

Ogawa, Tsuneko (1995), *Sokoku yo* [Oh, My Mother Country!] (Tokyo: Iwanami Shoten).

São Paulo Institute of Cultural Sciences (1992), *Burajiru Nikkeijin no Ishiki Chosa, 1991–1992* [Brazilian *Nikkeijin's* Awareness Surveyed] (São Paulo: Centro de Estudos Nipo-Brasileiros).

Suzuki, Joji (1992), *Nikkeijin Dekasegi Imin* [Japanese "*Dekasegi*" Emigration] (Tokyo: Heibonsha).

Suzuki, Yasuyuki (1995), "Alien Registration Statistics and Comments," mimeo, Tokyo.

Tsuchida, Motoko (1989), "The Making of the Americans: Journalism in the Politically Organized Society," *The Journal of American and Canadian Studies*, no. 4 (Autumn), pp. 71–113.

—— (1997), "Wakayama-ken Kihoku no Amerika Imin" [Emigrants to America from the North of Wakayama Prefecture], in *Nichi-Bei Kiki no Kigen to Hainichi Iminho* [The Origin of the Japan–US Crisis and the Anti-Japanese Immigration Law] (Tokyo: Ronsosha, 1997), pp. 89–118.

Tsurumi, Kazuko (1991), "Steveston no Nihon Kanadajin" [Canadians of Japanese Origin in Steveston], in John A. Schultz and Kimitada Miwa (eds), *Kanada to Nihon* [Canada and Japan in the Twentieth Century] (Tokyo: Sairyusha), pp. 43–66.

Wakatsuki, Yasuo and Suzuki, Joji (1975), *Kaigai Iju Seisaku Shi Ron* [On a History of Emigration Policies] (Tokyo: Fukumura Shuppan).

Wilson, Robert A. and Hosokawa, William K. (1980), *East to America* (New York: Quill).

Yano-Tsuneta Kinenkai (Tsuneta Yano Memorial Society) (1995), *Nihon Kokusei Zue* [A Charted Survey of Japan] 1995/96 (Tokyo: Kokuseisha).

5 The Challenge of Incorporating Foreigners in Japan: "Ethnic Japanese" and "Sociological Japanese"

Takamichi Kajita

THE INCORPORATION OF FOREIGNERS

The influx of foreign workers which began in the early 1980s with the arrival of female workers from Asia, increased greatly in the late 1980s. Fifteen years later, Japan finds that a number of foreign workers have become permanent residents and, like Western Europe, faces the problem of how to incorporate them into society. Even the reduced demand for foreign workers during the recent recession has not decreased the foreign population, which indicates that Japan's prosperity is not the only factor that keeps foreign workers in Japan.

Although the Japanese government does not officially permit the entry of foreign workers, it seems tacitly to permit their employment, because a large number of foreign workers have remained by overstaying their visas. In addition, *Nikkeijin*, immigrants of Japanese ancestry, are formally accepted; foreign students are permitted to work at part-time jobs; and some foreign workers are accepted under entertainment visas or the trainee system. In this regard, Japan seems to accept foreign workers through the "back door" or "side door" rather than the "front door" (Kajita, 1994, 1995). As a result, qualifications for stays in Japan vary considerably according to worker categories.

Foreigners in Japan can be roughly divided into three groups. The first group is made up of foreigners who have lived in Japan over three or four generations, while the second group is made up of *Nikkeijin* who have been officially permitted to work in Japan by the revision of Japan's immigration law. The third group is made up of Asians who are officially prohibited from working in Japan. These three groups must be discussed separately, because the conditions under which they are in Japan are different for each. All three have caused social tensions in Japanese society, although the nature of the tensions varies. The purpose of this paper is to discuss the incorporation of foreigners into Japanese society, in the fields of labor, education and the community.

The incorporation of the third group, illegal workers from Asia, is at the present legally impossible; nevertheless, they are increasing in number. Many of them have overstayed their visas. The number of children born of these illegal foreigners is gradually increasing, and since their nationality cannot be established under current law, controversy has arisen around whether they should be granted Japanese citizenship. In addition, a new question is being raised about the incorporation of these third-category foreigners, who are different both from foreigners who have settled down in Japan and from *Nikkeijin*, into Japanese society. Many points concerning this third category remain to be clarified, and further research will be required for a full understanding of the issue.

Besides these three groups, a group of foreigners, mainly Americans and Europeans, exists in Japan who are officially allowed to work in Japan as professionals and business people. They are generally staying in Japan temporarily and have no plans to settle there; their employment, being legal, causes few problems. However, some of these Americans and Europeans have settled in Japan. They seldom adapt to Japanese society; Japanese society is required to adapt itself to them through the internationalization of Japanese society to American and European cultures and the English language. The problem of adaptation of Americans and Europeans to Japanese society is thus different from that of *Nikkeijin* and Asians.

The special problem of Koreans who have lived in Japan since the colonial period from 1910 to 1945 will be discussed at some length in a later section of this paper. It should be distinguished from the larger foreign worker problem. These Koreans have a deep-rooted antipathy against assimilation into

Japanese society, even though more and more third- and fourth-generation Korean residents become naturalized Japanese citizens and marry Japanese. The Korean residents who resist assimilation are pressing the Japanese government to grant voting rights in local elections to foreigners living in Japan. Active discussion on naturalization and the suffrage of foreigners are thus about to start in Japan.

Three Immigrant Groups, Three Special Conditions

Let us look at the approximate number of people in each of the three groups. Table 5.1 shows the number of foreign residents in Japan according to nationality, as of December 1993. The figures refer to the number of legally resident foreigners, either permanent or temporary. Koreans, totaling about 680 000, are the largest in number, and many of them belong to the first group, that is, the group of foreigners who have

Table 5.1   *Foreign residents in Japan by nationality (December 1993)*

Nationality	Number
1. South and North Korea	682,276
2. China (including Taiwan)	210,138
3. Brazil	154,650
4. Philippines	73,057
5. USA	42,639
6. Peru	33,169
7. UK	12,244
8. Thailand	11,765
9. Vietnam	7,609
10. Iran	6,754
Total	**1,320,748**

SOURCE: Nyukan Kyokai (Association of Immigration) (1995), *Kokusai Jinryi* [International Flow of Persons], no. 92 (January) (Tokyo: Nyukan-Kyokni).

settled in Japan. Many foreigners from Brazil and Peru are *Nikkeijin* and belong to the second group. As shown in Table 5.2, the number of *Nikkeijin* is about 190 000, a sharp increase over 1990, when they were first officially permitted to work in Japan. The third group, made up of Asians, includes many people who have overstayed their visas. Their actual numbers cannot be determined based on Table 5.1.

Table 5.3 shows the difference between the number of foreigners who legally entered Japan and the number who left the country from 1985 to 1991. The number of Asians living in Japan can be estimated at about 200 000 based on the table, excluding *Nikkeijin*, who are officially permitted to work in Japan.

The number of foreigners in each group will not change considerably unless Japan goes through a rapid change in its economic conditions and its foreign worker policies. If the demand for foreign workers grows again with the recovery of the Japanese economy and a change in the country's foreign worker policy, foreign workers belonging to the third group will sharply increase in number.

Now, basic concepts should be explained before the main subject is embarked upon. In Japan, which puts relatively strong emphasis on the maintenance of cultural uniformity and ancestry, almost no difference can be seen in the meanings among the terms "absorption," "integration" and "incorporation," the key concepts for the foreign worker problem, subsumed under the term "incorporation" in Japan. Japanese society accepts foreigners in various ways, and controversy has arisen on how to accept them. In this article, the term "incorporation" is used to refer to the method of accepting foreigners in the broadest sense, including the various meanings mentioned above.

Foreigners must understand Japanese language and culture and acquire Japanese citizenship if they hope to be incorporated into Japanese society. This leaves little room for a multiple identity that would allow them to become naturalized Japanese citizens while maintaining their own ethnic identity and culture.

Japan has been sharply criticized as having little tolerance for "incorporation without assimilation", which is close to the concept of "insertion" in France, and which permits

Table 5.2 Number of Peruvians and Brazilians staying in Japan

	1986	1987	1988	1989	1990	1991	1992	1993
Peruvians	553	615	864	4,121	10,279	26,281	31,051	33,169
Brazilians	2,135	2,250	4,159	14,528	56,429	119,333	147,803	154,650
Total	2,688	2,865	5,023	18,649	66,708	145,614	178,854	187,819

SOURCE: The Japanese Ministry of Justice.

Table 5.3 Difference between the number of foreigners who legally entered Japan and the number of foreigners who left Japan (1985–91)

Nationality	1985	1986	1987	1988	1989	1990	1991
Philippines	2,517	24,556	18,019	9,587	9,781	18,080	18,225
China	−1,102	554	11,874	30,998	8,817	16,017	21,009
South Korea	1,077	2,637	5,519	14,814	21,717	19,677	23,718
Bangladesh	453	898	3,460	11,653	1,244	881	884
Pakistan	941	783	3,331	10,998	1,149	693	961
Brazil	450	231	400	2,464	12,310	42,696	54,948
Iran	−144	127	−15	76	1,081	11,252	32,595
Malaysia	5	339	908	2,944	8,858	10,938	26,257
Thailand	1,579	2,188	3,728	5,870	4,875	10,230	30,063
Peru	103	96	118	376	3,635	7,670	17,023
Total	**30,487**	**48,119**	**55,427**	**101,387**	**94,716**	**161,970**	**257,687**

NOTE: The table includes countries which recorded differences of more than 10 000 people a year between 1985 and 1991.

SOURCE: The Japanese Ministry of Justice.

multiculturalism. France, a nation that has engaged in multiple ways of accepting immigrants, including assimilation, integration and insertion (Costa-Lascoux, 1989; Kajita, 1992), often uses the term "insertion" to emphasize a multicultural sense of values leading to integration without assimilation. In another context, however, this seems to be used as a general term that contains various modes of acceptance, as "incorporation" as used in English-speaking countries. Currently, the need for multiculturalism and incorporation without assimilation is being increasingly recognized in Japan; the idea is disappearing that Japanese are only those people who have Japanese citizenship, speak Japanese and hold Japanese identity and culture, as will be discussed in a later section of this paper.

Generational differences among foreign residents should also be mentioned here. The problems they face are often discussed on the basis of their generation: *issei* (first-generation), *nisei* (second-generation) and *sansei* (third-generation). Such categories, often used by *Nikkeijin* who emigrated to the United States and Brazil, help to understand the generational differences in degree of assimilation to the communities that have accepted them. In the United States, the *issei* maintain their Japanese identity, but the *nisei* have a strong tendency to assimilate into American society, mainly because they grew up there during the Second World War; the *sansei* have completely assimilated into American society, but exhibit a strong inclination to return to Japanese culture and identity at a symbolic level. It is the *sansei* who filed a complaint against the United States government for its policy of sending *Nikkeijin* to internment camps during the Second World War (Takezawa, 1994).

Koreans have lived in Japan over three or four generations. Assimilation of third- and fourth-generation Koreans to Japanese society is progressing, while they are still under the strong influence of first- and second-generation Koreans. These third- and fourth-generation Koreans are comparable to the second-generation foreigners living in France and Germany whose existence has become a serious social problem in these countries. From the viewpoint of Korean residents, incorporation into Japanese society is equal to assimilation or naturalization, and many are reluctant to become naturalized Japanese citizens, fearing the loss of their own culture. Thus, Koreans in Japan have not yet fully assimilated to Japanese society nor become naturalized Japanese citizens, even though they have lived in Japan for three or four generations.

NIKKEIJIN – THE EMERGENCE OF "ETHNIC JAPANESE"

As a result of the labor shortages of the 1980s, the Japanese government, among other measures, allowed the employment of *Nikkeijin* – foreign workers of Japanese ancestry, mostly from Brazil or Peru. Their employment was permitted by the government in 1990, in the belief that this would relieve the demands of both employers and workers, while emphasizing the importance of cultural uniformity and ancestry. It was thought that they would be easily accepted by Japanese society, because they do not "look like foreign workers." Japan had already had a similar experience through the acceptance of mixed Chinese/Japanese children born during the Second World War.

Such a problem is not peculiar to Japan. *Nikkeijin*, who are ethnic immigrants, are similar to the *"Aussiedler"* – immigrants of German ancestry who immigrated to Germany from East Europe or the former Soviet Union, and to Jewish immigrants who went to Israel from the former Soviet Union; the concept "ethnic Japanese" is adapted from that of "ethnic German". Since ethnic ties will make it easier for these immigrants to enter and find employment in those countries, they become economically motivated, and their decision to immigrate is made.

Nikkeijin differ from other ethnic immigrants in that most of them come to Japan as temporary migrant workers. However, further observation is required, because it is doubtful whether this difference will continue. Many *Nikkeijin* go back to their home countries after a stay of several years in Japan, returning later with their families. Generally speaking, 30–40 percent of *Nikkeijin* who come to Japan seem to intend to settle down in the near future (Kitagawa, 1993), and a network of *Nikkeijin* is gradually forming. However, it is interesting to note that, except for those who originally emigrated from Okinawa

Prefecture, their ties with their Japanese families and relatives are weak. In most cases, they come to Japan with the help of brokers and middlemen.

The weak familial bonds of the *Nikkeijin* stand in a sharp contrast to those of overseas Chinese, who have strong networks of family and relatives. Compared with Chinese, Japanese do not attach importance to blood ancestry. Rather, they put emphasis on the continuance of *ie*, the "fictitious" family system, which may include close friends and even business ties.[1] In addition, since most early emigrants from Japan were second and third sons from poor regions, sent abroad to relieve the burden on their family and with no means of maintaining family ties, they were in many ways cut off from their families. This weak family bond relativizes the principle of *jus sanguinis* as it applies to Japanese citizenship.

Let us now turn to the field of labor. About 200 000 *Nikkeijin* were employed in Japan in 1994. The size of the *Nikkeijin* community in South America is limited, and the number of *Nikkeijin* workers there is several hundred thousand at most. All *Nikkeijin* working in Japan are legally employed; they are willing to work long hours, in jobs Japanese workers are unwilling to take. Their take-home pay, including overtime, is sometimes higher than that of Japanese workers. *Nikkeijin*, who can work legally in Japan, have an advantage over other foreign workers. Many of them work in the manufacturing industry which offers relatively better working conditions than other industries, and they live in company towns where large firms and their affiliates are concentrated (Inagami *et al.*, 1992).

The working conditions for *Nikkeijin* worsened slightly in the economic recession of the 1990s. Some lost their jobs and moved to other industries, such as food processing and construction, and to other regions. Many *Nikkeijin* depend upon brokers to find employment, but some Japanese Brazilians have become independent and look for work through a network of Brazilians living in Japan. A three-layered structure – Japanese workers, *Nikkeijin* workers and illegal foreign workers – has been formed in the Japanese labor market (Inagami *et al.*, 1992); there is little competition among these three categories. If the Japanese government changes its foreign worker policy, permitting Asian workers in Japan, *Nikkeijin* will lose their advantage.

Are the *Nikkeijin* incorporated into the community? Most of them are concentrated in company towns and live in company houses or in apartments provided by brokers. Since their living space is separate from that of Japanese, and since they do not speak Japanese, they do not have much contact with Japanese and are isolated in their own community. Finding a place to live in Japan is the most serious problem for foreigners. They not only must find a Japanese guarantor but must also pay a large deposit to rent an apartment. Brokers serve as guarantors, because it is difficult for *Nikkeijin* to find a Japanese guarantor by themselves. This prevents them from living independently in Japan.

On the other hand, many *Nikkeijin* live in company towns in Gunma, Kanagawa, Shizuoka and Aichi prefectures, and networks of *Nikkeijin* have formed in such relatively comfortable cities as Hamamatsu, Toyohashi, Ohta and Oizumi. In addition, since business circles in these cities actively accept *Nikkeijin* workers, and local governments have taken various measures to assist them, many *Nikkeijin* want to live in them.

Many *Nikkeijin* came to Japan with their families, and their children go to Japanese elementary and junior high schools in the company towns, which find themselves having to accept many foreign students who do not understand Japanese. This is quite a new experience in Japan. Since the Ministry of Education has not taken adequate measures to cope with it, the local municipal governments must find their own way through repeated trial and error, devising interesting experiments on ways to educate and incorporate many foreign students. Since this is a local problem, no special education for *Nikkeijin* has been introduced into schools in regions where few *Nikkeijin* live.

Children who came to Japan in the lower grades can easily learn to speak Japanese. However, since they have not yet mastered their mother tongue, such as Portuguese or Spanish, it is hard for them to learn how to write and read Japanese, which has negative effects on their performance in other subjects. On the other hand, since those who are in the upper grades of elementary schools were already fluent in their mother tongue, their grades tend to improve rapidly once they have mastered Japanese.[2]

The most serious problem for recently-arrived children of *Nikkeijin* is attending high school. They must enter into Japanese society, which attaches great importance to one's educational background, without adequate preparation, and it is difficult for them to compete with Japanese students. When they look for jobs, they are often forced to work as unskilled workers in the manufacturing industries, like their parents; their education tends to be sacrificed to their parents' repeated moves between Japan and their home country every 2 or 3 years, which prevent them from getting the background to seek a position as a professional or an engineer even in their home country. *Nikkeijin* may be able to obtain the maximum profits through international migration in the short run, but they make the worst choice in the long run in terms of the education of their children.

The biggest challenge for *Nikkeijin* is establishing a long-term life plan. It will be interesting to observe what kind of life plan they will choose in the near future. It is no wonder that some of them choose to settle down in Japan, because many of their families have already lost a foundation for life in Brazil or other home countries. The question of their naturalization will come up again in such cases. They will probably continue their current life-style of repeated moves between Japan and their home countries every 2 or 3 years for a while, taking advantage of their double nationality and employment opportunities in Japan that are offered only to *Nikkeijin*. However, some of them will settle down in Japan for some reason, such as the education of their children. They will face difficulties in assimilating into Japanese society, because they do not have a good command of Japanese. They are in some ways in a position similar to Puerto Ricans and Mexicans in the United States; the process of their incorporation into Japanese society will be similar to that of refugees from Indo-China and the Chinese/Japanese children of the Second World War who later came to Japan, whose incorporation into Japanese society is an example of integrating people with different cultural and linguistic backgrounds into a society and can be applied to the integration of today's foreigners, represented by *Nikkeijin*.

KOREANS LIVING IN JAPAN: "SOCIOLOGICAL JAPANESE"?

South and North Koreans living in Japan are descendants of those individuals who were brought to Japan by force during the colonial period or those who came to Japan voluntarily to look for employment. Their number reached about 2 million in 1944, but many of them returned to their homeland later. As of 1993, about 680 000 Koreans lived in Japan. In addition to them, a large number of Koreans have become naturalized Japanese citizens. Most of them are concentrated in the Osaka and Kobe districts, where they have lived and worked since pre-war days, but many Koreans also live in the city of Kawasaki in Kanagawa Prefecture, Adachi and Kita wards in Tokyo, and Kitakyushu, which is close to the Korean peninsula. A movement to grant foreigners voting rights in Japan, which will be discussed later, is quite active in the Osaka and Kobe districts.

Today, third- and fourth-generation Koreans live in Japan, and their settlement has become a *fait accompli*. To reflect this, an organization of South Koreans living in Japan changed its name from *Zainihon daikanminkoku kyoryu mindan* (the Korean Residents' Union in Japan) to *Zainihon daikanminkoku mindan* (the Korean Union in Japan) by taking out the word *kyoryu* (residents). Many Koreans living in Japan still have South or North Korean citizenship, although they have lived in Japan for many years. Thus, they are not "Korean Japanese", and they have established a strong ethnic community.

There are several reasons why Koreans have maintained such a strong ethnic community in Japan, beginning with Japan's invasion of the Korean peninsula. First- and second-generation Koreans who suffered under the Japanese invasion and subsequent discrimination against them still have a strong influence in the Korean community and prevent third- and fourth-generation Koreans from acquiring Japanese citizenship, which they view as ethnic betrayal. Koreans living in Japan have long been excluded from the primary labor market through social and economic discrimination, and as a result opened their own businesses and ethnic-oriented enterprises. For example, many of the pinball parlors, whose total sales surprisingly exceed that of the steel industry in Japan, are run by Koreans. These business activities have also hardened their relative separation from Japanese and made their assimilation into Japan more difficult.

Second, the division of their homeland into South and North Korea also divided the Korean community in Japan, prompting alignment with either South Korea or North Korea. Koreans have been much interested in national identity, because their homeland throughout its history has been surrounded by big powers such as China, the Soviet Union and its successor states, and Japan, and national independence has been difficult to maintain. Such national consciousness also applies to Koreans living in Japan. This topic is not directly related to the discussion here, but today, South Korea also faces an inflow of a large number of foreign workers such as Filipinos and Iranians, complicating Koreans' definition of themselves as a minority.[3]

Third, the problems between Japan and South and North Korea have yet to be completely solved. A lingering problem is that of the Korean women forced to provide sexual services for Japanese soldiers during the Second World War. Japan and other Asian countries represented by South and North Korea have repeatedly argued about the historical interpretation of Japan's invasion; in some ways this argument is similar to that about African–Americans' history in the United States.

In addition, Japan's security relations with North Korea have been strained. The Cold War has not yet come to an end in the Far East, and such international relations have negative effects on Koreans living in Japan, including harassment of Korean high school girls.

However, in a sociological sense the assimilation of Koreans living in Japan has been progressing steadily. The mother tongue of third- and fourth-generation Koreans is Japanese, and their life-style is quite similar to that of Japanese. More than half the third- and fourth-generation Koreans have married Japanese. The progress of assimilation and the maintenance of ethnic identity, existing side by side, place Koreans living in Japan in a unique situation. While their sociological assimilation has been progressing, historical problems between Japan and South and North Korea have not yet been solved, and there is still socio-economic discrimination against them.

In addition, they are an all but invisible minority, because they cannot easily be distinguished from Japanese; their ethnic background is generally revealed only by their names. The use of Japanese names, historically forced on them through the pressure to assimilate in Japanese society, has become popular among Koreans to avoid discrimination, but some also try to maintain their own identity by using their real Korean names. The maintenance of their Korean citizenship is closely related to their sense of ethnic identity. If Japan were similar to the United States, where Koreans are visible and can acquire American citizenship while keeping their ethnic identity, the situation would have changed, because they would not have to link their ethnic identity with their Korean nationality.

The unique ethnic identity held by Koreans is illustrated by their efforts to maintain, not a literal ethnicity, but ethnicity in a symbolic sense. Such symbolic ethnicity can be clearly seen in their protest against fingerprinting for alien registration in Japan, the movement to use their real name in schools and their attachment to their Korean citizenship. Such symbolic ethnicity leads to the creation of symbolic politics.[4] Unlike interest politics, which is characterized by negotiations, deals and compromise, symbolic politics is not based on rational judgments and calculations; what is important is legitimacy or correctness of historical interpretation.

The issues of Japan's responsibility for the war and foreign women who were forced to provide sexual services to Japanese soldiers during it are not only domestic but also international, making it difficult to discuss the problem of foreign residents in Japan purely in the context of interest politics and the social cost theory. In contrast, the problem of foreign workers who came to Japan relatively recently can to some extent be discussed in the context of interest politics, just as it is not very difficult to argue the issue of foreign workers in the United States from this viewpoint.

However, South and North Koreans living in Japan are Japanese in a sociological sense, and their ethnicity is not the same as that of South or North Koreans living in their home-lands. In fact, many third-generation Koreans living in Japan have gone to South Korea to study, but most of them returned to Japan to find employment and live. The problem of Koreans living in Japan is largely sociological. So, following the example of French sociologist Patrick Weil, who refers to "sociological French" (Weil, 1991), we can call them "sociological Japanese": third- and fourth-generation immigrants who are assimilated sociologically even if they are still foreigners in the juridical sense.

Employment, education and community life of Koreans in Japan should be outlined here to compare them with other foreigners living in Japan, especially with *Nikkeijin*. Discrimination against Koreans still continues in terms of employment, but not a few Japanese companies, including large firms, have opened their doors to foreigners living in Japan, as the abolition of discrimination, including sexual and ethnic discrimination, has been promoted through the improvement in Japan's international status and growing pressure by foreign governments.

Foreigners living in Japan are not allowed to enter the civil service, except for that of some local governments, a measure intended to maintain national security and prevent foreigners from taking part in national policy-making. The employment of foreigners by national and local governments, as well as their right to vote in local elections, has become a matter of debate in Japan.

As for education, many children of North Korean ancestry go to Korean schools in Japan, which educate students in the Korean tradition. These children, whose mother tongue is Japanese, master Korean and, paradoxically, they are relatively isolated from Japanese society and experience relatively little discrimination. However, since Korean schools do not conform to the Japanese Education Ministry's guidelines, their students – most of whom want to stay in Japan – are not qualified to take examinations for entrance to Japanese universities, but are forced to go to other schools to prepare for entrance examinations. The increase in the number of Koreans who reside permanently in Japan has thus had a noticeable impact on education.

In contrast, most children of South Korean ancestry go to Japanese elementary and junior high schools, and do not speak Korean. They have many contacts with Japanese students and want to assimilate into Japanese society, but often experience discrimination. Many of them go to Japanese universities, their ratio being the same as for Japanese students.

Yet in the Osaka district, where many South and North Koreans live, a movement has sprung up to keep their real Korean names to promote their ethnic identity, and many want to see the introduction of Korean-based education in Japanese schools.

Although Koreans in Japan tend to concentrate in the Osaka district and the city of Kawasaki in Kanagawa Prefecture, generally speaking no marked ethnic segregation can be observed in Japan. However, local governments in the regions where many Koreans live have played an active role in the movement to obtain voting rights for foreigners in local elections, and have attempted to set up an advisory organization for foreigners and to delete the requirement for Japanese nationality from eligibility for civil service. Nor is there noticeable discrimination against Koreans in terms of coverage by the national pension plan or availability of apartments built by the National Housing Corporation.

The city of Kawasaki plans to build a "Korean Town". Until now, discrimination has forced the Korean community to blend in, but today some attempts are being made to highlight diversity and even to use ethnic culture to attract tourists and consumers. Japanese society has gradually become more tolerant of other cultures.

Denizens or Citizens? The Two Korean Communities in Japan

Today, a generation gap is causing a split in the Korean community – South Korean and North Korean. North Koreans living in Japan view themselves as overseas citizens of North Korea and do not become naturalized Japanese citizens; many of their children go to Korean schools in Japan and are educated in the Korean tradition. In contrast, South Koreans do not ignore the fact that they reside in Japan, and send their children to Japanese schools. As a result, third- and fourth-generation Koreans living in Japan have a multi-based sense of values and identity, and can be divided into various groups (Fukuoka, 1993).

The first group is made up of those who intend to live discretely in Japan. They live in Japan, but resist not only assimilating into Japanese society, but also aligning themselves with either South or North Korea. They try to define themselves based on their own history of growing up in the Japanese community. This view is similar to that of "*les beurs*," as the second generation of Arab immigrants is called in France. The second group are individualists. They have weak ethnic identity, pursue equality and try to seek self-fulfillment based on their own abilities. Those who try to overcome discrimination through higher education and study abroad, frequently in the United States, often belong to this group. The third and largest group is made up of individuals who want to become naturalized Japanese citizens in order to avoid discrimination.

What is common to these three groups is their intention to remain in Japan and their tendency to think of their life and future in terms of the Japanese society in which they were raised. There is yet another group, made up of young people with North Korean citizenship who are strongly aligned with their homeland. They have never lost sight of the fact that their homeland is North Korea, and they do not intend to become involved in Japanese society, nor do they define themselves as residents of Japan.

A related topic is the problem of foreigners' voting rights in Japan (Suh, 1995). The views of established Korean ethnic organizations primarily reflect the opinions of first-generation Koreans living in Japan. The League of Koreans in Japan, made up of North Korean immigrants, refuses to consider the issue of the right to vote, insisting that they should stay out of Japan's internal affairs; the North Korean government is likewise opposed to their participation in Japanese policy, because they are North Korean citizens and the acquisition of the franchise may promote their assimilation into Japanese society. In contrast, the Korean Residents' Union in Japan, an organization of South Koreans living in Japan, wants suffrage (only for local elections), based on the fact that they actually live in Japan.

What is common to third- or fourth-generation young Koreans is that they were brought up in Japan and they are going to continue to live in Japan. In particular, young people of South Korean ancestry who intend to live together with Japanese are aware of their situation. An organization of foreigners living in Japan, called *Zainichito* (Party of Foreigners Living in Japan), tried to run candidates in the 1992 House of Councillors election and the 1993 House of Representatives election (Lee, 1993). Their attempt ended in failure, but sparked a controversy over the issue of suffrage for foreigners.

In parallel with this movement, some municipal assemblies in the Kansai region, where many Koreans live, have adopted resolutions to give foreigners the vote in local elections. The suffrage of foreigners will not be easily achieved; however, some local governments such as the city of Kawasaki plan to set up advisory councils for foreigners to promote their participation in local politics. Some Japanese political parties, such as Sinto-Sakigake, allow foreigners to become members, although membership in a political party is not directly connected to suffrage.

What is worthy of note here is the ruling by the Japanese Supreme Court in the spring of 1995 that granting foreigners the voting right in local elections does not violate the Japanese Constitution, but can be achieved by enacting a law. This is in contrast to the situation in France and Germany, where a constitutional amendment would be required. Thus it is possible that Japan may permit foreigners to vote in local elections earlier than either France or Germany.

The problem surrounding voting rights for foreigners in Western Europe is often referred to in similar discussions in Japan. Foreigners residing in Western Europe can be compared to Koreans living in Japan, rather than to more recent arrivals. Over 80 years have passed since the first Koreans came to Japan in 1910, and their fourth and fifth generations have been born; their incorporation, or that of other foreigners, into the body politic has been much later in Japan than in Western Europe. However, what is important here is not the number of years since the influx of foreigners started but the fact that both Japan and Western Europe are facing complaints and demands for rights from their foreign residents. Discussions on the issue of foreigners in Western Europe have had an impact on the situation in Japan, and Japan and Western Europe are experiencing the same problem.

The sociological assimilation of foreign residents is ongoing, but their nationality remains unchanged. However, something is inherently strange when a group retains its status as foreign after residing in the same place for nearly a century. Voting rights for foreigners tend to be the focus of attention in Japan, because no one wants to address directly the problem of granting foreigners Japanese citizenship or naturalization. In Germany, where the emphasis on lineage has prevented foreigners from becoming naturalized German citizens, the problem of the right of foreigners to vote tends to be highlighted to avoid discussion about naturalization. The situation in Japan is quite similar to that in Germany.

However, there is an increasing number of foreigners who have been granted Japanese citizenship through naturalization or marriage. Many Koreans living in Japan are expected to acquire Japanese citizenship when the first- and second-generation Koreans have passed away, when the Cold War in the Korean peninsula comes to an end or South Korea and North Korea are united, and when Japan's naturalization policy has changed. Many children who had not been granted Japanese citizenship were naturalized in Japan in 1985, when the Japanese nationality law was expanded to reflect the growing equality between the sexes, and children whose mothers are Japanese, in addition to those whose fathers are Japanese, were allowed to acquire Japanese citizenship.

The above case, which is related to marriage to Japanese, should be distinguished from the cases of other foreigners, but many foreigners will try to acquire Japanese citizenship if the procedure for its acquisition becomes straightforward and there is a fair chance for them to be naturalized in Japan by satisfying certain requirements. The problem of nationality, as well as that of foreigners' suffrage, should be fully discussed in Japan.

Even under these circumstances, the social and economic conditions of foreigners living in Japan have improved and a movement for foreigners' suffrage has become galvanized, as mentioned above. In such a social atmosphere, foreigners living in Japan may choose to stay in Japan as foreigners rather than to become naturalized Japanese citizens, because if they can be "denizens" (Hammer, 1990), their social, economic and political rights will be close to those of Japanese citizens, and the benefits of naturalization will become smaller, making naturalization less attractive; they will live in Japan as foreigners whether they are naturalized Japanese citizens or not. Giving foreigners the right to vote will not weaken but reinforce such tendencies. They are very likely to choose to be denizens on the assumption that their assimilation into

Japanese society and culture is progressing and that they can continue to maintain their symbolic ethnicity and symbolic politics. Such a situation may not actually exist in Japan at the moment, but the country is very likely to confront it in the near future. Japan may face the paradoxical situation that the closer denizens get to being citizens, the fewer denizens become naturalized citizens (Schuck, 1989).

At any rate, with the internationalization of Japan, the ethnic border between Japanese and non-Japanese has become vague. It is the time when the Japanese should consider what kind of people they are, along with the problem of nationality.

TWO KINDS OF ETHNICITY: "OLDCOMERS" AND "NEWCOMERS"

Japan has faced a slightly different problem than has Western Europe. While foreigners such as Koreans, who have stayed in Japan for a long time, are increasingly remaining in the country, many newcomers are arriving from Asian countries. Two kinds of immigration problems, clearly separate from each other, co-exist in Japan. Foreigners who have settled down in Japan ("oldcomers") and those newly arrived ("newcomers") are completely different from each other, not only in their ability to speak Japanese but also in the labor markets in which they participate. Many Koreans who have recently come to Japan were brought up in Korea, and they do not share the language and customs of longtime Korean residents, who maintain a symbolic ethnicity based on their names and their nationality, but whose daily life is Japanese.

A look at the relationship between longtime Korean residents and those who have come to Japan recently would be instructive. Culturally speaking, this relationship can be compared with that between Japanese visiting the United States and Brazil and *Nikkeijin* living in these countries, or that between Japanese and *Nikkeijin* visiting Japan. Japanese companies that have moved into the United States have had a certain impact on *Nikkeijin* in the United States, as has the inflow of newcomers on oldcomers in Japan. The coexistence of these two immigrant problems has resulted in an overlap of the discussions and comments on these issues. The following two points should be noted here.

The first point is the influence of oldcomers on newcomers. Many of the oldcomers, while facing discrimination and the pressure to assimilate in Japanese society, have demanded and expanded their rights – rights that would greatly benefit newcomers. Many newcomers depend upon a network of their relatives and try to find employment in the Korean community, and some Korean residents invite their relatives to come from South Korea and provide them with jobs during their stay.

The second is the influence of newcomers on oldcomers. Koreans who have settled down in Japan are close to Japanese sociologically and linguistically, although they have sought equality and the maintenance of their symbolic ethnicity. They have called upon the Japanese to recognize their existence, while newcomers have maintained a completely different ethnicity, and their heterogeneity is much more conspicuous than that of the oldcomers. This situation further expands the discussion on foreigners and different cultures.

When third-generation Koreans living in Japan visit South Korea on a trip or to study, the locals mistake them for Japanese. They cannot speak Korean well and are viewed as Japanized Koreans. Today, however, Koreans living in Japan are more likely to see South Koreans in Japan than to visit South Korea and see South Koreans there. Since the number of such newcomers from South Korea is increasing, they should be factored into any discussion on the problems of Koreans living in Japan.

Recently, oldcomers have tried to distinguish themselves from recent arrivals. When the Japanese immigration law was revised in 1990, the Korean Residents' Union in Japan submitted a request to the Japanese government to ensure that no revision would cause disadvantage to Koreans who have settled in Japan. Based on this request, the government modified the bill to provide a new certificate for foreigners qualified to be employed in Japan. The inflow of a large number of Koreans has caused a conflict with the long-term residents in Ikuno, Osaka, and job competition has sprung up between the groups.

The Japanese government's response to foreigners was polarized in the middle of the 1990s as foreigners living in Japan became more and more like Japanese citizens. While the Japanese government legalized the employment of *Nikkeijin* and introduced a foreign trainee system, when demand for foreign workers dropped during the recession it tightened controls on illegal foreign workers. In 1993, a volunteer in Kitakyushu who played an active role in supporting many Peruvian workers was arrested and charged with encouraging foreign workers to overstay and work illegally, becoming the first foreign worker supporter to be arrested for violating the immigration law.

These facts clearly underline the polarization of the policy toward foreigners by the Japanese national government, which is trying to shut illegal foreign workers out of the country while guaranteeing the rights of foreigners who have legally settled in Japan and permitting *Nikkeijin* and foreign trainees to work in Japan. In this regard, the Japanese situation has become more like that of Western Europe.

"Ethnic Japanese," "Sociological Japanese" and Japanese Nationality

There are two kinds of legal foreign residents in Japan: foreigners, such as Koreans, who have settled down in Japan and *Nikkeijin*, such as Japanese Brazilians. Each group's qualifications for staying in Japan are determined by law, and conditions of employment are different for each. As a result, how they are incorporated into Japanese society varies drastically.

One of the features of the Japanese foreign worker problem, as discussed above, is the coexistence of oldcomers and newcomers. Japan faces two kinds of immigrant problems, which can also be seen in Western Europe, except that the gap between the two groups is greater in Japan than in Western Europe.

Another feature is the appearance of a new category of foreigners, that is, the *Nikkeijin*. Like Germany and Israel, Japan is experiencing an inflow of ethnic immigrants. A broad interpretation of the *jus sanguinis* definition of lineage not only sets *Nikkeijin* apart socio-economically in South American society, but was also used to give them permission to work in Japan.

While this policy helps to emphasize lineage and reinforce nationalism, Japanese nationals who live in such countries as the United States, Australia and Brazil maintain their interest in Japanese politics and want to vote in its national elections. The progress of globalization and an increase in the international migration of labor not only let people view their nationality and nation from a relative point of view, but also give them a strong awareness of their own nationality.

As shown above, the boundary between Japanese and foreigners has become increasingly blurred in various fields. Foreigners who have settled down in Japan are foreigners in terms of their nationality and lineage, but they are often not different from Japanese from a socio-cultural point of view and can be referred to as "sociological Japanese." They, together with the Japanese, played an important role in Japan's postwar economic growth. In contrast, the *Nikkeijin* grew up in South America, which is very different from Japan, and are foreigners in a sociological sense. However, they can be called "ethnic Japanese," because to some extent they share the Japanese lineage and culture. Both foreigners who have settled in Japan and *Nikkeijin* are foreigners in one sense, but Japanese in another. The existence of these two kinds of foreigners will continue to raise such questions as what it means to be Japanese and how Japanese nationality should be defined.

THE NEW MIGRATION FROM ASIA

The number of foreign workers from Southeast Asia, East Asia and South Asia has increased since the late 1980s. Most come from the Philippines, Thailand, South Korea, China, Malaysia, Pakistan and Iran, with various visas and occupations. With the changes of the Japanese government's policies on visas and Japanese language schools, their number fluctuates dramatically. Since, except for professionals, the Japanese government does not permit foreigners to work in Japan, many foreigners overstay their visas and work illegally.

Because a foreigner can legally stay in Japan through marriage to a Japanese citizen, the number of so-called "mail-order brides" is increasing, and depopulated Japanese villages have accepted many brides from Asia. However, the number of foreigners who have married Japanese is larger in urban areas than in rural villages. Traditionally, more Japanese women than men married foreigners, but the situation has reversed today. The largest group of foreign brides is from the Philippines. Another way of remaining in Japan legally is with an entertainer's visa. While many Filipinas obtain visas to work as entertainers, too often they end up in an unsavory red-light district. They are far from being the entertainers for whom the entertainment visa was instituted.

In addition to them, many foreign women, called *japayuki-san*, are illegally working in Japanese businesses that offer food and entertainment. One reason why there are so many *japayuki-san* is that foreign women are not permitted to work as maids, nurses or factory workers; another is that the food and entertainment businesses need them to cope with a serious labor shortage caused by a general improvement in the status of women in Japanese society.

However, many workers from Asian countries are illegal aliens who have overstayed their visas or entered Japan with forged passports or by other illegal methods, making it impossible for them to be incorporated into Japanese society. The actual living conditions of these illegal workers are not well known, but routes for overstaying and working in Japan seem to have been well established, because more than 10 years have passed since Japan first faced the problem of illegal foreign workers. With the revision of the Japanese immigration law in 1990 that helped legalize the employment of *Nikkeijin*, a clear border was drawn between them and other foreign workers. As a result, Japanese employers tend to avoid hiring Asian workers who are clearly foreigners, because of potential legal troubles.

As for illegals' effect on education, Japan is not one of the few nations that educate the children of illegal residents. In any case, many of the illegal Asian workers are single and do not bring family members with them, so that their presence does not directly affect the Japanese schools.

In daily life, illegal foreigners face many problems. They have trouble renting apartments, with the result that many often share a small room with others, and problems occur constantly between them and their Japanese landlords and neighbors due to differences in customs, such as how to dispose of garbage. However, this does not attract public attention, as other foreigners have stayed in Japan for a long time and have learned Japanese customs. If employers provide apartments for foreign workers, regardless of whether they are legal or illegal, they are isolated from the Japanese in their neighborhood and there are few problems. This is also true when foreigners concentrate in company towns or in large cities such as Tokyo. *Nikkeijin* tend to gather in company towns, but because of the stagnation of the manufacturing industry, their jobs and the regions where they live have become diversified, and the border between them and other Asian workers is becoming fuzzy.

Brazilians and Filipinos are forming ethnic networks, which are not the same thing as ethnic communities. Many newspapers and magazines for *Nikkeijin* are published (for example, a Portuguese weekly magazine entitled "*International Press*" has a circulation of 33 000 copies), and stores and restaurants which cater to *Nikkeijin* are increasing in company towns. Many Filipinos are Catholic and often go to church, and churches are their greatest source of psychological support, as well as a place to exchange various information on areas such as employment.

Iranians used to get together at Yoyogi Park in Tokyo to exchange information, but the city of Tokyo temporarily closed the park in 1993 to shut them out, a move which symbolizes the toughened attitude of the Japanese national and local governments toward illegal aliens. The number of Iranians is decreasing, and their meeting places have been broken up, because their entry into Japan has been strictly controlled since then.

Since land prices are very high in Tokyo, the city has no impoverished neighborhoods and does not face the inner-city problems which plague large American cities. For the same reason, segregation of ethnic groups is not likely to occur in Tokyo. Therefore, ethnic networks are springing up via churches, ethnic media and telephones – characteristics that make their existence invisible to Japanese.

Thus, these foreigners' living environment in Japan is conditioned by the fact that they are not allowed to work in Japan; they have either overstayed their visas or been illegally employed. Under such circumstances, their incorporation into Japanese society is unlikely to occur. However, the situation may change rapidly if the Japanese government modifies its foreign worker policy.

The Japanese government started intervening in the foreign worker problem with the revision of the immigration law in 1990. Since the governmental agencies concerned have not yet reached an agreement on this matter, and a basic strategy concerning the foreign worker policy has not been mapped out, the Japanese government is trying to satisfy the labor needs of small and medium-size companies by accepting foreign workers "through the back door." Meanwhile, the governmental agencies have agreed among themselves that the acceptance of foreign workers should be avoided; the employment of foreigners in the general labor markets should not permitted; and their settlement in Japan should not be allowed.

However, judging from the findings of various public opinion polls, the Japanese people have become more receptive to the employment of foreign workers, including unskilled workers, although they do not welcome their permanent settlement in Japan. Demand for foreign workers lessened during the recession of the 1990s, but it may grow again in the near future. In that case, it is doubtful whether Japan's conventional back door policy would be accepted internationally; the Japanese government's foreign worker policy may then shift from the back door to a side or front door policy.

Developments in the trainee system introduced in 1993 should also be touched upon. During the recent recession, few companies have taken advantage of it, but there is the possibility that many companies will start using the system and that foreign workers will actually be accepted by its substantial expansion. In that case the situation of foreign workers in Japan would change drastically, and the problem of their incorporation into Japanese society is likely to attract public attention in Japan.

NOTES

1. Immigrants from Okinawa to Peru have maintained a close connection with their hometowns, while those from mainland Japan are said to have few ties with theirs. People from Okinawa may have different ethnic characteristics from those from mainland Japan in terms of *ie*. Further research will be required on this issue.

2. These findings came from a survey on *Nikkeijin* conducted in Toyohashi, Aichi Prefecture by a study group, including the author. The author also received useful suggestions from Haruo Ohta, a member of the study group.
3. The number of illegal foreign workers, such as Filipinos, is increasing in South Korea, and those who were arrested in 1990 totaled 1918. In 1992, however, those illegal foreign workers were granted a special pardon. The South Korean government permitted companies to accept foreign workers for the purpose of providing them with in-house training and issued visas to 10 000 foreign workers. South Korea is thus becoming a country that formally accepts foreign workers.
4. For concepts of symbolic politics and interest politics, see Dower (1993).

REFERENCES

Costa-Lascoux, Jacqueline (1989), *De l'immigré au citoyen* (Paris: La documentation française).

Dower, John (1993), "Peace and Democracy in Two Systems: External Policy and Internal Conflict," in Andrew Gordon (ed.), *Postwar Japan as History* (Berkeley, CA: University of California Press).

Fukuoka, Yasunori (1993), *Zainichi kankoku chosenjin* [South and North Koreans living in Japan] (Tokyo: Chuokoronsha).

Hammer, Tomas (1990), *Democracy and the Nation State: Aliens, Denizens and Citizens in a World of International Migration* (Aldershot, UK: Avebery).

Inagami, Takeshi, Kuwahara, Yasuo and Kokumin kin-yu koko sogo kenkyusho(eds) (1992), *Gaikokujin rodosha wo senryakukasuru chushokigyo* [Small and Mid-sized Companies Which Make Good Use of Foreign Workers] (Tokyo: Chushokigyo Research Center).

Kajita, Takamichi (1992), "Doka Togo Hennyu–Furansu no imin eno taio wo meguru ronso" [Assimilation Integration Insertion – Controversy over the French Immigration Policy], in Toshio Iyotani and Takamichi Kajita (eds), *Gaikokujin rodosha ron* [Theories of Foreign Workers] (Tokyo: Kobunsha).

—— (1994) *Gaikokujin rodosha to Nippon* [Foreign Workers and Japan] (Tokyo: Nihon hoso shuppan kyokai).

Kitagawa, Toyoie (1993), *Hamamatsushi ni okeru gaikokujin no seikatsu jittai – ishiki chosa* [Actual Conditions of Foreigners in the City of Hamamatsu – Survey of Their Attitudes] (Hamamatsu: City of Hamamatsu).

Lee, Yong Hwa (1993), *Zainichi kankoku chosenjin to Sanseiken* [South and North Koreans and Their Voting Right] (Tokyo: Akashi Shoten).

Suh Yong-Dal (ed.) (1995), *Kyosei shakai eno chiho sanseiken* [Suffrage in Local Elections Toward Symbiotic Society] (Tokyo: Nihon Hyoronsha).

Schuck, Peter H. (1989), "Membership in the Liberal Polity: The Devaluation of American Citizenship", in William R. Brubaker (ed.)

Immigration and the Politics of Citizenship in Europe and North America (Lanham, MD: University Press of America).

Takezawa, Yasuko (1994), *Nikkei amerikajin no ethnicity – kyosei shuyo to hosho undo niyoru hensen* [The Transition of Japanese American Ethnicity – The Effects of Internment and Redress] (Tokyo: University of Tokyo Press).

Weil, Patrick (1991), *La France et ses Etrangers: L'aventure d'une politique de l'immigration de 1938 à nos jours* (Paris: Calmann-Lévy).

Part III
Do Japan and the United States Need Immigrants?

Part III

6 Does Japan Need Immigrants?

Kazutoshi Koshiro

During Japan's 2000-year history, there have been four waves of large-scale immigration, beginning in the eighth century with the arrival of many intellectuals and skilled artisans, most of whom came from Korea, in a period of great cultural growth. The second wave occurred in the 1640s, under the Tokugawa Shogunate, when several noble families of the Chinese Ming dynasty sought asylum in Japan, escaping from political oppression by the newly established Ch'ing dynasty (Shiba, 1987, pp. 498–507). The third wave occurred during the 1930s and 1940s, when many Koreans and Chinese were imported as forced labor. Most of these returned at the end of the Second World War, but more than 100 000, mostly Koreans, remained. Except for this third wave, modern Japan remained a country of net emigration until the early 1960s (SOPEMI, 1993: 58–62).

Now Japan faces a fourth wave of immigration, which includes not only officially admitted intellectuals, skilled workers and artists, but also, for the first time, illegal unskilled migrant workers. In the industrial expansion of the late 1960s and early 1970s, Japan first began to experience labor shortages; seasonal employees of industries such as construction and road-building were not available, as their traditional source – farmers in the North, made idle by winter – shrank (Figure 6.1), and employers began to call for immigrant workers.

During the boom period of 1987–91 there was an active discussion of whether Japan should change its traditionally restrictive immigration policy toward unskilled foreign workers, a debate stimulated by expectations of a labor shortage early in the next century. At the same time, the remarkable appreciation of the yen beginning in the fall of 1985 stimulated the potential supply of immigrant workers from the developing countries of Asia, while migrant workers of Japanese descent

Figure 6.1 *Changes in the number of seasonal migrant workers, 1970–90*

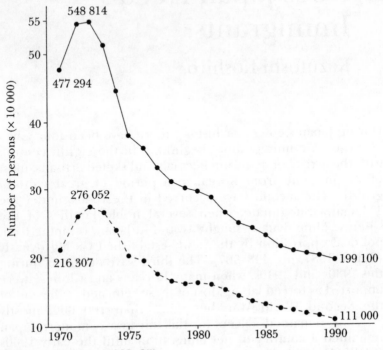

SOURCE: Koshiro (1992: 35)

from South America filled the supply/demand gap to some extent. With the end of the "bubble economy" and the onset of recession in the spring of 1991, industry began reducing its work force, producing a labor surplus by the fall of 1992. However, the recession has resulted in only a slight decrease in the estimated number of illegal immigrant workers, which remains at about 284 500 in May 1996. Some macroeconomic analyses estimate that the acceptance of foreign unskilled workers will cause a deterioration in the national economic welfare, causing a 1500 billion yen loss in national income if half a million foreign unskilled workers are accepted. This estimate is, however, based upon a set of strong assumptions, and there should be no optimism about the supply of native workers in the so-called "3D" (dirty, dangerous and demanding) jobs.

The government revised its immigration policy for skilled and professional workers in 1989, facilitating the immigration of specialists and technicians, but leaving unchanged the prohibition of unskilled immigrants. A study commissioned by the Ministry of Labor (1992c) estimates that the long-run social costs of accepting 2 million foreign immigrant workers and their families will amount to 1.4 trillion yen. The government still appears to be giving priority to public security. Because the recession has resulted in problems involving foreign immigrant workers, "Bright," the first labor union of foreign immigrant workers, was begun in Tokyo by Japanese volunteers in March 1993, organizing 4500 foreign immigrant workers and helping them to escape inhumane exploitation by greedy employers. Some local agencies of the Ministry of Labor have also exposed illegal intermediaries who were exploiting foreign immigrant workers.

Even if low economic growth continues, a labor shortage is expected to develop in Japan, particularly in sectors with "3D" jobs, early in the next century. The question of how Japan can overcome its labor shortage must be scrutinized carefully, not only from the viewpoint of economic welfare, but also considering public security and humanitarian factors. A continued appreciation of the yen would certainly facilitate overseas production and increasing imports, but improvement in these areas will not overcome the expected labor shortage in the service sector, including the expanding field of care for the aged.

BASIC POLICIES OF THE JAPANESE GOVERNMENT TOWARD FOREIGN IMMIGRANT WORKERS

The Japanese government has maintained a very conservative policy to restrict the inflow of foreign migrant workers seeking unskilled work. The Immigration Control Act of 1951 has been amended several times, notably in 1981, and again in 1989 when the system of differing categories of residence was introduced, making it easier for skilled workers to enter the country. An excellent summary of present foreign labor in Japan is provided by the SOPEMI Report of the OECD (1993: 59–62):

The government's current policy was formulated in 1992 as part of the Seventh Basic Plan for Employment Measures, and is designed to facilitate the immigration of specialists and technicians whose presence is consistent with the internationalization of the economy and Japanese society. However, the situation is very different for unskilled workers who are officially barred from entering the country. The government's strategy is to encourage employers to offset manpower shortages not by immigration but by improved efficiency and the use of labor-saving production techniques.

In 1991 the number of new foreign workers allowed to take up residence and employment in the country was 113,599, an increase of 20 percent from 1990 and a continuation of the upward trend of recent years. The vast majority of these were skilled workers. In addition, for the same year some 50,000 students were granted temporary work permits. The October 1990 census estimated the number of foreigners in the labor force at about 460,000 (including those with the right of permanent residence [mostly Koreans and Taiwanese who had lost their Japanese nationality as a consequence of the Peace Treaty of 1952]) of whom 300,000 were in salaried employment, 137,000 self-employed and about 23,000 unemployed.

In recent years, the inflows from South America of migrants of Japanese descent have increased rapidly: from 8 450 in 1988 to 76 150 in 1990 and 148 700 in 1991. In 1991, 80 percent came from Brazil and 12.1 percent from Peru.

Illegal immigration is a problem that is assuming greater proportions. The number of foreigners refused entry increased five-fold between 1986 and 1990 to a total of 13 934; between 1986 and 1991 the number of expulsions tripled to 35 903. In over 90 percent of cases these were illegal workers. According to estimates by the Ministry of Justice, the number of foreigners illicitly prolonging their stay totaled some 280 000 in May 1992. Among the nationalities concerned Thais were the most numerous (44 000), followed by Iranians, Koreans and Filipinos. ... To curb this growing trend, the 1989 Amendment to the Immigration Control Act introduced heavy fines and terms of imprisonment for employers and agents recruiting illegal workers....

Japan remains firmly opposed to immigration as a solution to its shortage of manpower. A study commissioned by the Ministry of Labor suggests that the alternative would be to encourage optimum use of manpower resources. It also recommends speeding up and extending the processes of automation, mechanization and the rationalization of employment in certain sectors such as construction, distribution and the wholesale and retail trades. The internal mobility of labor should be encouraged and working conditions in small and medium-sized enterprises improved so as to make employment in such firms more attractive, particularly to Japanese youth. In addition, the study suggests that labor market policy objectives would be better served by more effective placement and promotion of foreign workers. Lastly, international cooperation should continue to give priority to direct investment and job creation in the developing countries. ... Japan's direct investment in ASEAN countries has risen sharply, from $935 million in 1985 to $4 684 million in 1989.

Despite the government's restrictive immigration policy, there are an estimated 300 000 illegal immigrant workers in Japan, in addition to the legally admitted ones (skilled and professional workers, students and migrants of Japanese descent, totaling about 300 000). The six countries from which 73 percent of illegal immigrants come are Thailand, Korea, China, the Philippines, Malaysia and Iran (Table 6.1).

It is noteworthy that the number of illegal immigrant workers did not decrease considerably during the recession that began in the spring of 1991. This is at least partly because the large income differential between Japan and neighboring countries, accentuated by the appreciation of the yen, continues to attract migrant workers, while Japanese firms continue to suffer from a chronic shortage of native workers in the so-called "3K" ("3D") fields: *kitsui* (demanding), *kitanai* (dirty), *kiken* (dangerous).

Because of a decreasing population of young people predicted for the next century, this labor shortage is expected to worsen. The Ministry of Labor (1992c) estimates that the labor force under age 60 will decrease by 4 100 000, or 7.0 percent, between the years 2000 and 2010, while the over-60 labor force will increase by 2 340 000, or 25.1 percent. All told, the labor force will decrease by 1 760 000, or 2.6 percent, within the next decade.[1]

156

Table 6.1 *Estimated number of illegal immigrant workers*

		Major home countries					
As of	Total	Thailand	Korea	China	Philippines	Malaysia	Iran
1 July 1990	106,497	11,523	13,876	10,039	23,805	7,550	764
1 May 1991	159,828	19,093	25,848	17,535	27,228	14,413	10,915
1 November 1991	216,399	32,751	30,976	21,649	29,620	25,379	21,719
1 May 1992	278,892	44,354	35,687	25,737	31,974	38,529	40,001
1 November 1992	292,791	53,219	37,491	29,091	34,296	34,529	32,994
1 May 1993	298,646	55,383	39,455	33,312	35,392	30,840	28,437
1 November 1993	296,751	53,845	41,024	36,297	36,089	25,653	23,867

SOURCE: Bureau of Immigration, Ministry of Justice, "On the Number of Illegal Residents in Japan" (March 1994).

In December 1991, the government initiated a new on-the-job training program for foreign workers, which was put into effect in April 1993. Foreign trainees are officially admitted after passing screening examinations. They are allowed to stay in Japan for 2 years. During the first 10 months, employers provide classroom studies, including a Japanese language course, without overtime, followed by on-the-job training. The trainees are to be paid a monthly training allowance of 110 000 yen in addition to travel expenses and housing accommodation. This training system was expected to allow the employment of foreign workers as supplementary labor, but perhaps because of the rather high cost of bringing them, and also because of the recession, only 1147 trainees were brought to Japan under this program between April and November 1993.[2]

Why has the Japanese government maintained so restrictive an approach toward admitting unskilled foreign migrant workers? It may be because there are seventeen ministries and agencies involved. The Ministry of Justice, the major government agency responsible for immigration policy, takes the most conservative approach in order to maintain social peace and order; the Ministry of Foreign Affairs tends to insist upon the necessity of promoting international cooperation. Between these two, there is a spectrum of view points. Until a few years ago, the Ministry of Labor, which greatly feared an erosion of the unskilled labor market due to large inflows of efficient foreign workers, was one of the most conservative agencies.[3] Its stand was supported by labor unions, at least officially at the national level. The views of the Ministry of Construction and MITI are not expressed publicly. So far, no serious empirical study on this subject has been conducted by political scientists, although several sociological case studies have been published (Komai, 1989; Yorimitsu, 1993; Kuwahara, 1993).

THE EXPECTED LABOR SHORTAGE OF THE TWENTY-FIRST CENTURY

The 18-year-old population reached a peak in 1991 and began decreasing thereafter. The productive population above age

Table 6.2 *Estimated changes in labor force by age groups*

Age	1970	1980–90	1990–2000[a]	2000–2010[a]
15 and over	497	734	395	–176 (–2.6%)
Of which between				
15 and 59	421	529	196	–410 (–7.0%)
60 and over	74	205	199	+234 (+25.1%)

[a] Indicates the estimate of the Ministry of Labor (1992b). For more details, see Appendix in 1996 (see note 1 of this paper). These figures were modified by the *8th Basic Plan for Employment Measures.*

15 will begin to decrease in 1995 (Ministry of Welfare, 1992), and the labor force is expected to decrease by 1 760 000, or 2.6 percent, during the first decade of the next century (Table 6.2).

The labor force between the ages of 15 and 59 will decrease by 4 100 000, or 7.0 percent, in the coming decade, but the 65 and over labor force will increase by 2 340 000, or 25.1 percent, during the same period.[4] In the next century, this change will cause not only a general labor shortage if the economy continues to grow at a moderate rate of 1 or 2 percent annually, but also serious mismatches in some occupations, especially in "3D" fields demanding young unskilled workers. Industries have endeavored to develop robots and automated instruments in these fields to overcome the expected labor shortage, but their costs and efficiency are still unsatisfactory.

Official government reports (Ministry of Labor, 1991, 1992; Economic Planning Agency, 1991) envision a decreasing labor force early in the next century, but at the same time predict that the Japanese economy could continue to grow at a moderate rate if automation is introduced and if the labor force is reallocated from less productive to more productive sectors. For example, a report on foreign workers by the Ministry of Labor predicts,

> In Japan, it is expected that the rate of increase of the labor force will slow because of the decelerating rate of increase of the productive population between the ages 15 and 64.

However, the total labor force will continue to grow until 2000. Assuming an annual rate of economic growth of about 4 percent, the unemployment rate will fall to 2.0 percent by 1995, and 1.8 percent by 2000. This implies that a tight labor market will continue. The labor market is expected to be balanced at the macroeconomic level by such measures as promoting the employment of senior citizens, active participation by females in the labor force, increased labor productivity, and the transfer of production facilities abroad through foreign direct investment.   (Ministry of Labor, 1991: 23)

However, assuming that the elasticity of demand for labor in the economy as a whole will not decrease dramatically but remain at the 0.29 level observed in recent years (Table 6.3), a 2 percent economic growth rate will require an additional 380 000 workers per year, while the actual labor force will decrease by about 180 000 annually after 2000. Simple arithmetic shows that Japan should expect to need about half a million additional workers each year. As the official governmental reports suggest, some of these additional workers could be supplied by mobilizing the 2 million unemployed workers as well as through industrial reallocation, while others could be supplied by legally admitted foreign specialists and technicians. Even a portion of the demand for unskilled labor could be filled by migrant workers of Japanese descent or by foreign students, who are allowed to work 4 hours a day during weekdays and 8 hours a day on the weekend under the present Immigration Law. Furthermore, foreign trainees who are officially allowed to work after completing their required training might be able to fill the gap. The export of labor-intensive industries to Asian and other countries will be further promoted by the appreciation of the yen. Nevertheless, there is no cause for optimism about the possibility of maintaining moderate economic growth while excluding unskilled immigrant workers (Koshiro, 1991).

On the other hand, zero or negative growth is undesirable because the cost of social security will inevitably increase in the next century. Supporting an increasing aged population will require moderate economic growth of at least 1 or 2 percent (Takayama, 1994).

Table 6.3   *Elasticity of aggregate demand for labor in the Japanese Economy, 1965–92*

Observation period (fiscal year)	Elasticity of employed person to real GDP
1965–73	0.126
1974–85	0.266
1986–92	0.392
1974–92	0.290

NOTE: Calculated by ln (EMPD) = $a + b$ ln (YDR), where a = a constant term and b = elasticity shown in the table above.

SOURCE: Prime Ministry's Office, *Labor Force Survey,* for the number of employed persons (EMPD), Economic Planning Agency, *Annual Report on National Account,* for real gross domestic production (YDR).

THE DECREASING DEMAND FOR LABOR IN THE PRESENT RECESSION AND THEREAFTER

Because of the recession, labor supply and demand changed dramatically beginning in 1991, and calls for relaxing restrictions on unskilled immigrant workers appear to have faded away, although, as explained in the previous section, the number of illegal foreign workers did not substantially decrease.

Also during this period the continuous appreciation of the yen intensified apprehension that an acceleration of moves abroad in the automobile, electric appliance and precision machinery industries would lead to the export of jobs. In fact, television parts and sets are no longer made in Japan, but abroad, and the production of parts as well as the assembly of video cassette recorders have also been almost completely transferred to Southeast Asian countries. For example, a well-known producer of micro-motors for video cassette records has moved its main plant to Shen Yiang (*Shinyo*) in Manchuria (Seki, 1993).

An econometric analysis presented in a Labor White Paper (1994) shows that the net employment impact of overseas investment turned negative in 1991; the number of jobs exported as a result of the decreased export of goods has since

Figure 6.2   *Impact upon domestic employment of overseas production by manufacturing industry*

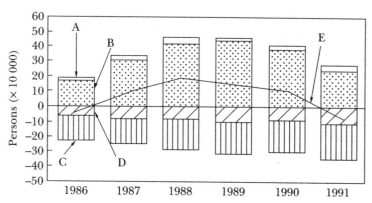

NOTE: A = employment growth through export of capital
            equipment
        B = employment growth through export of intermediary
            products
        C = employment loss due to decreased exports
        D = employment loss due to boomerang effect
        E = net employment effect: (A+B) − (C+D)
SOURCE: Ministry of Labor (1994: 144)

then exceeded the number of jobs created through the increased export of capital equipment and intermediate goods (parts) that accompanies overseas production (Figure 6.2).

This analysis implies that this tendency will accelerate if the yen continues to appreciate, and due to the increasing industrial capacity of Asian countries. The proportion of Japanese manufacturing production performed overseas is now about 6 percent of the total; this proportion will likely increase to 20 percent, comparable to levels in the United States (27%) or Germany (20%).

There is growing concern among Japanese employers that, even as the economy recovers from the present recession, the "jobless growth" experienced in the United States since the late 1980s will also appear in Japan because of the exodus of leading industries. It is very difficult to predict whether this exodus or the expected labor shortage will have a greater effect. If the labor market slackens due to the exodus of jobs, real wages will decline, which in turn will reduce the pressure of increasing labor costs resulting from a shortage of young workers. Price effects of this kind are highly complex and therefore need to be analyzed more precisely by a macroeconomic model that is based on a broad set of assumptions.

THE ECONOMIC IMPACT OF UNSKILLED FOREIGN IMMIGRANTS

Analyses of the economic impact of accepting foreign unskilled workers have produced conflicting views.

Erosion of the Domestic Unskilled Labor Market

Japan once had an abundant supply of unskilled labor. Even during the period of high economic growth in the 1960s, a relatively large supply of surplus labor existed in agricultural areas. By the mid-1970s, about half a million seasonal migrant workers were supplied to growing manufacturing and construction industries from snow-bound agricultural areas. However, because of industrialization and the retirement of farmers this labor resource decreased over the following decades (Figure 6.1).

The supply of young people has also shrunk as they remain in school longer, to prepare for higher-level jobs. In the mid-1950s a majority of students had 12 years of education and graduated from senior high school. The proportion of those who did not attend senior high school, but began to work after graduating from junior high school, declined to less than 20 percent by 1970 and was only 5 percent in 1992 (Ministry of Education, 1994).

These two phenomena indicate that the quality of unskilled labor in Japan has tended to deteriorate during the past decades. On the other hand, several sociological studies concerning foreign immigrant workers in Japan note that their quality is high and that they are ready to work even in "3D" jobs. For this reason, the first report of the Ministry of Labor (1988) on foreign immigrant workers warned that the domestic labor market of unskilled workers could deteriorate if the inflow of foreign immigrants were allowed without strictly controlling work permits.

Rather than permit the inflow of foreign immigrant workers, the report recommended reallocating and upgrading labor by increasing automation and other labor-saving devices. It appears that the government fears the introduction of heterogeneous elements to Japan, which has hitherto been largely homogeneous. A gradual learning process is needed. Furthermore, we must keep in mind the huge supply pressure of immigrants from neighboring countries, including China. On the basis of halving present productivity differentials between the two countries, one study (Hirose, 1992) estimates that if inflows were completely freed about 250 million workers would immigrate from China to Japan.

A Partial Equilibrium Analysis by Labor Economics

A simple partial equilibrium analysis by labor economics of the effects of accepting immigrant workers is illustrated in Figure 6.3. The curve *ABEG* indicates the marginal labor

Figure 6.3   *Impact of immigrant workers in a host country*

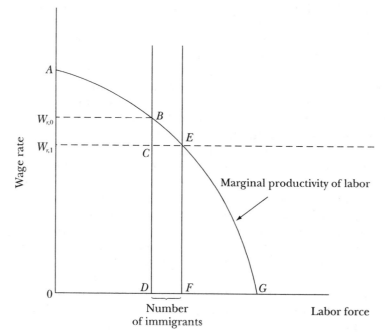

SOURCE: Goto (1990: 62)

productivity of the host country; $0D$ indicates the existing domestic labor of the host country, where workers are paid by the wage rate $W_{r,0}$ at point B, by which domestic workers receive total wages of $W_{r,0}DBO$, and capital's income in the host country is $AW_{r,0}B$.

Suppose the host country were to accept an inflow of foreign migrant workers amounting to DF from a foreign country. The new equilibrium point becomes E, at which the wage rate $W_{r,1}$ of the host country decreases. This enlarges capital's income in the host country to $AW_{r,1}E$. Foreign immigrant workers receive wages $CDFE$, while wages of domestic workers decrease to $W_{r,1}0DC$. However, the national income of the host country will increase from $A0DB$ to $A0FE$. The resulting difference between the two, BCE, indicates the net increase of the national income of the host country as a result of accepting immigrant workers. However, the interests of capital and those of domestic workers could conflict.

A Pluralistic Approach by International Economics

Mundell's Theorem (1957) predicts that free international movement of production factors creates price equalization through the equalization of factor prices between two countries, despite the existence of trade barriers.

Using this concept, Hamada (1977) clarifies the conflicting interests of workers in a host (receiving) country, immigrant workers and workers remaining in a home (sending) country. Figure 6.4 illustrates his point. Here, 0_1D is the original quantity of labor available in the host country; 0_2D is the original labor available in the home country; AD is the initial marginal productivity of labor in the host country; CD is the initial marginal productivity of labor in the home country; and wage rates in the home and host countries correspond to AD and CD, respectively. Since wages are higher in the host country, labor flows from the home to the host country until the wage rates of the two are equalized. Supposing immigration amounting to DH flows into the host country, the wage rate of the host country would decline to EH and that of the home country would increase to FH. As a result, immigrating workers would benefit by receiving an increase in wages equal to $BCGE$, while workers remaining in the home country would lose income equal to CGF.

Figure 6.4 *Conflicting interests generated by international labor migration*

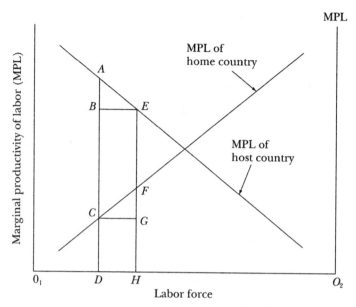

SOURCE: Goto (1990: 69)

A Macroeconomic Simulation of the Benefits of Accepting Immigrant Workers

Goto (1990) developed a more realistic analysis through a macroeconomic simulation model that considers the benefits of accepting immigrant workers. He assumes: (a) a three-sector model of export goods, import goods and non-tradable goods; (b) trade barriers; (c) equal wages for domestic and immigrant workers; (d) a trade pattern that does not change with the inflow of immigrant workers; and (e) that terms of trade, or the price relativity between export and import prices, are not affected by immigration.

Goto constructs a simulation based on a simple macroeconomic model consisting of 20 equations. As summarized in Table 6.4, his conclusion is that the benefit of accepting foreign immigrant workers is negative.

Table 6.4   *Estimated benefits of accepting foreign immigrant workers:*
a mid-term analysis

		Number of immigrant workers accepted	
		300,000	500,000
Social utility	(1)	9	–15
National income (billion yen)	(2)	–916	–1,511
Capital income (billon yen)		+330	+548
Labor income (billion yen)	(3)	–1,160	–1,918
Per-capita labor income lost (thousand yen)		–30	–49
Relative share of labor (%)	(4)	–0.23	–0.37

NOTE: (1) Ordinal utility.
　　　(2) Including transfer income raised by tariffs.
　　　(3) For wage income of domestic workers only.
　　　(4) Defined as employees' income/(capital income plus
　　　　　employees' income).

SOURCE: Goto (1990: 168).

Goto distinguishes short-, mid- and long-term analyses. A short-term analysis considers that immigrant workers are employed only in the non-tradable sector, in which wages are pulled down and total wages paid to immigrant workers are deleted from national income, but in which these shocks do not affect the other two sectors. In a mid-term analysis, the impact of the inflow of immigrant workers on wages spills over across sectors. As a result of widened wage differentials arising from the inflow of immigrant workers into the non-tradable sector, domestic workers move out of the non-tradable sector to export and import sectors, where higher wages are available. In the long run, capital will also move among the three sectors, but this element is not considered in the mid-term analysis.

According to Goto's simulation, an inflow of 300 000 illegal unskilled foreign workers causes a total decrease in labor income of 1160 billion yen, or a loss of 30 000 yen per employee, while total capital income (profit) increases by 330 billion yen. This yields a net loss of 916 billion yen in national income, or a decrease of ordinal social utility on the order of 9.

However, one cannot overlook the fact that Goto's conclusions are based on the set of strong assumptions mentioned above. They must be modified if: (a) the terms of trade improve; (b) foreign workers do not remit all of their wages to home countries; (c) the type of production function is not the Cobb–Douglas, but rather the productivity of scale is larger than unity; or (d) foreign workers' wages are less than those paid to equivalent domestic workers.

THE ESTIMATED SOCIAL COSTS OF ACCEPTING UNSKILLED IMMIGRANTS

Whatever the conclusions of economic analyses of accepting immigrant workers, there is concern about the social costs of such an inflow. A recent study of this problem (Ministry of Labor, 1992c) found that if foreign workers are officially admitted, there will be costs beyond the per-capita social expenditures that an ordinary Japanese citizen can expect from the central and local governments, including wages for interpreters, the preparation of pamphlets in foreign languages, classrooms and teachers for children of foreign workers, employment services, housing, special police officers who can speak foreign languages, special expenditures for maintaining health and sanitation, and so on. These costs tend to increase with the length of the foreigners' stay in Japan. It is assumed that at the initial stage, foreign workers will simply want to stay alone in Japan for 1 year or less, but in the second, "settlement," stage they will want to be accompanied by their spouses for 3–5 years, and in the final "integration" stage they will be blue-collar workers in the production processes of the manufacturing industry, will have lived in Japan for 5–10 years, and will have, on average, two children of school age. Thus a half-million first-stage immigrants will become a million in the second stage, and two million in the final stage.

Using these assumptions, the report estimates that the social costs of accepting foreign workers will increase exponentially from 80.6 billion yen in the first stage to 1413.4 billion yen in the final stage, while the social benefits (taxes and social insurance contributions paid by foreign workers)[5] will be larger than social costs only in the initial stage. The net social costs will exceed 1 trillion yen in the final stage (Table 6.5).

Besides these cost–benefit analyses, there are significant apprehensions about undesirable aspects of foreign immigra-

Table 6.5 *Estimated costs and benefits of accepting inflows of immigrant workers*

	Period I	Period II	Period III
(1) Annual social costs (billion yen)			
Expenditures by central government	12.8	77.8	353.8
Expenditures by local governments	15.5	486.1	901.5
Social insurance benefits	52.3	89.1	158.1
Total	**80.6**	**653.0**	**1,413.4**
(2) Annual social benefits (billion yen)			
Tax revenues to national government	181.1	93.1	77.5
Tax revenues to local governments	0	38.3	28.2
Social insurance contributions	145.5	180.2	193.2
Total	**326.6**	**311.6**	**298.9**

SOURCE: Ministry of Labor (1992c: 29, Appendix).

tion. Social problems such as crime, sickness, poor sanitation and other cultural conflicts have been increasingly reported by the mass media as the number of illegal immigrant workers grows.

The Ministry of Justices's *White Paper on Foreigners Residing in Japan in 1993* (1994) reveals that in 1993 the number of crimes committed by foreign residents increased several times faster than those committed by Japanese, and that during that year the police exposed 907 illegal labor brokers, an increase of 450, or 98.5 percent, over the previous year. We must be careful that sentiments arising from these social problems do not supersede rational considerations.

INCREASING CONCERN ABOUT INHUMANE TREATMENT OF ILLEGAL IMMIGRANT WORKERS

There have been many reports by sociologists, jurists and journalists showing that illegal immigrant workers often face inhumane working and living conditions. Komai (1989) uncovered the operation of greedy intermediaries and revealed the unsanitary conditions of immigrant worker housing. Through mail questionnaires collected from 261 companies employing trainees, Komai (1991a) also explored the difficulties faced by foreign "trainees", finding that 54.1 percent of the companies responding were employing these trainees in very questionable ways. He also found (1991b) that many illegal immigrant workers in Kanagawa Prefecture had higher educational levels than legally admitted foreign workers.

Some jurists and volunteers are deeply concerned about increasing discrimination against and inhumane treatment of illegal immigrant workers. Bright, the first Japanese labor union to help immigrant workers, was organized by Japanese volunteers in Tokyo in March 1993. This union has 4500 members, most of whom are overstaying their Japanese visas, and has revealed many terrible work accidents and incidents of intolerable exploitation by greedy employers who, because of the recession, sought to escape paying wages to foreign workers.

We must deal with these disturbing social problems, which are increasing. We must avoid the pitfall of believing that they will disappear if we admit a certain number of unskilled immigrant workers through bi-country agreements, as its done by other advanced industrialized countries. Hanami and Kuwahara (1989: 158–9) contend that discrimination against immigrant workers similar to that which has occurred in Germany (Wallraff, 1985) and in France (Hayashi, 1984) cannot be avoided even if Japan accepts a certain number of legal unskilled immigrants. Kuwahara (1991) proposes that a "moral contract" such as that recommended in Canada should be worthwhile in preventing cultural conflicts with immigrants. Yorimitsu (1992) fears that the formal introduction of foreign unskilled workers is inevitable if Japan attempts to preserve "low-tech" industries by allowing them to exploit illegal immigrants.

ALTERNATIVES TO UNSKILLED IMMIGRANT WORKERS

The severe labor shortage which existed until a few years ago almost disappeared with the onset of recession in the spring of 1991, and with it the urgent calls for allowing unskilled immigrant workers into Japan. However, during the recession the estimated number of these workers decreased only slightly. Given the demographic changes of the past decades, it is expected that Japan will face an annual 0.36 percent decrease in its total native labor force, beginning in the first decade of the next century.

There may be some alternatives to accepting unskilled immigrant workers as a way of meeting Japan's future labor shortages. The extension of the mandatory retirement age beyond 60, inducement of more women to join the labor force, and the improvement of labor productivity through shedding surplus labor in the service sector, are measures that have been discussed and will be discussed in the future; in fact, they are all taken into account when the Ministry of Labor and/or the Economic Planning Agency make quantitative projections of the future labor supply.

Legally enforcing the extension of the retirement age beyond 60 seems undesirable to all parties concerned. For employers, the cost would exorbitant unless some fundamental reforms of the seniority-linked pay system were available; for workers, particularly those who started worked early and have worked for 45 years or more, the right to retire is more important than that to continue working (Seike, 1993). For example, when Meitetsu, a large private railway-company in the Nagoya area, extended its mandatory retirement age to 65 during the past decade, only a third of the eligible workers preferred to extend their employment, while most preferred to retire because they were entitled not only to public old-age pension payments, but also to either a rather generous lump-sum retirement allowance or to a company pension. On top of these benefits, they were also to receive 300 days' "unemployment benefit" after retirement. Most of these workers had a small piece of farm land and a house, so that they had very little incentive to continue working unless they were supporting the education of their younger children.

Women workers are certainly an underutilized resource in Japan. Despite the passage of the Equal Employment Opportunity Law in 1986, discrimination against female workers is common, and many able female workers are obliged to retire when they marry or have children. In spite of this, the official labor force projections include the increasing participation of middle-aged and older women workers.

Modernization and rationalization of the service sector may help Japan to ameliorate future labor shortages. Westerners visiting Japan are often surprised by the number of young women in banks and department stores whose sole function appears to be to bow and smile to customers, or by the number of young men working in urban gas stations, practices that partly reflect traditional values and culture in Japan, but are also the result of excessive government regulation. The official labor supply projections take into account a considerable increase of labor productivity in these fields due to a reduction in workforce, but it is doubtful that such an improvement can really be achieved. Another factor is the number of older workers who will not be replaced upon retirement. Still another question is whether many workers can be successfully transferred to more productive jobs.

CONCLUSION

The Japanese government will probably continue to maintain a restrictive policy toward foreign unskilled workers, while making some allowances for the immigration of foreigners of Japanese descent, part-time work by foreign students, and officially admitted trainees. With these exceptions, current manpower policy focuses on increasing labor productivity through the reallocation of labor and modernization of the means of production.

The difficult question of whether or not the acceptance of foreign unskilled workers beyond the present framework will enhance social welfare must be carefully considered, not only from the perspective of social and cultural considerations, but also taking economic interests into account. A moderate rate of growth in the next century is indispensable to maintaining economic welfare, particularly social security for the aged, and it is clear that a certain number of additional workers will be needed to maintain that growth.

The accelerated appreciation of the yen has worsened the prospects for economic growth. Certainly, more production facilities will have to be exported, particularly to Asian countries. A combination of increased overseas production and technological progress provide an opportunity to reduce future reliance on the immigrant workforce, but the non-tradable sector, such as construction and services, cannot be fully automated, and cannot depend solely on the domestic workforce. A gradual moderation of immigration policy toward the next century seems inevitable. However, given the powerful geographical constraints on the population of Japan together with the potentially immense supply pressure from neighboring countries, the unlimited acceptance of un-skilled immigrants should not be considered. Some restrictions on the immigration of unskilled workers must be maintained.

APPENDIX

Table 6.6   *Changes in and estimation of the labor force*
(ten thousand persons)

Gender and age		1980	1990	2000*	2010*
Total	15 and over	5,650 (497)	6,384 (734)	6,779 (395)	6603 (1,176)
	15–29	1,361 (1,391)	1,475 (114)	1,556 (81)	1,190 (1,366)
	30–54	3,377 (730)	3,617 (240)	3,664 (47)	3,625 (139)
	55 and over	912 (156)	1,292 (380)	1,559 (267)	1,788 (229)
	55–59	385 (82)	560 (175)	628 (68)	623 (15)
	60–64	248 (26)	372 (124)	418 (46)	527 (109)
	65 and over	279 (48)	360 (81)	513 (153)	638 (125)
Males	15 and over	3,465 (336)	3,791 (326)	4,010 (219)	3,932 (179)
	15–29	792 (1,225)	817 (25)	862 (45)	650 (1,212)
	30–54	2,109 (486)	2,174 (65)	2,160 (114)	2,213 (137)
	55 and over	563 (74)	799 (236)	988 (189)	1,158 (170)
	55–59	228 (42)	348 (120)	392 (44)	392 (0)
	60–64	151 (6)	234 (83)	277 (43)	362 (85)
	65 and over	184 (26)	217 (33)	319 (102)	404 (85)

Table 6.6   *(Continued)*

Gender and age		1980	1990	2000*	2010*
Females	15 and over	2,185 (161)	3,593 (408)	2,769 (176)	2,672 (197)
	15–29	570 (1,165)	658 (88)	694 (36)	540 (1,154)
	30–54	1,268 (246)	1,444 (176)	1,504 (60)	1,502 (12)
	55 and over	348 (82)	493 (145)	571 (78)	630 (59)
	55–59	156 (40)	212 (56)	236 (24)	231 (15)
	60–64	97 (20)	138 (41)	141 (3)	165 (24)
	65 and over	95 (22)	143 (48)	194 (51)	234 (40)

NOTE: Figures in parentheses indicate changes in a 10-year period; * indicates estimated figure.

SOURCE: Figures for 1980 and 1990 are from Prime Minister's Office, Labor Force Survey; figures for 2000 and 2010 are based on population estimates provided by the Ministry of Welfare (September 1992). This estimate is now under review and will be modified (see note 1).

NOTES

1.   The Ministry of Labor is at the time of writing preparing the *Eighth Basic Plan for Employment Measures*, which includes a new estimation of the future labor supply. It differs a little from the previous estimates as follows: it estimates that the total labor force will continue to increase, from 66 450 000 in 1994 to 68 460 000 in 2000, an annual rate of increase of 0.3 percent; the labor force will further increase to 68 660 000 in 2005 but will then decrease to 67 450 000 by 2010. This is because the number of younger workers (below age 60) is expected to decrease by 416 000 between 2000 and 2010, whereas the number of older workers (above age 60) will increase by 315 000 during the same period, a net decrease of 101 000 (a net increase of

20 000 between 2000 and 2005, but a net decrease between 2005 and 2010 of 121 000).

2. Prior to the establishment of this foreign workers on-the-job training program, many companies were allowed to bring in foreign trainees under certain conditions. The total number of these trainees exceeded 40 000 in 1992, but began to decrease thereafter (*Nihon Keizai Shimbun* [Japan economic newspaper], 13 April 1994).

3. The first report on foreign migrant workers by the Ministry of Labor (1988) proposed to introduce a work permit system for unskilled immigrant workers, but the proposal was rejected by the Ministry of Justice.

4. These estimates must be replaced by the new ones upon publication of the Eighth Basic Plan, as explained in Note 1 above.

5. This statement does not take into account the economic benefits which Japanese society receives from immigrant workers in the form of additional economic growth and services.

REFERENCES

Economic Planning Agency (1991), *Choices for 2010*, in Japanese (Tokyo: Deliberation Council on the Economy, June).

Goto, J. (1990), *The Economics of Foreign Immigrant Workers*, in Japanese (Tokyo: Toyo Keizai Shinpo Sha).

Hamada, K. (1977), "Taxing the Brain Drain: A Global Point of View," in J. Bhagwati (ed.), *The New International Economic Order: The North–South Debate* (Cambridge, MA: MIT Press).

Hanami, T. and Y. Kuwahara (1989), *Tomorrow's Neighbor: Foreign Immigrant Workers*, in Japanese (Tokyo: Toyo Keizai Shinpo Sha).

Hayashi, M. (1984), *Foreigners in France – the Hardships of Immigrants, Asylum-seekers, and Minorities*, in Japanese (Tokyo: Chuo Koron Sha).

Hirose, T. (1992), "An Economic Analysis of International Labor Migration," in Japanese, Economic Planning Agency, *ESP*, 241 (May), pp. 49–52.

Komai, Y. (1989), *The Actual Situation of Foreign Workers in Japan*, in Japanese (Grant Report to the Ministry of Education).

—— (1991a), *A Study of the Work and Lives of Foreign Workers – An Analysis of Trainees*, in Japanese (Grant Report to the Ministry of Education).

—— (1991b), *Report on the Actual Situation of Foreign Workers*, in Japanese (Department of Labor, Kanagawa Prefectural Government).

Koshiro, K. (1991), "Labor Shortage and Employment Policies in Japan," in United Nations University (ed.), *International Labor Migration in East Asia* (Tokyo: United Nations University) pp. 179–96.

—— (1992), "Regional Movement of Seasonal Migrant Workers", in Japanese, Yokohama National University, *Economia*, 43(3), pp. 33–57.

Kuwahara, Y. (1991), *Workers Moving Across National Boundaries*, in Japanese (Tokyo: Iwanami Shoten).

—— (1993), "How Workers of Japanese Descent Come to Seek Employment in Japan," in Japanese, in Institute of Statistical Studies (ed.), *Survey on the Employment of Migrant Workers of Japanese Descent* (Tokyo: Institute of Statistical Studies), March, pp. 7–37.

Ministry of Education (1994), *Handbook of Statistics on Education*, in Japanese (Tokyo: Government Printing Office).

Ministry of Justice (1994), *White Paper on Foreigners Residing in Japan in 1993*, unpublished.

Ministry of Labor (1988), *Report of the Committee on Foreign Migrant Workers*, in Japanese (Tokyo: Romu Gyosei Kenkyujo), March.

Ministry of Labor (1991), *Report of the Study Committee on the Impact of Foreign Workers on Employment*, in Japanese, Chairman: Professor K. Yamaguchi (Tokyo: Ministry of Labor).

—— (1992a), *Mid-Term Employment Plan*, in Japanese (Tokyo: Ministry of Labor).

—— (1992b), *The Outlook for and Problems of Labor Demand and Supply*, Study Committee on Employment Policy, March; revised in March 1993 (Tokyo: Ministry of Labor).

—— (1992c), *Report of the Expert Committee on the Impact of Foreign Workers on Employment*, in Japanese, Chairman, Professor K. Yamaguchi (Tokyo: Ministry of Labor).

Ministry of Labor (1994), *Labor White Paper* (Tokyo: Japan Institute of Labor).

Ministry of Welfare (1992), *Population Projections for Japan: 1991–2000* (Tokyo: Kosei Tokei (Kyokai).

Mundell, R. A. (1957), "International Trade and Factor Mobility," *American Economic Review*, 47, pp. 321–35.

Seike, A. (1993), *The Labor Market in an Aging Society*, in Japanese (Tokyo: Toyo Keizai Shinpo Sha).

Seki, M. (1993), *Beyond the Full-Set Industrial Structure*, in Japanese (Tokyo: Chuo Koron Sha).

Shiba, R. (1987), *Dattan Shippu Roku* [Tales of a Squall in Tartary] (Tokyo: Chuo Koron Sha).

SOPEMI (1993), *Trends in International Migration*, Annual Report (Paris: Organization for Economic Cooperation and Development).

Takayama, N. (1994), "A Gradual Increase in Pension Premiums is Highly Desirable," in Japanese, *Nihon Keizai Shinbun*, 28 October, Classroom on the Economy.

Wallraff, G. (1985), *Ganz Unten*, Japanese translation (1986) (Tokyo: Iwanami Shoten).

Yorimitsu, M. (1992), "State of Foreign Workers' Problems and Policy Questions," in Japanese, Ministry of Labor, *Rodo Jiho*, May, pp. 14–17.

—— (1993), "Problems of Foreign Migrant Workers Observed by Interviews with Migrants of Japanese Descent", in Japanese (Tokyo: Institute of Statistical Studies), March, pp. 85–100.

7 The Economic Consequences of Immigration: Application to the United States and Japan

Barry R. Chiswick

INTRODUCTION

The issue of the economic impact of immigrants is often couched in terms of whether the economy, or a sector of the economy, "needs" immigrants. This is a common concept among political leaders, the media and representatives of industry and labor, yet it is a concept that makes no sense to economists. The purpose of this paper is to explore the issue of the economic impact of immigrants in an advanced industrial economy with abundant capital (or access to capital) and workers of various levels of skill.[1] It will also explore the implications for countries that differ in the domestic supply of low-skilled workers.

OUTLINE OF THE ANALYSIS

The first section begins by discussing the "social welfare function," a relationship that describes what it is that an economy seeks to maximize. It argues that for modern advanced societies both the level (or rate of change) of real output and the distribution of this output enter the social welfare function. It then examines the impact of immigration on an economy when there are two factors of production, homogeneous labor and capital, to develop the basic principles. It extends this to a more "realistic" model for describing a developed economy – a three-factor model, where the factors are high-level/professional (or skilled) labor, low-level (or unskilled) labor, and capital – and explores the impacts of immigration on the level and distribution of income.

The next section adds a modern income transfer system to the analysis and develops the implications of skilled and unskilled immigrant labor in its presence. The section that follows develops the implications of alternative immigration regimes using stylized facts regarding the United States and Japan, advanced economies intensive in physical and human capital, and with elaborate income transfer programs but with a large low-skilled native population in the former and shortages of low-skilled native labor in the latter. Four immigration regimes are considered: temporary (guest worker) and permanent immigration, and low-skilled and high-skilled workers. It is shown how differences in the economic circumstances of the native population of the receiving country may call for different immigration policies. The final section provides a summary of the analysis and the implications for immigration policy for the United States and Japan.

ARE IMMIGRANTS NEEDED?

The first item on the agenda is to dispense with the issue of whether an economy "needs" immigrants. Some argue that there are "jobs that native workers will not do". These jobs are variously characterized in different times and different places as very low paying, unpleasant, dirty, dangerous, demeaning, or in some other way undesirable to natives. There is a further assumption that there are large costs to society if these jobs are not done. Presumably, given the absence of native labor, if not for immigrant labor there would be bottlenecks in the production process which would have adverse impacts either "upstream" or "downstream" from the production bottleneck.

This view ignores the reality of markets and production processes. At what wage or working conditions will natives not do the job? Presumably at higher real wages and more desirable working conditions more native labor would be forthcoming. Alternative production techniques can come into play that native workers would find less unattractive. Furthermore, the output of the labor used in this job could be imported. The axiom in international trade theory regarding the consequences of trade barriers, "If you don't trade in goods you will trade in labor," can be turned around: "If you don't trade in labor you will trade in goods."

Thus, to the extent that substitution can take place, an economy will adjust to a "scarcity" of immigrant labor. This substitution can be among workers by nativity or skill level, among types of production, among products (for example, in my lawn I can substitute artificial grass for real grass that needs to be mowed) and among sources for the product. While bottlenecks may exist in the short run under special circumstances, unless artificial barriers are imposed substitution will, in the long run, eliminate bottlenecks.

An alternative extreme view is that "immigrant workers take jobs from native workers." Under this view there is a fixed number of jobs in the economy and the employment of immigrants in a particular job means that a native worker is unemployed. Thus, instead of immigrant labor lowering unemployment by relieving bottlenecks, they increase unemployment on a nearly one-for-one basis. This approach also denies the reality of an economy. The amount of labor employed is not fixed and, with increased competition in the labor market for a particular grade (skill level) of worker, relative wages do respond. A decline in relative wages expands the amount of such labor employed, and some native workers leave the sector for more attractive alternatives elsewhere.

The two lessons to be drawn from this discussion are that: (a) markets do operate and changing relative prices and wages send signals of relative scarcity to the economy; and (b) production and consumption relationships are not fixed, production functions and consumption patterns allow for substitution, and the shapes of physical capital and human capital are flexible in the long run if not in the short run.

Having dismissed the two extremes as irrelevant for understanding the functioning of a modern economy, this paper will focus on an economy that is characterized by a production process (production function) that allows for substitution among factors of production, including native and immigrant labor.

PITFALLS IN ESTIMATING THE IMPACT OF IMMIGRANTS

There has recently emerged a literature that estimates the impact of immigration (a flow concept) or the foreign-born population (a stock concept) on the earnings of the native-born population of the United States. This literature uses states or metropolitan areas as the unit of observation, and relates the earnings of the native-born to the presence of immigrants or the foreign born. The results have been inconclusive and therefore the unfortunate conclusion has emerged that immigrants have no adverse impact on the wages of the native-born population.

This line of research has been based on faulty methodology. It is not immigrants but skill groups that enter the aggregated production function. The impact of immigrants on native wages depends on the skills of the immigrants and the natives, as well as the parameters of the production function. By generally ignoring the issue of skill, these studies confound labor market effects, and hence obtain inconclusive patterns.

Even more serious, however, is the implicit assumption in this methodology that the units of observation (usually states or metropolitan areas) are closed economies. The choice of location by immigrants is not exogenous. Immigrants, at least initially, settle in areas close to their ports of entry, where previous waves of immigrants from their origin have settled, and where job opportunities for their skills are more attractive. Over time, their internal migration is even more heavily influenced by employment opportunities. If immigrants are attracted to high wage/low unemployment areas, their estimated impact on the labor market is biased statistically, unless their location is treated as endogenous in the econometric analysis.

Moreover, even if immigrants are not mobile in a destination, the internal mobility of native labor and capital will bring about factor price equalization. Adjustments of the native population to the labor market impacts of immigrants occur through the movement out of the area of factors of production that are substitutes in production (such as native labor of a similar skill level) and into the area of factors of production that are complements in production (such as capital and native labor of very different skill levels than that of the immigrants). Furthermore, the location of the production of goods and services responds to changes in relative factor prices. That is, the labor market effects of the immigration become dissipated as they are spread throughout the economy, rather than remaining concentrated in the locale of the initial settlement.

Due to a failure to account for the issues raised in the preceding three paragraphs, the cross-sectional studies for the United States provide no guide as to the impact of immigrants on the wages of the native-born population.

THE ECONOMIC MODEL

This analysis of the impact of immigration will be based on theoretical models of social welfare functions and production functions. Understanding these impacts is important for reasons beyond intellectual curiosity: it is only when the costs and benefits of alternative policies can be ascertained that public policy can be based on a rational decision-making process.

For purposes of exposition, a model of the world in which there are only two homogeneous factors of production – labor and capital – is developed to present a simple graphic treatment of the issue. This is followed by a more complex model in which workers are differentiated into those with high and low levels of skill. Although most of the essential elements in the conclusions do not change, this extension is necessary because much debate regarding immigration policy is based on the distinction between more-skilled and less-skilled workers.

These models will consider not only the effect of immigration on the aggregate level of income in the economy, but also its effect on the distribution of this income. An immigration policy that would increase average income, but with gainers outnumbered by losers, may not be adopted in a democratic society unless it is linked to income redistribution policies that spread the benefits more widely. Because it is difficult in practice to develop appropriate income redistribution programs, policies that increase aggregate economic welfare but in which the losers out number the gainers may not be adopted.

The Social Welfare Function

It is assumed that an economy seeks to maximize a "social welfare function", which is subject to the constraints of the limited resources available and which relates certain arguments to social value or utility. In an earlier period the main argument in the social welfare function was the level or rate of growth of national output; economic growth or development were of paramount concern. Over the course of the last six decades in the United States the social welfare function has changed. Issues in income distribution have become very important for public policy, not merely through the development of an elaborate income transfer (redistribution) system but also through the evaluation of particular policy issues. Then a social welfare function can be written $V = f(Y, E)$, where social welfare is a rising function of the level or rate of growth of income (Y) and a rising function of the equality of income (E). Policies that increase both Y and E unambiguously enhance social welfare. Policies that increase income level but decrease equality, or vice versa, are not unambiguously desirable. One can, for example, think in terms of some policies that increase aggregate income but reduce equality (increase inequality) as being either desirable or undesirable, depending on the magnitude of the income gain and the loss in equality.

In what follows an aggregate production function analysis is used to explicate the impact of immigrants on an economy. Implications for the level and distribution of income for the native population are explored. An interesting question, which is beyond the scope of this study, is: When do immigrants become absorbed into the body politic/social welfare function? When is their welfare incorporated into social decision making? This may occur immediately after immigration in some countries (for example, Israel), a few years after immigration in others (as in the United States), or not for several generations, if ever, for others.

The Two-factor Model

In a Ricardian model of the economy, there are two homogeneous factors of production, capital and labor, that are not perfect substitutes in production. For a given amount of capital, the marginal product of labor declines as the amount of labor in the economy increases, other things being the same. The wage rate is determined by the intersection of the labor supply curve and the downward sloping curve representing the marginal product of labor. This is shown schematically in Figure 7.1 for two countries, X and Y.

Countries X and Y have the same access to technological knowledge and they have the same aggregate production function where output is solely a function of the amount of capital and labor. The two countries differ, however, in their factor proportions; country X is capital intensive, that is, it has much more capital per unit of labor than country Y. The marginal product of labor, and therefore the wages of labor are greater in country X (e.g. the U.S. and Japan). In the absence of international migration, the supply of labor in country X is $S_{0,x}$, and the supply of labor in country Y is $S_{0,Y}$. Given their marginal product curves, the wage rates are $W_{0,x}$ and $W_{0,y}$ respectively. Since aggregate income in country X can be represented (Figure 7.1) by the area under the marginal product of labor curve, total income is area $O_x DAL_{0,x}$, of which labor receives the rectangle area $O_x W_{0,x} AL_{0,x}$ and the return to the

Figure 7.1   *Schematic representation of the effect of international migration on the level and distribution of income*

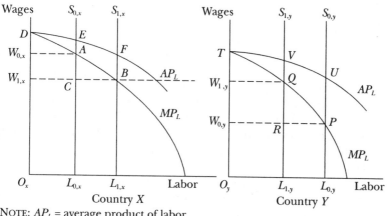

NOTE: AP_L = average product of labor
     MP_L = marginal product of labor

owners of the country's capital stock is the triangle area $W_{0,x}DA$. In country Y, total income is area $O_yTPL_{0,y}$ which is divided into labor's share, area $O_yW_{0,y}PL_{0,y}$, and capital's share, the triangle area $W_{0,y}TP$.

The situation portrayed by labor supply curves $S_{0,x}$ and $S_{0,y}$ is unstable if the present value of the stream of annual wage differentials ($D_0 = W_{0,x} - W_{0,y}$) exceeds the cost of migration. If there were no cost of migration (including no legal barriers), workers would move from country Y to country X until the wage differential was eliminated, as shown by the new labor supply curves $S_{1,x}$ and $S_{1,y}$ in Figure 7.1. As a result of the migration, labor supply in the two countries would shift and wages rise in the sending country and wages would decline in the receiving country. At the margin, there is no longer any gain from migrating, as the present value of the wage differential equals the cost of migration, and the net migration stream ceases. The earnings of the immigrants have increased, from a wage of $W_{0,y}$ to $W_{1,x}$. Costs of migration, including information about the labor market in the destination, can result in a persisting wage differential even if there are no legal barriers to migration.

In this model immigration has raised the aggregate income in the receiving country X, but it has also increased the number of workers. Because the capital stock was assumed unchanged, the marginal and average product of labor in X has declined, average income has fallen from the length $L_{0,x}E$ to the length $L_{1,x}F$. Yet the native population is better off. The average income of the native population has increased because its aggregate income has risen, the new aggregate income less the income received by immigrant workers being greater than the original aggregate income.

In addition to the increase in the average income of the native population in the receiving country, there is a change in its distribution by economic function. The total income of capital increases (from area $W_{0,x}DA$ to $W_{1,x}DB$) and the total income of native labor decreases (from area $OW_{0,x}AL_{0,x}$ to area $OW_{1,x}CL_{0,x}$).

The increase in the rate of return on capital provides incentives for more domestic investment and for the importation of foreign capital. This results in the long run in an outward movement of the marginal product of labor schedule and tends to increase wages for both native and foreign labor in the receiving country. The greater the extent of the increase in the capital stock, the smaller is the net decline in the wage received by native labor. In the limiting case, if the capital–labor ratio returns to its original level, and if there are constant returns to scale in the economy, the wage rate returns to its original level in the long run. The favorable effect on wages of the growth of the capital stock would encourage additional migration. These second-order effects are not shown in the figure.

The effect of the change in the distribution of income by function on the personal (or household) distribution of income depends on the distribution of ownership of labor and capital. If each native household owned the same amount of labor and capital, the inequality in the personal distribution of income would not change. At the other extreme, if all the capital were owned by one household and labor was the only factor of production owned by the other households, the inequality in the personal distribution of income as measured by the share of income received by the top wealth holder would experience the largest possible increase. Neither extreme characterizes the American or Japanese economy, and, depending on how capital is measured, an economy may be closer to one than the other.[2] If, however, the owners of capital are relatively few, immigration raises the aggregate income of the native population and increases the inequality of this income.

The level and distribution of income in the sending country also change in response to the emigration. As indicated in Figure 7.1, the decline in the supply of labor raises the marginal product of labor from $W_{0,y}$ to $W_{1,y}$ and average income increases from $L_{0,y}$ U to $L_{1,y}V$. The rise in average income among those who remain is accompanied by a change in the distribution of income by function; labor gains and capital loses. The relative decline in the return on capital would discourage investments in country Y and encourage a flight of capital to country X. The effect on the personal distribution of income again depends on the distribution of ownership of capital and labor resources. The more highly concentrated the ownership of capital, the larger is the decline in income inequality as a result of the emigration. Thus, in this model, emigration has the favorable effects of raising the level and narrowing the inequality of income.

For those accustomed to thinking in terms of "zero sum games," in which one party must lose if another party gains, the implication of the two-factor, two-country model in Figure 7.1 would appear inconsistent. How can each of the three major groups in the international migration model gain? The gains arise from the movement of some workers from where they are less productive to where they are more productive. Because factors of production are not perfect substitutes for each other, marginal products change as factors move; this results in gains to both the native population of the receiving country and the remaining population of the sending country, as well as to the immigrants.

The Three-factor Model

Although the two-factor model outlines the overall economic impact of immigrants on the native population, it is not useful for analyzing the differential impact on various groups in the labor market. A three-factor model, in which there is a capital, less-skilled labor, and more-skilled labor, provides greater realism regarding the economy and highlights some important issues regarding the distribution of the economic impact of immigration between more- and less-skilled workers. The "less-skilled" labor would be those engaged in the "3D" jobs – jobs that are dirty, dangerous and demanding, yet requiring little in the way of skills. The "more-skilled" labor would be the white-collar professional, technical and managerial workers, as well as the high-skilled craft workers. They are employed in jobs that generally require high levels of schooling and on-the-job training.

While the implications of immigration in the three-factor case are difficult to show using a two-dimensional graph, they are easy to show algebraically. The economy of a developed country can be described by a three-factor, constant-elasticity-of-substitution (CES) production function.[3] The three factors are high-level manpower (professionals, managers, and technical workers), other manpower, and physical capital, and the pair-wise elasticities are consistent with a CES (σ) equal to about 2.5 (Chiswick, 1979, 1986). Aggregate output (Q) may be written as

$$(1) \qquad Q = \left[\beta_1 H_1^{-p} + \beta_2 H_2^{-p} + \beta_3 K^{-p} \right]^{1/p}$$

where H_1 = low-level manpower, H_2 = high-level manpower, K = capital stock, and

$$\sigma = \frac{1}{1+p} = \text{elasticity of substitution.}$$

Within the context of a three-factor model, an increase in the supply of either type of worker due to immigration decreases the marginal product (wage) of that type of labor and increases the marginal product of both capital and the other type of labor. Since aggregate income in the economy increases by more than the total wages of the immigrants, the aggregate income of the native population is increased.

The marginal product of each factor of production is

$$(2) \qquad \begin{aligned} MPH_1 &= \beta_1 \left(\frac{Q}{H_1} \right)^{1/\sigma} \\[2mm] MPH_K &= \beta_3 \left(\frac{Q}{K} \right)^{1/\sigma} \\[2mm] MPH_2 &= \beta_2 \left(\frac{Q}{H_2} \right)^{1/\sigma}. \end{aligned}$$

An increase in the quantity of unskilled labor, H_1, increases output Q, but at a smaller rate than H_1, so that Q/H_1 declines. Thus, an increase in H_1 due to the immigration of unskilled workers decreases the marginal product of unskilled labor, MPH_1, and increases the marginal product of skilled workers, MPH_2, and capital, MPK. If the number of unskilled workers increases from $H_{1,0}$ to $H_{1,n}$, aggregate income in the economy increases by the integral

(3) $$\int_{H_{1,0}}^{H_{1,n}} \beta_1 (Q/H_1)^{1/\sigma} \, dH_1.$$

After the n immigrants arrive, the marginal product of unskilled workers is

(4) $$MPH_{1,n} = \beta_1 \left(Q_n/H_{1,n} \right)^{1/\sigma}$$

and their aggregate wages are $(MPH_{1,n}) H_1$. Because of the decreasing marginal product of unskilled labor, the increase in aggregate income exceeds the total wages of the immigrants. The change in the aggregate income of the native population is

(5) $$\int_{H_{1,0}}^{H_{1,n}} \left[\beta_1 \left(Q/H_1 \right)^{1/\sigma} - \beta_1 \left(Q_n/H_{1,n} \right)^{1/\sigma} \right] dH_1$$

which is necessarily positive for any elasticity of substitution between zero and infinity.

Thus, the immigration of unskilled workers widens the wage differentials between the two types of labor, increases the return to capital relative to the wages of the unskilled, raises the aggregate income of skilled workers and capital, and reduces the aggregate income of native unskilled workers. If the ownership of capital is concentrated, overall income inequality is increased. The immigration increases the return to investments in both physical and human capital. Unskilled native workers have a greater economic incentive to invest in schooling and on-the-job training, although this may be mitigated by the greater difficulty of self-financing human capital investments because of their lower level of wealth.

Suppose, however, that the immigrants are skilled workers. It can be shown algebraically (see marginal product equations above) that this decreases the marginal product of skilled workers and increases the marginal product of unskilled labor and capital. It therefore lowers wage differentials between skill levels and lowers the aggregate earnings of the native-born skilled workers, but raises the aggregate earnings of unskilled workers and the rate of return on capital. The immigration raises the return on investment in physical capital relative to human capital. The aggregate income of the native population as a whole also increases. Income inequality declines in the lower part of the personal income distribution (among skill levels), but inequality increases between skilled workers and the owners of capital in the upper part. The relative decline in the rate of return on human capital lowers the incentive for native-born unskilled workers to acquire additional schooling and on-the-job training, although their increased wealth facilitates the self-financing of the investments.

Economies of Scale

The model thus far assumes there are no economies or diseconomies of scale. That is, the production function in equation (1) assumes that if both labor inputs and capital inputs increase by say, x percent, aggregate output will also increase by x percent. There could be economies of scale, that is, aggregate output increasing by more than the same percentage increase in all factor inputs. This could arise from a larger economy having a greater specialization of function or from reduced per-unit costs of communication and transportation due to greater density of population or intensity of traffic. This may well have characterized the economy of the United States during the period of westward expansion, and possibly up to the early twentieth century.

Alternatively there can be diseconomies of scale, that is, aggregate output increasing by less than the same percent increase in all factors of production. This would arise if a greater population density or a larger economy resulted in costs associated with crowding, congestion and pollution, or costs associated with efforts to mitigate their adverse consequences. This can be thought of as due to a factor of production that does not directly enter the production function and cannot be expanded, such as land area, the air, and so on. Diseconomies of scale may characterize the economy of Japan at the close of the twentieth century.

Economies of scale can be incorporated into the model expressed in equation (1) in the following manner:

(6) $$Q^* = Q^\lambda,$$

where Q^* is actual aggregate output, λ is the measure of scale economies, where $\lambda = 1$ for no economies of scale, $\lambda > 1$ if they are positive and $0 < \lambda$ 1 if they are negative. Equation (1) above describes the economy if there were no economies of scale.

The parameter λ is not necessarily fixed for an economy. It can be expected to vary with the size of the population (P), the size of the land area and other characteristics of the environment (Z), and technological considerations (g). Thus, $\lambda = g(P,Z)$, where beyond some point a larger P relative to Z results in diseconomies of scale $(0 < \lambda < 1)$. It is easy to show that the marginal product of a factor of production is greater than or less than that shown in equation (2) depending on the magnitude of λ. That is,

(7) $$\frac{\delta Q^*}{\delta H_1} = \lambda Q^{\lambda-1} \frac{\delta Q}{\delta H_1}$$

which is greater than, equal to, or less than $\frac{\delta Q^*}{\delta H_1}$ = depending on whether $\lambda > 1$, $= 1$, or $0 < \lambda < 1$.

Economies characterized by economies (diseconomies) of scale will experience increases (decreases) in average income if all of the factors of production, such as labor and capital, increases by the same percentage. Thus, the effect of immigration on the income of the native population is that much more favorable if on balance there are strong economies of scale and that much less favorable if there are strong diseconomies of scale.

Immigrant Assimilation

The analysis becomes somewhat more complex if it incorporates the finding that the skills of immigrants vary with the number of years they have been in the destination.[4] As a result, the initial impact of a cohort of immigrants differs from its ultimate impact. In an extreme example, if the immigrants are initially all unskilled when they arrive at their destination, they lower the earnings of unskilled native workers and widen wage differentials. As the immigrants adjust, their productivity rises, and an increasing proportion (in an extreme case, perhaps nearly all) become skilled workers. As this occurs, wage differentials narrow, and the earnings of unskilled native workers increase. Ultimately, if the ratio of skilled to unskilled workers becomes larger among the immigrants than among the native population, relative wage differentials between skill levels are smaller, and the earnings of unskilled native workers are higher than prior to the immigration.

When there is a time path to the skill distribution of a cohort of immigrants, who gains and who loses among native workers, measured in terms of the present value of future income, depends on several factors. Of course, it depends in part on the initial and ultimate skill distribution of the immigrants compared with the native workers. It also depends on the time path of the change in relative skills of the immigrants. The greater the initial and ultimate skill level of the immigrants relative to native workers, and the faster they reach their ultimate skill level, the greater are the gains in income for native unskilled workers and the smaller the gains for skilled workers.

The discount rate of native workers, the rate at which they value today dollars received in the future, is also relevant. The higher the discount rate of unskilled native workers (that is, the smaller the valuation they place on future income), the smaller is the gain to them from the type of immigration just described. Under a high discount rate, the declines in current income are less likely to be offset by the rise in future incomes as the immigrants become skilled workers. On the other hand, the higher the discount rate of skilled workers, the more they would gain from a policy that raised their earnings initially, even though it lowered them in the future.

Unskilled workers are likely to have a higher discount rate than skilled workers (see, for example, Caplowitz, 1967). The difference in discount rates may account for the different level of investment in human capital that define the skill groups. In addition, high discount rates may be a consequence of the lower level of wealth of those with less human capital.

If the divergence in discount rates by skill level is sufficiently large, that is, if the unskilled place little value on the higher incomes received in the future while the skilled place little extra value on receiving higher incomes in the present, it is possible for both skilled and unskilled native labor to lose because of the immigration. The income received, however, by the native population as a whole and by the owners of capital would be larger in each and every year; hence the present value of these incomes would also be larger with the immigration.

Immigrants and Capital

There is often a presumption that immigrants have higher savings and investment rates than the native population. Immigrants appear to make greater investments in human capital, as evidenced by their investments in migration, including investments made to adjust for the imperfect transferability to the destination of the skills acquired in the country of origin. These greater investments in human capital may arise from a lower discount rate or from greater labor market ability, that is, a greater productivity of investments, due to the general favorable selectivity of immigrants. The hypothesis that immigrants have a high savings rate and make greater investments in nonhuman assets is consistent with much folk wisdom regarding immigrants in the United States, including their higher rate of non-farm, non-professional self-employment. It has, however, not been adequately tested empirically.

The impact of immigrants depends in part on their propensity for saving relative to that of the native population. Even if immigrants bring no nonhuman resources with them, if they have a higher savings rate than the native population, over time their capital stock increases faster than otherwise, increasing the ratio of immigrant-owned to native-owned capital. The increasing capital stock decreases the return on capital, and hence the income of native-born owners of capital and their incentive to invest in it. As long as the per-capital stock is increased, however, the earnings of labor (native and foreign born) and the total income of the native population increase in response to the greater savings rate of immigrants.

SHARING THE PIE: IMMIGRANTS AND TRANSFERS

Let us now introduce an income transfer system that taxes the population as a whole to subsidize low-income persons. The income transfer system includes a welfare program or negative income tax, social services targeted to the poor, or social overhead capital financed prior to the immigration. It will be assumed that the income transfer system is invariant with the immigration policy; that is, the criteria for eligibility and the schedule of benefits do not change as the number and characteristics of the immigrants change.

The Economic Models

The immigration of unskilled workers can increase the aggregate of income transfers in two ways. First, the immigrants themselves may qualify for benefits. Second, as immigration depresses the wages of unskilled workers, a larger proportion of native unskilled workers qualify for some benefits, and some of those already receiving benefits may receive a larger transfer.

In the simple two-factor, capital-labor model of the receiving country in Figure 7.1, through a tax on capital, each of the $L_{0,x}$ native workers can receive a subsidy of AC to raise their earnings to the pre-immigration level $W_{0,x}$, with capital still receiving a net increase in income, although the increase in income to capital is reduced to area ABC instead of area $W_{1,x} W_{0,x}AB$. This can occur because aggregate income among the native population has increased. Thus, if the immigrants are excluded from participating in the transfer system, income could be transferred from capital to native labor so as to make everyone at least as well off as before the immigration.

Suppose, however, the transfer system is not permitted to differentiate between natives and immigrants. If both native and immigrant workers are to be brought up to the income level of native workers prior to the immigration, the aggregate income (after taxes) of capital must be lowered. If all $L_{1,x}$ workers in Figure 7.1 are to receive the subsidy of AC, the aggregate income of capital must be lower than before the immigration.

The impact of immigrants can also be considered explicitly within the context of a three-factor production function when there is an income transfer system. Suppose the immigrants are unskilled workers and the transfers are to bring the earnings of unskilled native workers up to the level it would have been without the immigration, with the skilled workers and the owners of capital made no worse off than before. Because the aggregate income of the native population is increased, this can be accomplished if the immigrants are excluded from the income transfer system, but not if they are included in it on the same basis as native workers. Thus, if the progressive-tax transfer system is invariant with immigration policy, the greater the extent to which unskilled immigrants are net recipients of income transfers (welfare benefits, social services, capital dilution), the smaller the optimal size of unskilled immigration.

This can be shown algebraically. The rise in the aggregate income of skilled workers and capital exceeds the transfer that would return native unskilled workers to their pre-immigration income but not the transfer required to bring all unskilled workers up to this level. That is, the gain in income exceeds the transfer of

$$(8a) \qquad \beta_1 [Q_0/H_{1,0})^{1/\sigma} - (Q_n/H_{1,n})^{1/\sigma}] dH_{1,0}$$

but not the transfer of

$$(8b) \qquad \beta_1 [Q_0/H_{1,0})^{1/\sigma} - (Q_n/H_{1,n})^{1/\sigma}] dH_{1,n}$$

that would be needed to bring the unskilled native workers and immigrants to the pre-immigration level of earnings for unskilled native-born workers. Thus, if both native and immigrant unskilled workers are to be brought up to the income level of native-born unskilled workers prior to immigration, the aggregate income (after taxes) of skilled workers and capital must be lowered.

If the immigrants are skilled workers, however, the wages of native-born skilled workers decline, while the wages of the unskilled increase. The wage differential between skill levels becomes smaller. If the structure of the transfer system does not change, aggregate net transfers received by low-income native workers would decline as their earnings rise. The additional revenues from the taxation of the higher income of capital and lower transfer expenditures could be used to lower the tax rate paid by skilled labor. In principle, native-born skilled workers could be made at least as well off as before the immigration, without eliminating the net gain to the other factors of production.

The guest worker programs in several European countries may have been designed with the foregoing model in mind. Under these programs, unskilled workers enter the country, but they do not bring their families with them and they are generally not eligible for income transfers. In the United States, the Bracero Program (1942–64) and other temporary worker programs prohibit participants from receiving welfare benefits and most social services. The same situation exists *de jure* (although perhaps not *de facto*) for illegal aliens in the United States. When the status of nearly three million illegal aliens in the United States was "regularized" under the 1986 Immigration Reform and Control Act and many families were allowed to join them, their greater use of welfare benefits and social services would reduce their net contribution to the economic well-being of the native population. For illegal aliens with low levels of skill and nonworking dependents, the net impact on the native population is likely to change from positive to negative if they bring their dependent family members.

Additions to the Economic Models

The transfer system itself may serve as a means of attracting immigrants. For some, the calculus of the costs and benefits of migration to a destination is the comparison of earnings in the country of origin with income transfers in the destination. For others who intend to work, the potential availability of transfers acts as an insurance that cushions the loss of income in the destination due to unemployment, ill health or other factors. This would both encourage low-skilled immigration and discourage the return migration of low-skilled immigrants during periods of low income.

Immigrants consume a share, as a first approximation a proportionate share, of social overhead capital, such as roads, schools, hospitals and flood control projects. The greater the magnitude of the "capital dilution," that is, the greater the extent to which immigrants receive benefits from social overhead capital without contributing to its cost, the smaller the net gain (or the larger the net loss) to the native population from immigration. Most social overhead capital is financed, however, by bonds that are retired by direct and indirect fees levied on the users (for example, gasoline taxes, water taxes), or through general taxes as the social overhead capital is consumed. Thus, immigrants pay for the consumption of social overhead capital. Social overhead capital that is paid for by the taxpayers as it is constructed can be subsumed within the income transfer system, and its impact can be analyzed as in the preceding discussion.

Synthesis

In summary, if immigrants are not included in the income transfer system, the increase in the aggregate income of the native population means that appropriate income redistribution policies can, in principle, be devised to transfer some income from the native groups that gain to the native groups that lose, so that no native group loses from the immigration. The welfare and tax systems can be the mechanism for this transfer. This cannot be accomplished, however, if the immigrants themselves are to be substantial recipients of income transfers, that is, if they receive an income in excess of their productivity. Thus, an important issue is the number of years that must pass following immigration before immigrants become eligible for public income transfers. Moreover, redistribution policies that may exist "in principle" may not exist in practice. If these policies cannot be implemented, even if immigrants cannot receive income transfers, the low-skilled native population experiences a decline in their economic well-being. If individuals vote their economic self-interest, low-skilled workers would then oppose low-skilled immigration.

Even if immigrants are not recipients of any net income transfers, unskilled immigrants decrease the earnings and employment of unskilled native workers, thereby increasing the aggregate resources that flow through the income transfer system. The increased administrative costs and the adverse effects of increased taxes and transfers on labor supply and capital formation from an enlarged tax-transfer system would reduce the aggregate net output of the native population.

Thus, in terms of maximizing the income of the native population, the optimal level of immigration would be highest if the immigrants are skilled workers, lower if they are unskilled workers but do not receive income transfers, and lowest (and possibly negative) if the immigrants are unskilled and receive income transfers on the same basis as the native population. Thus, the length of time before low-skilled immigrants are eligible for benefits from income transfers and the extent to which they may bring dependent family members with them are critical issues.

IMMIGRATION POLICIES FOR POST-INDUSTRIAL ECONOMIES

An optimal immigration policy cannot be designed in the abstract. It requires some specification of the social welfare function of the country, as well as the level of development, relative factor supplies, and relative factor prices.

Schematic Representation

The analysis developed here will focus on the models of advanced *post-industrial* (as opposed to *industrial*) economies in which there is a highly developed income transfer system, technologically advanced economies in a time-frame extending well into the "computer age" or "information age". Much of the industrial employment characteristic of the mid-twentieth century has been shipped overseas or uses high-level technology. The seemingly unlimited employment opportunities in industry and mining, which in previous decades had been satisfied by internal migrants or by immigrants, are no longer available. The low-skilled employment that would exist in the absence of immigration is in the service sector, but even low-skilled service employment is shrinking in contrast to high-skilled service employment.

Two separate country models will be considered. One country is characterized by a large inequality in wealth and

especially in skills, with a large low-skilled native-born population, many of whom are in economic distress. This will be referred to as *Inequalityland*. The other is characterized by a
relatively small, low-skilled native-born population or at least a
low-skilled native population that remains heavily subsidized
in the countryside. Let this country also be characterized by
crowding, or at least a belief that the population is beyond the
level at which there are economies of scale from additional
population growth and that possibly it is in the range of diseconomies of scale. Let us call this *Crowdedland*.

Now consider four alternative immigration policies (see
Figure 7.2):

(1) **Low-skilled worker/family immigration policy**. Under this
policy immigrants are selected either because of their low
level of skill or this is the consequence of a selection
mechanism independent of skill level. The immigrants
can stay indefinitely and can bring dependent family
members with them. This immigration would exacerbate
the already existing downward pressure on wages in the
low-skilled labor market, especially in Inequalityland. A

Figure 7.2   *Schematic representation of desirability of policy options*

	Type of Immigrant worker	
Skill level	Guest or temporary worker	Permanent immigrant
Low-skilled		
Inequalityland	No	No
Crowdedland	Yes	No
High-skilled		
Inequalityland	Yes	Yes
Crowdedland	Yes	No

Code: Desirable policy: Yes
      Undesirable policy: No

net loss to the native population in both receiving countries, but especially in Inequalityland, could arise from the income transfer system. This loss would be smaller, or the gains larger, if the immigrants are denied access to the transfers and if they do not bring or acquire dependent family members. Yet, both are difficult to prevent among long-term immigrants.

(2) **Low-skilled guest worker policy**. Under this policy low-skilled workers can enter the country but it is expected (required) that their duration of stay is short (say, up to 6 months) and is not renewable. If it is always renewable this is the equivalent of long-term immigration. Moreover, dependent family members do not accompany the worker. While this policy, in principle, solves many of the policy problems with the low-skilled immigrant worker policy, in practice it is difficult to prevent "guest workers" from becoming "permanent immigrants". This policy is more effective the more stringently enforced are the rules regarding duration and accompanying family members. It is also more successful if the worker does not acquire skills that are specific to the destination, as the acquisition of these skills discourages departing. Because of the existing relatively low wages in the low-skilled labor market, this policy could run counter to the interests of the native-born population in Inequalityland, but could relax some of the labor shortages in the low-skilled sectors in Crowdedland.

(3) **High-skilled worker/family immigration policy**.[5] A high-skilled worker immigration policy can be achieved by focusing the selection process on the skill level of the applicant and by severely limiting the sponsorship of relatives. These immigrants would make little use of the income transfer system. The depressing effect on the earnings of high-skilled workers in the labor market and the positive effect on the earnings of low-skilled workers would narrow skill differentials and income inequality, and would be especially beneficial in Inequalityland. There is a temptation in a high-skilled worker immigration policy to adopt a "targeted labor" policy, as is done in

the occupational categories in US immigration law.[6] Under a targeted labor policy employers petition for a specific worker for a specific job slot. This encourages counterproductive industry-/occupational-/region-specific lobbying efforts to favor (by employers) or to discourage (by competing workers) specific job categories. A more effective high-skilled worker policy calls for focusing on skill level and letting the market forces allocate these workers across employers and sectors of the economy. This can be accomplished through a skill-based point system, as is used in Canada and Australia, or by various mechanisms for charging large visa fees, including auctioning visas. Except for a spouse and minor children, these immigrants should have no rights to bring in other relatives. Moreover, under this program there would be no kinship sponsorship, even for citizens, except for the spouse, minor children and perhaps aged parents of citizens, where the sponsor is held liable for the financial support of the relatives they sponsor. A high-skilled worker policy is less attractive, however, if the size of the population is perceived as having reached the point of diseconomies of scale. It is most attractive for Inequalityland and less so for Crowdedland.

(4) **High-skilled guest worker policy**. Either in the absence of or as a supplement to a high-skilled worker/family immigration policy there can be economic gains from a high-skilled temporary worker policy. This policy instrument can address "bottlenecks" or shortages in particular sectors at particular times, even if the applicant might not otherwise satisfy conditions for a permanent visa. Presumably it would be limited to specialized jobs for which there is little need for training specific to the destination, even though it involves high levels of internationally transferable skills. Characteristics of this program would include petitions by employers for specific job slots, and employment contracts with a relatively short and finite duration. Because of the higher level of skill, these employment contracts would have as a maximum a longer duration than those for low-skilled guest workers, perhaps of up to 3 years.

Application to the United States and Japan

The characterizations of Inequalityland and Crowdedland were based on stylized facts regarding the United States and Japan, respectively.[7] Both countries have reached very high levels of per-capita output (Table 7.1). They are in the post-industrial stage of economic development in which future employment growth will occur in high-technology areas in manufacturing and especially in the service sector, while opportunities for low-skilled workers in the once abundant dirty, dangerous and demanding jobs will continue to shrink. Both countries also have elaborate income transfer programs for their citizens, and both countries have fertility rates below the level necessary for replacement, 2.1 births per woman (Table 7.1).

Yet the United States and Japan differ in some important respects. The United States encourages immigrants to become citizens and has more lenient requirements, and at least up to the present has been more open to aliens' receiving income transfers. Moreover, relative skill differentials, the ratio of the wages of high-skilled to low-skilled workers, are greater in the United States, as is the degree of income inequality. The United States has a relatively large native-born low-skilled pool of workers that are in direct competition in the labor market with low-skilled immigrants.

Furthermore the United States and Japan have vastly different immigration histories.[8] The United States has historically been a country of immigration, with a very low rate of emigration among the native born. Although the Japanese immigration/emigration experience is more episodic, Japan was a country of emigration for much of the last century, until the 1980s (Tsuchida, 1995). In 1990 the foreign-born comprised 8 percent of the population of the United States (20 million people) in contrast to 1 percent for Japan (1.2 million people).[9] The migration rate (annual immigration per 1000 population) is much higher in the United States than in Japan. The United States granted about twice as many temporary worker visas in recent years as has Japan, with a roughly similar rate per 1000 population (Table 7.1).

The two countries differ in the degree of "crowding," As a crude index, the population per square mile in Japan in 1990

Table 7.1 *Selected characteristics regarding the United States and Japan, 1990*[a]

Item	United States	Japan
Population	255 million	125 million
Population per square mile	71	814
Annual population growth rate (percent)	0.7	0.4
Total fertility rate	1.85	1.56
Crude birth rate (births per 1,000 population)	14.6	10.2
GNP per capita ($)	21,863	23,558
Employment ratio for women	54.4	48.0
Foreign origin Number (Percentage of population)	20 million (foreign born) (8.0%)	1.3 million (all) (1.1%) 0.4 million (excluding Koreans and Chinese) (0.3%)

Table 7.1 (Continued)

Item	United States	Japan
Immigration rate – 1980s (annual immigration per 1,000 population)	3.2	–
Temporary worker visas (1993)	165,238[b]	97,101 76,242 (entertainers) 28,859 (all others)
Illegal aliens (1993) (approx.)	3 million	300,000

[a] The data refer to 1990 unless noted otherwise.

[b] Temporary workers and trainees, excluding spouses and children, and excluding those on student visas (*Statistical Yearbook of the Immigration and Naturalization Service 1993*).

SOURCE: Unless indicated otherwise the source is US Bureau of Census, *Statistical Abstract of the United States, 1992* (Washington, 1992), various tables. Immigration and foreign worker data for Japan are from OECD (1993), Kazutoshi Koshiro (1995) and Yasuo Kuwahara (1995).

was 814, in contrast to 71 for the United States. More relevant for public policy may be the sense of whether a country is "too crowded." With a renewed interest in the environment in the United States, and increased concerns regarding environmental degradation due to population growth, a greater sense of population crowding, or diseconomies of population scale, is playing an increasing role in the US public policy debate over immigration. However, the diseconomies of scale argument plays a larger role in the public policy debate in Japan.

Thus, at this point, Inequalityland best characterizes the United States and Crowdedland best characterizes Japan. The policy implications are that the United States should avoid low-skilled worker immigration and focus on a high-skilled permanent immigration program that stresses skill levels in general and a high-skilled targeted labor policy for temporary migrants or guest workers. On the other hand, the implications are that Japan should focus on targeted temporary migrant (guest worker) policies in both the low-skilled and high-skilled labor markets. There will be some leakage as some temporary workers become permanent residents, but this is a side effect of temporary worker policies that cannot be completely eliminated.

SUMMARY AND IMPLICATIONS FOR IMMIGRATION POLICY

This paper has developed an analysis of the effects of immigration on the economy of the destination country. Special attention is given to the implications of immigrants that differ by skill level, as well as their impacts on the level and distribution of income in the destination. The existence of an income transfer system and whether immigrants are eligible for benefits on the same basis as natives, and public policy concerns over inequality, as well as economies or diseconomies of population size, also enter the analysis. The analysis is developed for a two-factor (labor and capital) model of the economy, which has the advantage of simplicity, and a three-factor (skilled labor, unskilled labor and capital) model which offers greater realism and richer implications.

It is shown that an optimal immigration policy, in terms of the skills and permanence of the migrants, depends on the characteristics of the host economy. A policy optimal for one environment maybe sub-optimal for another. Moreover it is shown that the arguments that the economy "needs" immigrants (i.e. that immigrants will take jobs "natives will not do") or that they "take jobs from natives" are polar cases that do not describe the reality of labor markets and the impact of immigrants.

The United States and Japan are characterized as post-industrial welfare states with limited job opportunities for low-skilled workers but with highly developed income transfer systems. They differ in that the United States is characterized by a larger income inequality and a larger low-skilled native-born population. On the other hand, Japan is characterized as a crowded country which may have reached or may be beyond economies of scale for additions to its population.

Four broad policy alternatives are considered: permanent versus temporary (guest) workers for both high-skilled (professional, managerial and technical and high-skilled craft) and low-skilled (all other occupations) workers. It is shown that an optimal policy for the United States would involve both high-skilled permanent immigration and high-skilled temporary worker migration, with severe restrictions on the sponsorship of extended family members. For Japan, on the other hand, the analysis implies both low-skilled and high-skilled guest worker policies, but again with severe limits on the sponsorship of family members.

NOTES

1. This paper draws, in part, on the author's earlier research on the impact of immigrants, in particular B. Chiswick (1982) and C. Chiswick *et al.* (1992). For an analysis of the historical flows of immigrants and the characteristics of the current foreign-born population of the United States, see B. Chiswick and Sullivan (1995) and for Japan see Cornelius (1994).
2. The inequality in the ownership of capital is smaller if the equity of owner-occupied dwellings, automobiles, and wealth in asset-holding pension plans are included in the household's stock of capital.
3. Using the Drymes–Kurz generalization of the constant-elasticity-of-substitution (CES) production notion, Carmel U. Chiswick has shown

that the data for US manufacturing are consistent with a constant elasticity of substitution, where the pairwise elasticity is about 2.5. She used a two-equation supply-and-demand model in which the demand for professional manpower relative to other factors of production is derived from a three-factor production function in which non-professional manpower and capital are the other factors. See C. Chiswick (1979).

4.   The pattern of low earnings on arrival in the destination and a subsequent rise in earnings with duration of residence is a robust finding in the immigrant adjustment literature. Immigrants make investments to increase the transferability to the destination of pre-immigration skills, as well as to acquire new skills. Recent research has demonstrated that these skills include knowledge of the dominant language of the destination, including fluency and literacy. The pattern of increases in earnings with duration of residence is more intense the lower the transferability of the skills of the origin to the destination and among refugees than among economic migrants. See, for example, B. Chiswick (1978, 1979) and B. Chiswick and Miller (1995).

5.   For a fuller development of mechanisms for implementing a high-skilled worker immigration policy see B. Chiswick (1981).

6.   Current US immigration policy selects workers for the occupational preferences as if they were to be temporary workers (i.e. an employer petitions for a particular worker for a specific job slot), but grants them permanent resident visas and rights to bring in the family members.

7.   Regarding Japan, see Koshiro (1995) and Kuwahara (1995).

8.   For a review of the history and rights of recent foreign-origin groups in Japan see Hanami (1995), Kajita (1995), Tsuchida (1995) and Cornelius (1994).

9.   The approximately 1.3 million foreigners residing legally in Japan for 90 days or more as of December 1993 comprise 1.1 percent of the Japanese population of 125 million. The percentage distribution by country of origin of the foreign nationals is as follows (Kajita, 1995):

Korea	51.7
China (including Taiwan)	15.9
Brazil	11.7
Philippines	5.5
United States	3.2
Peru	2.5
United Kingdom	0.9
Vietnam	0.6
All others and country unknown	7.0
Total	**100.0**

The Korean and Chinese nationals (nearly 900 000 persons) are primarily individuals (and their Japan-born descendents) brought to Japan as workers prior to and during the Second World War (1910–45). The Brazilians and Peruvians (nearly 190 000 individuals) are *Nikkeijin*, immigrants of Japanese ancestry, who started returning to Japan in the late 1980s. Not counting the Koreans and Chinese, the *Nikkeijin* and the approximately 240 000 other foreign nationals make up 0.3 percent of the Japanese population.

In addition, it is estimated that there are about 300 000 illegal aliens in Japan, primarily low-skilled workers from various parts of Asia who are working in violation of their temporary (tourist or student) visa or have stayed longer than their visa allowed (Koshiro, 1995; Y. Kuwahara, 1995). Including the illegal aliens, nearly 0.6 percent of the population of Japan immigrated since 1945. The comparable rate for the United States is over 8.0 percent.

REFERENCES

Caplowitz, David (1967), *The Poor Pay More* (New York: The Free Press), ch 6–8.

Chiswick, Barry R. (1978), "The Effect of Americanization on the Earnings of Foreign-Born Men," *Journal of Political Economy*, 86:5, pp. 897–922.

—— (1979), "The Economic Progress of Immigrants: Some Apparently Universal Patterns," in William Fellner (ed.), *Contemporary Economic Problems, 1979* (Washington, DC: American Enterprise Institute), pp. 357–99.

—— (1981), "Guidelines for the Reform of Immigration Policy," in William Fellner (ed.), *Essays in Contemporary Economic Problems, 1981–82* (Washington, DC: American Enterprise Institute), pp. 309–47.

—— (1982), "The Impact of Immigrants on the Level and Distribution of Economic Well Being," in Barry R. Chiswick (ed.), *The Gateway: US Immigration Issues and Policies* (Washington, DC: American Enterprise Institute), pp. 289–313.

Chiswick, Barry R. and Miller, Paul W. (1995), "The Endogeneity Between Language and Earnings: International Analyses," *Journal of Labor Economics*, 13:2, April, pp. 245–87.

Chiswick, Barry R. and Sullivan, Teresa A. (1995), "The New Immigrants," in Reynolds Farley (ed.), *State of the Union: America in the 1990s* (New York: Russell Sage Foundation), pp. 211–70.

Chiswick, Carmel U. (1979), "The Rise of Professional Occupations in US Manufacturing: 1900 to 1973," in I. Sirageldin (ed.), *Research in Human Capital and Development*, vol. 1 (Greenwich, CT: JAI Press), pp. 191–217.

—— (1986), "The Elasticity of Substitution Revisited: The Effects of Secular Changes in Labor Force Structure," *Journal of Labor Economics*, 4:4, October, pp. 490–507.

Chiswick, Carmel U., Chiswick, Barry R. and Karras, Georgios (1992), "The Impact of Immigrants on the Macroeconomy," *Carnegie–Rochester Conference Series on Public Policy*, 37 (December), pp. 279–316.

Cornelius, Wayne A. (1994), "Japan: The Illusion of Immigration Control," in Wayne A. Cornelius, Philip L. Martin and James E. Hollifield (eds), *Controlling Immigration: A Global Perspective* (Stanford: Stanford University Press), pp. 375–410.

Hanami, Tadashi (1995), "Japanese Policies on the Rights and Benefits of Foreign Workers, Residents, Refugees and Illegals" (Tokyo: School of Law, Sophia University, xerox).

Kajita, Takamichi (1995), "The Challenge of Incorporating Foreign Workers in Japan" (Tokyo: Faculty of Social Studies, Hitotsubashi University, xerox).

Koshiro, Kazutoshi (1995), "Does Japan Need Immigrants? A Preliminary Investigation" (Yokohama: Yokohama National University, xerox).

Kuwahara, Yasuo (1995), "Illegal Migrant Workers in Japan – Japan's Dilemma, Can International Migration be Controlled" (Tokyo: Faculty of Economics, Dokkyo University, xerox).

OECD, Continuous Reporting System on Migration (SOPEMI) (1993), "Japan and International Migration," in *Trends in International Migration: OECD)* (Paris), pp. 57–62.

Tsuchida, Motoko, (1995), "A History of Japanese Emigration and Immigration: 1860s–1990s" (Tokyo: Sophia University, xerox).

US Bureau of the Census (1992), *Statistical Abstract of the United States* (Washington, DC).

US Immigration and Naturalization Service (1993), *Statistical Yearbook, 1993* (Washington, DC) p. 104.

Part IV
Rights and Benefits

8 Japanese Policies on the Rights and Benefits Granted to Foreign Workers, Residents, Refugees and Illegals

Tadashi Hanami

INTRODUCTION

The principal difference between Japanese and US immigration, refugee and citizenship policies is that the United States considers itself a country of immigration, while Japan does not. Should Japan become a country of immigration and accept foreigners as migrants? Such a question, which seems to me impossible to ask, will be discussed as a policy matter elsewhere in this volume; this paper discusses how foreigners coming to Japan are treated, given their legal status, and what kinds of rights and benefits accrue to them. Foreigners who work fall into several categories: foreign citizens with permanent resident status, foreign visitors with work permits, refugees (who will be discussed in Chapter 14 by Isami Takeda), descendents of Japanese, and so-called "illegal" foreign workers who are overstaying visas and/or employed without work permits. The rights and benefits discussed here are related to visa status, registration, naturalization, marriage, application of the employment laws, social security, education, criminal liability and community life.

BASIC PRINCIPLES OF THE LEGAL STATUS OF FOREIGNERS

Article 14 of the Constitution of Japan of 1946 prohibits discrimination because of race, creed, sex, social status or family origin. However, the legal status of foreign citizens is not addressed in the Constitution, and there is no consensus among legal theories or opinions about which fundamental human rights guaranteed by the Constitution are awarded only to Japanese citizens and which are granted to all residents. In some provisions of the Constitution "every person" (*nanibito*) and in some others "every citizen" (*kokumin*), is identified as the subject of the guaranteed right. There is another term, *jyumin* ("resident"), in connection with the right to participate in local community affairs. Partly based on such distinctions, some theories contend that some rights, such as voting rights and eligibility for public positions, are accorded only to Japanese citizens (*kokumin*). The Supreme Court laid down that constitutionally guaranteed fundamental human rights should also be given to foreigners staying in Japan, except for some which are reserved to Japanese citizens "because of their nature" (Supreme Court, Grand Bench, 1978, 10, 4, 32 *Minshu* 1223).

Foreigners may obtain Japanese citizenship by applying for naturalization under the procedures of the Nationality Act of 1950. However, there are prerequisites, such as good behavior and a 5-year stay in Japan. The requirement for obtaining citizenship is regarded as rather restrictive, partly because the law does not permit dual nationality. (For more details, see the section on naturalization, below).

The fundamental principles of the visa status of foreigners are prescribed by the Immigration Control and Refugee Recognition Act of 1951 (amended in 1989 – hereafter referred to as the ICA). The basic scheme of immigration control in Japan is not particularly different from other major advanced countries as far as passport control, visa requirements and visa status are concerned. There are 27 categories of visa, for some of which work permits are granted. Generally foreign workers are accepted only in professional and technical fields; unskilled workers are excluded except as trainees. The visa categories allowing work permits include the following:

- Investor and business manager
- Professor
- Entertainer

- Engineer
- Skilled labor
- Artist
- Religious activities
- Journalist
- Legal and accounting services
- Medical services
- Researcher
- Instructor
- Specialist in humanities and international services
- Intra-company transfer

Table 8.1 *Stock of foreign workers registered by residence status (thousands)*

	1990	1992	1993	1994	1995
Investor, business manager	7.3	5.1	4.4	4.5	4.6
Professor	1.8	2.6	3.2	3.8	4.1
Entertainer	21.1	22.8	28.5	34.8	15.9
Engineer	3.4	9.2	9.9	10.1	9.9
Skilled labour	2.0	5.4	5.9	6.8	7.4
Artist	0.6	0.2	0.2	0.2	0.2
Religious activities	5.5	5.6	5.7	5.6	5.3
Journalist	0.4	0.4	0.4	0.4	0.4
Legal and accounting services	0.1	0.1	0.1	0.1	0.1
Medical services	0.4	0.2	0.2	0.2	0.2
Researcher	1.0	1.3	1.5	1.7	1.7
Instructor	7.6	5.8	6.2	6.8	7.2
Specialist in humanities/ international services	14.4	21.9	23.5	24.8	25.0
Intra-company transferee	1.5	5.1	5.7	5.8	5.9
Total	**68.0**	**85.5**	**95.4**	**105.6**	**87.9**

SOURCE: Immigration Bureau, Ministry of Justice.

These categories are not particularly restrictive, and may be broader than the categories of work permits in many European countries and in the United States[1] although the total number of foreign workers in Japan is small and thus their impact on the labour market is rather limited (see Table 8.8).

SPECIAL CATEGORIES OF FOREIGN RESIDENTS

Certain groups of foreigners are permitted a special residence status in Japan because of historical and/or political considerations. First, *permanent resident* status has been given to Koreans and Chinese who were living in Japan before the Second World War and to their descendants; they make up 47.8 percent of all registered foreigners (631 812 of the total 1 320 748 foreigners in Japan at the end of 1993). Second, a total of 221 458 persons were naturalized between 28 April, 1952, when the Treaty of Peace was implemented, and 1992 (see Table 8.2).

Indochinese refugees granted long-term residence in Japan totaled 8 899 in June 1993, including 3357 boat people, 3789 Indo-Chinese refugees temporarily staying in Asian countries, 742 former students who entered Japan before the political change (these were granted long-term residence in 1981) and 1011 Vietnamese in the Orderly Departure Program (see Tables 8.3 and 8.4).

Table 8.2 *Naturalizations by country/area of former nationality*

	Korea	China	Others	Total
28 April 1952–1987	140,977	35,827	8,853	185,657
1988	4,595	990	182	5,767
1989	4,759	1,066	264	6,089
1990	5,216	1,349	229	6,794
1991	5,665	1,818	305	7,788
1992	7,244	1,794	325	9,363
Total	**168,456**	**42,844**	**10,158**	**221,458**

SOURCE: Civil Affairs Bureau, Ministry of Justice.

Table 8.3 *Permission for temporary refuge, 1982–92*

	1982–9	1990	1991	1992	1993	1994	Total
Applied for	7,024	374	366	17	638	21	8,440
Granted	4,197	154	20	100	17	0	4,488
Refused	2,824	39	86	238	390	262	3,839

NOTE: The screening system was introduced for Indo-Chinese refugees in 1989, and as a certain period of time is necessary for the examination, the number applying does not necessarily correspond to the total number of those granted and refused.

SOURCE: Immigration Bureau, Ministry of Justice.

Aside from the residents of Japan, the boat people who left for the United States made up the largest share with 3977, about 60 percent of all the 6759 persons who departed for third countries by 1994 (see Table 8.5). Between the institutionalization of refugee recognition in January 1982 and June 1993, 1090 people had applied for refugee status of whom 203 had been recognized (see Table 8.6).

Under the "Comprehensive Plan of Action" adopted at the International Conference on Indo-Chinese Refugees, boat people arriving in Japan since 13 September, 1989 are subject to a screening system. Screening has been implemented for 342 out of 702 eligible persons, and 136 have passed (Iguchi and Koyama, 1993).

Second-, third- and fourth-generation Japanese descendents arriving from Latin American countries such as Brazil and Peru may work legally as the "spouse or child of a Japanese national" or as a "long-term resident." These were estimated by the Ministry of Foreign Affairs to total some 150 000 as of June 1991.

IMMIGRATION CONTROL AND THE VISA SYSTEM

In order to obtain one of the above-mentioned 14 categories of visas that permit the holder to work, a foreigner must make an application at the relevant Japanese delegation in his or

Table 8.4 *Long-term residence permits granted to Indo-Chinese refugees*

	1978–87	1988	1989	1990	1991	1992	1993	Total
Those staying temporarily (boat people)	2,327	164	152	171	263	239	41	3,357
Those coming from refugee camps abroad	2,205	193	194	321	370	411	95	3,789
Former students who entered Japan before the change of government	742 (1,981)							742
Orderly Departure Program	147	143	115	242	147	142	75	1,011
Total	**5,421**	**500**	**461**	**734**	**780**	**792**	**216**	**8,899**

SOURCE: Immigration Bureau, Ministry of Justice.

Table 8.5 *Boat people leaving for a third country*

	1975–89	1990	1991	1992	1993	1994	Total
USA	3,703	230	10	31	0	3	3,977
Canada	640	39	41	13	4	4	741
Australia	689	8	11	8	3	0	719
Norway	694	1	0	0	0	0	695
Others	613	5	5	3	1	0	627
Total	**6,339**	**67**	**67**	**55**	**8**	**7**	**6,759**

SOURCE: Immigration Bureau, Ministry of Justice.

Table 8.6 *Applications for refugee recognition and number processed*

	1982–9	1990	1991	1992	1993	1994	Total
Applied	864	32	42	45	473	73	1,129
Processed							
Recognized	194	2	1	3	6	1	207
Not recognized	484	31	13	41	33	41	643
Withdrawn	137	4	5	2	16	9	173
Unprocessed	80	44	67	66	84	106	190

SOURCE: Immigration Bureau, Ministry of Justice.

her home country and present a certificate of employment issued by a local immigration office upon application by a prospective employer. Since the majority of foreign workers coming to Japan are unable to obtain an employment contract before leaving their home countries, those who do not use the services of a labor contractor come with tourist or student visas. As for the student visa, Japan is rather lenient, permitting students with such a visa to work 4 hours per day (8 hours during the summer, for university students) with permission of the Minister of Justice given on a case-by-case basis.

For those with either tourist or student visas there is always the possibility of changing visa status if there is a compelling reason. In practice, the local immigration office takes a rather

Table 8.7 *Trends in workforce and number of foreign workers*
(estimate: 10,000 persons)

Classification		1990	1991	1992
Workforce	(A)	6,384	6,505	6,578
Number of employees	(B)	4,835	5,002	5,119
Foreign workers	(C)	30	50	59
Overstayers		10.6	21.6	29.2[a]
Ratio of foreign workers	(C)/(A)	0.5%	0.8%	0.9%
	(C)/(B)	0.6%	1.0%	1.2%

[a] 293,800 in May 1994.

SOURCE: Employment Security Bureau – Trends, Ministry of Labor.

Table 8.8 *Impact of foreigners on the labor market (ratio of foreign workers to total number employed in professional technical jobs)*

Impact on the labor market for professional categories (ratio of foreign workers with professional technical jobs	(1) Number of persons employed in professional and technical jobs = 7,550,000 (2) Number of foreigners who can be employed = 62,767 (0.8%)	(1) Management and Coordination Agency, "Work Force Survey" (1992) (2) Ministry of Justice Immigration Bureau. Total number of registered foreigners as of the end of 1992[a]
Impact on the labor market of college graduates obtaining employment (ratio of foreign students to total number of college graduates employed	(1) Number of college students employed = 345,040 (2) Number of foreign students employed = 2,184 (0.6%)	(1) Ministry of Labor Employment Security Bureau "Statistics on Employment Security" (1993) (2) Ministry of Justice Immigration Control Bureau "Changes in visa status accompanying employment of foreign graduates"

Table 8.8 *(Continued)*

Impact on the labor market of temporary and seasonal workers.	(1) Number of temporary workers = 3,940,000 (2) Number of Japanese descendants = 152,120 (3.7%)	(1) Management and Coordination Agency, "Work Force Survey". Temporary workers with an employment contract for more than 1 month but less than 1 year (non-agricultural, non-forestry)[b] (2) Estimate by Ministry of Foreign Affairs (as of June 1991)
Impact on part-time labor market (ratio of college and pre-college students who work part-time to total number of such workers)	(1) Number of part-time workers = 8,680,000 (2) College students and pre-college students working part-time −61,792 (0.07%)	(1) Management and Coordination Agency, "Work Force Survey". Workers working under 35 hours per week (non-agricultural, non-forestry)[b] (2) Unofficial estimates by Labour Ministry

[a] The statuses of residence are "Engineer," "Specialist in humanities/international services" "Skilled labor," and others, excluding "Entertainer."

[b] Averages for 1992.

SOURCE: See column 3 for details.

strict approach to avoid evasion of the law, and in most cases the applicants are advised to go back to the home country and make another application with appropriate documents to obtain a different type of visa. However, permission may be granted in cases where the Minister finds appropriate reasons for a change, such as possible employment of students who finished their education and obtained the qualifications appropriate to one of the 14 visa categories that permit work.

Once a work permit is issued, it is not a problem to change jobs if the new job falls in the same category of activities permitted under the present visa. If the new job belongs to a different category, an application for another type of visa must be made, of which the requirements are in substance the same as for a new application.

REGISTRATION OF FOREIGN RESIDENTS

Foreigners staying in Japan longer than 90 days must be registered at their local community office, and must always carry the certificate of registration issued by that office. The requirement of carrying a registration card has been criticized, as has the requirement of fingerprinting in the registration procedure. The fingerprint requirement became a serious political issue, as it was picked up by the Korean government in connection with the legal status of Korean descendents living in Japan. Finally, in 1993 it was abolished for Koreans and Taiwanese, and replaced by submission of a photograph, a signature and a report of family relationship. But as a general issue for other foreigners, the government is in a rather awkward situation because of its serious concern with the growing number of "illegal" workers entering the country, with fake passports or in other ways, sometimes entering repeatedly under different names; there is a lack of effective means to identify them other than by fingerprints.

NATURALIZATION

In addition to the already-mentioned requirements of a 5-year stay and no dual nationality, naturalization is granted to those older than 20 years, with enough income for themselves together with spouse or other family members to live on and not having attempted or advocated the violent overthrow of the Constitution or the government, nor belonging to an organization including a political party which attempted or advocated such actions. The 5-year requirement may be fulfilled as a result of the accumulation of a number of years during renewed periods of legal stay. The spouse of the naturalized or to-be-naturalized person may be naturalized after a 3-year stay; their children are automatically granted permission to be naturalized. After 3 year of marriage and having been resident in Japan for longer than a year, the spouse of a Japanese citizen may also be naturalized.

There are certain problems concerning the naturalization of Koreans and Chinese and their descendents remaining in Japan from the pre-war period. Their Japanese citizenship was forfeited regardless of their wishes in April 1952, when the Peace Treaty became effective. As a result, their legal status was uncertain until 1991, when they were given the status of "special permanent resident" under the Special Law. Under this law Koreans and Taiwanese are given the most stable residential status, that is, they may be forced to leave only if they are sentenced to imprisonment for life or longer than 7 years, and if the Ministry of Justice finds a serious infringement of Japanese national interests by the crime of which they are convicted. Other foreign residents are forced to leave if they are sentenced to imprisonment for longer than a year. The re-entry period is also extended for Koreans and Taiwanese to 5 years, while other foreigners are given less than a 1 year re-entry period.

In spite of such a stable permanent residence status, providing an opportunity for them to choose their nationality should be considered as a policy alternative, because most of these residents have, in fact, been fairly well integrated into Japanese society. However, at the same time there still exist some strong political trends that emphasize national identity and pride, among both Korean residents in Japan and their counterparts in Korea. As a result only a limited number of them take Japanese nationality (Table 8.2). Thus the issue is still a delicate political matter between the two countries.

MARRIAGE AND FAMILY STATUS

Foreigners staying in Japan may marry under Japanese law, provided both parties are qualified to be married under the laws of their own home countries. For a marriage registration, they are required to submit to the local community office certain documents such as a passport, certificate of qualification for marriage from the official delegation of their country and, in the case of Koreans and Taiwanese, a copy of the family register.

Foreigners staying in Japan without legal qualifications, such as illegal entrants or those overstaying the permitted period, must get special permission for their stay from the Minister of Justice in order to marry a Japanese citizen. For that purpose they must report to the Immigration Office; immigration officers then determine whether there has been any violation of the ICA or other law which justifies a forced departure. The procedure permits three appeals. Finally the Minister makes a decision as to whether to grant special permission for the stay, taking into consideration other factors such as living conditions and the family relationship. If the request is granted, the foreigner is given the legal qualifications to stay as the spouse of a Japanese citizen. However, the investigation often takes a long time, and sometimes it is advisable for the applicant to go back home and return with the required legal documents, depending upon the circumstances.

Those foreigners who are married to Japanese, and their dependent family members, are not subject to any restrictions on their activities. But permission for their stay is normally granted for a shorter period (6 months, 1 year, or 3 years) initially and for longer after some renewals. However, a foreign spouse with such a status will lose it if he or she is divorced or if the other party dies. In such a case the Minister may grant permanent resident status after taking into consideration the degree of the applicant's integration into Japanese society.

Such status is to be granted only to those who are legally married to Japanese citizens; a common-law marriage is not regarded as a legal marriage in this context. The Immigration Office is rather cautious in its investigation, even in cases of registered marriages, because of the recently growing number of fake marriages by illegal foreign workers desperately seeking employment in Japan.

EMPLOYMENT LAWS

As already explained, except for those with permanent residence, spouses and dependent family members of Japanese citizens, who may work without special work permits, foreigners are permitted to work in only the above-mentioned 14 job categories. The total number of those with working visas was 95 367 at the end of 1993, while people of Japanese descent (*Nikkeijin*) numbered 152 120 as of June 1991. College students and pre-college students working part-time were estimated at about 60 000 in 1992. In addition, illegal workers who were overstaying their visas were estimated to number 293 800 in 1994. Thus, the Labor Ministry estimates that a total of some 590 000 foreigners were employed, 1.2 percent of the total employment in Japan in 1992 (see Table 8.1).

In principle, the protective labor laws are applied to all workers regardless of their status, even including illegal workers. The labor law is interpreted to apply to *de facto* labor relations, including those without a legal contract. [For instance, under the Labor Standards Law of 1947 (LSL), overtime work is prohibited and penalized unless agreements for overtime between labor and management are submitted to the Labor Inspection Office. However, wage claims on overtime rates for illegal work are permitted.] Besides the LSL, protective labor statutes include the Minimum Wage Law of 1959, the Industrial Safety and Health Law of 1972 (ISHL) and the Workmen's Accident Compensation Insurance Law of 1947 (WACIL). The LSL prohibits discrimination in working conditions because of the nationality of workers.

In case of industrial accidents, workers are entitled to various benefits under the compulsory insurance system of the WACIL, such as medical benefits, temporary disability, physical disability benefits, survivors' benefits, funeral expenses, and injury and disease compensation benefits. Insurance fees are paid solely by employers; workers are automatically entitled to benefits whether or not the employer has paid the fees. Workers who have met with an industrial accident must apply for benefits at the Labor Inspection Office and the employer is obliged to submit evidence on the accident. In the case of illegal foreign workers, the Labor Inspection Office must refrain from reporting to the Immigration Office, at least until the accident investigation is complete. According to the administration guidelines set out by the Labor Ministry, the Labor Inspection Office will report illegal employment to the Immigration Office only in cases of serious violations of the protective labor law; such prosecution or order to prohibit employment against the employer is to be initiated if a number of illegal foreign workers are involved.

In addition to the minimum benefits provided under the WACIL, workers are entitled to additional compensation based on the employer's liability of torts or employment contracts. In such civil lawsuits involving foreign workers, the amount of damages is often controversial: whether the damages should be calculated based on the economic level of Japan or of the worker's home country. For example, in the case of an accident involving a Pakistani, the Higher Court sustained a District Court decision which calculated the worker's possible income for the first 3 years at the Japanese level and thereafter at the Pakistani level (Bobby Macsudo *v.* Kaisinsha, Tokyo District Court, 24 September 1992, 618 *Rohan* 15). The court's attitude is still not fixed, since decision in cases of traffic accidents are divided, some calculating lost income on the Japanese level, some on the home country level.

In the case of an individual with a trainee's visa, the WACIL is, in principle, not applied because he or she is not supposed to "work" as an employee. However, regardless of the kind of visa, if there is *de facto* employment instead of training the WACIL could be formally applied. In any case, trainees are entitled to civil law damages against training institutions, which are required to carry commercial nonlife insurance. For trainees in general, see below, under Education.

Pensions

Registered foreigners between 20 and 60 years of age are covered by the Basic Pension Scheme under the 1982 Amendment of the National Pension Law of 1959, which abolished the requirement of citizenship. Those employed by enterprises subject to the Welfare Pension Law of 1947 are covered by the Welfare Pension Scheme. However, most foreign workers are not actually entitled to pensions because 25 years of affiliation with the scheme is required for eligibility. However, pensions for survivors and handicapped persons are not subject to this requirement.

In the case of Welfare Pensions, foreigners waste the fees they pay in, because they are compulsorily collected and foreigners are often not entitled to a pension, mostly because of their brief period of membership in the plan. However, the law was amended in 1994 so that they can receive a lump-sum payment upon application within 2 months of leaving Japan.

Health Insurance

All residents of a local community, including foreigners, except those living in Japan less than 1 year, are covered by the National Health Insurance Law (NHIL) of 1958, amended in 1986 to abolish the citizenship requirement. They must make application and pay fees at the local community offices. Those employed by private employers with more than five employees, who are subject to the Health Insurance Law (HIL), are entitled to better benefits than those covered only by the NHIL. However, since illegal foreign workers do not join the NHI scheme, nor do their employers pay fees under the HIL, payment of such illegal foreign workers' medical costs is becoming a serious issue. Doctors and hospitals are beginning to refuse to accept foreign patients without proof of health insurance, particularly after their bills become overdue. Local communities and volunteer groups are trying to help such foreigners, but there seems to be no solution if the unpaid medical cost is very large. This issue should be handled as a part of livelihood protection (see below).

On 19 May, 1995, a Health and Welfare Ministry panel submitted a report to the Ministry proposing that the state allow foreigners living illegally in Japan to join the health insurance plan if they are regularly employed. Based on the proposal, the Ministry plans to review related systems and laws, such as the Health Insurance Law, with a view to their revision. The report urges the state to provide financial assistance to local governments to help hospitals recover their costs in cases where illegal immigrants die following treatment.[2]

Employment Insurance

There is no requirement for citizenship under the Employment Insurance Law of 1974. However, a visa with a work permit is issued only for employment at a particular job, not for general employment. In other words, foreigners with such visas are not supposed to seek work and therefore are not "unemployed" in the sense that they are entitled to unemployment benefits. Upon their request employers make an application at the Public Employment Office for cancellation of their qualification to be insured, and fees already paid in are reimbursed.

Livelihood Protection

The Livelihood Protection Law of 1950 in principle applies only to "Japanese people". But recognized refugees and registered foreigners living in poverty without protection or assistance from their home country's representatives are covered on a temporary basis under the 1954 administrative guidelines of the Ministry of Welfare. However, there are apparently limits to the protection this law can afford to the growing number of overstayers.

EDUCATION

College students may obtain student visas by applying at a Japanese delegation in their home countries, submitting certificates of their student qualifications. A certificate will be issued by the local immigration office upon receiving an application with a copy of the college's letter of acceptance, the applicant's *curriculum vitae,* evidence of financial condition, and other documents related to the intended study, with a written statement by a guarantor. A pre-college student visa is issued to foreign students who study at a high school, professional or technical school, through similar documentation.

Students receive a 1-year or 6-months visa (usually for 1 year) and pre-college students receive a 3-month, 6-month or 1-year visa (usually for 6 months). As already mentioned, either may obtain permission from the Ministry of Justice to work up to 4 hours a day; only college students are allowed to work up to 8 hours a day during the summer. At the end of 1993 there were about 60 000 students and more than 44 000 pre-college students in Japan; the Ministry of Labor estimates that about 60 percent of them were working and could be disguised workers. Many of the pre-college students in particular study at Japanese language schools, including some questionable ones that lend legitimacy to disguised workers.

Thus the Immigration Office rather carefully investigates applications for student visas, especially pre-college student visas. The visa can be renewed upon application with reasonable grounds for the purposes of study, but in the renewal procedure the Immigration Office carefully investigates the students' grades and attendance to discover disguised workers. If students are working without permission or beyond the permitted number of hours, they are liable to be charged with violation of the Immigration Law and even deported if they are found to be "entirely" working.

As already mentioned, at the end of their study in Japan a change of visa status from student to one of the 14 categories of working visa is possible if they can find appropriate employment in Japan based on the qualifications they gained during their education.

Foreign trainees are permitted to stay with special trainee visas (trainees entering Japan during 1993 totaled about 40 000). With this type of visa they are not supposed to engage in regular employment, and thus are not permitted to receive wages. But they are permitted to receive a stipend for housing, food, teaching materials and daily necessities. In order to avoid their being disguised workers, they are accepted only under certain conditions: (1) they must be older than 18 years; (2) their aim must be to gain a skill, technique or knowledge which they are unable to get in their home country; (3) they must return to the home country ready to work at a job which requires the skill, technique or knowledge gained during their stay in Japan; (4) the skill, technique or knowledge gained through training must not be acquired by mere repetition of the same activities; and (5) training must be conducted under the leadership of regular employees with more than 5 years' experience. In addition, trainees may be accepted only by certain qualified enterprises. Such an enterprise (1) is permitted to accept a number of trainees up to 5 percent of the number of its regular employees; (2) is required to provide housing and teaching facilities for trainees and the training staff; (3) must have employees responsible for the care of foreign trainees; (4) must be responsible for industrial accidents by being insured against damages in case of death, injury or illness of trainees; and (5) must meet the ISHL requirements applying to training facilities. These requirements do not apply to training operated by certain institutions such as a local community, Chamber of Commerce or other public entity, including international organizations.

As shown above, trainees are not supposed to be employed and thus the employment law is not, in principle, applicable. However, if trainees are in fact working and are actually-disguised workers, they fall under the protection of the employment law, and employment rights and benefits will apply. Of course, at the same time they could be regarded as violating the ICA; thus they face the contradiction of either being protected by the employment law and risking admission of their illegal status, or being protected under the ICA but giving up their rights and benefits under the employment law.

As a result of the increase in the number of foreigners living in Japan, the lack of a policy to meet the educational needs of their children is becoming a serious issue. According to a recent survey undertaken by the Ministry of Education, there are more than 10 000 children of foreign resident workers in need of Japanese-language instruction. Altogether these children speak some 48 different languages. The survey also showed that the number of schools accommodating such students has more than doubled over the past few years. This means that foreigners with children are now spread throughout the country, whereas they were previously concentrated in the metropolitan regions. In the past, education of such children was taken care of in the small number of schools in which they were concentrated, under the initiative of local communities. But now the Ministry of Education should be responsible for coping with their needs on a more national scale, including special language instruction. So far, the Ministry has only designated a facility to train teachers and compile teaching materials for foreign children, and the overall effort remains at the formative stage.

CRIMINAL ACTIVITY

The Justice Ministry's 1994 White Paper on Crime had emblazoned across its cover, under the main title, the words "Internationalization of Crime and Criminals." Nearly a third of the report's 437 pages were devoted to crimes attributed to foreigners. Arrests of foreign nationals rose in 1993, reaching 12 182, an increase of 1375 over 1992; more than half of these people – 7276 – were short-term visitors. In that category, the number of arrests was more than five times that of 10 years earlier. Some of the crimes committed by foreigners are serious, accounting for 5.9 percent of the 1233 homicides and 6.8 percent of the 2466 felonious robberies in Japan, figures the Ministry points out are higher than the demographic ratio of foreigners to the native population. Foreigners accounted for 2.4 percent of the total 2 437 252 registered crimes in 1993, whereas they account for 1.06 percent of Japan's total population of 125 million.

In respect of criminal activities, language is also a serious issue. The number of interpreter-assisted court cases increased eightfold between 1989 and 1993, to 3524 in 1993, with as many as 25 languages being used. Today, courts register about 1050 interpreters for 35 languages throughout the country.[3] The language problem is not limited to court procedures; as soon as foreigners are arrested they face a serious language barrier. The official language in court is, of course, Japanese, and in prison a foreign language may be spoken during conversation with visitors only when the director of detention or the prison permits it. At police and prosecutors' offices there are few interpreters available. In June 1995 the Yokohama District Court began providing outlines of indictments in foreign languages to prosecuted foreigners. In the first case of this service, on 2 June the Court issued an outline in Chinese. At the time of writing, the Court is ready to provide such outlines in English, Korean and Spanish, as well as Chinese. This practice was begun in Yokohama District Court, in accordance with the policy of the Supreme Court, which intends to provide such service in the future in 20 languages, including Tagalog, Thai and Vietnamese. It has also provided sample forms to use in appointing lawyers, and subpoenas in foreign languages, to all the law courts.[4]

Lawyers defending suspects in custody may be accompanied by interpreters by submitting a form available at criminal courts. Persons other than lawyers are permitted to meet with the suspects only when an interpreter is available, and are thus sometimes precluded from doing so simply because of the lack of an interpreter. It is pointed out that correspondence with foreign suspects in custody is also disrupted by censorship by the detention director, because it is often slowed by the language barrier.

In court procedures the court has sole discretion as to whether the suspects are permitted to use an interpreter because of their inability to speak Japanese well. The law requires that interpreters must be able to make "the meaning of the court process" understandable; that is, they must have a command of the language that includes an understanding of legal terms. However, particularly in cases of an uncommon language, it is not easy to find enough qualified interpreters. A more serious problem due to the shortage of interpreters is the fact that the same person who worked as an interpreter during the police or prosecutor's investigation, who may have certain preliminary knowledge and therefore be prejudiced, may work again in the courtroom proceedings.

Foreigners enjoy the same legal rights as Japanese citizens in criminal procedures. However, it is pointed out that courts maintain a rather strict policy in permitting parole to foreigners. Except for those with diplomatic immunity, members of the US and UN armed forces and their families, foreigners are subject to Japanese criminal law and the jurisdiction of Japanese courts when the crime was committed in Japan; if they are sentenced to imprisonment they are imprisoned in Japan.

When a foreigner is forced to overstay his visa as a result of imprisonment or of being in custody, parole may not be denied by the court, as the foreigner could be put into immigration camp even if he or she were ultimately to receive a suspended sentence. In order to avoid such an inconvenience, an extension of the visa may be applied for at the Immigration Office. The visa-holder will not be treated as staying illegally until the criminal procedures are complete, since the Immigration Office normally waits to decide on the application for extension pending the court ruling.

Foreigners committing serious crimes, such as bodily injury resulting in death, leading to a sentence of longer than 1 year of imprisonment, and crimes related to drugs or prostitution, are to be deported. Special permanent residents will be deported only if they are sentenced to a life term, or longer than 7 years of imprisonment, and if the Minister of Justice finds the interests of Japan seriously impaired by the crime.

DEPORTATION

Foreigners are to be deported in cases of: (1) entry without permission; (2) illegal entry; (3) unqualified activities; (4) illegal overstay; and (5) crimes and other disorderly activities specified in Article 24, Section 4 of the ICA. The Minister of Justice makes a decision on deportation based on an examination and interview by immigration officers. During 1991 a total of 35 536 notices of deportation were issued, and in only 393 of these cases, as a result of examinations and interviews, were special residence permissions granted for humanistic reasons, mostly to those who had been living in Japan since before the end of the Second World War, or to their descendants. Foreigners may come to court to challenge the legality of a notice or decision of deportation, or to suspend enforcement of the notice. During the 5 years between 1986 and 1991, 36 of the former and 31 of the latter cases were brought to the courts. In the former, plantiffs lost in six cases, 28 cases were withdrawn, and two were pending at the end of the year. In the latter, the plaintiffs lost 19 cases, won three, partly won eight, and one was withdrawn.

More than 95 percent of those deported (35 017 out of the total 36 275 deported during 1991) left Japan at their own expense. A few were returned by the agencies that had brought them. Groups of foreigners who came without permission, including disguised refugees and the small number who had a mental disease, refused to leave or were without means of transport, were deported at government expense (Homusho, 1993: 112ff).

COMMUNITY LIFE

Public housing facilities are now available to foreigners, provided they meet the same requirements as Japanese citizens, such as income level and family makeup, depending upon the type of such facilities. A public condominium may be purchased only by permanent residents who have lived in Japan longer than a certain period (1 year, in the case of the City of Tokyo). Public loans for purchasing housing facilities are also available to foreigners.

However, private owners and real-estate agencies sometimes refuse to rent or even to show a house or room to foreigners, offering reasons or excuses such as the language barrier, the possibility of their moving out while owing rent, different living styles, and so on. The Tokyo Metropolitan government in 1992 introduced a provision in its housing ordinance to the effect that it will endeavor to enlighten landlords and related persons to avoid discrimination due to age, handicaps, nationality or other situations of renters or applicants. As recently as June 1994, the Osaka District Court laid down a pioneering decision which ordered payment of damages by a landlord who refused to rent an apartment to a Korean resident because of his nationality. In this case the court held the landlord responsible, but not the realtor or the Osaka Metropolitan government.[5] In another case the Tokyo District Court awarded damages to a South Korean resident against a golf club operator who refused him membership on the grounds of his nationality.[6] Appropriate legal remedies against discrimination available to foreigners will be discussed below.

Foreigners are excluded from employment in local government offices except in certain job categories. Such exceptions are different from one community to another. The general principle is based on the assumption that such public positions involving administration, command of authority and participation in decision-making should be exclusively reserved to Japanese citizens. Thus in most communities foreigners are accepted only in teaching positions (professors, teachers), medicine (doctors, dentists, nurses, X-ray technicians, nutritionists, midwives, etc.), transportation, technical jobs and the like, although some communities have recently been expanding the list of jobs available to foreigners.

Also there is a trend to permit suffrage to foreigners on the local community level. According to a survey by the Korean Residents' Union in Japan (*Mindan*) in 1994, more than a hundred local bodies, including nine prefectural assemblies, adopted nonbinding resolutions urging voting rights for non-Japanese residents in local elections. The Kawasaki city government announced in October 1994 that in fiscal 1995, as an experimental measure, it will establish a panel of non-Japanese residents, similar to those set up by local governments in France and Germany, to give them a voice in local affairs.[7]

The Home Affairs Ministry, which is in charge of local elections, is inclined toward a negative view of this trend, pointing to the legal question of the concept of "people" (*kokumin*) who are guaranteed suffrage by Article 15 of the Constitution (see above). However, there is another provision in the Constitution, Article 93, which gives the right to elect governers, mayors and assembly members of a locality to "residents" (*jyumin*) of the community. The Supreme Court laid down in its decision (3rd Bench, 28 February 1995) that Article 15 guarantees voting rights only to *kokumin*, and thus the provision does not apply to foreigners. This decision also added that the term *jyumin* in Article 93 should be interpreted solely as meaning *nihon kokumin* (Japanese citizens) and thus also does not apply to foreigners. The media paid much attention to this decision because it indicated that the Constitution does not exclude the possibility of giving voting rights through legislation to those foreigners closely related to the local community, including those with permanent residential status.[8]

EQUAL RIGHTS UNDER JAPANESE LAW

In recent years Japan has been criticized from outside, particularly by the American media, as being racist and sexist, mainly because of the careless utterances of some politicians[9] and the discriminatory employment practices of some Japanese enterprises doing business in the United States.[10] At the same time, inside Japan, foreigners seeking employment and those already living in Japan complain of discriminatory treatment, particularly in employment and housing. This is not the place for a full discussion of equal rights under Japanese law, which the author has done elsewhere (Hanami, 1991).

To sum up, Japanese and American laws are similar in regard to the basic principles of equality under the law. Article 14 of the Constitution of Japan sets forth the principle of equality regardless of "race, creed, sex, social status or family origin," a statement almost identical with Title VII of the American Civil Rights Act of 1964 prohibiting discrimination because of race, color, religion, sex or national origin. Both cover all kinds of discrimination based on race (color), creed (religion), sex, social status and family (national) origin. However, the similarity ends there.

There is a significant difference in how effectively anti-discrimination laws and remedies against discrimination are enforced in the United States and Japan. In the United States, Title VII established an effective enforcement mechanism, particularly in the field of employment, through the Equal Employment Opportunity Commission (EECC) and court procedures; in Japan, except for the rather abstract legal principles of the Constitution, there are no effective enforcement mechanisms for anti-discrimination laws. The sole substantial statute in the field, the Equal Employment Opportunity Act (EECA) of 1985, which covers only sex discrimination in employment, has established only a mediation agency. Thus in Japan civil courts have no authority to issue enforcement orders enjoining discriminatory treatment, or to order specific performance, not to mention ordering affirmative action. Courts may order only recovery of damages based on the legal theory of torts, and punitive damages is not a notion recognized by Japanese courts. As already mentioned, the LSL prohibits discrimination in working conditions because of the nationality of workers; this prohibition is enforced, and penalties exacted, by the Labor Standards Inspection Office. But the LSL prohibits only a narrow range of discrimination in working conditions; there are no prohibitions against discrimination in recruitment, hiring, job assignment and promotion.

The EEOA also prohibits sex discrimination only in working conditions, training, company welfare and termination.[11]

As a result, there are no laws that effectively cope with serious discrimination in the form of job segregation resulting from Japan's labor market structure, in which traditionally only Japanese males are regular employees, with better working conditions and strong job security, while women, minorities and foreigners are mostly employed in auxiliary jobs – temporary, part-time and contract employees, with inferior working conditions and no job security.

To summarize, for a non-immigration country Japan's immigration law, particularly its acceptance of foreign workers, is not particularly restrictive. In what numbers, and at what rate of inflow, should Japan accept foreign labor? For what kinds of labor and under what conditions should it accept such workers – as a temporary work force, as permanent residents, or even as immigrants? All these questions are matters for policy consideration.

At the same time, how foreign workers should be treated once they are accepted and issued work permits, is a legal question. As seen above, the general Japanese law relating to the legal status of foreigners is not particularly discriminatory. However, the most serious legal problem in the Japanese law granting equality is not the legal principle or the legal text, but its application and enforcement, and the remedies available to victims of discrimination. What is most needed is a statute that would provide courts with the power to enforce the principle of equality in general, and for foreigners in particular, in the fields of housing and employment, at least as a first step, later to include education and other community services, and finally, suffrage.

NOTES

1. In these countries migrants are accepted only in the following higher-qualified categories, except in accordance with other standards such as family relationship or investment: in France, university professors, teachers in specified high-level institutions, researchers at highly qualified research institutes and high-ranking managers of enter-

prises; in England, qualified professionals, managers, specified occupations with higher or rare qualifications, experienced workers at hotels or restaurants as high-ranking managers with longer than 2 years of training; in the United States, professionals or persons with rare ability in science and skilled and unskilled workers in undersupplied fields (Koyokaihatu Centre, 1991: 285ff).

2. *The Japan Times*, 22 May 1995.
3. *The Japan Times*, 28 October 1994.
4. *Asahi Shinbun*, 6 June 1995.
5. *Asahi Shinbun*, 18 June 1994.
6. *Asahi Shinbun*, 24 March 1995; *The Japan Times*, 24 March 1995.
7. "Suffrage for foreigners urged," *The Japan Times*, 31 October 1994.
8. Supreme Court, III Bench, 2 February 1995, 49 *Hanrei Jiho* 1523.
9. Several high-ranking Japanese politicians, including former Prime Minister Y. Nakasone and former Minister of Foreign Affairs M. Watanabe, have in recent years made a series of bantering remarks implying that the high crime rates and low efficiency of American society are caused by the presence of ethnic minorities. These careless comments by unsophisticated politicians were picked up by American correspondents and contributed to the anti-Japan campaign by the American media in the early 1990s.
10. In the early 1990s, a number of Japanese subsidiaries in the United States were accused of racial, sexual and age discrimination. This trend was highlighted by the series of public hearings held by the Employment and Housing Subcommittee of the US House of Representatives Government Operations Committee in 1991 and 1992.
11. The EEOA does not prohibit discrimination in recruitment, hiring, promotion, or job assignment, but introduced employers' obligations to "endeavor" not discriminate in such manners. As a result the law has been ineffectual in reducing job segregation by sex ever since its implementation in 1986 (see Hanami, 1991).

REFERENCES

Hanami, Tadashi (1991), "Discrimination in the U.S. and Japan – From a Legal Viewpoint," *The Journal of American and Canadian Studies*, pp. 1–31.

Homusho Nyuukoku Kanrikyoku (ed.) (1993), *Heisei 4 Nenban Syutunyuukoku Kanri* [Immigration Control, 1992 edn] (Tokyo: Okurasyou Insatsukyoku).

Iguchi, Y. and Koyama, M. (1993), "Report on SOPEMI" (Tokyo: unpublished paper).

Koyokaihatu Center (1991), *Gaikokujin Rodosha Mondai Shiryoshu* [Data on Issues of Foreign Labor] (Tokyo: Koyokaihatu Centre).

9 The Legal Rights of Citizens and Aliens in the United States

Peter H. Schuck

The United States is not a nation-state like Japan. Instead, it is a state of diversities. These diversities multiply and ramify across every dimension of American social life as religious, racial, ethnic, ancestral, linguistic, economic and regional differences in turn engender other enduring diversities of a political and cultural nature. Occasionally, an ultraconservative politician like Pat Robertson or Pat Buchanan seeks to deny this fact by insisting that the United States is a Christian nation with English or European roots. To the vast majority of Americans, however, these narrow ethnocentric definitions deny what common observation confirms – the extraordinary, multidimensional, polyglot composition of the American "family." Immigration has always driven this diversity. It will do so even more powerfully in the future.

In this paper, I focus on the legal rights and statuses of various categories of immigrants and aliens once they are in the United States – what has been called "immigrant policy" – and the way in which the events of the 1980s and 1990s have shaped these rights and statuses. The first section provides necessary context for the discussion that follows; the next discusses the legal rights of US citizens, legal resident aliens, refugee and asylum claimants, and illegal aliens. The final section explores four issues bearing on aliens' rights, issues that are now being intensely debated in the United States and were the subject of major Legislative changes enacted in 1996. These are: (1) the treatment of aliens who commit crimes in the United States; (2) aliens' rights to public benefits; (3) the allocation of immigration-related costs between different levels of government; and (4) the significance of citizenship.

THE LEGAL AND POLICY CONTEXT

This section summarizes four aspects of the legal and policy context: the demographic changes that immigration is spawning; the state of public opinion about immigration, which ultimately frames and shapes the legal and policy responses to these changes; the historical evolution of the immigration control system in the United States; and the current form of that system.

Demographics

Immigration is producing profound demographic changes in the United States.[1] During the last decade, the number of new immigrants (legal and illegal) exceeded those in any other decade in American history, including the 1905–14 period when 10.1 million immigrants were admitted. From 1987 to 1996, approximately 10 million immigrants were legally admitted, but several million more came or remained in the United States illegally during the decade, and an estimated 5 million of them were resident at the end of 1996.[2]

The level of legal admissions remains high. Not counting the almost 2.7 million aliens legalized under the amnesty program (who by 1994 had little inflationary effect on the admissions numbers), 915 000 were admitted in 1996, a large increase over the 720 000 admitted in 1995, and the 804 000 in 1994. As for emigration, an estimated 200 000 Americans leave the United States more or less permanently each year (Warren and Kraly, 1985; Dunn, 1994). Today, almost 10 percent of the US population – more than 24 million people – are foreign-born. This fraction is well below the 14 percent share in the first decade of this century, and remains somewhat below the share of foreign-born today in France, Germany and Canada, but it has nearly doubled since 1970.

Because immigrants tend to be younger and have higher fertility rates than the native-born, this proportion is rising steadily; immigrants now account for more than one-third of the population growth in the United States. This may significantly alter the racial and ethnic composition of the population, not only in states like California but in the nation as a whole, although it will have relatively little effect on the nation's median age (Espenshade, 1994). New studies by the

US Census Bureau predict that by the year 2020, whites will shrink to 78.2 percent of the total population, people of Hispanic descent (most of whom call themselves white) will increase to 15.7 percent, blacks will increase to 13.9 percent, Asians and Pacific Islanders will increase to 6.9 percent, and Native Americans will increase to 0.9 percent. These changes, moreover, are occurring even faster than the Census Bureau had only recently predicted (Roberts, 1994; *New York Times*, 1994a)

Public Attitudes

Almost all Americans favor some restrictions on immigration. The principal public debates center on the questions of how much immigration should be permitted, the appropriate criteria and mix for whatever immigration is permitted, and the moral and policy justifications for these criteria. Virtually all Americans want stronger enforcement of existing restrictions, and most also favor reducing legal immigration below current levels, which in 1995 totaled 720 461 aliens admitted as legal permanent residents.[3] In 1996 Congress considered a number of proposals for restrictions on legal immigration, ranging from modest adjustments to major reductions, but these proposals were defeated.

Although those who favor restrictions are commonly seen as monolithic in their views, they are actually a diverse group motivated by different emotions, principles, and interests, some of which are misrepresented in public debate. In order to understand restrictionists' views, it is useful to distinguish broadly among four ideological positions, which I call xenophobia, nativism, principled restrictionism, and pragmatic restrictionism. Although these positions can be distinguished analytically, they are often conflated in the political debate over immigration policy. This conflation occurs both because advocates of different positions may advance similar policy proposals and justifications and because conflating them may confer rhetorical and political advantage on particular groups in the intense policy debate.

Although I focus here on restrictionist views, the diversity of expansionist positions should also be noted. Some (like the author) favor moderate increases in legal immigration but tighter controls on illegal aliens. Principled expansionists – libertarians, some economists, and the editorial page of the *Wall Street Journal* – assert that essentially open borders will maximize individuals' rights to engage in voluntary transactions with other individuals and otherwise to do as they like; government, they believe, should not limit these rights by impeding such transactions. Pragmatic expansionists, including many agricultural and other business interests seeking cheap labor or skills in short supply, ethnic groups desiring more members in the United States, and human rights organizations advocating larger refugee quotas, also favor increased immigration.

Xenophobia is an undifferentiated fear of foreigners or strangers as such. Who counts as a foreigner or stranger, of course, depends on the domain of one's primary reference group, which is often much smaller than the nation-state. It may be that the sources of xenophobia are congenital, reflecting some deeply embedded, universal feature of human psychology and identity by which individuals seeks to distance themselves from those whom they define as "others" or "strangers". Fortunately, most Americans seem capable of overcoming or "unlearning" this fear as they are exposed to those outside their primary group. In this sense, the scope of xenophobia – the domain of perceived "otherness" – seems to be contracting over time.

One might predict, then, that the development of the so-called global village through advanced communications and transportation technologies and the integration of the world economy would tend to homogenize cultures and reduce the fear of otherness on which xenophobia feeds. No doubt this has occurred to some extent. Public attitudes toward Asians, for example, have grown markedly more favorable and less fearful than they were several decades ago, even as heightened economic competition between the United States and Japan has strained the newer tolerance. On the other hand, the advance of transcendent, cosmopolitan values can engender a sharp backlash in the more parochial enclaves where xenophobia tends to flourish. Sudden migration flows can inflame these attitudes, as has occurred recently in the United States and especially in Europe, including Germany. Some people in these enclaves engage in violence against those whom they view as foreign because of their race, language, appearance, or behavior. This may explain some of the crimes committed in recent years by blacks against Korean-Americans and other immigrant minorities in Los Angeles and Washington, DC. In general, however, the level of xenophobia in the United States has steadily declined and is probably not a significant force today.

Nativism is a more discriminating, specific position than xenophobia. Nativists believe in the moral or racial superiority of the indigenous stock. (In the US context, this refers not to the indigenous stock, which was, of course, Native American, but to the Anglo-Saxons who became demographically, politically, and culturally dominant.) Nativism holds that members of this stock alone exemplify the distinctive values that the nativist associates with the nation-state. The nativist insists that immigrant cultures are inimical to these values and, at least in that sense, inferior. Nativism, then, is a species of racism; it maintains that cultural values inhere in particular racial, ethnic, or national groups and cannot be learned. It demands not only exclusion of the inferior groups but leads ineluctably to doctrines that justify nativist domination of the members of the other groups who are already inside the country.

Nativism, unlike xenophobia, has been a perennial theme in US history; it is as constant as the motifs of welcome, succor, and assimilation mentioned earlier. It has erupted with special force during periods of social upheaval and economic crisis. But even in more stable times, groups of Americans have organized politically for the explicit purposes of ostracizing, excluding, and repatriating immigrants. In his classic study of American nativism during the late nineteenth and early twentieth centuries, John Higham (1970) showed that nativism has appealed to all strata of society at different times. But it has especially attracted those whose economic and social positions are the least secure and who search most desperately for simple explanations, scapegoats, and conspiracies to assuage their painful sense of status vulnerability.

American nativism has assumed many repellent forms. Before (and even after) the Civil War, prominent Americans, including President Abraham Lincoln, proposed sending US blacks back to Africa. Nativist premises have led the federal and state governments to enact harshly discriminatory laws, among them the Chinese Exclusion acts, the national origins quotas, and anti-Japanese policies such as the Gentleman's Agreement and World War II internment. Nativist groups have fomented violence against Catholics, Jews, and other immigrant groups.

As with xenophobia, however, nativism – as distinct from other restrictionist theories – is probably not a significant force in US politics today. Although the question is controversial among immigration scholars and the answer is far from clear (Schuck, 1966, n.18, 1996a), I believe that the support for Proposition 187 in California in 1994 is best understood as an expression of widespread public frustrations with the failures of federal immigration enforcement and the perceived erosion of US sovereignty and control over its borders and demographic destiny, not as a spasm of nativist hatred (Schuck, 1995). The openly nativist candidacy of Patrick Buchanan during the 1992 and 1996 Republican primary campaigns indicates that it does survive and is capable of being mobilized to some extent; the public's decisive rejection of that candidacy, however, suggests that nativism is no longer widespread, even in the conservative wing of the Republican Party. Indeed, some of the most prominent members of that wing, such as the House's Richard Army of Texas, vice presidential candidate Jack Kemp, and commentator William Bennett, are openly pro-immigration, while others such as Speaker Newt Gingrich claim to favor immigration.

In contrast to xenophobia and nativism, *Principled restrictionism* is a commonly held position in the United States today. Principled restrictionism is driven neither by a generalized fear of strangers nor by a belief that only certain categories of Americans are capable of civic virtue. Instead, it is the view that current levels of immigration threaten particular policy goals or values advocated by the restrictionist.

Today, the leading principled restrictionists in the United States include some advocates of environmental and demographic controls who maintain that zero (or even negative) population growth is essential to preserve ecological stability and that both the number of immigrants and their high fertility rates threaten that stability. The leading example here is the Federation for American Immigration Reform (FAIR). Some of FAIR's board members are environmental and population control activists, labor union professionals, demographers, and politicians – for example, presidential candidate and former Colorado governor Richard Lamm – who in other areas subscribe to liberal public policy positions.[4]

Many principled restrictionists also express a concern for the effects of contemporary immigration on the interests of low-income Americans. They believe, with some labor economists, that today's levels of immigration – especially illegal (and some legal) migration by low-skill Mexican and Central American workers – displace native workers from jobs, drain scarce welfare benefits intended primarily for American indigent citizens, and consume already overburdened public services (primarily education and health care). Some also point to the adverse effects that large numbers of non-voting aliens (legal and illegal) have on the political effectiveness of Mexican Americans and other new immigrant groups.

Some principled restrictionists place greater emphasis on values such as national solidarity, linguistic unity, religious tolerance, or cultural coherence. These themes are commonly sounded in congressional speeches, organization newsletters, and private conversations. An example of such a group is US English, founded by the late senator (and linguist) S. I. Hayakawa. These principled restrictionists appear to be more conservative in their social policy views than those of the FAIR stripe, but, again, they are well within the mainstream of US politics.

Unlike nativism, which most Americans regard as a disreputable position, principled restrictionism contributes significantly to the overt debate about US immigration policy. Because the etiquette of acceptable public discourse forces nativists' views underground, nativists may seek political legitimacy and influence by publicly couching their racist views in the less-objectionable rhetoric of principled restrictionism. Thus it is difficult to determine the extent to which principled restrictionist positions are in fact motivated by nativist and racist views (Schuck, 1996a: 1965, n. 14).

Ideally, only the merits of a speaker's position would be relevant in the public debate over immigration, not the speaker's motives. This debate, however, usually proceeds as if motives matter a great deal. Many immigration advocates seek to stigmatize their restrictionist opponents, whether principled or pragmatic, by tarring them with the nativist brush. The reverse is also true: restrictionists deride those favoring more liberal immigration policies as unpatriotic "one-worlders" and "open-borders" advocates. Principled restrictionists are especially vulnerable to this tactic; they cannot easily refute such charges even when they are false.

Pragmatic restrictionism is a common perspective on immigration levels. It resembles principled restrictionism in the policy positions that it supports, but it differs in one important respect. Where principled restrictionists see the threat that immigration poses to their preferred goals or values as inherent in the nature and fact of immigration, pragmatic restrictionists view such conflicts as contingent, not inevitable.

Pragmatists believe, for example, that immigration's actual effects on population, the environment, national unity, cultural consensus, and so forth are empirical questions whose answers depend on a variety of factors. They do not oppose immigration in principle or in general. They may even be prepared to support it if they can be persuaded, for example, that immigrants actually create jobs rather than taking them away from native workers, that they are mastering the English language without undue delay, and that they do not exploit the welfare system or otherwise threaten social cohesion. Although certain labor unions, taxpayer groups, and other interest groups may have closed their minds on these factual questions, the pragmatic restrictionist remains open to persuasion by contrary evidence.

Most Americans, I suspect, are pragmatic restrictionists, although one cannot be certain. That is, they favor lower levels of immigration but are open to argument and evidence about what those levels should be and about what immigration's actual effects are. Thus their views about the wisdom and level of restriction are capable of being changed. In a recent study, political scientists Paul Sniderman and Thomas Piazza examined public attitudes toward race-oriented policy issues and found them notably tractable to counter-argument.[5]

The evidence just cited did not specifically concern attitudes toward immigration policy. But if Americans are open to argument and evidence with respect to the explosive issues surrounding race and welfare, issues on which they presumably have already developed firm attitudes, it must be even truer of immigration about which (as I discuss immediately below) they are already profoundly ambivalent. Attitudes toward aliens, of course, are not the same as attitudes toward either racial minorities or people on public assistance. Nevertheless, two central facts about American society – that white Americans' hostility toward blacks and other racial minorities has declined sharply and that public benefits for the poor sharply increased between the 1960s and the enactment of the 1996 Welfare Reform Law (Schuck, 1996a: 2010–11) – suggest that negative attitudes toward aliens as (as distinguished from attitudes concerning the optional number who should be admitted to the US) have probably softened as well. I have already noted the markedly more favorable views to Asians since 1965, when they began immigrating to the United States in large numbers.

Surveys of public opinion that specifically inquire about immigration tend to support my claim that most Americans are pragmatic restrictionists (Espenshade and Hempstead, 1996). Survey data about many public policy issues often seem puzzling or even incoherent, of course, and those concerning attitudes toward immigration are no exception. These data are sensitive to the respondents' own perceptions about economic and social conditions, the specific wording of the question being asked, and the respondents' willingness to share strong, sometimes stigmatized feelings with interviewers who are strangers (Lewontin, 1995). In part, however, the data are hard to interpret because of Americans' ambivalent views about immigration.[6]

Some of the evidence of ambivalent or conflicting American attitudes toward immigration may reflect this propensity to draw subtle but important distinctions. According to the survey data, for example, Americans like immigrants more than they like immigration, favor past immigration more than recent immigration, prefer legal immigrants to illegal ones, prefer refugees to other immigrants, support immigrants' access to educational and health benefits but not to welfare or Social Security, and feel that immigrants' distinctive cultures have contributed positively to American life and that diversity continues to strengthen American society today. At the same time, they overwhelmingly resist any conception of multiculturalism that discourages immigrants from learning and using the English language.[7]

One tension most deeply pervades current immigration policy debates: Americans treasure their immigrant roots yet believe that current immigration levels are too high. Anxiety about immigration, it seems, is aroused by the newer immigrant groups, a bias that a 1982 Gallup poll places in a revealing historical light. When asked about its views on the contributions of particular immigrant groups, the public gave the highest scores to precisely the groups that had been widely reviled in the nineteenth and early twentieth centuries; the lowest scoring groups were the newer arrivals (in 1982 Cubans and Haitians). Professor Rita Simon has captured this ambivalence in an arresting metaphor: "We view immigrants with rose-colored glasses turned backwards" (1995). The optimist might infer from this that 75 years hence the public will view today's newcomers – who by then may be seen as old, established groups – with the same solicitude and admiration now generally reserved for Italians, Jews, Slovaks, and other well-assimilated groups. The pessimist, of course, will reject this postdictive prediction, insisting that things really have changed for the worse.

When viewed over time, however, the polling evidence suggests that in attitudes toward immigration as in so many other areas, the more things seem to change, the more they stay the same. The public, it appears, has *always* thought that the immigration levels of their day were too high. Over the course of the past fifty years, Americans asked (in slightly different formulations) whether immigration levels should be increased, reduced, or kept the same have responded in remarkably similar ways. During that period, only 4–13 percent have favored an increase, while 33–66 percent have favored a decrease. In 1993 only 7 percent favored an increase, 61 percent favored a decrease, and 27 percent preferred no change.[8] The trend in attitudes has been toward greater negativity. In 1965, the percentage favoring reduced immigration began rising steadily until the late 1970s, then rose more sharply until the mid-1980s, then declined somewhat for several years, fluctuating until the early 1990s when it again rose sharply. Since about 1980, this attitudinal trend has tracked the trend in the unemployment rate very closely. Hence attitudes can and do change abruptly (Espenshade and Hempstead, 1996: 539, 557).

In sum, the survey data indicate that Americans are quite favorably disposed in principle to legal immigration and to cultural diversity but want less of it. They harbor concerns about the impact of immigration and diversity on specific aspects of American life, and also worry about how quickly and completely the newer immigrant groups can be assimilated. As I have noted, these concerns troubled earlier generations of Americans as well.

These data raise another intriguing question: if Americans are indeed ambivalent about immigration and desire even less *legal* immigration, how can we explain the adoption of the Immigration Act of 1990? This was a law, after all, that expanded immigration levels by about 40 percent and will continue those higher levels for the foreseeable future, a law that will thus maintain and perhaps even increase the ethnic and racial diversity of the immigration streams to the United States.[9] This puzzle only deepens when we note that Congress passed the 1990 act during a national and international economic recession, a time when virtually all other immigrant-receiving countries were moving to restrict normal immigration and limit asylum claiming. Why did these enormous anti-immigration pressures fail to convince Congress to follow suit, as so many restrictionists (principled and pragmatic alike) strongly urged it to do? And why did a strenuous restrictionist effort in 1996 fail to cut back these higher legal immigration levels even as it succeeded in restricting legal immigrants' procedual and substantive rights?

One answer is that restrictionist pressures, which often build up in particular regions and localities as a result of the high residential concentration of immigrants in a handful of states and localities, tend to dissipate somewhat when legislation is considered at the national level, where the US Constitution lodges exclusive jurisdiction over immigration policy. In 1995 two-thirds of the legal immigrants intended to settle in only six states: California, New York, Texas, Florida, New Jersey, and Illinois. Almost one in four hoped to live in either of two metropolitan areas, New York or Los Angeles (US Dept. of Justice, 1996: 8). The pronounced regionalization of immigration means that the majority of Americans (and their political leaders) who reside elsewhere only feel its effects on jobs, public service budgets, and cultural unity in an indirect, muted form. Public attitudes about desired immigration levels vary by region (Espenshade and Hempstead, 1996: 546, 548).

In addition (and not surprisingly), immigrant enclaves are in precisely those areas where the political groups with a powerful stake in increased immigration, such as growers, church groups, and ethnic organizations, are located. These groups, which enjoy excellent access to the mass media, are often strong enough to counteract the restrictionist pressures that concentrated immigrant populations generate.[10] For whatever reasons, national political leaders, media, prominent commentators, business executives, and other elite groups generally support immigration more than the general public does, and immigration policy tends to reflect their pro-immigration positions.[11]

The Evolution of the System of Immigration Control

For the first century of American history, the law was not much concerned with immigration. Apart from some state-enforced public health restrictions, US borders were essentially open to both entry and exit (with the notable exception of slavery). Migration patterns were shaped by economic, political, ethnic and religious developments, not by legal rules (Neuman, 1993).

In 1875, Congress enacted the first federal limitation on immigration (again, apart from laws dealing with the slave trade).[12] Anti-immigrant sentiment increased during subsequent years as immigration from southern and eastern Europe grew rapidly. In 1906, Congress passed a statute requiring English-language proficiency for naturalization, but failed to enact a literacy test for admission. In 1907, as immigration levels swelled, Congress established a national study group (the Dillingham Commission) to review the problem; its massive 1911 report recommended significant restrictions, but none was adopted for another decade. Meanwhile, Congress twice passed literacy requirements for admission, but Presidents Taft and Wilson, like Cleveland before them, vetoed the provisions. In 1917 Congress, reflecting the nationalist passion of the First World War, overrode Wilson's veto and enacted the literacy requirement, while also banning almost all Asian immigration. In 1921, Congress finally adopted the Dillingham approach, enacting a provisional but comprehensive scheme of immigration control. Three years later, this system was institutionalized in the Johnson–Reed legislation. This National Origins Act provided for an annual limit of 150 000 Europeans, a complete prohibition on Japanese immigration, and a system of quotas that favored migrants from the traditional source countries (primarily the British Isles, Germany and Scandinavia). Under these quotas, immigration to the United States remained relatively low but rising during the next four decades: 528 000 in the 1930s, 1 million in the 1940s, 2.5 million in the 1950s, and 3.3 million in the 1960s.

Under the powerful influence of the civil rights revolution, the national origins system was finally abandoned in 1965. Under the new law, Asian, African and Caribbean immigrants became eligible to seek admission, although both the Congress and the Johnson Administration predicted that few non-Europeans, especially Asians, would come. The 1965 law established many elements of what continues to be the structure of the legal immigration system today. These elements included identical per-country quotas and a categorical preference system that emphasized family unification and, to a much lesser degree, occupational skills and refugee status. In 1976 the system was changed to equalize the treatment of Eastern and Western Hemisphere countries, including Mexico, and in 1978 the the hemispheric quotas were combined into a single, global total of 290 000 visas per year. During the 1970s, legal admissions totaled 4.5 million, the highest since the second decade of the century. It was during this decade, moreover, that concern about illegal migration became a high-visibility political issue in the United States. Most of these migrants were Mexican agricultural workers who had been marooned in the mid-1960s when the long-standing Bracero program was terminated, and in the mid-1970s when the per-country limits were applied for the first time to Mexico.

The period since 1980, as we have seen, has witnessed an enormous increase in immigration levels. Continuing a trend generated by the 1965 law, the source country composition of the migration stream changed dramatically. Between 1985 and

1990, for example, only 8.9 percent of the legal immigrants came from Europe. In contrast, 34 percent were Asian and 54 percent (as well as the vast majority of illegal migrants) were from Mexico, Central America, South America and the Caribbean. In 1996, when the 1986 amnesty program had ceased dominating these statistics, the shares were 16, 34 and 37 percent, respectively (US Dept. of Justice, 1997). The five leading source countries for legal immigrants in 1996 were Mexico, the Philippines, India, Vietnam, and mainland China. The new immigrants' residential patterns in the United States are highly concentrated, with two thirds of the legal and amnestied immigrants settling in only six states: California (especially the Los Angeles area), New York, Texas, Florida, New Jersey and Illinois (US Department of Justice, 1994).

As immigration levels soared in the 1980s, so did the level of immigration-related political activity at the federal, state and local levels (Schuck, 1992). In the Refugee Act of 1980, Congress established for the first time a systematic legal structure for controlling refugee admissions and adjudicating refugee and asylum claims. Six years later, in the Immigration Reform and Control Act of 1986 (IRCA), Congress made sweeping changes in immigration enforcement and in admissions. On the enforcement side, it enacted an employer sanctions program that prohibited employers from hiring undocumented workers. The Immigration Marriage Fraud Amendments, passed just before IRCA, also bolstered enforcement by seeking to prevent aliens from using sham marriages to gain admission. Congress also adopted a number of criminal enforcement provisions relating to alien drug trafficking and other criminal conduct. Legislation enacted in the late 1980s was directed at criminal aliens.

On the admissions side, IRCA established several amnesty programs (for agricultural workers, other workers, and Cubans and Haitians) authorizing aliens in the United States illegally since 1 January 1982 to apply for temporary legal status, which could eventually lead to permanent legal status and citizenship. Of the 2.76 million who applied, 2.67 million were granted legal status. IRCA also created a temporary "diversity" program designed to favor European (especially Irish) immigrants who would not otherwise qualify for visas. These provisions, which ended up favoring both Irish and

Asian immigrants, were extended throughout the 1980s and in the 1990 Act. Finally, IRCA adopted a new anti-discrimination program, discussed in the following section, which was intended to protect legal Hispanic workers against the discrimination that might result from the imposition of sanctions on employers who hired illegals.

The Current System

Only 4 years later, Congress passed and President Bush signed the Immigration Act of 1990, the most far-reaching reform of immigration and naturalization law since 1965, which defines and governs almost all legal admissions under the current immigration and naturalization system. (Legislation enacted in 1996 changes the law relating to asylum claims, aliens convicted of crimes in the US, and the procedures for the deportation and exclusion [now consolidated into "removal" proceedings] of aliens.) This system is very complex, but four major elements can (with some necessary simplifications) be briefly summarized.

(1) Broadly speaking, three categories of aliens can be admitted: "immigrants", who enjoy the status of permanent resident aliens; "nonimmigrants", who are admitted under restrictions as to the purposes and duration of their visit; and "parolees", who despite their entry are treated legally as if they stood at the border seeking entry.

(2) The law establishes an overall cap on non-refugee admissions of 675 000 per year. This cap can be breached, however, if the number of "immediate relatives" (spouses, minor children, and parents of US citizens), who are exempt from this numerical cap, exceeds a certain level. There were 302 000 immediate relative admissions in 1996. The number of overseas refugees is fixed according to the procedures established by the 1980 Act, and asylees are not limited in number. In 1996, more than 128 000 refugees and asylees were adjusted to permanent legal status. Also exempt from this numerical cap were Amerasians, "diversity" admissions (from so-called "low-admission" countries), those legalized under IRCA, parolees from the former Soviet Union and Indo-China, and some others.

(3) The numerical ceiling of 675 000 is divided into three major categories of immigrants, each governed by its own intricate rules. These categories are: family-sponsored (480 000, further divided into four sub-categories with ceilings); employment-based (140 000, further divided into five sub-categories with ceilings); and diversity (55 000). Although the new system places somewhat greater emphasis than the earlier one did on employment-based admissions (and especially those with higher-level skills), the family-sponsored admissions (including the unlimited "immediate relatives") still account for over two-thirds of the total.

(4) Within the overall preference ceilings, every country is subject to a further annual ceiling of at least 25 620 with respect to family-sponsored and employment-based admissions. Diversity admissions are subject to a per-country annual ceiling of 3850. Chargeability to these ceilings depends on the immigrant's country of birth, not country of nationality.

THE LEGAL RIGHTS OF CITIZENS, LEGAL RESIDENTS, REFUGEE AND ASYLUM CLAIMANTS, AND ILLEGAL AND PRUCOL ALIENS

The institutional, legal and political contexts in which the rights of citizens and various categories of aliens are defined and enforced (and, all too often, violated) changed in a number of important ways during the 1980s. Together, these changes have given great prominence to the public debate over the character and extent of these rights.

During the 1980s a more cosmopolitan legal culture began to permeate the parochial bureaucratic culture of the INS. For a variety of reasons, immigration law began to shed its shadowy reputation as a backwater legal specialty of interest largely to marginal, low-status practitioners and the INS. More lawyers of demonstrated professional competence and high repute were attracted to the private, public-interest, and government sectors of immigration practice. Some of the elite law schools began to offer academic and clinical courses in immigration law. Legal scholars began to scrutinize the INS and immigration law more carefully. Publications devoted to monitoring and reporting on the INS and the courts' immigration decisions were established (Schuck, 1989a). An analogous change occurred during the 1980s in the federal courts, which have exclusive jurisdiction over immigration law (Schuck, 1984; Schuck and Wang, 1992). Abandoning much of their traditional deference to the INS, they were drawn into a more detailed supervision of the agency's administration of the law. They entertained a flood of immigration cases, which mirrored the rising immigration levels. Although the government won the vast majority of these cases, the courts did invalidate statutory provisions and INS procedures and policies with an alacrity that would have astonished an earlier generation of immigration lawyers.

Still, old habits are hard to change, especially in law, and the long tradition of judicial deference to Congress (as distinguished from deference to the INS) continues in matters of immigration policy. The Supreme Court has strongly reaffirmed this tradition in a number of its recent decisions.[13] Even so, the recent judicial assertiveness in immigration cases is unmistakable. Indeed, the courts are likely to engage in even closer constitutional review as Congress, driven by deep public anxieties about drug trafficking, smuggling, and terrorism, increasingly emphasizes the use of criminal sanctions against aliens. Many of the immigration enforcement provisions of the anti-terrorism law and other immigration reforms enacted in 1996, which are potentially far-reaching, are being challenged in the courts.

A third factor that has conditioned immigrants' rights, of course, is politics (Schuck, 1992). The forces favoring immigration restriction and those favoring immigration expansion are always in tension in the United States, and the balance of power changes over time. During much of the 1980s the interests that traditionally favor liberal immigration policies – primarily western growers and many business organizations – were joined by newer, less conventional allies: ethnic groups, religious organizations, libertarians, the influential *Wall Street Journal*, human-rights activists, and many politicians in both parties. These interests gained greater power at the expense of traditional restrictionists such as organized labor. Black civil rights organizations, which historically looked askance at immigration (Fuchs, 1990), joined the expansionist coalition. In many states and localities, opposition to US policies in Central America led many citizens with little interest in immigration policy to favor sanctuary for asylum claimants and to advocate other forms of non-cooperation with the federal immigration authorities, all in furtherance of immigrant rights and ultimately of expanded immigration through the legalization under the 1986 law of millions of unsuccessful asylum claimants and other illegals. As noted earlier, the 1990 act further increased immigration levels well into the future.

By the 1994 congressional campaign, the expansionist tide had receded as many erstwhile proponents of liberal immigration policies began to join restrictionists in demanding curtailment of the rights of illegal, and in some cases even legal, aliens.[14] This reversal was first evident in California, which was suffering from a protracted economic recession, but it became manifest on a national scale in 1996 with the enactment of three statutes – the Anti-Terrorism and Effective Death Penalty Act, the welfare reform legislation, and the Illegal Immigration Reform and Immigrant Responsibility Act – which sharply limited the procedural and substantive rights of both legal and illegal aliens under the federal immigration laws as well as their eligibility for many governmental benefits. These developments underscore the larger point that within the leeways permitted by the Constitution – and indeed beyond those leeways, as the legally doubtful Proposition 187 suggests (*League of United Latin American Citizens v. Wilson*, 908 F. Supp. 755 [C.D. Cal. 1995]) – immigrant rights are inevitably shaped by the forces of public opinion.

An important aspect of these changes in the political environment is the rapid expansion of the INS since the mid-1980s, a period when the federal government has been under intense budgetary pressures. The priority accorded to immigration enforcement has been so high that, despite these constraints, INS funding and staff have grown steadily. Today, the agency's annual budget is over $3 billion and it employs 26 000 employees.

Citizenship

As we saw earlier, US immigration law has experienced frequent and significant changes during the last three decades. In contrast, US citizenship law exhibits a remarkable stability.

Since the very first Congress enacted a naturalization statute in 1790, citizenship law has undergone few fundamental and enduring changes – with the notable exception of the Citizenship Clause of the Fourteenth Amendment, ratified in 1868.[15] The 1990 Act made relatively minor changes, streamlining the administration of the naturalization process and permitting the INS, and not just the backlogged courts, to administer the naturalization oath. Congress has also considered reducing the period of required residency from 5 to 3 years, the period required in Canada and several European states, but there seems to be little support for this change.

US citizenship can be obtained in three ways. The most common way – citizenship by birth in the United States – reflects the Anglo-American tradition of *jus soli* (although the United Kingdom no longer strongly adheres to it) and is protected by the Fourteenth Amendment's Citizenship Clause. (Customary exceptions to the *jus soli* rule exist; these include, for example, children born on foreign vessels and children of diplomatic personnel.) The courts' interpretation of the Citizenship Clause has long been deemed to extend that status to the native-born children of aliens who are in the country illegally or on a non-immigrant (temporary) visa. This extension has never been seriously questioned in the courts, although it has recently come under scrutiny, and in some cases criticism, by some politicians, commentators and scholars (Schuck and Smith, 1986a). This issue is discussed in the final section.

A second route to citizenship is through naturalization. In 1996, approximately 1.3 million individuals petitioned to naturalize, more than six times the number who petitioned only five years earlier, and the total is expected to approach 1.8 million in 1997. More than 446 000 immigrants were naturized in 1995, and 965 000 petitions were pending in March 1997. In order to naturalize, a permanent resident alien must have resided in the United States with that status continuously for 5 years; be of good moral character; demonstrate an ability to speak, read and write English; and demonstrate a basic knowledge of US government and history. More than 85 percent of all naturalizations take place under these general provisions, although some people are permitted to use less restrictive procedures. Spouses of American citizens can naturalize after only 3 years; children who immigrate with their parents can be naturalized more or less automatically (simply by obtaining a certificate) when their parents naturalize; and adopted children of US citizens can also naturalize in that fashion. Certain aliens who served with the American military during past wars may naturalize easily. Some individual or categorical naturalizations are effectuated directly by statute. As a result of both the dramatic increase in the number of applications for naturalization during the last few years and Republican Party allegations that the Clinton administration abused the naturalization laws in order to increase the number of voters for the 1996 election, Congress is likely to reconsider the legal requirements for naturalization.

An important social fact in the United States is that a large number of eligible aliens choose not to naturalize.[16] Indeed, an INS study of the cohort of aliens who immigrated to the United States in 1977 found that 54 percent had not naturalized by the end of 1995, 18 years later, when they had already been eligible for at least a decade. Moreover, most aliens who do naturalize do not apply until well after they become eligible; their median period of US residency is now 9 years. There are, however, important regional and country variations in speed of naturalization. Of those who naturalize, Asians and Africans tend to do it relatively quickly (7 and 6 years respectively),[17] while those from North America take longer (14 years). As for country-by-country variations, 65.4 percent of immigrants from the Soviet Union in the 1977 cohort had naturalized through 1995, while only 18.1 percent of the Canadians and 22.2 percent of the Mexicans had done so. There are also important differences in naturalization rates among immigrants from different countries within a given region (US Department of Justice, 1997).

Aliens who wish to naturalize are required to renounce any prior allegiance, which may or may not be effective in terminating that foreign citizenship. Because of this, dual (and even triple) citizenship is increasingly common in the United States due to the combination of the American *jus soli* rule with the various *jus sanguinis* rules of other countries. Although the US government does not favor dual citizenship, it nonetheless tolerates and legally protects such status (Neuman, 1995; Schuck, 1995c).

The third route to citizenship is through descent from one or more American parents. The principle of *jus sanguinis* is codified in the statute, which identifies a number of parentage categories, sometimes augmented by residency requirements, that confer elibility for statutory citizenship on children who are born abroad of American parents. Over time, Congress has liberalized these eligibility requirements.

US citizenship, once acquired, is almost impossible to lose without the citizen's express consent. Supreme Court decisions since the 1960s have severely restricted the government's power to denationalize a citizen for reasons of disloyalty, divided allegiance, or otherwise. Today, the government cannot prevail against a birthright citizen unless it can prove that the citizen specifically intended to renounce his or her citizenship. This standard is difficult to satisfy – as it should be. Relatively few denationalization proceedings are brought and the number of successful ones is probably declining. Denaturalization proceedings against citizens who procured citizenship by misrepresenting their backgrounds or through other illegality are largely directed against Nazi and Soviet persecutors, and under a 1988 decision of the Supreme Court, the standards that the government must satisfy to prevail are quite demanding (Kungys v. United States, 1988).

Resident Aliens

Until very recently, the differences in legal rights between legal permanent resident aliens (LPRs) and citizens in the United States were quite modest, more political than legal or economic. These differences, however, increased dramatically in 1996 when Congress, in a series of bipartisan votes, sharply reduced LPRs' legal rights. This issue is discussed at greater length in the section "Current Policy Issues", below.

Earlier, US courts had established that the constitutionality of government-imposed discriminations between citizens and aliens turned on whether the discrimination being challenged was imposed by the federal government or by a state, and in certain circumstances also on the strength of the justifications for the discrimination advanced by the enacting government. In several Supreme Court decisions during the 1970s, the Court held that Congress could exclude some LPRs from public benefits under Medicare (and presumably under other federal programs as well) but that the states could not do so (*Mathews v. Diaz*, 426 US 67 [1976]; *Graham v. Richardson*, 403

US 365 [1971]. Since then, the constitutional rationale for decisions restricting the states' power to discriminate may have changed. The Court originally seemed to view state law discriminations on the basis of alienage as a "suspect classification" like race, which would impose a very heavy, probably impossible, burden on the state to demonstrate that its interest in discriminating against aliens was "compelling" and narrowly tailored to achieve its purpose. But in subsequent cases, the Court seemed to favor a different constitutional theory, one based on the Supremacy Clause rather than the Equal Protection Clause. Stressing the dominant federal interest in regulating immigration, this "federal preemption" theory holds that a state cannot legislate about aliens if doing so could interfere with this federal interest. On the other hand, states may enact legislation that merely mirrors or reinforces federal immigration policy (Tribe, 1988). It seems to follow that federal law may constitutionally *require* the states to discriminate against legal aliens or *authorize* them to discriminate. In the 1996 Welfare Reform Law, which differentiates among benefit programs and between federal and state laws, the federal government did both.

Even before the 1996 law was enacted, some noteworthy differences in legal rights existed, and each of them remains. Three are political in nature: the right to vote, the right to serve on federal and many state juries, and the right to run for certain high elective offices and to be appointed to some high (and not-so-high) appointive ones. Each of these restrictions seems to be premised on one or more of the following assumptions: that aliens' political socialization is too fragmentary and embryonic to be trusted in matters of public choice; that confining political participation of this kind to citizens carries an important symbolic message about the value and significance of full membership; and that exclusion of aliens from such participation encourages them to naturalize as soon as possible (Schuck, 1989b).

Although aliens enjoyed the franchise in some states until 1926, when Arkansas repealed its law, only US citizens may exercise it today, a limitation that applies in virtually all countries, at least in national elections.[18] Tacoma Park, Maryland, and some other communities have granted aliens the right to vote in their local elections, and similar proposals have been advanced in some larger cities including Washington, DC, and Los Angeles. Some academic commentary supports such a reform as well (Rosberg, 1977; Raskin, 1993). However, extending the vote to aliens is highly unlikely.

The individual LPR (as distinct from immigrants' rights advocates) probably does not view this inability to vote or serve on juries as a significant, unfair deprivation. Aliens' inability to vote certainly limits their collective political influence *qua* aliens, but their collective political identities have focused more on their ethnicity than on their alienage. Even so, the many measures pending before Congress that seek to disadvantage legal aliens broadly as a class have clearly increased the political salience of alienage *per se* and hence the value that aliens will place on the vote in the future (Verhovek, 1995). This certainly accounts for some of the dramatic increases in petitions for naturalization filed in the last few years.

Citizenship requirements for jury service are not much of an issue in the United States. In the framing of the Bill of Rights, which protected the right to trial by jury in both criminal and civil cases, jury service was seen as an important political, as well as legal, institution protecting the people from the oppression of governmental and private elites (Amar, 1991). Today, Americans continue to esteem juries and serve on them conscientiously. Still, many view such service as less of a privilege than a burden; Americans, after all, generally refer to it as jury *duty*. Unlike the right to vote, the notion of extending jury service to aliens has not surfaced in the public debate about improving the jury system.

Aliens' ineligibility for federal employment, which is similar to the practice in virtually all nations (Schuck, 1994a), is likely to be of greater concern to many of them than is their inability to serve on juries. As a practical political matter, few LPRs would seek high elective or appointive offices during the period prior to naturalization even if the law permitted them to do so. But many might want immediately to pursue employment in the federal, state, and local civil service systems. In the mid-1970s two Supreme Court decisions elaborated the constitutional principles relating to discrimination against aliens in the civil service setting. The Court held that the Constitution permitted Congress and the president to limit federal civil service jobs to citizens (which has been done since the 1880s) but that the states could not impose citizenship requirements for their civil service systems (*Hampton v. Mow Sun Wong,* 426 US 88 [1976]; *Sugarman v. Dougall,* 413 US 634 [1973]). Although it emphasized the exclusive federal interest in regulating immigration, a principle that is discussed more fully below, the Court did recognize the states' power to exclude LPRs from particular job categories that represented their "political function," such as schoolteaching and police work. This distinction has proved difficult to apply but continues to enjoy the Court's support (Tribe, 1988: 1544–53).

Two other inequalities are worth mentioning. First, LPRs have a lesser right to sponsor their family members for immigration than do US citizens. "Immediate relatives" of citizens receive preferred immigration status without regard to numerical quotas, and citizens' siblings and adult children have preferred status under the numerical quota system. In contrast, the spouses and unmarried children of resident aliens qualify for only a numerically limited preference, and their siblings receive no preference at all (Aleinikoff, Martin, and Motomura, 1995).

Second, citizens and LPRs differ with respect to their right to remain in the United States. Citizens, whether through birthright or naturalization, are not subject to deportation, but LPRs are. Deportation of a long-term resident can wreak enormous deprivation on aliens and their families and friends. Although the Supreme Court has repeatedly held that deportation is not punishment and therefore does not implicate the due process and other constitutional guarantees that surround the imposition of criminal sanctions, the fact is that, as Justice Douglas put it, deportation "may deprive a man and his family of all that makes life worthwhile" (*Harisiades v. Shaughnessy,* 342 US 580 [1952], Justice Douglas, dissenting).

Still, this risk should be viewed in a realistic context. Deportation may indeed be devastating to individual aliens and their families and friends. Before Congress amended the immigration laws in 1996, however, the probability of an LPR actually being deported was in fact exceedingly low, unless he or she had been convicted of a serious crime and was in custody. Moreover, the courts require government to observe high standards of procedural fairness in adjudicating individual rights, including the qualified right of deportable LPRs to remain in the United States. Deportable LPRs can also invoke extensive procedural safeguards established by statute and regulation, as well as by judicial decision.[19]

In truth, long-term resident aliens faced a vanishingly small risk of deportation unless they were convicted of certain crimes. In 1995, for example, only 45 000 aliens were formally deported or removed "under docket control," and virtually all of these were illegal entrants, out-of-status non-immigrants, violators of narcotics laws, or convicted criminals. A far larger number (1.3 million) were expelled without formal proceedings, but almost all of these fell into the same four categories.[20] In addition, relatively few of those who were deported or expelled had been in the United States for a long period of time. Finally, severe administrative failures and resource constraints limit the INS's ability to implement even the relatively few formal deportation orders, and the far more numerous informal departure agreements, that it does manage to obtain. The INS's current efforts to improve its dismal removal record are focused almost entirely on deportable aliens who commit crimes in the United States. As a practical and legal matter, then, the ability of non-criminal long-term resident aliens to remain in the United States if they wish was remarkably secure, although they did not quite equal those of US citizens.

The 1996 changes to the immigration statute sharply limited the procedural rights and ability to avoid deportation of even long-term LPRs if they are convicted of an "aggravated felony." As noted below, this category has been steadily expanded to encompass a large number of offenses punishable by more than one year of imprisonment, including a broad range of weapons and drug offenses. It is not yet clear how many LPRs will be affected by these changes.

Today, the most controversial issue concerning the rights of LPRs (and other alien categories) involves their access to public benefits, an issue discussed in more detail in the "Current Policy Issues" section, below. Until federal law was amended in 1996, LPRs were entitled to many cash assistance, medical care, food, education,[21] housing, and other social programs. These benefits were often also available to certain other categories of aliens who were present in the United States legally and would probably gain LPR status in the future, though they did not enjoy it yet: family members of amnestied aliens, refugees and asylees, parolees, Cuban/ Haitian entrants, and so-called PRUCOLs (individuals "permanently residing under color of law" whom the INS knows to be illegal but declines to deport). In addition, LPRs were often eligible for state benefit programs such as low tuition fees in state university systems.

Even before the 1996 changes, these rights were limited in certain respects. First, so-called deeming provisions applied to many federal and state benefit programs. Even aliens with visas to enter as LPRs could be excluded from the United States if they were "likely at any time to become ... public charge[s]," and LPRs or other aliens already in the country could be deported if they had become public charges within five years after entry, unless they could show that their poverty was caused by conditions that arose *after* entry. Very few deportations were enforced under this provision. All entering aliens (except for refugees) had to show that they would maintain a steady source of support through employment, family resources, or otherwise. If they could not do so, a portion of the income of their US resident sponsors was deemed to be available to the alien for a number of years after arrival, which would ordinarily render him or her ineligible for public benefits. Until the 1996 welfare reforms, the deeming period was five years in the case of SSI, a means-tested cash assistance program for the aged, blind, and disabled that was used by a rapidly growing number of elderly aliens, much to the consternation of Congress. An alien who received welfare would probably be unable to sponsor other family members as immigrants. Finally, aliens who received legal status under the 1986 amnesty program were not permitted to receive most federal benefits except emergency health care for five years after they were legalized, a period that has now ended for most of them.

These older limitations, as well as the new ones adopted in 1996, are palliated somewhat by the fact that they need only be temporary. The vast majority of LPRs can easily remove them by naturalizing in five years (three if they have a citizen spouse), although fewer than 14 percent of LPRs have naturalized that quickly in recent years. Indeed, the median period of US residence lengthened to ten years for those individuals who naturalized in 1994, and only 45.9 percent of the cohort that was admitted as LPRs in 1977 had naturalized by the end of 1995, more than eighteen years later (US Dept. of Justice, 1997: 135). Although naturalization rates vary a great deal among different nationality groups, even those groups that traditionally naturalized at relatively low rates have recently begun to petition for naturalization at much higher levels.[22]

The marginal incentive of LPRs to naturalize is presumably affected by the importance of the rights they can obtain only by becoming citizens. Many Americans, noting the low naturalization rate among LPRs as a group, believe that US citizenship, as a distinctive status carrying special rights, has counted for less than it once did or perhaps than it should. This belief, among others, has fueled a debate over the significance of citizenship and the appropriateness of imposing disadvantages on LPR status, a debate that culminated in the 1996 statutory changes that sharply curtailed certain rights of LPRs, especially those receiving public assistance. I discuss these changes further in the "Current Policy Issues" Section, below.

Another legal regime bearing on the rights of resident aliens in the United States is the corpus of anti-discrimination law. In 1986, as part of IRCA, Congress adopted an anti-discrimination remedy for aliens in order to balance the employer sanctions program and fill a remedial gap in employment discrimination law. Many immigrant advocates feared that the new employer sanctions provisions would encourage employers to discriminate against job applicants, especially Hispanics, whose national origin or citizenship status made them statistically more likely to be undocumented. These groups also argued that existing remedies for such discrimination were inadequate since Title VII of the Civil Rights Act of 1964, which bars discrimination on the basis of race and national origin (among other factors), has been held to be inapplicable to alienage-based discrimination.

When these concerns threatened to fracture the coalition supporting the legislation, a compromise was forged. In the end, IRCA created a Special Counsel for Immigration-Related Unfair Employment Practices in the US Department of Justice. The special counsel is authorized to investigate and prosecute alienage-based discrimination claims against employers, referral agencies, or recruiters. Enforcement activity by the special counsel appears to have been very limited so far.[23] It is hard to know, however, whether that is because alienage discrimination is rare or because the new anti-discrimination program has simply been ineffective. In 1996, moreover, Congress amended this law to make it easier for employers to defend against discrimination complaints. A decade after IRCA, then, the issues of how much alienage-based job discrimination exists, how much of that is caused by employer sanctions, and how the law should be enforced remain hotly contested.

The employer sanctions program itself has been only indifferently enforced, as a steady stream of congressional reports and private studies has established. Employer non-compliance is due to several factors, including ignorance about the program's complex provisions, the inadequate penalties assessed against violators, and the notorious document fraud that the program has engendered. In any event, employer sanctions have squandered whatever small credibility they began with: employers and illegal aliens know that they have little to fear from them. To be sure, the level of illegal border crossings is lower than it would have been without the program. Illegal entry, however, has returned to pre-IRCA levels.[24] The best estimate is that 5 million illegal aliens were living in the United States (more or less permanently) at the end of 1996. This total grows by about 250 000 each year. Roughly half of these are believed to be illegal entrants, with the other half being people who entered legally but then over-stayed their visas (Espenshade, 1995).

Finally, Congress has adopted increasingly stringent provisions governing the deportability of resident aliens who commit crimes in the United States and severely limiting the procedural and other immigration-related rights of those who have committed "aggravated felonies." This category, created in the late 1980s, is peculiar to immigration law. Already defined quite broadly, it has been constantly expanded by Congress, most recently in the anti-terrorism legislation enacted in April 1996. The issue of criminal aliens is discussed in the "Current Policy Issues" Section below.

Refugees and Asylees

The Refugee Act of 1980 created a legal structure for the adjudication of the status of individuals who claim to be refugees.[25]

Refugees are defined as individuals who possess a "well-founded fear of persecution" in their country of nationality or habitual residence "on account of race, religion, nationality, membership in a particular social group, or political opinion." "Refugees" are located outside the United States when they claim the protection of American officials; if they are physically present in, or at the border of, the United States when they present their claims, they are "asylees." In general, refugees receive more favorable treatment than asylees under US law. The major differences are mentioned below.

The 1980 law made five major innovations. First, its definition of "refugee" tracked the language of the 1951 Refugee Convention, and established a legal duty of *nonrefoulement*, a duty not to deport or return a refugee to any country "if the Attorney General determines that such alien's life or freedom would be threatened [there] on account of race, religion, nationality, membership in a particular social group, or political opinion." Second, it established an annual process of consultation between the President and the relevant congressional committees; this process produces annual refugee ceilings and allocates that number among the regions of the world, although both the numbers and the allocations can be changed to reflect unforeseen circumstances during that year. Third, it established a public–private system for providing social welfare benefits to refugees once a decision to give them legal protection has been made. Fourth, it created a regular legal status for refugees, one that enables the refugee to adjust to the status of permanent resident alien and eventually to apply for citizenship. Finally, it required the Attorney General to establish a procedure permitting asylum claims by any alien meeting the refugee definition who is "physically present in the United States or at a land border or port of entry, irrespective of such alien's status" but giving the Attorney General discretion as to whether to grant asylum to eligible claimants.

An alien who is found to be a refugee under either program initially occupies an uncertain legal position. Refugee or asylee status may be revoked if conditions in the source country change in ways that eliminate the alien's fear of persecution there. Refugees and asylees automatically qualify for the full range of federal benefits, and since they are not assumed to have any independent sources of support, they are not subject to the "deeming" provisions discussed above in connection with LPRs. Eligibility for state and local public benefits varies with the particular jurisdiction's law.

In the United States, the general expectation is that refugees and asylees will acquire permanent legal residence status within a relatively short period of time, perhaps as soon as 1 year, and will move toward eventual citizenship. Under the 1980 law, refugees must regularize their legal status by adjusting to permanent resident status 1 year after their arrival if they are otherwise admissible; asylees who would otherwise be admissible may seek to adjust status, but they (unlike refugees) are subject to an annual ceiling of 10 000 such adjustments; 7837 asylees adjusted status in 1995.

Although the refugee program and the asylum program employ the same refugee definition, they differ in important respects. The refugee program screens and selects people overseas, usually in refugee camps, for resettlement in the United States, and the refugee definition is applied more loosely in overseas screening than in asylum decision-making. Although the statutory "normal flow" ceiling for overseas refugees is 50 000, the negotiated ceiling is always higher; for 1996 it was 90 000. Special legislation that favors particular groups, such as Jews and Pentecostals from the former Soviet Union, may effectively increase even this number.

The asylum program is quite different. First, the number of asylum claims is not subject to specified limits. More than 154 000 new applications were filed during 1995, although many of these were filed before the new regulations (discussed below) took effect, and many others were related to a settlement in a particular litigation. More than 450 000 cases were pending at the beginning of 1996 and more than 486 000 were pending six months later. Under the complex, legalistic procedures adopted in 1990, aliens applying for asylum (or withholding of deportation, a related but slightly different status) filed their claims with a corps of professional, specially-trained "Asylum Officers" within the INS. The Officer had to rule on the application and produce a written opinion explaining the grant or denial. If the Officer denied the claim, the applicant could renew it before an immigration judge (an employee of the Justice Department but independent of the INS, who adjudicates deportation and exclusion cases) if the

INS later charged the alien with an immigration violation. The immigration judge then had exclusive jurisdiction over the asylum claim, deciding it *de novo*. If the judge denied the claim, the alien could appeal to the Board of Immigration Appeals (BIA), and if the BIA denied it, then to the federal courts. Stays of deportation pending decision are easily obtained; if the alien appeals to the courts, a stay is automatic.

A very important feature of the asylum-claiming system under the 1990 regulations was that an applicant could apply immediately for work authorization and the INS was obliged to act quickly on that application and grant it unless it was "frivolous," defined as "manifestly unfounded or abusive." This generous procedure and standard, coupled with protracted delays before asylum officers and immigration judges made even initial determinations, meant that aliens with weak but non-frivolous asylum claims were able to work unhindered for long periods of time in the United States.

The new regulations, which took effect in January 1995, are designed to simplify and expedite these procedures and to limit the right to a work authorization pending resolution of the asylum claim. The Officer, in the case of excludable and deportable aliens, must either grant the asylum application or refer the case to the immigration judge to initiate enforcement proceedings in which the claim will be considered. The Officer need not conduct a personal interview and simply refers weak claims for enforcement action. No longer must Asylum Officers and immigration judges wait for a State Department opinion on a claim. Most important, asylum claimants must now wait 150 days before applying for a work authorization, denied asylum claims are ineligible for it, and other restrictions on such authorization have been imposed. Early indications are that the new regulations are effectively reducing the number of asylum claims. Much depends on the additional resources that the Justice Department can commit to the processing of the enormous backlog, a commitment that President Clinton made as part of his program to strengthen immigration enforcement.

The 1996 amendments to the immigration made far-reaching changes in the asylum procedures. Congress authorized INS officials to summarily exclude at the border all non-LPR aliens lacking proper documents or making false statements unless the aliens can establish that they have a "credible fear" of persecution if returned, in which case they are granted a hearing on their asylum claims. No judicial review of the summary exclusion decision is authorized by the new statute.

One final category of asylee-like aliens should be mentioned. These are aliens who, while not Convention refugees, nevertheless qualify for "temporary protected status" (TPS), the statutory safe haven program authorized by the 1990 Act, by reason of an armed conflict, natural disaster, or other "extraordinary and dangerous conditions" in their home country that prevent them from returning there in safety. Such individuals enjoy a right to remain in the United States so long as the Attorney General continues to designate their country for such treatment. TPS aliens are ineligible for most but not all federal social benefits.

The largest group of TPS aliens is the approximately 187 000 Salvadorans, for whom the Congress showed special solicitude in the 1990 Act by creating a distinct TPS program for their benefit. Shortly after the November 1994 elections, which revealed intense public concern about illegal migration, the Clinton administration indicated its intention to bring this program to an end and deport those Salvadorans, presumably the vast majority, who could not qualify for legal status under the ordinary standards for asylum or some other relief category. The administration is understandably concerned about the credibility of its "temporary" programs of protection when they allow aliens to remain in the United States indefinitely, long after the conditions in the home country that justified the creation of the program cease to exist. Despite this concern, it is highly doubtful that the INS will ever succeed in removing most of them.

Illegal Aliens

Many individual rights protected by the Constitution apply to "persons", not just "citizens". For this reason, aliens who are in the United States illegally – whether because they entered illegally or, as is often the case, because they remain in violation of their visa restrictions – enjoy some of the basic legal rights of citizens. The question of whether and to what extent government may treat them differently once they are in the country, as distinct from expelling them for their illegal status, has no clear answer.[26] In principle, they are entitled to sue in the courts, claim the protection of the Due Process Clause, and enforce civil rights like anyone else, although as a practical matter they may risk detection if they attempt to do so (unless, for example, they can assert their rights more or less anonymously through class action, an organization, or a "John Doe" claim).

The Supreme Court has directly addressed the question of the rights of illegal aliens in only one case, *Plyler v. Doe.*[27] In *Plyler*, illegal alien children challenged the constitutionality of a Texas statute that barred them from attending public schools. A closely divided Court struck down the statute as a violation of the Equal Protection Clause, holding that because the statute failed to further a substantial state interest, it was irrational under equal protection jurisprudence. Texas had cited its interests in deterring illegal migration, its fiscal obligations to its own citizens and resident aliens, and its desire to use its resources to benefit those who were likely to remain in Texas. The Court, however, rejected these reasons, emphasizing that whatever laws their parents might have violated, the children were innocent. To deny them basic education would force them into a permanent caste or underclass, which Texas could not rationally pursue as a public goal.

In order for the Court to strike down the Texas statute, it had to fashion what Professor Laurence Tribe has called a "curious new species of equal protection review" (1988: 1552); this is a kind of "intermediate scrutiny" between the strict scrutiny reserved for racial and other "discrete and insular minorities" (*United States v. Carolene Products*, 304 US 144, 152 n. 4 [1938]) and the minimal scrutiny accorded to most other classifications. The strict logic of the Court's opinion in *Plyler* is not altogether convincing, but its special solicitude for the "innocent" children of illegal parents nevertheless remains attractive. Despite this solicitude, however, the INS can legally deport illegal parents even when doing so means that, as a practical matter, their citizen children must also leave the United States.[28]

It is not clear how far the reasoning of *Plyler* extends beyond the category of illegal alien children and the domain of public education. Its logic, however, might conceivably protect illegal alien children's access to other social services on the theory that these services are needed to prevent them from forming a permanent underclass. I know of no court decisions establishing a legal right to such services, however, and public education may indeed be a special case. In 1996, Congress narrowly rejected an effort to deny such children the right to attend public schools, a right that became a central element of the presidential campaign.

Indirect access by illegal alien children to public benefits also occurs in the situation of mixed-status families in which some children may be US citizens, others may be LPRs or in other valid statuses, and still others are illegal aliens. The citizen and LPR children may be entitled to welfare and other public benefits, while the illegal alien children are not – although the parents (who themselves are probably illegal in such cases) will inevitably allocate some of the benefits the citizen and LPR children receive (e.g., cash and food stamps) to their illegal alien children as well. The mixed-status family claiming welfare benefits is increasingly common; citizen children of illegal aliens accounted for an estimated 2 percent of total AFDC benefit costs in 1992. The 1996 welfare reform legislation, by excluding LPRs from some but not all public benefit programs, will confuse the situation even more.

In recent years, restrictionists and others opposed to the growth of welfare budgets have intensified their efforts to deny access to public programs not only to illegal aliens but also to an ill-defined category of aliens who are not LPRs but whom the government allows to remain in PRUCOL status. Illegal aliens (but not PRUCOLs) are expressly barred from almost all major federal assistance programs with the important exception of emergency services under Medicaid (including labor and delivery services). Before the 1996 welfare reform law was enacted, they still remained eligible for certain other federal programs as well, such as school lunches, Head Start, social services, and earthquake disaster relief.[29] Under the new law, however, both illegal and PRUCOL aliens will be barred from participating in most or all of these programs unless the states enact laws specifically making them eligible.

California has led other states seeking to go beyond these federal restrictions (Rosen, 1995). In November 1994 the state's voters, by a margin of 59 to 41 percent, approved Proposition 187, which would deny illegal alien children the right to attend public schools, in apparent violation of their rights under *Plyler*, and allow access only to emergency medical care, while requiring teachers and other social service providers to report suspected illegal aliens to the INS. A federal court has enjoined the enforcement of this law pending trial (*League of United Latin American Citizens v. Wilson,* 908 F. Supp. 755 [C.D. Cal. 1995]). I discuss the implications of these events below.

CURRENT POLICY ISSUES

Some of the developments that contributed to Proposition 187's political success are also shaping the major immigrant policy issues today. Perhaps the most important of these are the large number of illegal aliens in the United States, particularly in California, and voters' opposition to welfare benefits for aliens. Illegal migration to the United States is a striking example of the law of unanticipated and unintended consequences. Few would have predicted that a series of immigration control measures would in fact increase the level of illegal migration. Yet that is precisely what occurred when the federal government terminated the bracero program in 1964, established an asylum program in 1980, and made it easy for agricultural workers (but not their families) to gain legal status and for employers to comply with employment authorization verification requirements in 1986.

All observers now agree that two decades of enforcement reforms, of which employer sanctions formed the centerpiece, have failed to reverse the tide of undocumented workers and visa abusers. Recent data suggest, moreover, that the composition of this flow is changing, as women, children, and the elderly – the very groups most likely both to remain permanently and to demand costly public services – migrate or remain illegally (Espenshade, 1995). This volume and kind of illegal migration, however, is at least as much a political problem as a fiscal one. It inflames Americans' fears and antagonisms by stoking a widespread sense that the United States can no longer control its borders (if it ever did), that US sovereignty is in grave jeopardy, that the national destiny is increasingly in the hands of strangers, and that taxpayers' generosity is being abused by those same strangers.

Several analyses of voters' attitudes toward Proposition 187 shed some additional light on these fears. A still-unpublished analysis of registered voters' reasons for supporting Proposition 187 indicates that 90 percent of them thought (and hoped) that it would send a message to the federal government to do more to protect the border; this was also the consequence cited most frequently (Citrin, 1995). Exit polls indicated that the measure attracted the support of a majority of Asian Americans, African Americans, and non-Hispanic whites as well as 22 percent of Latinos. Another survey, conducted by Ron Unz, an immigration advocate who unsuccessfully challenged Governor Wilson in the Republican primary, indicated that Republican primary voters did not feel a generalized anxiety about immigrants or even much concern about their impact on unemployment or crime so much as they resented that illegal aliens were receiving welfare benefits and that both legal and illegal aliens were not learning English in the schools and would benefit unfairly from affirmative action. If this survey is correct, voters' anger may have more to do with concerns about illegal migration, welfare abuse, multiculturalism, and affirmative action than with opposition to legal immigrants *per se* (Schuck, 1995).

In this final section, I briefly discuss four issues that are being shaped by these and other similar anxieties: criminal aliens; aliens' rights to public benefits; the distribution of immigrant-related costs among the various levels of government; and the nature and significance of US citizenship.

Criminal Aliens

No aspect of current immigration policy evokes more public indignation and dismay than the problem of aliens who commit serious crimes but nevertheless remain in the United States. As the Urban Institute demonstrated in the study that I discuss below, the direct cost to states of incarcerating aliens convicted of crimes is quite high; the indirect costs imposed by the crimes themselves, of course, are far higher. Although the vast majority of legal and illegal aliens are law abiding (excepting, of course, for immigration offenses committed by the latter), foreign-born individuals constitute a significant and growing fraction of the inmates in US prisons, both federal and state. The overwhelming majority of these inmate aliens, moreover, are legally deportable and have few if any avenues of relief available to them.

Congress has enacted many laws and held many hearings on this issue in the last decade. It has imposed expedited procedures for deporting criminal aliens, required that they be detained and kept in custody until they can actually be removed (which may sometimes mean indefinite or even lifetime incarceration), denied them immigration benefits, made them ineligible for discretionary relief from deportation, imposed severe criminal sanctions on their re-entry, and instructed the INS to deport them as swiftly and unceremoniously as possible. The 1996 amendments strengthened these sanctions.

As with so many other immigration policies, however, the INS has failed to implement these congressional directives effectively, although its performance in this respect is improving. Remarkably, no one knows how many convicted criminal aliens are in US prisons and jails. The INS succeeded in deporting almost 70 000 criminal aliens in 1996, but this still amounted to a small fraction of the deportable aliens under criminal justice supervision. According to one newspaper account, 87 percent of the criminal aliens in New York City who received three-day deportation notices (which even the INS calls "run letters") disappeared from the system (Sontag, 1994). The INS is now placing a high priority on this problem; it hopes to deport 93 000 criminal aliens in 1997, many through a program that commences (and hopefully completes) their deportation hearings while they are still serving their criminal sentences in federal or state prisons.[30]

Some states, tired of waiting for the INS to remove criminal aliens, have taken direct action. In 1992 New York State sued the federal government to force it to take custody of illegal aliens in the state's prisons and deport them (Lyall, 1992). In 1994 Florida won the INS's permission to pull convicted aliens out of prison and deport them, and the state announced in October that it would begin to deport aliens accused of minor and nonviolent offenses even before they were tried if they agreed not to return to the United States. Florida claims to have saved $5 million in incarceration costs through these programs ("Florida", 1994). Other states are likely to try to do the same.

Aliens' Right to Public Benefits

As noted earlier, federal law bars illegal aliens from participating in the major federal assistance programs (except for emergency medical and disaster relief benefits and public schools), while legal aliens were entitled to participate in all of them (although "deeming" and "public charge" limitations applied) until Congress amended the law in 1996. But while these differences in welfare rights between legal and illegal aliens were clear to lawyers, the public was understandably confused on this point. This confusion contributed to the closer, more hostile scrutiny to which legal aliens' access to public benefits has recently been subjected.

We have seen that the public views legal immigrants much more favorably than illegal ones. Even so, politicians who wish to attack illegal aliens must tread carefully in order to avoid antagonizing legal aliens (many of whom will vote soon enough) and citizens (many of whom support legal immigration and may also sympathize with the plight of illegal aliens even while favoring enforcement activity against them). For this reason, politicians across the political spectrum tend to couple any attack on illegal immigrants with expressions of support for the rights of legal immigrants.[31] In the debate over Proposition 187, for example, California governor Pete Wilson and other prominent advocates of the measure took pains to defend and even praise legal immigrants (although the new law's reporting requirements might in fact adversely affect them), pointing out that one of every four Californians is a legal immigrant and that the state had benefited from their presence. Still, the passionate intensity of immigration politics can easily obscure the distinction between legals and illegals, as some of the hostility to the latter spills over and taints the former as well (Schuck, 1995).

Another reason why the public conflates legal and illegal aliens, is that illegal aliens, who are specifically barred from almost all public programs, nevertheless do receive significant public resources. The precise amount, of course, is impossible to determine because of methodological obstacles and variations among the studies (Vernez and McCarthy, 1995). A 1994 study by the Urban Institute provided the first systematic assessment of some (not all) of the fiscal impacts occasioned by illegal aliens. The study, which has been criticized by restrictionist groups, which think that it underestimates the net costs imposed by illegal aliens, focused on seven states in which an estimated 86.4 percent of the nation's illegal aliens live; the largest, of course, is California, whose 1.4 million illegals comprise 4.6 percent of the state's population. The study found the following costs in the seven states: criminal incarceration, $471 million; education, $3.1 billion; and Medicaid, $200–300 million. (Partly offsetting these costs are $1.9 billion in revenues generated from sales, property, and state income taxes on illegal aliens in the seven states surveyed.) The Urban Institute's estimates focused on illegal aliens' use of those services to which they are entitled (e.g., emergency care under Medicaid); thus they do not include benefits that illegal aliens obtain fraudulently. On this point, congressional testimony in May 1994 indicated that little fraud could be detected by the federal eligibility verification system for aliens (SAVE); the fraudulent claims that SAVE could *not* detect may be much greater (Clark *et al.*, 1994).

Legal aliens, as noted, until recently enjoyed a right to public benefits that was essentially equal to that of US citizens, and a large and growing number of them in fact claimed and received these benefits. With Americans fervently denouncing welfare dependency and desperately searching for spending reductions to lower budgetary deficits, aliens' use of welfare benefits – which is already substantial and seems to be increasing for refugees and certain other subgroups (Schuck, 1996a; 1984) – generated considerable public controversy and resentment.

This public opposition has taken an enormous toll on aliens' welfare entitlements in recent years. Congress in 1994 extended the deeming period for SSI benefits for legal aliens from three to five years, and limited illegal aliens' access to earthquake disaster funds to emergency relief and temporary housing of up to ninety days. The 1996 welfare reform law adopted far more sweeping restrictions, barring most *current* LPRs (except for refugees/asylees in their first five years in the United States, veterans and soldiers, and those who have worked for ten years in the United States and not taken public assistance during that period) from cash assistance and food stamps, and most *new* LPRs from most federal means-tested programs for five years. It also imposes restrictions on LPR eligibility for most *state* benefit programs. In addition, the new law extends and enforces more rigorously the deeming provisions against the family and employer sponsors of legal aliens who might apply for public benefits, tightens income requirements for sponsors, and requires stricter application of the "public charge" provisions to facilitate deportation of legal aliens who receive benefits, especially during their first few years in the United States. These changes are expected to produce very large budgetary savings (more than twenty billion dollars over five years [Fix and Passel, 1994: 65–7]), a factor that makes them politically irresistible to "deficit hawks" as well as to welfare opponents and immigration restrictionists.

Many of these provisions raise difficult constitutional questions, which will soon be tested in the courts. As a policy matter, denying public support to LPRs, especially children, may have dire and unpredictable consequences. Enforcing the complex new eligibility restrictions may involve high administrative and political costs. Moreover, federal limits on aliens' benefits will displace many of these costs onto those state and local governments that seek to fill the gap (where the new law permits these governments to do so). This raises the intergovernmental cost allocation issue, to which I now turn.

Intergovernmental Allocation of Immigration-Related Costs

In a federal system, the allocation of costs among different levels of government raises difficult problems. This issue, which the states and localities tendentiously but correctly call the question of "unfunded federal mandates", has several different aspects. First, federal law until 1996 required the states to provide to legal aliens the same welfare, health care, food programs, and other social services that the states provided to their own citizens, while paying only a portion of their cost. Indeed, federal constitutional principles require the states to provide the same benefits and services to legal aliens that they provide to citizens, even if the federal government contributes *nothing* to those benefits and services. The 1996 law permits, and in some cases requires, the states to avoid these fiscal burdens, but as just noted those states and localities that decide to pick up the slack will end up with *greater* burdens. Finally, these principles (as interpreted in *Plyler v. Doe*) still require the state to provide public education, by far the most costly public service of all, even to illegal aliens.

In addition to these features of the system, a large fiscal mismatch exists among the different levels of government. Most of the costs of public benefits and services that legal and illegal aliens use (two-thirds, according to state government estimates) are borne by state and local governments, while most of the taxes (again an estimated two-thirds) paid by those aliens go to the federal government. (The states and localities, however, tend to ignore the likelihood that most of the other economic benefits that aliens generate are received by the local communities in which they live and work.) In the case of illegal aliens, the federal government enjoys a further fiscal advantage; the workers pay Social Security taxes but do not ordinarily claim Social Security benefits.

This mismatch between cost bearers and tax receivers is a subject of bitter intergovernmental dispute, and the 1996 welfare reform law has in some ways exacerbated the conflict (Espenshade, 1996a). By restricting aliens' access to federal benefits, the law will aggravate the mismatch as states and localities move to defray the costs of indigent aliens through their general assistance and other programs, which are politically unpopular. Although the new law bars the states from assisting some non-LPR aliens with some benefits, it leaves them free to extend many benefits to legal aliens and actually requires them to provide certain benefits, including the very costly Medicaid program, to favored categories of aliens. It is unclear how the new law, which transforms federal entitlements into block grants to the states, will affect those costs. State and local governments' inability to shift their immigration-related costs to the federal government, which possesses exclusive policy control in this area, mirror their long-standing frustrations with unfunded federal mandates in numerous other areas of public policy, frustrations that led Congress in 1995 to impose limits on unfunded mandates. This legislation is prospective only, however, and it is not yet clear to what extent immigration-related costs will be affected.

Long before the 1995 unfunded mandate law, some desperate states mounted a number of attention-getting challenges. Florida and California sued the federal government, demanding reimbursement for certain costs generated by both illegal and legal aliens residing in these states. Although these suits will probably fail, they helped to secure the unfunded mandates legislation. In addition, some states are adopting new restrictions on illegal aliens' access to public services. In addition to Proposition 187 in California, Virginia required its schools to verify the legal status of students over eighteen years of age who are enrolled in English as a second language (ESL) programs and of all students over twenty who entered the United States after the age of twelve. Failure to do so might lead to the loss of some state funding. These laws probably foreshadow similar efforts elsewhere.

The Significance of Citizenship

Alexander Bickel, a leading constitutional lawyer, wrote that US citizenship "is at best a simple idea for a simple government" (1975: 54). By this he meant that full membership in the American polity has been widely and easily available (at least to males) since the Fourteenth Amendment was ratified in 1868 and that the nature of this inclusive citizenship – in particular, the legal rights and obligations attached to that status – has long ceased to be an important or divisive issue. In a 1989 essay on US citizenship, I wrote that Bickel's observation "is probably truer today than in 1973 when he made it" (Schuck, 1989b: 1).

Today, I am not so sure. In the last few years, public discourse about citizenship has returned to first principles: its nature, sources, and significance. This discourse has been prompted by a number of developments since the late 1960s, most of them related to high levels of illegal immigration from the Caribbean Basin and of legal immigration by individuals with linguistic and cultural backgrounds vastly different from those of earlier waves of immigrants. These developments have raised concerns about the unity and coherence of the American civic culture, concerns that have in turn raised fundamental questions about how US citizenship affects that culture. I shall briefly note five of these concerns: multicultural pressures; the loss of a unifying ideology; technological change; the expansion and consolidation of the welfare state; and the devaluation of citizenship. With the enactment of the 1965 immigration reforms law, the composition of the immigration stream to the United States changed radically. Of the top ten source countries, only the Philippines and India were sending immigrants who spoke English well. Bilingual education thus became a major curricular issue in public education, and teaching in dozens of languages became necessary in many urban school systems. With the growing politicization of ethnicity and widespread attacks on the traditional assimilative ideal, anxieties about linguistic and cultural fragmentation increased. These anxieties have led to public measures establishing English as the official language in California and more than twenty other states. They also pre-empted House passage of a national official-language requirement in August 1996, and the 1996 restrictions on the rights of legal and illegal aliens. The civil rights movement, moreover, took a turn toward separatism after 1965. African Americans, already severely disadvantaged, were obliged increasingly to cede political and economic influence to more recently arrived Hispanic and Asian voters. Certain economic sectors came to depend almost entirely on immigrant workers, legal and illegal. Relatively parochial immigrant enclaves grew larger. These multicultural pressures caused many Americans to feel more and more like strangers in their own country.

The end of the cold war rendered largely irrelevant the anticommunist ideology that had served for many decades as a unifying, coherent force in American political culture and as an obsessive preoccupation and goal in US foreign policy. No alternative ideology has yet emerged to replace it. Only constitutionalism, the American civic religion, seems potentially capable of performing this function of binding together a nation of diverse peoples.

Rapid changes in transportation and communication technologies have transformed a world of sovereign nations into a global web of interdependent societies and multinational enterprises. Migration is now inexpensive and reversible. Immigrants no longer need to make an irrevocable commitment to their new society; they can more easily retain emotional ties to their countries and cultures of origin. Studies by sociologists of immigration such as Alejandro Portes and others indicate that TV and other cultural forces help to assimilate second-generation immigrant youths into an underclass culture rather than into mainstream American life, and that divorce rates and other indications of social dysfunction tend to increase with the length of immigrants' residence in the United States. With the welfare state's expansion, the behavior, values, and economic progress of immigrants have become matters of fiscal significance and public policy concern. In contrast to the historical pattern, immigration no longer ebbs and flows with the business cycle, presumably because of a stronger social safety net. The welfare state, by pitting citizens and aliens against one another in competition for scarce public resources, has raised the stakes in the perennial debate over how the polity should conceive of community, affinity, and civic obligation.

Until the 1996 legislation reversed the tide, the welfare state's egalitarian thrust, its nourishing of entitlement as an ideal, and the growth of a dependent population had diluted citizenship as a distinctive status bearing special privileges and demanding special commitments and obligations. The rights of legal aliens had converged with those of citizens until there was little to separate them; as noted above, only the franchise, immigration sponsorship privileges, and eligibility for the federal civil service remained the special prerogative of citizens. Americans began to feel that US citizenship had lost much of its value, that it should somehow count for more.[32] As the practice of dual nationality became more widespread and the US government grudgingly acquiesced to it, many US citizens participated actively in the politics of their countries of origin.

These changes led to calls for a revitalization of citizenship. One type of proposal, which prompted the enactment in 1993 of the National Community Service Corps, looks to the creation of a spirit of public service to the nation among young people. Another approach, embodied in the federal welfare reform laws adopted in 1988 and 1996 and in many state programs, sought to undermine the entitlement mentality by insisting that able-bodied applicants for cash assistance perform some kind of socially useful work as a condition of receiving it. The 1996 reform, of course, limited welfare programs for US citizens as well. A further, related strategy, exemplified by the 1996 restrictions on LPRs' rights to public benefits, was motivated by more than the desire to save scarce public resources. Congress also wanted to favor citizens in allocating those resources, to dismantle portions of the welfare state, and to increase citizenship's value by widening the gap between the rights of citizens and aliens, thus strengthening aliens' incentives to naturalize. As noted earlier, the recent spurt in naturalization petitions at least partly reflects the changing incentives generated by policy changes reducing LPRs' eligibility for governmental benefits.

Other types of reforms are aimed directly at citizenship *per se*. The INS has attempted to make the naturalization process easier, faster, and more attractive. Indeed, the INS has succeeded so well at this that it has been accused of tolerating widespread fraud in the naturalization process as a way to attract new voters to be the Democratic party during the 1996 elections and Congress will hold hearings on these accusations in 1997. The Commission on Immigration Reform has proposed a 1990s version of the "Americanization" movement that sought to foster rapid assimilation and naturalization around the World War I era. Another approach, which would encourage naturalization but also risk dividing the loyalties of US citizens, would adopt policies more tolerant of dual nationality. It is striking that while Germany and other European states are seriously considering such changes (along with some limited adoption of *jus soli* principles), the United States continues its official opposition to dual nationality, requiring all who naturalize in the US explicitly to renounce all other allegiances.

A far more radical proposal, which is not at all inconsistent with the policies designed to encourage naturalization, would deny citizenship to some who, under existing law, are entitled to it. In the traditional understanding of the *jus soli* rule embodied in the Citizenship Clause of the Fourteenth Amendment, one automatically becomes a citizen merely by being born on US soil, even if one's parents are in the country illegally or only as temporary residents. Those who challenge this understanding emphasize the importance of mutual consent – the polity's as well as the alien's – in legitimating US citizenship. They also point to the perversity of permitting a Mexican woman with no claims on the United States to confer citizenship on her new child simply by crossing the border and giving birth, perhaps at public expense, in a US hospital. While not favoring this common practice, defenders of birthright citizenship wish to avoid creating and perpetuating an underclass of long-term residents who do not qualify as citizens. Many guest workers and their descendants who live in European countries that reject the *jus soli* principle suffer this disadvantage (Schuck and Smith, 1986; Schuck, 1996b; Neuman, 1996).

This change would require either a constitutional amendment or a Supreme Court reinterpretation of the Citizenship Clause. Congress considered and rejected proposals in 1996 to eliminate birthright citizenship for the children of illegal aliens, although the Republican Party platform supported such proposals in the 1996 presidential campaign (Schuck and Smith, 1996). The US is not alone in maintaining a birthright citizenship rule (Adams, 1993), and some, notably Germany, have been moving toward – although remaining well short of – the traditional US position. Elimination of the traditional birthright citizenship rule is most unlikely. Nevertheless, some modification of the rule – for example, allowing those who are born in the United States in illegal status and remain as long-term residents to seek naturalization – could possibly attract wider support. A similar change was adopted in France (Schuck, 1996b).

NOTES

1. Most of the numbers that follow in this section are drawn from US Department of Justice (1997).
2. In principle, none of the illegals arriving after 1981 should have been eligible for the amnesty program, which established a cut-off arrival date of 1 January 1982.
3. This total was 10.4 percent below the 1994 total of 804 000 and 20.3 percent below the 1993 total of 904 000 – in effect, the largest two-year decline since the 1930–2 period (US Dept. of Justice,1997).
4. FAIR's former executive director Roger Conner now heads a group (the American Alliance for Rights and Responsibilities) that advocates so-called communitarian norms, especially the promotion of public safety and public values in local public spaces. Here, too, the board members are decidedly mainstream in status and largely liberal in their politics.

5.   Employing an unusual methodology, they elicited the respondents'
      answers to standard survey questions and then followed up with addi-
      tional questions in a process designed to resemble, albeit crudely, the
      give-and-take of ordinary conversation about public issues. Sniderman
      and Piazza found that the respondents' views on race-oriented issues
      differed considerably from issue to issue. That is, attitudes about
      affirmative action were not the same as attitudes about fair-housing
      policies or about government spending on behalf of minorities. For
      my purposes, the more interesting finding is that respondents' initial
      views on issues (except for affirmative action) changed when those
      views were even weakly challenged or met with additional informa-
      tion. The authors summarized this finding as follows: "Finally, and
      perhaps most importantly, the positions that whites take on issues of
      race are pliable to a degree never suspected. Substantial numbers – on
      some issues as many as four in every ten – can be talked out of the
      positions they have taken by relatively weak counter-arguments,
      affirmative action not surprisingly being a major exception" 1993;
      13–14).

         A somewhat analogous positional shift appears in a recent *New York
      Times*/CBS opinion poll on welfare reform. When the respondents
      were asked about their attitudes toward government spending on
      welfare," 48 percent favored cuts, and only 13 percent favored
      increases. But when they were asked about "spending on programs for
      poor children," 47 percent favored increases, and only 9 percent
      favored cuts (DeParle, 1994).

6.   Indeed, the word *ambivalent* appears in the title of a comprehensive
      survey of public attitudes toward immigration (Simon and Alexander,
      1993) and in the subtitle of a recent study of Mexican immigrants'
      political identities in the United States (Skerry, 1993).

7.   Some of these attitudinal distinctions are arguably inconsistent.
      Although respondents believe that immigrants take jobs away from
      Americans, for example, they also believe that immigrants take jobs
      that Americans do not want and that immigrants threaten neither
      their own jobs nor the jobs of people whom they know (Simon and
      Alexander, 1993).

8.   Even more interesting, roughly similar patterns have been found from
      polling over time in Canada, Australia, Britain, and France. The
      survey data discussed in this and the preceding paragraph appear in
      Simon (1995).

9.   Similar questions can be raised about the enactment of the
      Immigration Reform and Control Act of 1986, which was expansionist
      on balance although it contained important control measures, notably
      employer sanctions. For a discussion of both the 1986 and 1990 acts
      and the role of ideas in immigration politics, see Schuck (1992).

10.   This point is not necessarily contradicted by California's adoption of
      Proposition 187, for the measure was directed not at legal immigrants
      but at illegal ones, about whom political attitudes are considerable
      different (Schuck, 1995). The political significance of Proposition 187
      is discussed below.

11. See Graham (1986). The publications of FAIR, the restrictionist group described above and one of which Graham is a leading member, frequently emphasize this attitudinal gap.

12. The historical summary that follows is largely drawn from Aleinikoff, Martin and Motomura (1995, ch. 1).

13. A recent example is *Stone v. I.N.S.*, 115 S.Ct 1537 (1995) (filing of motion to reopen or reconsider the Board of Immigration Appeals' final deportation order does not toll statute period for seeking judicial review). Lower courts occasionally strike down some legislative provisions, even on constitutional grounds. See, e.g., *American–Arab Anti-Discrimination Committee v Meese*, 714 F. Supp. 1060 (C.D. Cal. 1989), vacated as moot, 940 F.2d 445 (9th Cir. 1991).

14. Perhaps the most dramatic example of this shift is Pete Wilson, who, as a US senator, obtained expansionist provisions in IRCA at the behest of California growers but less than a decade later made immigration restriction the keystone of his re-election strategy (Schuck, 1995).

15. The infamous Alien and Sedition Acts of 1798 were short-lived, and by the time that Congress added a literacy requirement to the naturalization requirements in 1906, it had relatively little effect in excluding applicants from citizenship.

16. A remarkable spurt occurred during 1995 and 1996 in the number of naturalization petitions being filed. The possible reasons for this are discussed under "Current Policy Issues".

17. According to the INS study, however, "few Japanese immigrants become citizens" (US Department of Justice, 1994: 130).

18. Even US citizens vote at low levels: only 49% of eligible citizens voted in the 1996 presidential election, and only 38 percent voted in the 1994 congressional elections, a higher rate than in recent off-year elections. Because of several factors, including the relatively large number of elections in the United States, cross-national comparisons of voting rates should be interpreted with care.

19. For a recent judicial reaffirmation of these rights, see *Arab–American Anti-Discrimination Committee v. Reno*, 883 F. Supp. 1365 (C.D. Cal. 1995).

20. In 1995 70% of the aliens who were removed were charged with crimes or narcotics activity (US Dept. of Justice, 1997, Part VI).

21. According to a summary of a recent report by the National Center for Educational Statistics, a large number of alien students (including LPRs, non-immigrants, and perhaps other categories) received sizable educational grants as well as loans on the same basis as students who are US citizens (FAIR, 1995). Some of these benefits are being criticized (Johnson, 1996).

22. Verhovek (1995). Several reasons may account for this sudden spike in naturalizations: for example, Congress threatened (and in the 1996 Welfare Reform Law fulfilled the threat) to withhold public benefits from LPRs; millions of aliens legalized under IRCA are now becoming eligible to naturalize; and the INS's fees for renewing green cards have made naturalization more of a financial bargain.

23. According to summary data obtained from the special counsel in November 1994, seven years of enforcement have yielded a grand total of $1.5 million in back pay and $550 000 in penalties (US Dept. of Justice, Office of Special Counsel 1994). Many states and localities have established human rights commissions authorized to investigate and prosecute allegations of discrimination based on a number of characteristics, including national origin. It is unclear whether any of these provisions apply to alienage discrimination and, if so, how effectively they have been enforced. New York City has established a Mayor's Office of Immigrant Affairs, which seeks to protect and advance the interests of aliens.

24. The INS reported 1.3 million apprehensions in 1995, approximately the figure for 1985 (although below that for 1986, when IRCA was enacted and when an unusual amount of illegal entry probably occurred in anticipation of the new law) (US Dept. of Justice, 1997: 164).

25. Dr Teitelbaum's paper (chapter 15) reviews the history of US asylum and refugee policies.

26. The 1996 anti-terrorism law permits the government to exclude even long resident illegal entrants rather than deport them with a consequent limitation of their procedural, and perhaps also substantive, rights.

27. 457 US 202 (1982). For discussions of this case, see Tribe (1988: 1551–3); Schuck (1984: 54–8); and Schuck (1995).

28. Under existing law, citizen children cannot petition for an "immediate relative" visa (which is essentially outside the numerical quotas) for their parents until they reach the age of eighteen.

29. It took fifteen years to implement a 1980 statute prohibiting federal housing aid to illegal aliens (*Federal Register* 60 [20 Mar. 1995]: 14816). An amendment to the 1994 crime bill would have barred illegal and PRUCOL aliens from these and other federal programs from which they were not expressly excluded now, but it was ultimately defeated in conference. The 1996 law now bars them.

30. Schuck (1996a: 1989–90). Not all of the incarcerated criminal aliens are subject to immediate deportation in any given year, as their sentences expire at different times.

31. Indeed, former governors Mario Cuomo of New York and Michael Dukakis of Massachusetts, as well as several New York City mayors, including the incumbent Rudolph Giuliani, have voiced vigorous support for *illegal* aliens. See Schmitt (1996). See also Nathan Glazer, "Governmental and Nongovernmental Roles in the Absorption of Immigrants in the United States," in this volume. Leaders in many other communities did the same during the 1980s, when granting sanctuary to asylum-seeking Salvadorans and Guatemalans symbolized opposition to President Reagan's policies in Central America, although many of these same leaders are now in the vanguard of anti-immigration sentiment.

32. Very recently, nationalistic anger, populist resentment, and the politics of tax reform have fused in a bitter condemnation of very wealthy

Americans who renounce their US citizenship, apparently in order to reduce their tax liabilities. Many Americans fear that this practice confirms a disturbing trend toward a purely instrumental, self-interested conception of citizenship (De Witt, 1995). Another widely publicized example was Rupert Murdoch's decision to naturalize in order to become eligible to purchase additional media properties (Safire, 1985).

REFERENCES

Adams, Sarah A. (1993), "The Basic Right of Citizenship: A Comparative Study," Center for Immigration Studies Backgrounder no. 7–93 (Washington, DC: Center for Immigration Studies).

Aleinikoff, T. A., David A. Martin, and Hiroshi Motomura (1995), *Immigration Process and Policy*, 3rd edn (St Paul, MN: West Publishing).

Amar, Akhil (1991), "The Bill of Rights as a Constitution," *Yale Law Journal*, 100 (Mar.): 1131–210.

Bickel, Alexander M. (1975), *The Morality of Consent* (New Haven, CT: Yale University Press).

Borjas, George (1994) "Immigration and Welfare, 1970–1990," National Bureau of Economic Research, Working Paper no. 4872 (Cambridge, MA: National Bureau of Economic Research).

Citrin, Jack (1995), unpublished data sent to author on 6 April 1995.

Clark, Rebecca L., Passel, Jeffrey, Zimmermann, Wendy, and Fix, Michael (1994), *Fiscal Impacts of Undocumented Aliens: Selected Estimates for Seven States* (Report to the Office of OMB and the Department of Justice; Washington, DC: Urban Institute).

DeParle, Jason (1994), "Despising Welfare, Pitying its Young," *New York Times*, 18 December, E5.

De Witt, Karen (1995), "One Way to Save a Bundle: Become a Former American," *New York Times*, 12 April, Al.

Dunn, Ashley (1994), "Skilled Asians Leaving US for High-tech Jobs at Home," *New York Times*, 21 Feb., p. A1.

Espenshade, Thomas J. (1994), "Can Immigration Slow US Population Aging?," *Journal of Policy Analyses and Management*, 13, p. 759.

—— (1995), "Unauthorized Immigration to the United States", *Annual Review of Sociology*, 21:195–216.

—— (1996) "Fiscal Impacts of Immigrants and the Shrinking Welfare State," Princeton University, Office of Population Research, Working Paper no. 96–1.

Espenshade, Thomas J. and Hempstead, Katherine (1997), "Contemporary American Attitudes Toward US Immigration", *International Migration Review*, 30 (Summer): 535–70.

FAIR (Federation for American Immigration Reform) (1995), "While Congress Cuts Student Aid, Taxpayers Still Pay Over a Billion Dollars a Year to Educate Foreign Students," FAIR Immigration Report, 2 June.

Federal Register (1995), 60, 20 March, p. 14816.

Fix, Michael, and Passel, Jeffrey S. (1994), *Immigration and Immigrants: Setting the Record Straight* (Washington, DC: Urban Institute).

"Florida to Try Early Deportation" (1994) *New York Times*, 28 Oct., A25.

Fuchs, Lawrence H. (1990), "The Reactions of Black Americans to Immigration", in *Immigration Reconsidered: History, Sociology, and Politics*, ed. V. Yans-McLaughlin (New York: Oxford University Press), pp. 293–314.

Graham, Otis L. (1986), "Uses and Misuses of History in the Debate over Immigration Reform, "*Public Historian*, 8 (Spring): 41–64.

Greenhouse, Steven (1995), "U.S. Will Return Refugees of Cuba in Policy Switch," *New York Times*, 3 May, p. A1.

Hampton *v.* Mow Sun Wong, 426 US 88 (1976).

Harisiades *v.* Shaughnessy, 342 US, 580 (1952).

Higham, John (1970), *Strangers in the Land: Patterns of American Nativism, 1860–1925*, 2nd edn (New York: Atheneum).

Johnson, Dirk (1996), "Scholarship Restrictions Make Refugee Feel Scorned," *New York Times*, 12 May, p. 12.

Lavoie v. The Queen, Federal Court of Canada, Trial Division, 21 April 1995.

Lewontin, Richard C. (1995), "Sex, Lies, and Social Science," *New York Review of Books*, 20 Apr. p. 24

Lyall, Sarah (1992), "Albany Sues US on Aliens Held in Prison," *New York Times*, 28 Apr., B1.

Martin, David A (1985) "Membership and Consent: Abstract or Organic?," *Yale Journal of International Law*, 11, p. 278.

Neuman, Gerald (1992), "'We Are the People': Alien Suffrage in German and American Perspective," *Michigan Journal of International Law*, 13 (Winter): pp. 259–335.

—— (1994), "Justifying US Naturalization Policies," *Virginia Journal of International Law*, 35 (fall): pp. 237–78.

—— (1996), *Strangers to the Constitution: Immigration, Borders, and Fundamental Law* (Princeton: Princeton University Press).

New York Times. (1994a), "Americans in 2020: Less White, More Southern," 22 April, p. A1.

—— (1994b), "Florida to Try Early Deportation", 28 October, p. A25.

—— (1995), "Low-Income Voters" Turnout Fell in 1994, Census Reports," 11 June, p. 28.

Plyler *v.* Doe, 457, US 202 (1982).

Raskin, Jamin B. (1993), "Legal Aliens, Local Citizens: The Historical, Constitutional, and Theoretical Meanings of Alien Suffrage," *University of Pennsylvania Law Review*, 141 (Apr.): pp. 1391–1470.

Rosberg, Gerald A. (1977), "Aliens and Equal Protection: Why Not the Right to Vote," *Michigan Law Review*, 75 (Apr.–May): pp. 1092–136.

Rosen, Jeffrey (1995), "The War on Immigrants," *New Republic*, 30 Jan., pp. 22–6

Safire, William (1985), "Citizen of the World," *New York Times*, 16 May, A31.

Schmitt, Eric (1996), "Giuliani Criticizes GOP and Dole on Immigration," *New York Times*, 7 June, B3.

Schuck, Peter H. (1984), "The Transformation of Immigration Law," *Columbia Law Review*, 84 (Jan.): pp. 1–90.

—— (1989a), "Introduction: Immigration Law and Policy in the 1990s", *Yale Law and Policy Review*, 7, no. 1: pp. 1–19.

—— (1989b), "Membership in the Liberal Polity: The Devaluation of American Citizenship", *Georgetown Immigration Law Journal*, 3 (spring): pp. 1–18.

—— (1992), "The Politics of Rapid Legal Change: Immigration Policy in the 1980s," *Studies in American Political Development*, 6: pp. 37–92.

—— (1994a), Expert testimony delivered Oct. 1994 in *Lavoie v. The Queen*, Federal Court of Canada, Trial Division.

—— (1994b), "Whose Membership Is It, Anyway? Comments on Gerald Neuman", *Virginia Journal of International Law*, 35 (fall): pp. 321–31.

—— (1995), "The Message of 187", *American Prospect*, no. 21, pp. 85–92

—— (1996a), "Alien Rumination", *Yale Law Journal*, 105, no. 7: pp. 1963–2012.

—— (1996b), Testimony before House Judiciary Subcommittees on Immigration and Claims and on the Constitution, 13 Dec. 1995, and supplemental letter dated 14 Feb. 1996.

Schuck, Peter H., and Rogers M. Smith (1986a), *Citizenship without Consent: Illegal Aliens in the American Polity* (New Haven, CT: Yale University Press).

—— (1996), Letter to the editor, *New York Times*, 12 Aug., A14.

—— (1986b), "Membership and Consent: Actual or Mythic? A Reply to David Martin", *Yale Journal of International Law*, 11, p. 545.

Schuck, Peter H., and Theodore Hsien Wang (1992), "Continuity and Change: Patterns of Immigration Litigation in the Courts, 1979–1990," *Stanford Law Review*, 45 (Nov.): pp. 115–83.

Simon, Rita J. (1995), "Immigration and Public Opinion," Paper presented at National Legal Conference on Immigration and Refugee Policy, Washington, DC, 30 Mar.

Simon, Rita J., and Susan H. Alexander (1993), *The Ambivalent Welcome: Print Media, Public Opinion, and Immigration* (Westport, CT: Praeger).

Skerry, Peter (1993) *Mexican Americans: The Ambivalent Minority* (New York: Free Press).

Sniderman, Paul, and Thomas Piazza (1993), *The Scar of Race* (Cambridge: Harvard University (Press).

Sontag, Deborah (1994), "Porous Deportation System Gives Criminals Little to Fear," *New York Times*, 13 September, p. A1.

Sugarman v. Dougall, 413 US 634 (1973).

Tribe, Laurence H. (1988), *American Constitutional Law*, 2nd edn (Mineola: Foundation).

US Department of Justice (1994), *US Immigration and Naturalization Service, 1994: Statistical Yearbook* (Washington, DC: US Government Printing Office).

—— (1997), *Immigration and Naturalization Service, 1995 Statistical Yearbook* (Washington, DC: US Government Printing Office).

United States Department of Justice, Office of Special Counsel for Immigration-Related Unfair Employment Practices (1994), Weekly Report, 28 Nov.

Verhovek, Sam Howe (1995), "Legal Immigrants in Record Numbers Want Citizenship", *New York Times*, 2 Apr., p. 1.

Vernez, Georges, and Kevin McCarthy (1995), "The Fiscal Costs of Immigration: Analytical and Policy Issues," paper no. DRU-958-1-IF (Santa Monica, CA: RAND Center for Research on Immigration Policy).

Warren, Robert, and Kraly, Ellen Percy (1985), *The Elusive Exodus: Emigration from the United States* (Washington, DC: Population Reference Bureau).

Part V
Germany's Migration Policies Through American and Japanese Eyes

10 What We Can Learn from the German Experiences Concerning Foreign Labor

Yasushi Iguchi

INTRODUCTION

Since the late 1980s, member countries of the Organization for Economic Cooperation and Development (OECD) have experienced an enormous increase in international migration. According to the OECD, these countries' migration policies should focus on the selection and programming of migratory flows, integration of (legal) immigrants within the countries, and international cooperation to reduce sending pressures by developing countries (Garçon, 1995; OECD, 1994a).

OECD member countries exchange information on the development of migration and migration policies and strengthen their cooperation, particularly on these focal issues, an exchange which provides a firm basis for policy-oriented study as well as for policy-making (Iguchi, 1995b). But this does not mean that migration policy experiences are directly transferable from one country to another. Traditional immigration countries like the United States, Canada and Australia have very different capacities to manage international migration, compared with countries like Japan and those in the European Union (EU). Some countries, such as Italy, Spain and Japan, are called "new immigration countries": traditionally sending countries, they have only recently become receiving countries (OECD, 1994d), and as a result the presence of a foreign worker population has different effects from one country to another (Table 10.1).

Table 10.1 *Stock of foreign residents or foreign-born in population and labor force*

Country	Share of foreigners	
	Population	*Labor force*
Japan[a]	0.7 (1980)	
	1.2 (1993)	0.9 (1993)
European Union		
Belgium	8.9 (1980)	
	9.1 (1991)	7.4 (1991)
Denmark	2.0 (1980)	
	3.5 (1991)	
France	6.8 (1982)	6.5 (1982)
	6.5 (1991)	6.2 (1991)
Germany	7.6 (1980)	
	8.7 (1991)	8.9 (1991)
Italy	0.5 (1980)	
	1.5 (1991)	
Luxembourg	25.9 (1980)	
	27.9 (1991)	33.3 (1991)
Netherlands	3.7 (1980)	
	4.8 (1991)	
Spain	0.5 (1980)	
	0.9 (1991)	0.4 (1991)
Austria	3.7 (1980)	6.3 (1980)
	6.6 (1991)	9.1 (1991)
Finland	0.3 (1980)	
	0.7 (1991)	
Sweden	5.1 (1980)	5.4 (1980)
	5.6 (1991)	5.6 (1991)
EFTA		
Norway	2.0 (1980)	
	3.5 (1991)	
Switzerland	14.1 (1980)	15.6 (1980)
	17.6 (1992)	20.1 (1992)
Other		
Australia	20.6 (1981)	25.7 (1981)
	22.7 (1991)	25.8 (1991)
Canada	16.1 (1981)	20.1 (1981)
	15.6 (1986)	21.9 (1986)

Table 10.1   *(Continued)*

Country	Share of foreigners	
	Population	*Labor force*
Other		
United States	6.2 (1990)	6.7 (1980)
	7.9 (1980)	9.3 (1990)

ᵃ Figures include illegal overstayers but not permanent residents.

SOURCE: OECD (1994c); Japan Ministry of Labor (1995).

Also, in Europe, North America and Asia the regional integration of economies and the labor market are different in nature. The European Union (EU) and the European Economic Area (EEA) labor market is based upon a principle of free movement; the North American Free Trade Association (NAFTA) encourages movement of highly skilled personnel institutionally; but the increasing movement of people in Asia is induced by market-led regionalization (Pang, 1988, 1995).

Although migration policy is not always transferable under different circumstances in general terms, Japan and Germany have been the subjects of international comparison. This chapter will touch upon some aspects of international migration in Japan and Germany and will attempt to make the differences and similarities between the two countries' experiences clearer.

THE LABOR MARKET AND MIGRATION TRENDS

Why has Japan adopted a restrictive immigration policy, especially toward unskilled labor, while Germany, not only in the 1960s, but also at the beginning of the 1990s, has tried to recruit unskilled labor? These policy differences cannot be understood without reviewing the labor situation and migration trends in each country (Table 10.2).

Table 10.2 Labor market situation and trends of labor migration

Year	Japan		Germany (West)	
	Migration trends			Migration trends
1950s	Excess labor supply	Increasing emigration	Separation of East and West Germany	Inflow of Germans from East Germany
1960s	Turning to limited labor supply	Decreasing emigration	Decreasing German labor force	Recruitment of foreign labor
1970s	Employment adjustment after Oil Shock	Continued ban on unskilled workers	Employment adjustment after Oil Shock	End of recruitment of foreign labor (1973)

Table 10.2 (*Continued*)

Year	Japan		Germany (West)	
		Migration trends		*Migration trends*
1980s	Regionalization in Asia; excess labor demand	Massive influx Open to highly skilled	Single European market. Reunification of East and West Germany / economic restructuring	Massive influx. Exceptional recruitment from East
1990s	Regionalization in Asia; excess labor demand			
2000s (Projection)	Globalization/ decreasing labor force	Restriction deregulation	Globalization/ enlargement of European Union	Selection/ programming

Experiences before the Oil Crisis

In the 1950s, at the beginning of Japan's rapid economic growth period, while its manufacturing industry began to absorb its rural work force it remained an emigration country which sent 10 000 or more emigrants per year, mainly to Latin American countries. In the same period Germany, as the Federal Republic of Germany and the German Democratic Republic, experienced a steady migration from East to West which supplied additional workers to West German industries.

Thus, in the 1960s, sharply contrasting situations developed in the two countries. In Japan, the labor market reached what development theory would call a turning point (Lewis, 1954; Minami, 1992) when emigration to Latin American countries ceased (Iguchi, 1995a), while the inflow of young workers continued uninterrupted. In Germany, after the establishment of the Berlin Wall, not only was the supply of German workers from outside almost stopped, but also the economically active population in the Federal Republic of Germany began to shrink. According to estimates by Spitznagel (1987: 243–86), migration compensated for this drop in the German work force (Table 10.3).

The political debates concerning acceptance of foreign workers in the two countries had something in common, in that trade unions in both opposed replacement of native workers by foreign workers (Dohse, 1985; Ministry of Labor, 1992c) even though the German economy was facing an absolute decline in its work force while the Japanese economy was still enjoying an abundant labor supply.

Experiences after the Oil Crisis

In the 1970s, during the recession that followed the Oil Crisis, the policy responses of Japan and Germany were different but related. In the face of its labor shortage Japan saw no reason to lift the ban on unskilled labor, and also continued to accept skilled foreign workers whose knowledge or skill was unavailable or scarce in Japan. Facing a very different labor situation, Germany suspended bilateral labor arrangements and ended international placement services.

Table 10.3 Growth and employment in (West) Germany

Phase	Period (year)	Real GDP growth (%)[a]	Productivity (%)[b]	Change of employment (thousands)		
				Total[c]	Germans[c]	Foreigners[c]
Expansion	1961–6	+4.5	+5.1	+102	–62	+164
Expansion	1967–73	+4.3	+5.4	+25	–149	+174
Lowering growth	1974–84	+1.7	+3.0	–142	–74	–68

[a] Per year.
[b] Per year, man-hour basis.
[c] Absolute change per year.

SOURCE: Spitznagel (1987).

In spite of this suspension, the German Federal Ministry of Internal Affairs and Federal Ministry of Labor and Social Affairs issued an internal memorandum that permitted acceptance of foreign labor. The memorandum contained a list of acceptable occupations and nationalities which was incorporated into the 1990 amendment of the Aliens Law and Employment Promotion Law. Germany has been evolving its immigration policy since the 1980s. It consists of three principles: integration of foreigners who are legal residents, especially foreign workers recruited from abroad and their families; limitation of further migration from countries outside the EC; and the encouragement of voluntary return to the home country (Bundes ministerium des Innern (BMI), 1989).

During the 1980s, especially after the 1985 Plaza Accord, the Japanese economy began to encounter serious trade discord accompanied by a rapid rise in the value of the yen. Moreover, Japan's increasing direct investment in Asian countries has caused a new horizontal division of labor between Japan and its neighbors. Before the 1990s recession, Japanese direct investment in Asian countries increased dramatically and was expected to create more employment opportunities, especially in ASEAN countries (Ito and Iguchi, 1994).

The German economy is also growing in the direction of regional integration. The single European market established at the end of 1992 was expected to create the free movement of capital, goods, services and people within the EU member countries, which might mean that the labor market authority will lose control of its national labor supply. This movement will be promoted through expansion of the EU, especially to members of the European Free Trade Association (EFTA) beginning in 1995 and to East European countries in the future.

In these changing environments, Japan and Germany experienced an enormous influx of foreign labor in the second half of the 1980s. In 1988, the Government of Japan decided to establish new principles for its foreign worker policy: Japan would accept as many highly skilled foreigners as possible, while the acceptance of unskilled workers would be carefully studied (Ministry of Labor, 1992a). Japanese policy could thus be characterized as a dichotomy: liberalization for skilled workers and restrictions for unskilled and semi-skilled workers, a policy orientation that corresponded with the modernization of Japanese industry. At the same time, international cooperation to reduce sending pressures from developing countries became a very important issue in Asia (Iguchi, 1995a).

In 1991, even though Germany had previously ended recruitment from abroad in the wake of reunification, it introduced an exceptional measure to accept foreign labor, based on new labor agreements with East European countries (BA, 1991a and b). To realize this, the new Aliens Law also established new categories of residence permits that could not be extended. These permits form the legal basis of the "rotation system," which did not have a legal foundation in the 1960s. Now, "seasonal workers" and "guest workers" must return to their home countries after their residence permits expire (BMI, 1990).

Effects of Globalization

According to the preliminary results of the OECD (1994c, d) Jobs Study, the effect of globalization on employment in the OECD labor market is "still small." However, industrialization in the East and Southeast Asian economies, or other newly developing economies, may prove damaging to labor-intensive employment sectors, so that pressures for industrial structural adjustment will grow, especially in the developed economies.

Regarding the effects of trade on employment or wages, several US studies in the 1980s suggested that the need for unskilled labor in the manufacturing sector would shrink as a result of adopting labor-saving technologies and due to increasing importation from developing countries (Beckman *et al.*, 1994: 367–97). In Japan, the problem of "hollowization" in the manufacturing industry has been intensively under discussion and there are several preliminary studies (Ministry of Labor 1994b).

These concerns are supported by labor market projections, some of which suggest that low-skill jobs will not grow and may even decrease by the year 2000 (Ministry of Labor, 1992; Ministry of International Trade and Industry (MITI), 1994). This trend coincides with a German labor market projection by Tessering (1993).

Expectations that the demand for low-skilled labor will continue to decrease with the rapid globalization of developed economies, accompanied by the development of information technologies, lead the developed countries to adopt restrictive migration policies toward unskilled labor (United Nations Development Plan, 1994).

At the same time, other studies indicate that foreign workers have become indispensable in some employment sectors (OECD, 1993), and that they are often complementary rather than substitutable (OECD, 1994b). This also suggests that the availability of foreign workers may be influencing the structure of production and employment management in some economic sectors, leading to a chronic shortage of unskilled labor as these sectors postpone modernization.

Another issue is the promotion of technology transfer in both Asia and Europe, where liberalization of unskilled labor controls may have the short-term effect of upgrading industrial and employment structures. But regionalization of economies in Asia and Europe also requires human resource development. A shortage of skilled workers, including managers, engineers, technicians and so-called intermediate-skilled workers will become a serious problem. Therefore, international migration for technology transfer as well as human resource development will become important.

INSTITUTIONAL FRAMEWORK OF FOREIGN LABOR

Various measures are taken at national frontiers to select the kinds of foreign workers that will meet the needs of the local labor market. Table 10.4 shows different types of institutional apparatuses widely used in labor market adjustment. In examining Japanese and German approaches toward foreign labor, first it is necessary to compare the measures taken by the two countries and to consider their possibilities and limitations for the future.

A labor market authority should adjust the supply and demand of domestic workers and, taking foreign labor into account, should determine how to protect the domestic labor market and to what extent foreign labor may be introduced (Iguchi, 1993). In the case of Japan, the Employment Security

Table 10.4 *Measures of immigration control from the standpoint of the labor market*

Criteria	Countries	Limitations
Positive list with no labor market test or numerical quotas	Japan United States and European Union (limited to intra-corporate transfers)	Not flexible according to situation of labor market
Labor market test	EU member countries	Not always practicable; should be simplified
Numerical quotas	Germany (from E. Europe) Switzerland United States (specialty occupations)	Rationale should be re-examined

NOTE: The "point system" of accepting migrants, used in Canada and Australia, is excluded here because such a system is used for permanent, not temporary migrants.

SOURCE: Compiled by author using text of General Agreement of Trade in Services (GATS) and official documents and legal texts of the countries concerned.

Law prescribes equal treatment among nationalities but does not explicitly deal with foreign workers. While the labor market authority is to take responsibility for the "proper adjustment of demand and supply of work force," the "Criteria for Disembarkation Examination" under the Immigration Control and Refugees Recognition Act, must take "the situation of industry and national life" into account. In the common understanding of the ministries concerned, the labor market situation should also be reflected in the "Criteria for Disembarkation Examination" (Iguchi, 1993). Under present law, a foreigner may not be refused entry because of some numerical ceiling or the availability or priority of Japanese workers in the labor market. Therefore, the Japanese system falls under "Positive list" in Table 10.4.

On the other hand, the German "Employment Promotion Law" prescribes that special work permits must be based on conditions in the labor market, the "labor market test" of Table 10.4. There are exceptions: if the foreign worker has been legally employed for over 5 years, this test will not be required; nor will it be required for some exceptional nationalities and jobs. This work permit/labor market test requirement goes back to 1923, when unemployment was a social problem and trade unions insisted on determining the availability of German workers before hiring foreigners. The work permit system operates independently from the residence permit system (Dohse, 1985).

Japan has not experienced high unemployment coupled with an inflow of large numbers of foreign workers; should this occur, Japan should consider the introduction of a labor market test to identify areas of labor shortage and the availability of native workers to fill the jobs. The probable administrative costs of such a test and practical ways to implement it should also be considered.

At this time, Japan has no numerical quotas for immigrants; Germany in 1991 established new regulations intended to enable the government to conclude bilateral agreements for the establishment of such quotas (BMI, 1990).

From the standpoint of liberalization of trade in services and the movement of the workers who supply them, the labor market test and numerical quotas may be an infringement of Article 16 of the General Agreement on Trade in Services (GATS). Therefore, many countries, including Japan, the EU members, the United States and Canada, may not apply the labor market test in the case of some persons, such as inter-company transferees employed by a foreign service supplier. In any case, protection of the domestic labor market and further acceptance of foreign labor should be reconciled by some kind of institutional devices. The German and Japanese experiences should be examined from such viewpoints to help these nations adapt to changing international and domestic environments.

BILATERAL ARRANGEMENTS AND ILLEGAL WORKERS

In the area of bilateral arrangements concerning foreign workers, Germany and Japan provide interesting examples for comparison (Table 10.5).

In the 1960s Germany concluded bilateral labor agreements with eight countries. In those days, a "rotation system" had not yet been promulgated, employment contracts were renewable, and the duration of stay could be prolonged. In the 1990s, guest-worker agreements, mainly with East European countries, supply (skilled) guest workers, seasonal workers, sub contracted workers and, with some countries, frontier workers; all are subject to the rotation system under the 1990 Aliens Act (Bundesanstalt für Arbeit, 1991a and b).

Labor agreements are a recent development in Japan. In 1993 a new scheme, the "Technical Intern Traineeship Program," was introduced and the Japan International Training Co-operation Organization was established under the joint control of the Ministries of Justice, Labor, Foreign Affairs, International Trade and Industry, and Construction. The traineeship program can be compared to the German guest-worker agreement to a limited extent, in that the guest-worker program is also used to provide practical training to personnel of German enterprises in Eastern Europe (Japan Institute of Labor, 1994; Kuptsch and Oishi, 1995).

Controlling Return Migration

The potential number of migrants from East Europe to Germany under its "law of return" may be 3.5 million; there are 1.6 million *Nikkeijin* – descendents of Japanese immigrants

Table 10.5 *Bilateral arrangements or agreements concerning foreign labor (1994)*

Category	Japan	Germany
International traineeship under employment contract	Technical intern trainees from: China Thailand, the Philippines, Indonesia, Vietnam, Peru and Laos **(approx. 2000 in 1994)**	Guest workers for on-the-job training (OJT) with quotas from: Albania, Bulgaria, Czech Republic, Hungary, Latvia, Poland, Romania and Slovakia **(approx. 4200)**
International placement	Japanese–Brazilians from: Brazil **(approx. 152 000)** (The Employment Center for Japanese–Brazilians in São Paolo has been the official placement channel to Japan since 1994	Seasonal workers with labor market test from: Hungary, Poland, Czech Republic, Slovakia, Albania, Bulgaria, Romania, Latvia and Lithuania **(approx. 180 000)** Frontier workers with labor market test from: Czech Republic, Poland, Austria and Switzerland
International subcontracting		Subcontracted workers with quotas from: Bulgaria, Czech Republic, Hungary, Latvia, Poland, Romania, Turkey, Ex-Yugoslavia, Bosnia–Herzegovina, Croatia, Macedonia and Slovenia **(approx. 55 000)**

– in Latin America. It will be useful to compare the laws governing these groups' return to their ethnic homelands.

The legal framework for acceptance of ethnic Germans is the most generous in the world: if they can verify that their ancestors were German, they can apply for German citizenship. In the case of Japan, those who are second- or third-generation descendents of emigrants from Japan, and their spouses, are entitled to a residence status that permits every kind of activity, including employment. Most of these return migrants are from Brazil; although there is no formal agreement, there has been an understanding between the two countries on the need to protect *Nikkeijin* who wish to work in Japan from illegal recruiters or brokers. Within Japan, the network of the public employment service has been strengthened by introducing interpretation and counselling services for foreigners. Such official international placement services are not intended to promote labor importation from Brazil, but to eliminate illegal or inadequate placements between the two countries and to guarantee the rights of the workers. In 1993 approximately 152 000 *Nikkeijin* were estimated to be working in Japan. Some of them regularly return for a year or two to Latin American countries, which creates integration problems in their everyday lives. In the case of ethnic Germans, on the other hand, extensive integration measures are taken, but, as the potential numbers are greater than the possibility of absorbing them, a new quota system was introduced in 1993, limiting acceptance to 230 000 ethnic Germans per year.

Legal and Illegal Workers

The above-mentioned schemes are the official channels for foreign workers to obtain entry. But many foreigners come to Japan or Germany and work illegally, simply by overstaying their tourist visas. In Japan, out of 2.8 million tourists, 290 000 are estimated to be overstaying visas. In Germany in 1992, 1.4 million tourists arrived from East Europe and the former Soviet Union alone. Although there are no official estimates of illegal workers, many of these tourists may be working illegally. In addition, about 360 000 asylum-seekers and their families may have been working legally in 1993. We should have no illusions on the replacement effects of official channels, but without them it is very difficult to exert influence on commercially based illegal recruitment. Both the German and Japanese experiences suggest that official channels should be strengthened and supported by the governments of both sending and receiving countries to combat clandestine migration.

INTEGRATION OF FOREIGN WORKERS AND THEIR FAMILIES

To what extent can foreign workers be integrated into Japan or Germany? In terms of integration, the two countries have some aspects in common. Both accept the principle of "*jus sanguinis*" concerning nationality; neither intends to accept foreign workers as permanent settlers, and each permits renewal of temporary residence permits; in both cases, return migrants account for a large percentage of foreign workers; and, finally, both countries find integration of the second and third generations of their foreign workers to be problematic.

The development of integration measures in Germany goes back to the 1960s, as non-governmental organizations, especially Christian volunteer groups, offered services to foreign workers such as guidance and counseling. Beginning in the 1970s, trade unions have also aided foreign workers, promoting their equal status in the workplace (Dohse, 1982b). ·Because there were many Turkish workers in the trade unions, workplace integration was achieved rapidly.

In contrast, in Japan studies of integration measures are still underdeveloped. Integration of foreign workers and their families will be considered more fully elsewhere in this volume; however, it is significant that while administrative costs for such measures were a billion dollars in West Germany in 1989 (an underestimate, since it includes budgets of state and central governments, but not of communes), the estimated expenditures at the prefectural and local level in Japan amounted to only 51.2 million dollars. According to a new survey in 1993, services to foreigners by local governments have improved substantially.

Table 10.6   *Estimates of administrative cost of specific measures for foreign inhabitants (in dollars)*

	Germany (West) 1989[a]	Italy 1989[b]	Japan 1991[c]
Administrative cost (estimates)	1 billion	76.7 million	51.2 million
Share of foreign residents[d]	7.6% (1988)	0.8% (1988)	0.6% (1991)

[a] Estimates of administrative cost of specific measure for foreign inhabitants in the budgets of the Federal government (*Bund*) and state governments (*Länder*). Costs include language education for foreign workers and their families, vocational training, subsidies for consultation services provided by private institutions, and aid for returning to their home countries in 1991. The costs do not cover social insurance and social services provided by regional governments such as cities and communes.

[b] Estimates of administrative cost of the national government which subsidizes regional governments and private institutions undertaking integration measures for foreign inhabitants in 1991.

[c] Estimates of administrative cost of specific measures for foreign inhabitants in the budgets of prefectural governments and local governments. The costs include those for employing teachers for foreign languages, distribution of pamphlets for foreign citizens, establishment of language schools for inhabitants and subsidies for volunteer groups etc.

[d] Ratio of foreign inhabitants to total population in each country.

SOURCE: Japan Ministry of Labor (1992a).

THE MIGRATION POLICY-MAKING PROCESS

It is hard to compare the migration policy-making processes of Japan and Germany; the process is different depending upon the economic and social factors involved in each. Some issues must be decided by the parliament, while others are left to administrative discretion. In some cases, trade unions and employer associations play active roles; in others, political parties debate the issues.

Migration Policy-making in Germany

In Germany, there have been three turning points in policy orientation. The first was in 1955, with the agreement between Germany and Italy which initiated labor recruitment from abroad. In 1973, recruitment from abroad, which by then included eight bilateral agreements, was suspended because of the worsening labor market after the Oil Shock. The third was the amendment of the Aliens Law and conclusion of bilateral labor agreements with East European countries following the collapse of the Eastern Bloc. The following summary of policy-making in these three cases relies mainly upon the work of Dohse (1985) and the Japan Ministry of Labor.

In 1955, the Baden-Wurtenberg Farmers' Association intensified its demands that the regional governments, the Federal Ministry of Labor and Social Affairs and the Federal Employment Agency begin recruiting foreign workers – demands that had been made since 1952. The German Trade Union Federation (DGB) did not object to the introduction of foreign workers in agriculture in principle, but it imposed stringent conditions: (1) priority of employing German workers; (2) equal treatment of German and foreign workers in wages and other working conditions; (3) precise identification of sectoral and regional needs; (4) restriction of work permits for foreigners to fill seasonally urgent needs.

Germany had been negotiating with the Italian government on placement of Italian workers in Germany since 1952, with the Italians much more interested in concluding an agreement than the Germans. In 1954 the Federal Employment Agency expressed its opposition to the introduction of foreign agricultural workers, following protests not only by trade unions but also by several government agencies including the Federal Ministry of Economy. The Federal Minister of Labor and Social Affairs stated that importation of labor from Italy should not take place before 1957; in Parliament, no political parties supported the importation of Italian labor.

However, in September 1955 Federal Economic Minister Erhard said that there was no reserve labor force in Germany and it was therefore necessary to prepare for importation of foreign labor. In October the Federal Ministry of Economy had planned to establish the Program for Stabilization of the

Economy and Exchange Rate. This program contained some deliberations on wage policy, among them that wages should be decided by social partners, taking into account the German macroeconomic environment. To provide such an environment and as part of its Stabilization Program, the Ministry of Economy announced that the tight labor market situation caused by the shortage of German workers must be improved by the importation of foreign labor.

The Federal Ministry of Labor and Social Affairs, accepting this rationale, agreed with the change of policy regarding foreign workers. Two months after establishment of the Stabilization Program, the Federal Ministry of Labor, which was responsible for the negotiations with Italy in substance, concluded an agreement in Rome. As a ministerial action this arrangement was not subject to parliamentary approval; after 1955, arrangements with other countries were also concluded under administrative discretion and without parliamentary ratification. Foreign worker policy was thus in the hands of the Federal Government rather than those of political parties until the late 1980s, when the extension of foreign workers' rights became a political issue that resulted in the 1990 amendment of the Aliens Law.

The second turning point in German foreign labor policy, in 1973, was the "*Anwerbestop*", the suspension of recruitment from abroad. After the Oil Shock, as economic recession and unemployment increased, international arrangements for recruitment of foreign workers were suspended. This suspension, announced on 23 November 1973, 3 months after a strike of Turkish workers in Ford AG, was intended to be long-term, and the Federal Ministry of Labor and Social Affairs stressed that the employment of German workers should be a high priority. This decision invoked many protests from employers. The German Employers Federation insisted upon the need to recruit foreign seasonal workers. But since the government refused to introduce a rotation system or the obligation to return to home countries, employers had the choice to recruit foreign workers or not; there was no way to recruit seasonal workers only.

During the 1980s, although the inflow of foreign workers was strictly regulated and they were encouraged to return to their home countries, the number of foreign residents was growing steadily. In 1990 over half the foreign workers had been living in Germany for 10 years or longer. The second generation of foreign workers were growing up and entering the labor market having never lived in their home countries. Given these developments, foreign workers' right to stay and work became an important political issue during the 1980s. The new political parties, especially the Green Party (*die Grünen*), insisted that Germany had already become an "*Einwanderungsland*" (a country of settlement migration), and those foreigners who had been residents for a long time should acquire permanent resident status as well as the right to vote in local elections. While the Social Democrats and the Green Party were willing to guarantee the rights of long-term residents, the coalition of the Christian Democrats/Christian Socialists and the Free Democrats were very cautious about extending these rights, and wanted to impose limits on the second generation, awarding a stable legal status only to those who had successfully integrated. In some state governments (*Länder*) such as Hambourg and Nordrhein-Westfalen, the voting rights of long-term foreign residents were acknowledged in *Länder* laws, a ruling later set aside by the Constitutional Court, which said these *Länder* laws are inconsistent with the Basic Law (the German constitution).

With the collapse of the Soviet Union, culminating in the destruction of the Berlin Wall on 9 November 1989, migration from the East increased dramatically. Germany found itself coping with the new tidal wave not only from the standpoints of immigration and labor market authorities, but also from that of international cooperation with the East European countries that contributed to the unification process. The introduction of new labor agreements with East European countries became a keen political issue. In December 1990 Labor Minister Brüm promised in Warsaw to accept a certain number of Polish workers as an exception to the "*Anwerbestop*". The legal basis of such an exception had already been provided by the Parliament, and a new ordinance by the Federal Ministry of Labor and Social Affairs was introduced. This ordinance needed to be examined and recognized also by the the *Bundesrat* (the Upper House, which consists of representatives of the *Länder*). Thus an important change in policy-making occurred, as the political parties took the lead in the debates on the issue of rights of foreign workers and their families.

Migration Policy-making in Japan

During the era of high economic growth, the Minister of Labor commented at a Cabinet meeting that unskilled foreign workers should not be permitted to enter and stay in Japan (Ministry of Labor 1992c). In the 1989 Economic Plan and the Basic Plan of Employment Policy, the government's basic policies concerning foreign workers were formalized. The document was prepared by a committee made up of university professors and business managers representing employers and trade unions. The process included hearings at which draft proposals prepared by the secretariat were discussed, as were several academic studies and proposals. For example, against a background of the growing number of foreigners in Japan who are working illegally or who are there because of the internationalization of economic activities, the Ministry of Labor and the Ministry of Justice took opposite stands. The Ministry of Labor favored a broadened scope for foreigners who are permitted to enter, stay and work in Japan, and the institutionalization of an employment permit system (Ministry of Labor, 1989); the Ministry of Justice was preparing an amendment of the Immigration Control and Refugee Recognition Act that would make the residence status system more transparent and combat illegal employment. A logical compromise between the two ministries should be to broaden the categories of accepted foreign workers to include those who posess special technical skills or knowledge, and to intro- duce employer sanctions in the case of illegal employment.

During the above discussions the Liberal Democratic Party (LDP) held a strong majority in the Upper House and Parliament, so that the political discussions concerning Japan's foreign worker policy occurred mainly within the party. There, various factions within the LDP supported the proposals of the various ministries; any draft of an economic plan or an employment plan had to be recognized within the LDP. This basic decision-making mechanism was maintained in 1992, as the economic plan and employment plan were amended.

An extraordinary process was needed to bring about inauguration of the Technical Intern Training System. Within the LDP, influential Parliament members insisted on the acceptance of unskilled workers, who had previously been rigorously excluded. This development was brought about by the circumstances of the "bubble economy," with its high demand for workers and the accompanying severe labor shortage. The Tokyo Chamber of Commerce also drew up a proposal to introduce unskilled workers for the purpose of technology transfer through on-the-job training.

To cope with this discussion and to protect its basic policy, the Ministry of Labor issued a proposal to accept foreigners as trainees, and then to allow them a certain period of employment if the training was formally acknowledged as having been successful. In 1992, the Prime Minister's Provisional Committee for Administrative Reform presented its conclusions on measures against illegal employment, and proposals for acceptance of additional foreign workers. Although the idea of Tokyo Chamber of Commerce seems to have been taken into account by the Committee, it was the proposal of the Ministry of Labor that was eventually accepted. The Committee then proposed a "Technical Intern Traineeship Program" for the purpose of international cooperation in the field of human resource development. As the Cabinet decided that the proposal should be respected, the ministries concerned were urged to cooperate in the establishment of the new training system. The Ministry of Justice and the Ministry of Labor have cooperated to realize the new scheme, as have other ministries, such as the Ministry of Foreign Affairs, the Ministry of International Trade and Industries, and the Ministry of Construction.

Meanwhile, the National Police Agency, the Ministry of Justice and the Ministry of Labor have begun cooperating to cope with illegal workers and visa overstayers, an issue that has attracted wide social and political attention.

In sum, decision-making in Japan depends primarily on cooperation among the ministries concerned, and any drastic change of policy is impossible without a new consensus among them. As a coordinating organ, the Cabinet or the Prime Minister's Office must play an important role, if there should be a fundamental change of policy orientation, since the political parties' leadership has not always been strong enough.

Practically speaking, the future of the basic foreign worker policy depends on effective cooperation among ministries, although the parliament may also play an active role in realizing a more comprehensive approach

CONCLUSION

Germany's highly refined system for "selection and programming" of migratory flows – the labor market test in the domestic labor market, bilateral labor agreements with numerical quotas and cooperation of labor market authorities with neighbouring countries – is based on a long European tradition, and the renewal or strengthening of such a system after the reunification of 1990 should be understood from the viewpoint of European integration. Germany was forced to deal with an unprecedented inflow from the East European countries, and subsequently not only to curb illegal migration but also to promote development of human resources and to facilitate Eastern Europe's transition to a market economy.

The effectiveness of Germany's system seems to be limited, if one examines the country's experience since the 1950s. The labor market test is not always feasible, as its full implementation is very complicated. Such a test, if it is to prove that employment of a foreign worker will not damage the employment opportunities of a German worker, should be limited to certain occupations, sectors or schemes. This is also the case for the rotation system, if it is expanded to cover greater numbers of foreign workers in a growing variety of jobs. The growing need for integration of foreign workers and their families will give rise to more exceptions, as the history of the German guest worker policy shows.

The scheme that began in 1991 should be viewed as a kind of experiment, an exception to the ban on recruitment from abroad. The scope and size of this exception should not exceed the capacity of the labor market authority or the capacity of integration, either in the labor market or in society.

In Asia, where there is an enormous surplus of labor and the potential for the international migration of unskilled labor is very great, efforts to create employment through export-led development strategies and the improvement of living standards are very promising. Industrialized countries should not rely upon importing unskilled labor, but upon industrial upgrading. Japan in particular should not become a major importer of unskilled labor, but should improve the qualification spectrum of its work force. Furthermore, Japan should make more efforts to reduce sending pressures from abroad through international cooperation. The German experience has been and will be very instructive for the Japanese labor market authority inasmuch as bilateral efforts to create an orderly channel of migration are of great importance, but such official channels should seek to enhance technology transfer and the exchange of skilled personnel in accordance with the structural adjustment of the economies. Finally, the policy-making process should be reviewed and rationalized, in order to realize an orderly and beneficial movement of people in an integrated world economy.

REFERENCES

Beckman, E., Bound, J. and Gilliches, Z. (1994), "Changes in Demand for Skilled Labour within US Manufacturing," *Quarterly Journal of Economics*, pp. 367–97.

Bundesministerium des Innern (1989), *Aufzeichnuung zur Ausländerpolitik und zum Ausländer der Bundesrepublik Deutschland.*

—— (1990), *Das neue Ausländerrecht der Bundesrepublik Deutschland.*

Bundesanstalt für Arbeit (1991a), *Dienstblatt betreff Vermittlung ausländischer Arbeitnehmer für eine bis 3 monatige Beschäftigung in der Bundesrepublik Deutschland* (Nürnberg): Bundesanstalt für Arbeit).

—— (1991b), *Dienstblatt betreff Deutsch-polnische Regierungsvereinbarung über die Beschäftigung polnischer Arbeitnehmer auf der Grundlage von Werkverträgen* (Nürnberg Bundesanstalt für Arbeit).

Dohse, K. (1982a), *Foreign Workers in the Federal Republic of Germany: Government Policy and Discrimination in Employment* (Berlin: Wissenschaftszentrum, IIVG).

—— (1982b), "Auslänische Arbeiter und betriebliche Personalpolitik," *Gewerkschaftliche Monatshefte*, No. 7.

—— (1985), *Auslänische Arbeiter und bürgerlicher Staat* (Berlin: Express Edition).

Garçon, J. (1995), "Recent Trends in Migration Movements and Policies in OECD Countries," paper presented to the symposium on Migration and Labour Markets in Asia in the Year 2000, sponsored by OECD, Government of Japan and Japan Institute of Labour, Tokyo, January 19–20.

Iguchi, Y. (1993), "Japanese Labour Market and Employment Policy for Foreign Workers," in *Study Report of Historical Development of Foreign Workers Policy*, in Japanese (Tokyo: Rondomondai Research Center).

—— (1995a), "Integrated Labour Market Policies to Meet the Challenges of International Migration," paper presented to the symposium on Migration and Labour Markets in Asia in the Year 2000, sponsored by OECD, Government of Japan and Japan Institute of Labour, Tokyo, January 19–20.

—— (1995b), "International Migration in the 1990s," in *Rodojiho* (Tokyo: Ministry of Labour).

Ito, S. Y. and Iguchi, Y. (1994), "Japanese Direct Investment and its Impact on Migration in the ASEAN 4," *Journal of Asian and Pacific Migration*, 3 (2–3).

Japan Institute of Labour (JIL) (1994), *Traineeship for Foreigners in UK, France and Germany*, in Japanese (Tokyo: JIL).

Kuptsch, C., and Oishi, N. (1995), *Training Abroad: German and Japanese Schemes for Workers from Transition Economies or Developing Countries* (Geneva: International Labour Organization).

Lewis, W. A. (1954), "Economic Development with Unlimited Supply of Labour," *Manchester School of Economics and Social Studies*, 22 (May).

Minami, R. (1992), *Economic Development in Japan*, 2nd edn, in Japanese (Tokyo: Toyokeizai-shiopo-sha).

Ministry of International Trade and Industry (MITI) (1994), *Industrial Structure in the 21st Century*, in Japanese (Tokyo: MITI).

Ministry of Labour (MOL) (1989), *Report of the Study Committee on Foreign Workers' Affairs*, in Japanese (Tokyo: MOL).

—— (1992a), *Report of the Study Committee on the Effects of Foreign Workers on the Labour Market*, in Japanese (Tokyo: MOL).

—— (1992b), *Report of the Study Committee on Employment Policy*, in Japanese (Tokyo: MOL).

—— (1992c), *Documentation of Employment Policy for Foreign Workers*, in Japanese (Tokyo: MOL).

—— (1994a), *Report of the Study Committee on Employment Policy on Medium-term Employment Prospects*, in Japanese (Tokyo: MOL).

—— (1994b), *On the Issue of Hollowization in the Manufacturing Industry*, in Japanese (Tokyo: MOL).

—— (1995), *Present Situation of Employment Policy for Foreign Workers* (in Japanese) (Tokyo: MOL). OECD (1993), SOPEMI, *Continuous Reporting System for International Migration* (Paris: OECD).

—— (1994a), *Migration and Development* (Paris: OECD).

—— (1994b), *Jobs Study* (Paris: OECD).

—— (1994c), *Jobs Study Part I, Evidence and Explanations* (Paris: OECD)

—— (1994d), *Jobs Study Part II, Evidence and Explanations* (Paris: OECD)

Pang, E. F. (1988), "Structural Change and Labour Market Developments: The Comparative Experience of Five ASEAN Countries and Australia", in E. F. Pang (ed.), *Labour Market Developments and Structural Change* (Singapore: Singapore University Press).

—— (1995), "Structural Change and International Migration in Selected ASEAN Countries", paper presented to the symposium on Migration and

Labour Markets in Asia in the Year 2000, sponsored by OECD, Government of Japan and Japan Institute of Labour, Tokyo, January 19–20.

Spitznagel, E. (1987), "Gesamtwirtschaftliche Aspecte der Ausländerbeschäftigung," in E. Hönekopp (ed.), *Aspecke der Ausländerbeschäftigung in der Bundesrepublik Deutschland* (Nürnberg: Institut der Arbeitsmarkt und Berufsforschung), Betr. AB 114.

Tessering, M. (1993), *Manpower Requirement by Levels of Qualification in West Germany Until 2010* (Nürnberg: Institut für Arbeitsmarkt und Berufsforschung Werkstatt Bericht no. 4)

UNDP (1994), *Human Resource Development Report* (New York: UNDP).

11 The Perils and Promise of Pluralism: Lessons from the German Case for Japan

Thomas U. Berger

From their emergence as late industrializing military powers in the mid-nineteenth century to their reconstruction after the Second World War as peaceful trading nations allied with the United States, modern Germany and Japan have followed remarkably similar trajectories of development.[1] Because of the many striking parallels between the two countries, and because Germany modernized at an earlier date, Japan has a long tradition of seeking to draw lessons from the German experience. As early as the Meiji period, Japan's oligarchical leadership treated Wilhelmine Germany as a model, importing its legal, constitutional and military institutions.[2] Germany's cultural influence on Japan continued after the Meiji period, at times with negative consequences, as when during the 1920s and 1930s German ideas of the totalitarian state inspired the Japanese militarists (Peattie, 1975). Since 1945, Japan has looked more to the United States than to Germany for inspiration. Nonetheless, the affinity between Germany and Japan remains strong, and in certain respects may even be increasing.[3]

This affinity is especially striking in the area of immigration and national identity. Like Japan, German nationality has historically been defined in terms of a shared history, culture and ethnic background, as opposed to attachment to a particular set of ideals and institutions, as in the United States, France and England.[4] One concrete reflection of this approach to national identity is the two nations' nationality codes, which base citizenship on blood ties – the principle of *jus sanguinis*.[5]

Like Japan, Germany has had a troubled history of dealing with foreigners in its midst, traditionally viewing them as a threat to the cultural unity of the nation and seeking to minimize their impact on society. These tendencies reached murderous dimensions during the Nazi regime, leading to a violent rejection of such virulent racist doctrines in the post-war period. Yet, despite democratization and considerable liberalization of its attitudes toward foreigners, like Japan, Germany continues to define itself in ethnic terms and remains highly ambivalent about the growing resident population of foreigners.

Unlike Japan, however, post-war Germany has had extensive experience with immigration. Beginning in the mid-1950s the Federal Republic of Germany (and to a lesser extent the East German Democratic Republic) set out to actively recruit foreign workers to meet the labor needs of a rapidly expanding economy. As a result of this decision, the Federal Republic has become a *de facto* country of immigration, even while the German government continues steadfastly to maintain Germany's non-immigration status. In July 1992 German government statistics showed that there were 6 496 000 foreigners living in Germany, representing almost 8 percent of the total population. In addition, the majority of foreigners – over 61 percent in 1993 – had lived in Germany for more than 10 years (Press and Information Office, 1993: 108–9). In contrast, when Japan began to face similar pressures in the late 1960s, the government of Sato Eisaku decided against foreign labor recruitment and instead encouraged Japanese firms to transfer low-level production operations overseas.

A number of Japanese observers, most notably Nishio Kanji, have seen in the German experience with immigration a cautionary tale for Japan. Pointing to Germany's problems with integrating its immigrants into society, as well as to the bitter political controversy that immigration has triggered there, they argue that Japan should continue to prohibit the entry of foreign workers (Nishio, 1992). Other Japanese analysts, such as Shimada Haruo, while somewhat more positive in their assessment of immigration, still view the consequences of the German decision to allow foreign labor migration in a largely negative light (Tezuka, 1989: Hosomi, 1992; Chs 9, 10).

However, in recent years both the push and the pull factors in favoring immigration to Japan have grown considerably;

Table 11.1 Length of residence (years) in Germany, total and largest ten nationalities, December 1991

	Total	Less than 1 year	1–4	4–6	6–8	8–10	10–15	15–20	20+
EU	1,487,400	72,300	192,500	80,700	58,700	52,600	185,400	242,300	604,800
Turkey	1,779,600	71,100	247,800	116,400	74,000	71,000	415,300	443,200	340,000
Yugoslavia	775,100	110,600	92,000	24,400	18,700	18,400	82,500	148,600	281,800
Greece	336,900	17,400	58,700	14,900	8,500	9,500	29,700	53,600	146,200
Spain	135,200	3,000	6,900	3,600	2,700	2,800	10,300	25,300	80,800
Portugal	93,000	7,500	11,200	4,000	2,100	2,200	11,500	30,200	24,300
Italy	560,100	18,200	57,800	32,900	23,900	22,000	87,000	89,400	228,100
Morocco	75,100	4,500	15,200	8,300	5,500	4,900	15,500	10,000	11,300
Tunisia	27,200	1,200	4,000	2,100	1,700	1,700	5,500	4,900	6,100
Total	**5,882,300**	**511,800**	**1,128,500**	**406,800**	**279,300**	**220,400**	**894,400**	**850,400**	**1,490,800**

SOURCE: Cornelia Schmalz-Jacobsen *et al.* (1993).

today a substantial increase in the influx of foreign labor to Japan appears almost inevitable. Once again, it appears that the Japanese experience parallels developments in Germany, this time in the area of immigration. In this context, a re-examination of the impact of immigration on Germany may be instructive in identifying the problems that Japan is likely to encounter.

In what follows we shall briefly survey the impact of immi-gration on Germany in three distinct areas: (1) immigration and the economy; (2) immigration and the society at large; (3) the politics of immigration. In the concluding section we will examine the comparability of the German and Japanese situations, and tentatively explore the lessons that Japan may draw from the German experience.

If the German experience is any guide, the influx of for-eigners into Japan is likely to lead to a growing resident foreign population, triggering severe social and political tensions which will compel the political authorities to increase efforts at controlling the influx of both legal and illegal im-migrants. At the same time, Japanese policy-makers will try to better integrate those foreigners who do settle in Japan in order to avoid creating a permanent underclass and damaging diplomatic relations with neighboring Asian countries. Managing these conflicting pressures will be one of the most difficult tasks that Japan will face in the twenty-first century, but a careful comparison of the social and political conditions in the two countries suggests that there is no *a priori* reason to believe that Japan will be any more or less capable of meeting this challenge than Germany or other advanced industrial nations.

THE ECONOMIC IMPACT OF IMMIGRATION

The economic costs and benefits of immigration are a matter of some dispute among economists and immigration experts worldwide. On the one hand, there are those who look to im-migration for the salvation of advanced industrial societies beset by the labor shortages and growing deficits in the pension and state health insurance systems caused by de-clining birth rates. Others, however, point out that there are already high levels of unemployment in those occupational categories that attract immigrants, and that encouraging further immigration to meet short-term labor market needs will, in the long run, exacerbate social inequality and actually increase the burden on the welfare state.[6] These debates are unlikely to be resolved any time soon. Regardless of what the actual economic impact of immigration may be, it appears to be the consensus among German experts that immigration has had a positive effect on the German economy and that further immigration will be necessary in the future. German analyses of the economic effects of immigration have focused on three central questions: the impact of immigration on the German labor market, how the influx of foreign workers affects economic growth; and the potential burdens placed by immigration on the welfare state.

With reference to labor market issues, German advocates of a harder policy stance on immigration frequently point out that when foreign workers were originally recruited, unemployment levels in the German economy were low (around 2–3 percent). Since then, however, unemployment rates, among both native Germans and foreign workers, have increased dramatically, to approximately 10 percent in 1992. Yet, despite having unemployment rates 4–6 percent higher than the native German population, foreign workers have chosen to remain in Germany.[7] Some critics acerbically maintain that the "guest workers" – *Gastarbeiter*, the term used to differentiate foreign workers in the post-war period from the forced laborers of the Nazi era – have become "guests" without "work."[8] The general implications of this line of criticism are that foreigners are taking jobs away from Germans, and that those foreigners who do not work prefer to live off the largesse of the German welfare state. Asylum seekers, in particular, are seen as a drain on the German system, a perception reinforced by much publicized incidents of abuse of the welfare system – such as asylum seekers drawing welfare benefits while working on the black market, or using false papers to receive benefits under as many as a dozen different names.[9]

Most German economists, however, argue that high unemployment rates in the German economy have little to do with the presence of foreign workers. They point to statistics showing that those Germans who are unemployed suffer from a variety of disabilities and are unable to perform the work that foreigners do.[10] Rather than displacing German workers, the evidence suggests that, for the most part, foreigners have taken over work that Germans are no longer willing to perform themselves.[11] Consequently, even if all foreign workers were to leave Germany, there would be little significant change in the overall German unemployment rate.

Indeed, were such a development to take place, there is even evidence which suggests that the unemployment rate might increase, because a drop in economic activity is likely to follow. A study conducted for the city of Düsseldorf projects that if the foreign population were to move out over the space of 2–3 years, severe shortages would develop in economic spheres, including transportation, construction and service industries such as sanitation, food services and nursing. The disappearance of foreign students, foreign commuters and foreign customers would push down the demand for goods and services, leading to the closing of many schools and shops and making large portions of the local infrastructure superfluous (Landeshauptstadt Düsseldorf, Sozialdezernat, 1992; Hermann, 1992b; Schumacher, 1993).

Other analysts note that the rapid integration of nearly 4.2 million immigrants in the period between 1988 and 1992 – including ethnic Germans from Eastern Europe (*Aussiedler*) and the former German Democratic Republic (*Übersiedler*) – suggests that there remains a large, unsatisfied demand for low- to medium-skilled labor in the German economy which the domestic labor market has been unable to meet (Gieseck, *et al.*, 1993: 30–6). Some economists suggest that the presence of foreign workers has helped overcome bottlenecks in the labor market, increasing the total number of jobs available and allowing German workers to take on more highly-skilled, better-paying types of work (Gieseck *et al.*, 1993: 35–6).

Finally, the evolution of the foreign labor force strongly suggests that on balance foreign workers have served as a buffer against variations in the business cycle. Over the past 35 years, the number of foreign workers has increased whenever there has been an upturn in economic growth, while economic downturns have witnessed a net departure of foreign workers from the German economy. Without foreign workers, it is argued, the social costs of the business cycle would have to be entirely borne by the native German workforce (Castles and Kosack, 1985).

In terms of economic growth, a number of experts have pointed to the ready supply of immigrant labor as a major factor in the German economic "miracle" of the 1950s and 1960s (Kindleberger, 1967). More recently, econometric analyses suggest that the influx of foreign workers contributed to economic growth during the economic boom of 1988–92, raising growth rates to an average of 3.5 percent a year. Without immigration it is estimated that the growth rate during this time period would have remained at around 2 percent a year. Per-capita growth, on the other hand, remains largely unaffected by the influx of workers (Gieseck et al., 1993: 39–40).

On the other hand, the evidence is mixed as to whether the availability of foreign labor may have slowed down the structural evolution of the German economy by allowing out-dated, lower value-added branches of industry to survive longer then they otherwise might have done (Wehrmann, 1989). It should be pointed out, however, that while some of the industries in which foreign labor is concentrated, such as steel, are by international standards uncompetitive, other branches of industry dependent on foreign workers are counted among Germany's export leaders, such as the automobile industry, where 25 percent of all workers are foreigners.

Perhaps the most difficult question to resolve is whether the presence of a large, low- to medium-skilled foreign population represents a burden on the German welfare state. A number of studies suggest that, on balance, immigration has had a positive impact on government finances. According to one analysis produced by the Rheinische Wirtschafts Institut in Köln, public spending on immigrants including ethnic German *Aussiedler* and *Übersiedler* totaled 37.2 billion Marks in 1991 (including 17.2 billion Marks in direct welfare payments to immigrants as well as 20 billion Marks in increased spending on social infrastructure such as schools and public housing). Against these costs must be balanced the 30.2 billion Marks immigrants pay in taxes and contributions to health insurance, pension and unemployment funds, along with the estimated 20.5 billion Marks in increased revenues from German taxpayers that result from the boost in economic growth attributable to foreigners.[12] The study concluded that, on balance, immigration has brought a net increase in government revenues of 13.4 billion marks during the 1988–91 period.

This rather optimistic assessment of the costs and benefits of immigration to the German welfare state rests on two assumptions, one purely economic in nature, the other more social. First, it assumes positive growth in the economy. During periods of economic downturn, however, larger numbers of foreigners are likely to become unemployed and forced to draw unemployment benefits. If the economic downturn in severe and protracted, the net costs to state finances incurred by foreign workers and their families may outweigh the benefits (Giesek *et al.*, 1993: 40–1). Second, and more importantly, the demographic profile of different ethnic groups in Germany has historically come to approximate that of the native German population. Early in the post-war immigration cycle, the foreign population consisted largely of young, employed males. As they settled down in German society, however, they brought their wives and children, built homes and eventually retired. Whether their children will be able to replicate their parents' successful integration into the German economy is open to question. First, the modern economy increasingly demands a high level of skills and specialized knowledge that foreign workers frequently lack; second, the new generation of young foreigners increasingly hold attitudes and expectations of work and the welfare state similar to those of their native German counterparts, but frequently lack the qualifications for social and professional mobility. Even if the types of jobs performed by their parents were available, the children of the guest workers appear increasingly unwilling to accept them. Many of the discussions in Germany today revolve around the dangers of creating a permanent underclass of unemployed and unemployable foreigners.

In this context, many analysts note that in the long term the German welfare system is faced with a crisis posed by low birth rates and an ever-aging society. A number of demographic projections show that by the year 2010 over 20 percent of the German population will be over the age of 65. Under such conditions the entire German welfare system is likely to collapse, as there will be too few contributors relative to the numbers of beneficiaries (Klauder, 1992; Hof, 1992). On problems with the German pension system see Smith (1994; 213–16). Even if a number of far-reaching reforms are instituted, including boosting productivity, raising the retirement age and encouraging greater participation of women in the labor market, a number of German studies suggest that as many as 200 000–400 000 additional foreign workers will be needed per year to maintain the current German standard of living.[13] Critics point out, however, that such a level of immigration may well prove politically impossible.[14]

In sum, from an economic point of view, immigration seems to have had an overall positive impact on the German economy in the past, despite cyclical downturns associated with the business cycle; whether immigration will continue to have a beneficial impact in the future remains an open question.

SOCIAL COSTS

In contrast to the overall positive evaluation of the economic impact of immigration, there exists a general consensus among German experts that its social costs have been high. For a variety of reasons, including discriminatory housing practices, economic pressures, and a simple desire on the part of immigrants to remain separate, the foreign population in Germany has formed large ethnic enclaves largely isolated from wider German society, a geographical separation that has contributed to a clearly visible social division between Germans and foreigner (Huttman *et al.*, 1991: Blotevogel *et al.*, 1993; Introduction). Although contacts between the two groups have improved steadily over the past forty years, in 1990 nearly 70 percent of all Germans reported having no personal contact with foreigners, whether in the neighborhoods they live, the places they work, or among the people they befriend and with whom they associate (Kuechler, 1994: 56). This deep social gulf between native Germans and foreigners residing in Germany has exacerbated tensions between the two groups and fueled anti-foreign sentiments.

The popular perception that foreigners are especially prone to crime has in no small measure contributed to these tensions. This perception is not totally without some basis in fact. The percentage of persons suspected of crime who are foreigners (30 percent of all in 1992) far exceeds the overall share of foreigners in the population (8 percent). Moreover, over the past decade the percentage of crimes committed by foreigners in Germany has increased steadily.

Although approximately one-quarter of the crimes for which foreigners are arrested are related to their immigrant status (such as visa and work permit violations), the crime rate among foreigners remains disproportionately high, and certain types of crime are disproportionately committed by foreigners. For example, in 1991, 74.1 percent of those accused of being pickpockets were foreigners, 65.9 percent of gamblers, and 57.1 percent of cocaine smugglers (*Bulletin der Bundesregierung*, 18 May 1993: 363). Similarly, in many cities organized crime and narcotics are firmly in the hands of foreign syndicates, especially of Italian and East European origin. This pattern resembles the American experience, where successive waves of ethnic groups have dominated the organized crime scene since the middle of the nineteenth century.

Table 11.2 *Foreigners as a percentage of the total number of criminal suspects in Germany, 1984–92*

Area	Year	Non-German suspects	As a percentage of the total number of suspects
Federal	1984	207,612	16.6
Republic	1985	231,868	18.0
of Germany	1986	252,018	19.3
	1987	258,329	20.0
	1988	286,741	21.8
	1989	336,011	24.5
	1990	383,583	26.7
FRG plus all of	1991	405,545	27.6
Berlin	1992	509,305	32.2
FRG including the former GDR	1992	550 583	30.0

SOURCE: *Bulletin der Bundesregiereung*, no. 40, 18 May 1993, p. 363.

There is therefore some evidence for the view that the presence of foreigners has increased the overall crime rate in Germany. On the other hand, when variables such as age, gender and income are controlled for the gap between foreigners and Germans in terms of their propensity towards crime, the percentage decreases markedly. Moreover, there are significant differences between distinct groups of foreigners. In general, those groups who have been settled longer in Germany and enjoy a more secure social–economic and legal position are far less likely to be involved in criminal activities than more recent arrivals. Particular ethnic groups, such as long-time Yugoslav residents, have an even lower propensity toward crime than the German population as a whole. Other groups, such as Greeks and Turks, have become increasingly less prone to crime over time (see Table 11.3), a trend that suggests that their patterns of behavior are gradually coming to resemble those of the local German population (Der Beauftragten der Budesregierung, 1993).

The highly restrictive German citizenship law, based on a code developed in 1913 and setting high requirements for German citizenship, is yet another factor contributing to the gulf between immigrants and Germans. Under the present law, the candidate must have resided in Germany for a minimum of 10 years, must have led a "clean life" (*unbescholtener Lebenswandel*), must have obtained adequate housing, must be capable of supporting him/herself and his or her family, and must demonstrate a minimum level of cultural and political assimilation, including most importantly command of the German language and a willingness to renounce his or her previous citizenship. Even when these formal conditions have been met, however, it is still at the discretion of German bureaucrats whether citizenship is actually awarded or not.[15]

In recent years, a number of steps have been taken to facilitate naturalization of foreigners. Most recently, in the fall of 1994 the Christian Democrats and the Free Democrats agreed in principle to allow the limited introduction of *jus soli* for the third generation of foreigners born in Germany.[16] Yet, despite these improvements, the naturalization rate of foreigners – although increasing – remains low and is outstripped by the increase in the number of foreigners in Germany.[17] This low rate of naturalization even among second- and third-generation

Table 11.3 Share of nationalities in crimes committed by foreigners[a]

Nationality	Number	1992	1991	1990	1989	1988	1987	1986	1985	1984
Turkey	90,995	17.9	20.8	21.4	23.9	24.7	25.4	25.3	26.3	29.0
Yugoslavia	83,270	16.3	12.9	12.1	12.5	12.7	11.9	10.9	11.2	11.7
Rumania	74,994	14.7	9.8	6.5	1.8	1.3	1.0	0.8	0.7	0.6
Poland	41,444	8.1	8.8	14.0	13.2	9.4	7.2	5.6	5.6	4.6
Italy	21,773	4.3	5.3	5.5	6.2	7.3	8.0	7.7	8.1	8.5
Soviet Union	11,554	2.3	1.7	1.0	0.4	0.3	0.2	0.1	0.1	0.1
Czechoslovakia	10,216	2.0	2.7	2.6	1.7	1.5	1.3	1.2	1.4	1.6
Greece	9,469	1.9	2.2	2.2	2.5	2.8	3.1	3.1	3.5	3.7
Lebanon	9,401	1.8	2.8	3.4	2.8	2.6	2.9	4.1	2.1	1.3
Morocco	8,022	1.6	1.6	1.4	1.3	1.3	1.2	1.1	1.1	1.0
USA	7,393	1.5	2.1	2.5	3.0	3.6	4.1	4.1	4.4	4.7
Iran	6,919	1.4	2.0	2.3	2.7	3.6	3.4	2.9	2.4	1.7
Albania	6,686	1.3	1.2	0.4	0.0	0.0	0.0	0.0	0.0	0.0
Nigeria	6,471	1.3	1.4	0.8	0.4	0.3	0.2	0.2	0.2	0.1
Algeria	5,688	1.1	0.6	0.5	0.4	0.3	0.2	0.2	0.3	0.3
Austria	5,480	1.1	1.3	1.6	2.1	2.0	1.9	2.0	3.0	3.3

Table 11.3 *(Continued)*

Nationality	Number	1992	1991	1990	1989	1988	1987	1986	1985	1984
Ghana	5,316	1.0	1.6	1.6	1.6	1.5	2.4	3.3	2.5	2.0
GBR	5,142	1.0	1.2	1.2	1.3	1.6	1.7	1.8	1.9	2.2
Other	85,345	16.8	18.2	18.2	21.8	23.0	23.7	25.4	25.2	23.6
Total	**509 305**	**100.0**	**100.0**	**100.0**	**100.0**	**100.0**	**100.0**	**100.0**	**100.0**	**100.0**

a In the territory of the old Federal Republic, including united East and West Berlin.

SOURCE: Der Beauftragten der Bundesregierung für die Belange der Ausländer (1993), *In der Diskussion: 'Ausländerkriminalität' oder 'Kriminelle Ausländer' Anmerkungen zu einen sensiblen Thema* (Bonn).

foreigners in Germany threatens to further deepen the gulf between foreigners and the host society and heightens the danger of creating a growing population of young people who in terms of language and lifestyle are largely German, but who are alienated from the rest of society and lack any loyalty toward the German state.

Despite these tensions, public opinion data reveal a complex picture of both increased anxiety concerning the economic impact of continued immigration and growing acceptance of the resident foreign population as a part of German society. On the one hand, many Germans, both East and West, are uncomfortable with the presence of large numbers of foreigners in Germany. In 1993 approximately 30 percent of West Germans and 45 percent of East Germans felt that it is "not OK" that there are many foreigners in Germany. Likewise, growing numbers agree with the demand for "Germany for the Germans."[18] On the other hand, increasing numbers of Germans appear to believe that foreigners are necessary for the maintenance of the economy. Whereas in August 1986 only 47 percent of all Germans felt that the economy requires guest workers, in June 1987 the figure had risen to 55 percent, and by 1992 the number went up even further, to over 75 percent (Kuechler, 1994: 55–8).

Recent hostile acts toward foreigners appear to be motivated not so much by racial prejudice as by a sense that Germans are competing with foreigners for jobs and welfare benefits,[19] and, on the whole, negative attitudes toward foreigners as a group appear to have decreased significantly since 1980. This decrease is reflected in a growing social acceptance of foreigners. So, for instance, increasing numbers of Germans support marriages with foreigners (33.7 percent in 1980, 52.5 percent in 1984, and 52.9 percent in 1988) while those expressing opposition to such marriages have declined concomitantly (52.2 percent in 1980 to 34.1 percent in 1984, and 32.8 percent in 1988) (Scheuch, 1991: 171). Shifts in overall attitudes toward foreigners are matched by changes in behavior. The number of marriages between Germans and other nationalities has increased dramatically over the course of the post-1945 period, rising from 3.6 percent of the total number of marriages in Germany in 1950 to 9.6 percent in 1990, with the largest numbers being marriages to Poles and Turks, followed by Americans.[20]

The view that much of the opposition to the presence of foreigners is motivated more by a sense of competition rather than ethnic prejudice is reinforced by survey data that indicate that similarly high percentages of Germans express support for restrictions on the entry of EU nationals and *Aussiedler* as well as non-European immigrants from Turkey and elsewhere. In fact, support for *Aussiedler* in-migration dropped from 56 percent in November 1988 to less than 40 percent in August 1989 (Kuechler, 1994: 59). A form of "welfare chauvinism" rather than classical racism appears to be the chief factor driving German attitudes in favor of restrictive immigration policies.

These tensions erupted during the reunification period, when a wave of anti-foreign violence committed by gangs of young Germans gained national and international attention. Beginning in 1989 there was a rapid upsurge of attacks on foreigners, escalating from a mere 50 offenses in 1985 to 152 offenses in 1990, then soaring to 1257 incidents in 1991 and 2283 in 1992, before finally decreasing considerably in 1993. In 1992 alone, 17 people, including seven foreigners, lost their lives as a result of racially motivated attacks (Press and Information Office, 1993: 47–9). Among the more spectacular incidents were a virtual pogrom in the city of Rostock in 1992, where the local police stood by for hours as gangs of youths viciously attacked a hostel housing asylum seekers, and the tragic fire-bombing of an apartment in Mölln in which a Turkish woman and her two daughters, all long-time residents, were killed (*Der Spiegel,* 31 August and 30 November 1992). In response, many young foreigners became increasingly militant and clashed violently with German skinheads. These developments have contributed to a deepening sense of alienation among foreigners that threatens to undo the progress that has been made toward integrating the foreign population into German society.

Although there is little evidence that these attacks were centrally guided or organized, they evoked powerful memories of the Nazi period both at home and abroad. After the fire-bombings in Mölln Chancellor Kohl went so far as to declare a state of emergency and threatened to invoke emergency national security measures to combat the menace of right-wing extremism. Public opinion, as well, recoiled from the violence. Although survey data revealed that a sizeable plurality of Germans express some degree of "understanding" for anti-foreign sentiments and strongly support a reduction of the influx of foreigners into the country, the overwhelming majority of Germans condemned acts of violence against foreigners (*Aktuell,* January and June 1993).

In conclusion, it can be observed that immigration clearly has led to serious social tensions and problems in Germany. Although there exist signs of more supportive social attitudes toward foreigners in the broader society, there has also emerged a growing sense of competition with foreigners for jobs and increasingly scarce resources. At the same time, immigrants continue to encounter a great number of obstacles in their efforts to settle into German society. In the wake of German reunification long-simmering social tensions developed into a full-blown political crisis.

THE POLITICAL IMPLICATIONS

Beginning in the late 1970s, immigration has become one of the most controversial and volatile issues in German politics, representing one of the central dividing lines between the different political parties. Yet, despite their differences, German political elites have recognized that it is in their mutual interest to contain the forces of resentment and xenophobia. Their response, however, has been slow and hesitating, increasing the danger that the social tensions described above will be allowed to fester to the point where the integration of foreigners into German society becomes next to impossible.

Initially, in the mid-1950s, there was considerable resistance to the idea of recruiting foreign labor. The powerful German labor unions feared that foreign workers might form a Marxist industrial "reserve army" that would endanger the interests of native German workers. Various organizations representing the interests of displaced ethnic German refugees sought to ensure that ethnic Germans continued to receive preferential treatment in employment and housing. After an intense bout of neocorporatist-style bargaining, these groups dropped their opposition in return for guarantees that foreign workers would be allowed to work in Germany for limited periods of time (the "rotation principle") and that foreign workers would receive the same wages and benefits as German workers.[21]

Once these concessions had been successfully negotiated, the recruitment of foreign workers proceeded with exceptional efficiency and without any significant social or political tensions. As Peter Katzenstein has noted, migration during the 1960s "was remarkable for the lack of public debate that it provoked" (Katzenstein, 1987: 213). A major contributing factor to this absence of tension was the fact that the German public and the majority of German elites alike expected that the foreign workers would return to their home countries when no longer needed and that the rotation policy would, in fact, work. For the most part, it should be pointed out, this view was shared by the foreign workers themselves.

With time, however, the rotation scheme broke down and foreign workers became permanent fixtures in the German economy. While many ultimately did return to their home countries, a good proportion discovered that they either had become accustomed to German standards of living or no longer felt at home in their countries of origin. Many decided to settle on a more-or-less permanent basis in the Federal Republic; their children, and by now grandchildren, are even less motivated to leave.

Three sets of factors helped facilitate permanent settlement and the breakdown of the original rotation scheme. First, German industry proved reluctant to periodically lose the workers whom they had gone to considerable lengths to train. Industry representatives lobbied the Federal Government to extend the periods of time that foreign workers were allowed to stay in the country.[22] More importantly, however, the German courts slowly but surely increased the legal rights of foreigners in Germany. In a series of important decisions, German courts ruled in favor of foreigners in cases involving their rights: to remain in the country after a certain period of time; to family reunification; and to judicial review of government efforts to deport them (Barwig *et al.*, 1991; Kanstroom, 1993: 188–93). Finally, the ongoing process of European integration helped strengthen the legal position of the many foreign workers who came from West European societies, notably Italy, Spain, Greece and Portugal.[23] Slowly but surely, and without the general population being fully aware of it, the rotation principle became an empty formula.

After the Oil Shock of 1973, the Federal Republic, along with other West European governments, declared a moratorium on the further recruitment of foreign workers, and during the next 2 years over 500 000 foreign workers left Germany. At the same time, those foreign workers who remained exercised their right to family reunion under German and international law and brought their wives and children into the country.[24] While legal labor immigration to Germany had ceased, the number of foreigners applying for political asylum in Germany skyrocketed, backed by Article 16 of the German constitution which baldly states, "all persons who are politically persecuted enjoy the right to asylum." While the majority of applicants were eventually rejected, the review and appeals process sometimes took years, during which time the applicants enjoyed generous welfare benefits from the German state and often could find work either legally or on the black market. While many asylum seekers were, in fact, the victims of political persecution, clearly many others were economic migrants so that the Federal Republic was *de facto* subsidizing illegal labor migration.[25] As a result of these two trends – family reunification and the increase in asylum seekers – by 1980 the foreign population in Germany, far from having decreased, actually had grown by over 1 million.

Government efforts to restrict further immigration and encourage repatriation of the guest workers for the most part proved unsuccessful, or even counterproductive. In order to discourage family reunification, the German government announced that foreigners could not move to cities where foreigners represented more than 12 percent of the population. This rule, however, proved difficult to implement and was challenged in the courts, leading to its abandonment in 1978. Likewise, in 1983 and 1984 the newly elected Christian Democratic–Free Democratic coalition under Helmut Kohl offered financial incentives for foreigners to return to their native countries. The foreign population dropped only moderately, from 4.5 million in 1982 to 4.7 million in 1984, before springing back up to 4.5 million in 1986. Studies showed that for the most part, the returnees were foreigners who would have returned anyway, and many cases began to appear of repatriated guest workers who returned after a year or two of what had in effect been an extended vacation paid for by the German Federal Government (Martin, 1994: 203–4).

As the realization began to sink in that the foreigners were not about to leave Germany, the immigration issue moved into the realm of high politics. During the 1980 elections, the CDU/CSU attempted to use the asylum issue against the Social Democratic government of Helmut Schmidt. In response, Schmidt sought to accelerate the asylum review process but was constrained by judicial interpretations of the German Basic Law. After the CDU/CSU took over in 1982 it found itself hampered by many of the same political and institutional factors. Efforts to encourage return migration through financial incentives proved entirely unsuccessful.

Sharply diverging interests with respect to immigration served to further deepen the ideological divide separating the two major West German parties. The various organizations representing ethnic German expellees have been among the strongest constituencies of the CDU/CSU. As a result, the Christian Democrats have tended to favor an ethno-cultural definition of citizenship and have promoted policies favoring the influx of ethnic Germans as an alternative to relying on non-German foreign laborers. On the other hand, electoral analyses and survey data showed that foreigners, if given the right to vote, would in all likelihood overwhelmingly cast their ballots for either the Greens or the Social Democrats. Given the size of the foreign population and its concentration in key urban centers, if foreigners were allowed to vote even only on the local level they might decisively tip the electoral balance of power in favor of the German Left. Consequently, the SPD has consistently lobbied for restrictions on the influx of ethnic Germans and for the increased incorporation of foreigners into the German political system. The CDU/CSU, on the other hand, naturally resists these demands and prefers to continue to give priority to *Aussiedler* (Faist, 1994: 56–61). These divisions, driven by party-political interests between the two main German political parties, have made it more difficult to reach bipartisan compromises on immigration law and for a long time made it virtually impossible to achieve the two-thirds majority needed to reform the Basic Law's Article 16 on asylum.[26]

Throughout the 1980s, repeated efforts were made to deal with the asylum issue, yet for the most part these measures had only a short-term effect and distracted attention from broader immigration issues. Increasingly the German public came to view the established political parties as incapable of coping with asylum and other immigration problems, leading growing numbers of voters to cast their ballots for the far-right wing Republikaner party.[27]

At first, some Social Democrats welcomed the emergence of the far Right, hoping that the Republikaners would split the conservative vote and cripple the Christian Democrats in much the same way that the rise of the Greens had weakened the Left in the early 1980s (Glotz, 1989). During the late 1980s, however, the Republikaners along with other small right-wing parties won a series of important victories in local and European elections. Fears began to grow that the German political party landscape would become fragmented, leading to governmental paralysis and increasing political instability. Many political commentators began to talk of a "Weimarization of German politics" and warned that the emergence of a right-wing extremist party might polarize German society and potentially undermine post-war German democracy. At the same time, it became increasingly clear that the Republikaners were not only siphoning off conservative Christian Democratic votes, but were attracting many of the SPD's traditional blue-collar supporters as well.

These fears were greatly magnified after the eruption of anti-foreigner violence in 1991. The CDU and the SPD finally managed to overcome their ideological and political differences and agreed to a substantive revision of Article 16 along with restrictions on the further influx of *Aussiedler* and the adoption of various measures designed to ease the naturalization of certain categories of foreigners.[28] As a result the number of asylum seekers dropped dramatically and popular interest in the issue declined concomitantly. In the 1994 elections the Republikaners, stigmatized by their associated with extreme right-wing violence and robbed of their chief political issue, received only 1.9 percent of the vote, far below the 5 percent needed to gain representation in the German Bundestag.[29]

The election results of 1994 demonstrated once again the remarkable durability of the German political system. For the third time since the founding of the Federal Republic the German political parties had managed to stave off a challenge from the far-right end of the political spectrum.[30] The social tensions generated by immigration, however, remained, creating a potential rallying point for far-right-wing and protest voters and forcing German politicians to approach immigration with extreme caution. Strong differences in the two leading parties' views and interest with respect to immigration continue to compound the reluctance of German leaders to tackle the thorny dilemmas associated with the influx of foreigners into the society, leading to what one is tempted to label a policy of "malign neglect". Various reforms which the leaderships of all the major parties view as being necessary have been postponed, including such measures as a new immigration law that establishes rational criteria for the recruitment of foreign workers and a further liberalization of naturalization procedures.[31] The economic, social and long-term political costs of delaying the passage of such measures promises to be high.

CONCLUSIONS AND LESSONS FOR JAPAN

On balance, the German experience supports the position of those in Japan who describe themselves as being neither advocates of open borders (*kaikokuronsha*) nor of a "fortress Japan" (*sakokuronsha*), but rather as subscribers to the thesis that a limited degree of immigration is probably inevitable (*hitsuzen-ronsha*). Like Japan, Germany is an advanced industrial society with an aging population and a highly developed welfare system. Although Japan's population compared to that of most other highly industrialized nations is still fairly youthful, its extremely low birth rate (particularly during the past decade) makes it highly likely that in the near future it will face the same sort of shortage in certain sectors of its labor markets as Germany. By the same token, the Japanese welfare state, though still relatively small today, is likely to evolve along lines similar to those established in Western European countries, making an explosion of welfare spending over the course of the next few decades a near certainty (Campbell, 1992: 390–5).

At present, it seems likely that the apparent attractiveness of foreign workers to certain sectors of industry, as well as the difficulties in trying to keep them out, makes it likely that the foreign population in Japan will grow substantially over the coming decades. If so, clearly the German experience suggests that this influx will be very difficult to control. Once settled, foreign workers will be reluctant to leave, and efforts to encourage return migration through financial incentives have only limited effect and often backfire. Domestic political pressures, from businesses eager to retain trained workers, and international pressures, from foreign governments interested in the remittances foreign workers send home, are likely to make the enforcement of a strict rotation regime very difficult. Efforts to reduce the number of foreigners through expulsions likewise may be foiled by a combination of domestic and international political pressures. Over time, the foreign workers will want to bring their families to Japan and will create their own ethnic communities, much as many of the ethnic Koreans have already done, which in turn act as a magnet for further immigration. The question that then needs to be addressed is whether the social and political costs of immigration may differ from the German experience.

Like Germany, Japan historically has been a closed society with a strong ethno-cultural identity, and like the Federal Republic there are many signs that since 1945 Japanese society has become considerably more liberal than it was in the past (for a broad overview, see Iwao, 1990). One of the prime lessons that Japan can draw from the German experience is that even a country with as strong a tradition of ethno-nationalism as Germany's can eventually learn to accept the presence of a large foreign population, although the process is likely to be slow (three decades at least) and accompanied by considerable social and political friction.[32] There is even reason to hope that tensions might be less in Japan than in Germany. Current Japanese unemployment rates (under 3 percent) are lower than they were in Germany in the 1970s and 1980s, and the Japanese housing market, while expensive, is not as tight as the contemporary German housing market.

On the other hand, membership figures of far-right-wing organizations in Japan (*uyokudantai*) are far greater (at 90 000) than similar far-right organizations in Germany (49 800 in 1992, a seven fold increase over the levels of membership prevalent before the recent rash of anti-foreigner violence began). In addition, the Japanese organized crime syndicates (*Yakuza*) are numerically much larger than their European or even American counterparts and espouse far-right-wing views. Whether the *Yakuza* will prove as successful in incorporating the new waves of foreigners as they were with the Koreans and the native *Dowa* (a relatively small subgroup within the Japanese population that historically has been the target of severe discrimination) populations in the past remains uncertain (Kaplan and Dubro, 1987). If a social consensus emerges in Japan that foreigners have become an undesirable presence, the potential for anti-foreigner violence may prove even greater than in Germany.

Likewise, Japan has had a history of segregating its resident Korean and *Dowa* populations from the rest of society. As in Germany, current Japanese citizenship and electoral laws are unlikely to encourage the development of political loyalty to their new homeland on the part of foreigners. Thus the new foreign population of Japan is as likely as its German counterpart to feel alienated from the broader Japanese society, enhancing the potential for inter-ethnic tensions, especially in periods of economic downturn.

How the Japanese political system will respond to this challenge remains to be seen. In certain respects, the Japanese political leadership is likely to enjoy some advantages compared to their German counterparts. Since Japan is an island, border control should be relatively easier for Japan. Unlike Germany during the Cold War, Japan is not partitioned and the overseas Japanese population is relatively small. There are therefore no pressing international political reasons to retain the current citizenship law, nor does there exist a powerful domestic lobby like the German expellee organizations, with a concrete interest in an ethno-cultural definition of Japanese national identity (although certainly Japanese right-wing organizations would have powerful ideological reasons for such an interest). Finally, and perhaps most importantly, there is no tradition of judicial activism in post-war Japan of the sort that may be seen in either Germany or the United States. Japanese politicians may therefore have greater leeway in restricting the rights of foreigners in accordance with political necessity than has been true of their counterparts in Germany and the United States.[33]

Against this must be weighed the fact that the Japanese postwar political system has on the whole been even more prone to paralysis than is the case in most other democracies. In contrast, the German system has powerful institutional incentives favoring inter-party cooperation and a tradition of militant democracy that has united main-stream political parties when faced with a threat from the Right. Both these features of the German political system were very much in evidence in 1993 when the German Bundestag amended the Basic Law to resolve the asylum crisis. While for much of the Cold War period, Japanese politics was dominated by a single party, the Liberal Democrats (LDP), factional infighting and a high rate of turnover among leaders since the early 1970s has greatly weakened political leadership.[34] At the same time, the Japanese bureaucracy, while highly efficient, has been plagued by interministerial conflicts and turf wars. In dealing with an issue like immigration, which crosses many bureaucratic jurisdictional boundaries, the potential for fragmented policymaking is especially high. Finally, in light of the current political turmoil in the Japanese political system, it seems highly unlikely that in the near future Japan will develop the political leadership needed to coordinate its response to the challenge of integrating the foreign population.

Ultimately, however, Japan will be compelled to face the immigration issue head-on. When it does so, it is likely to find itself walking the same tightrope that Germany does today. On the one hand, if Japan adopts policies that are overly permissive of immigration, or it fails to cope with the social and political pressures that immigration is likely to generate, it runs the risk of triggering a dangerous social and political backlash. Anti-foreigner movements and political parties may emerge and incidents of anti-foreigner violence may well occur. On the other hand, if Japan adopts overly restrictive policies with respect to immigrants and immigration, it will both incur serious economic costs and create a large, alienated underclass of resident foreigners. Whether Japan will be able to pull off this balancing act successfully will be one of the most important tests of its political maturity in the coming decades.

APPENDIX

Table 11.4 *Points of similarity and contrast between Japan, Germany and the United States*

	Japan	*Germany*	*United States*
1. Borders	Island	Fairly long, with 11 neighbors	Long, with two neighbors
2. Bureaucratic strength	High, Severe coordination problems	High	Moderate
3. Church–state relations	Division	Support	Division
4. Citizenship	*Jus sanguinis*	*Jus sanguinis*	*Jus soli*
5. Civil rights tradition	Weak	Strong	Strong
6. Conception of the nation	Cultural/religious	Ethnic/cultural	Republican values
7. Crime	Very low	Moderate	High
8. Education system	Centralized	Decentralized	Decentralized
9. Ethnic diversity	Very low	Low	Very high

Table 11.4 (Continued)

	Japan	Germany	United States
10. IR sensitivity	High	Very high	Low
11. Judiciary	Weak	Very strong	Very strong
12. Military	Volunteer	Draft	Volunteer
13. Percent of population over 65 in 2020	High	High	Moderate
14. Political system	Multi-party (two-party dominant?)	Multi-party with two party dominance	Two-party
15. Regional integration	Weak but growing	Great	Weak but growing
16. Right-wing organizations	Moderate and centralized	Moderate and decentralized	Weak
17. Unemployment	3 percent	9 percent	6 percent
18. Unions	Increasingly strong and centralized	Very strong and centralized	Moderately strong and decentralized

ACKNOWLEDGMENT

The author would like to express his thanks to Mr Jürgen Haberland of the German Ministry of the Interior for the insights that he provided regarding issues of German immigration law.

NOTES

1. For the classical analysis of the impact of late development, see Gerschonkron (1989). For the effects of late development on Japan, see Johnson (1982). For a more recent comparison of German and Japanese approaches to defense and national security, see Berger (Johns Hopkins University Press, forthcoming).
2. On the Prussian influence on Meiji Japan, see Presseisen (1965), Siemes (1964) and Dale (1986, Ch. 12).
    At least part of the affinity between the two nations can be explained by the fact that the ruling political and social elites were military aristocrats who prided themselves on their martial valor and discipline – the Prussian Junkers and the Samurai. The Meiji Oligarch, Yamagata Aritomo, when he visited the West, reportedly was most at home in Berlin, where he wrote such enthusiastic *Haiku* as "Berlin, Where the air is free and the military bearing is not Uncommon" (Hackett, 1976).
3. This is especially true in the area of foreign policy, where Germany and Japan both are applying for membership for a permanent seat on the UN Security Council, have for the first time sent their forces abroad on UN peacekeeping missions, and are seeking ways of strengthening economic and political integration in their respective regions. Domestically as well there are signs of increasing convergence. For instance, the emergence of a Japanese federation of Trade Labor Unions (*Rengo*) as a powerful political force seems to be moving Japan closer to the German model of neocorporatism. Likewise, the Japanese are becoming more open in acknowledging the atrocities their forces committed in Asia during the Second World War.
4. Naturally, in all of these countries there are contending views on how to define national identity and at different points of time some of these other traditions played a larger role in the national self-understanding than they do today. So, for example, historically national identity in many countries, including Britain, France, the United States, Prussia and Japan, had a strong religious component that in recent decades has become considerably less salient than was the case in the past. For the purpose of the present discussion this complex historical issue has been simplified and national identity

here refers only to the approach to national identity that has been ascendant since the Second World War.

5. For an interesting analysis of Japanese nationalism which places it in the same category of cultural or holistic nationalism associated with the German idea of the *Volksgeist*, see Yoshino (1992, especially Chapter 3). The concept of ethnic nationalism was originally invented by Meinecke (1970) and further developed by Kohn (1967). For a recent expression of this point of view which links it directly to French and German citizenship law, see Brubaker (1992).

6. For a critical analysis of the utility of immigration for western Europe, see Coleman (1992, 1993).

7. For example, in 1991 the unemployment rate among foreigners was 10.7 percent, versus 6 percent among German workers. See Hermann (1992a: 12–15). A similar tendency has been observed in Japan recently, where despite the recent, protracted economic downturn the number of illegal foreign workers in the country apparently has not been reduced.

8. See for example Werner (1992: 80–7).

9. See Lummer (1992). It should be noted, however, that similar abuses of the welfare system committed by native Germans are rampant.

10. Forty-seven percent lack work qualifications, 27 percent suffer from physical disabilities, and 20 percent are too old to find work again easily (Schumacher, 1993: 35–6).

11. The same phenomenon is identifiable in Japan, where young Japanese are no longer willing to perform so-called "three-D" jobs (dirty, dangerous and demanding, *san k rodo* in Japanese).

12. A recent study by the Japanese Ministry of Labor of the costs and benefits of immigration came to the opposite conclusion largely because it left out the question of whether increased labor immigration would increase overall tax revenues by boosting economic activity (see *Nikkei*, 4 July 1992, p. 6).

13. Hof (1992). The Institut der deutschen Wirtschaft in Köln, which has close ties to the German Federation of Industry, estimated that Germany will need 400,000 immigrants per year until at least the year 2020 (see *Frankfurter Rundschau*, 27 November 1993).

14. Interview by the author with Dr Jürgen Haberland, Ministry of the Interior, Bonn, 26 November 1993.

15. The standard work on German citizenship law is Weidelener and Hemberger (1993), including the text of the 1993 additions to the German citizenship law on pp. 114–16. For a critical commentary, see Cohn-Bendit and Schmid (1993: 331–9).

16. See *Frankfurter Allgemeine Zeitung*, 15 November 1994, p. 2. This agreement has not yet, it should be emphasized, led to a corresponding alteration of German naturalization law.

17. Obvious parallels can be drawn between the German experience with trying to encourage the naturalization of former guest workers and the relative lack of Japanese success in absorbing its resident Korean population.

18. In 1992 51 percent of West Germans and 49 percent of East Germans expressed full or substantial agreement with the slogan "Germany for

the Germans", while 47 percent of West Germans and 46 percent of East Germans rejected it. (see Konrad Adenauer Stiftung, 1993).

19. In 1991 54 percent of East Germans and 46 percent of West Germans felt that their jobs were endangered by immigrants. Likewise, 57 percent of West Germans and 48 percent of East Germans felt that increased competition from foreigners for housing was depriving the local population of apartments. Similarly, ethnic Germans from Eastern Europe and asylum seekers were viewed as threats to jobs and housing (*Aktuell*, 20 October 1991). The author wishes to thank Wolfgang Glüchowski of the Adenauer Stiftung for kindly sharing the results of survey data collected by Infas.

20. Harald Schumacher (1993: 143–6). In 1990 there were 39 784 marriages between Germans and non-Germans, with the largest number of non-German marriage partners coming from Poland (10.6 percent), Turkey (8.7 percent), the United States (8.6 percent), Yugoslavia (8.3 percent), Italy (7.3 percent), Austria (5.5 percent), Great Britain (3.8 percent), Holland (3.6 percent), France (3.0 percent) and the Philippines (3.0 percent).

21. For an overview of this period, see Herbert (1986, Ch. 5).

22. A similar phenomenon is observable in Japan, where Japanese firms are lobbying the government to extend the period of time that foreign trainees, ostensibly in Japan only as part of foreign aid programs, are allowed to remain in the country.

23. For an overview of German immigration laws, see Kanstroom (1993).

24. On the German law regarding family reunification see Schmid (1991). In general, the courts have held that a constitutional right to family reunification exists under the provisions of Article 6, Family Protection (*Familienschutz*), of the German constitution.

25. See Münch (1993). For a critical view see Lummer (1992).

26. The two other established German political parties, the Free Democrats and the Greens, both favorably disposed toward immigration and increasing the rights of resident foreigners, albeit for totally different reasons. The Free Democrats' electoral base is in the German professional classes and small and medium businesses, which either benefit from immigration, or at least do not view themselves as threatened by the influx of low-skilled foreign workers. Ideologically, the FDP has views itself as the champion of economic liberalism and the guardian of civil liberties, and thus in principle it favors more open labor markets and opposes the expansion of police powers that would be needed to crack down on the employment of legal foreign workers and effect their mass expulsion. Cynics also point out that the FDP is the only major political party with virtually no representation in government at the local level, thus insulating it from many of the pressures that feed anti-foreigner sentiment in the other major parties, including the SPD.

The Greens are even more effusive in their support of foreign workers and continued immigration. Green voters for the most part are in occupational groups that do not compete for jobs with immigrants, and their high educational backgrounds makes them among the most cosmopolitan groups in the German population.

Ideologically, the Greens are intensely hostile to the very concept of the nation state and are fervent supporters of human rights and grass-roots democracy both at home and abroad. Consequently many Greens are oppose to any form of border controls at all, and they are profoundly critical of the other parties' efforts to restrict the right to asylum, efforts which they believe are motivated by old-style German chauvinism and nationalism.

27. On the rise of the Republikaners see Leggewie (1989), Eley (1993: 235–68), and Betz (1991: 110–32).

28. On the background leading up to the great compromise on the asylum issue, see *Frankfurter Allgemeine Zeitung*, 26 May 1993, p. 2. For the stormy events surrounding the final vote, see *Das Parlament*, 28 May – 4 June 1993, p. 1, and the *Frankfurter Allgemeine Zeitung*, 27 May 1993, pp. 1, 2, 4.

29. Although the Republikaner garnered an abysmally low 1.9 percent of the vote, they did succeed in forcing the other German parties to move on the right on the asylum and immigration issues (see Young, 1995).

30. For an overview of the development of right-wing extremism over the history of the Federal republic, see Zimmerman and Saalfeld (1993). For an excellent analysis of the relationship between immigration and the rise of right wing in Western Europe in general, see Betz (1994, especially Ch. 3).

31. Interviews by the author with the CDU, FDP and SPD members of the Bundestag committee for Internal Affairs (*Innenausschuß*) and their staffs, Bonn, November 1993. The chief exception, however, is the CSU, which remains strongly committed to the current system of encouraging the influx of ethnic Germans and discouraging other forms of immigration.

32. It is worth noting in passing that anti-foreigner sentiments, when they do emerge in Japan, may well be similar to the "welfare chauvinism" that we see in Germany, i.e. motivated more by anxieties concerning competition for jobs and welfare benefits than by ideological racism. If so, the second- and third-generation Japanese (*Nikkeijin*) are likely to be as much the focus of popular resentment as other, non-ethnic Japanese, much as the *Aussiedler* have become the target of criticism by the far Right in Germany.

33. See Ramseyer and Rosenbluth (1993, Ch. 7 and 8), and Upham (1987). On the powerful postwar German *Rechtsstaat* tradition, see Sontheimer (1988); and Kommers (1989, Ch. 6).

34. The precariousness of the Japanese Prime Minister's position is a rather deep-rooted phenomenon and not only the result of the recent turmoil in Japanese politics. See Hayao (1993). In contrast, the German Chancellor has far-reaching powers and cannot be easily removed from office. One reflection of this is that whereas Japan had twelve Prime Ministers between 1952 and 1992, Germany had only six chancellors. On the institutional position of the German chancellor, see Smith (1991: 48–61).

REFERENCES

Barwig, Klaus, Lörcher, Klaus and Schumacher, Christoph (1991), "Einleitende Bemerkungen zum neuen Ausländerrecht im westeuropäischen Kontext," in Klaus Barwig *et al.*, *Das neue Ausländerrecht: Kommentierte Einführung mit Gesetzestexten und Durchführungsverordnungen* (Baden-Baden: Nomos Verlagsgesellschaft), pp. 13–22.

Der Beauftragten der Bundesregierung für die Belange der Ausländer (1993), *In der Diskussion: "Ausländerkriminalität" oder "Kriminelle Ausländer" Anmerkungen zu einem sensiblen Thema* (Bonn).

Berger, Thomas U. (1996), "Norms and National Security in Germany and Japan," in Peter Katzenstein (ed.), *Constructing Security* (New York: Columbia University Press), pp. 317–56.

Betz, Hans-Georg (1991), *Postmodern Politics in Germany: The Politics of Resentment* (New York: St Martin's Press).

—— (1994), *Radical Right-Wing Populism in Western Europe* (New York: St Martin's Press).

Blotevogel, V. Hans Heinrich, Müller-Jung, Ursula and Wood, Gerald (1993), "From Itinerant Worker to Immigrant? The Geography of Guestworkers in Germany," in Russel King (ed.), *Mass Migration in Europe: The Legacy and the Future* (London: Belhaven).

Brubaker, Rogers (1992), *The Politics of Citizenship in France and Germany* (Cambridge, MA: Harvard University Press).

Campbell, John C. (1992), *How Policies Change: The Japanese Government and the Aging Society* (Princeton, NJ: Princeton University Press).

Castles, Stephen and Kosack, Godulda (1985), *Immigrant Workers and Class Structure in Western Europe* (London: Oxford University Press).

Cohn-Bendit, Daniel and Schmid, Thomas (1993), *Heimat Babylon: Das Wagnis der multikulturellen Demokratie* (Frankfurt: Hoffman & Campe),

Coleman, David A. (1992), "Does Europe Need Immigrants? Population and Workforce Projections," *International Immigration Review*, 26 (2) (Spring), pp. 413–61.

—— (1993), "Contrasting Age Structures of Western Europe and of Eastern Europe and the Former Soviet Union: Demographic Curiosity or Labor Resource," *Population and Development Review*, 19 (3) (September), pp. 523–55.

Dale, Richard N. (1986), *The Myth of Japanese Uniqueness* (New York: St Martins Press).

Eley, John (1993), "The Black-Brown Hazelnut in a Bigger Germany: The Rise of the Radical Right as a Structural feature," in Michael G. Huelshoff, Andrei S. Markovits and Simon Reich (eds), *From Bundesrepublik to Deutschland: German Politics after Unification* (Ann Arbor, MI: University of Michigan Press), pp. 235–68.

Faist, Thomas (1994), "How to Define a Foreigner: The Symbolic Politics of Immigration in German Partisan Discourse, 1978–1992," *West European Politics*, 17 (2) (April), pp. 50–71.

Gerschonkron, Alexander (1989), *Bread and Democracy in Germany* (Ithaca, NY: Cornell University Press; originally published in 1943).

Gieseck, Arne, Heilemann, Ullrich and von Loeffelholz, Hans Dietrich (1993), "Wirtschafts – und sozialpolitische Aspekte der Zuwanderung in die Bundesrepublik," *Aus Politik und Zeitgeschichte*, B 7/93 (12 February).

Glotz, Peter (1989), *Die deutsche Rechte: eine Streitschrift* (Stuttgart: Deutsche Verlags-Anstalt).

Hackett, Roger (1976), *Yamagata Aritomo and the Rise of Modern Japan* (Stanford, CA: Stanford University Press).

Hayao, Kenji (1993), *The Japanese Prime Minister and Public Policy* (Pittsburgh, PA: Pittsburgh University Press).

Herbert, Ulrich (1990), *A History of Foreign Labor in Germany, 1880–1990: Seasonal Workers/Forced Laborers/Guest Workers* (Ann Arbor, MI: University of Michigan Press; German original, 1986).

Hermann, Helga (1992a), "Ausländer am Arbeitsplatz," *Information zur Politischen Bildung*, 237, pp. 12–15.

—— (1992b), *Ausländer. Vom Gastarbeiter zum Wirtschaftsfaktor* (Köln: Beiträge zur Gesellschafts – und Bildungspolitik No. 173 des Instituts der deutschen Wirtschaft).

Hof, Bernd (1992), "Arbeitskraftbedarf der Wirtschaft. Arbeits-marktchancen für Zuwanderer," in Friedrich Ebert Stiftung (ed.), *Zuwanderungspolitik der Zukunft* (Bonn: Reihe Gesprächskreis, Arbeit und Soziales, No. 3).

Hosomi, Takashi, (ed.) (1992), *Gaigokujin Rodosha: Nihon to Doitsu* (Tokyo: Kawai Shuppan).

Huttman, E. D., Blau, W. and Saltman, J. (eds) (1991), *Urban Housing Segregation of Minorities in Western Europe and the United States* (Durham, NC: Duke University Press).

Iwao, Sumiko (1990), "Recent Changes in Japanese Social Attitudes," in Alan D. Romberg and Tadashi Yamamoto, (eds), *Same Bed, Different Dreams: American and Japanese Societies in Transition* (New York: Council on Foreign Relations) pp. 41–66.

Johnson, Chalmers (1982), *MITI and the Japanese Miracle: The Growth of Industrial Policy 1925 to 1975* (Stanford, CA: Stanford University Press).

Kanstroom, Daniel (1993), "Wer Sind Wir Wieder? Laws of Asylum Immigration, and Citizenship and the Struggle for the Soul of the New Germany," *Yale Journal of International Law*, 18 (155) pp. 155–211.

Kaplan, David E. and Dubro, Alec (1987), *Yakuza* (New York: Macmillan).

Katzenstein, Peter J. (1987), *Policy and Politics in West Germany: The Growth of a Semisovereign State* (Philadelphia, PA: Temple University Press).

Kindelberger, Charles P. (1967), *Europe's Post-war Growth: The Role of the Labor Supply* (Cambridge, MA: Harvard University Press).

Klauder, Wolfgang (1992), "Deutschland im Jahr 2030: Modellrechnungen und Visioner," in Klaus J. Bade (ed.), *Deutschland im Ausland, Fremde in Deutschland* (München: C. H. Beck), pp. 455–64.

Kohn, Hans (1967), *The Idea of Nationalism: The Study of its Origin and Background* (New York: Collier; originally published in 1944).

Kommers, Donald P. (1989), "The Basic Law of the Federal Republic of Germany: An Assessment after Forty Years," in Peter H. Merkl (ed.), *The Federal Republic at Forty* (New York: New York University Press), pp. 133–59.

Konrad Adenauer Stiftung paper (1993), "Ausländerfeindlichkeit in Deutschland" (November).

Kuechler, Manfred (1994), "Germans and 'others': Racism, Xenophobia, or 'Legitimate Conservatism'?," *German Politics*, (1) (April), pp. 47–74.

Landeshauptstadt Düsseldorf, Sozialdezernat (ed.) (1992), *Ausländer raus!?* "Stunde Null". Ausländer verlassen die Stadt Düsseldorf (Düsseldorf, January).

Leggewie, Claus (1989), *Die Republikaner* (Berlin: Rotbuch Verlag).

Lummer, Heinrich (1992), *Asyl: Ein Mißbrauchtes Recht* (Frankfurt: Ullstein).

Martin, Philip L. (1994), "Germany: Reluctant Land of Immigration," in Wayne Cornelius, Philip L. Martin and James E. Hollifield (eds), *Controlling Immigration: A Global Perspective* (Stanford, CA: Stanford University Press), pp. 83–99.

Meinecke, Friedrich (1970), *Cosmoplitansim and the Nation State* (Princeton, NJ: Princeton University Press).

Münch, Ursula (1993), *Asylpolitik in der Bundesrepublik Deutschland Entwicklungen und Alternativen 2*, Aktualisierte Auflage (Opladen: Leske & Budrich).

Nishio, Kanji (1992), *Rodosakoku no Susume* (Tokyo: PHP Bunko).

Peattie, Mark (1975), *Ishiwara Kanj and Japan's Confrontation with the West* (Princeton, NJ: Princeton University Press).

Press and Information Office of the Federal Government, Foreign Affairs Division (1993), *Hostility towards Foreigners in Germany: New Facts, Analysis, Arguments*, (Bonn).

Presseisen, Ernest (1965), *Before Aggression: Europeans Prepare the Japanese Army* (Tucson, AZ: University of Arizona Press).

Ramseyer, Mark J. and McCall Rosenbluth, Frances (1993), *Japan's Political Marketplace* (Cambridge, MA: Harvard University Press).

Scheuch, Erwin (1991), *Wie Deutsch sind die Deutschen?* (Bergisch Gladsbach: Bastei Lübbe).

Schmalz-Jacobsen, Cornelia, *et al.* (1993), *Einwanderung – und Dann?* (Munich: Kanuer), pp. 312–13.

Schmid, Rainer (1991), "Familiennachzug/Eigenständigkeit des Aufenthaltsstatus von Familienangehörigen," in Klaus Barwig *et al.* (eds), *Das nene Ausländerrecht: Kommentierte Einführung mit Gesetzestexten und Durchführungsverordnungen* (Baden-Baden: Nomos Verlagsgesellschaft), pp. 121–34.

Schumacher, Harald (1993), *Einwanderungsland BRD: Warum die deutsche Wirtschaft weiter Ausläner braucht* (Düsseldorf: Zebulon Verlag).

Siemes, Johannes, S. J. (1964), *Hermann Roessler and the Making of the Meiji State* (Tokyo: Sophia University Press).

Smith, Eric Owen (1994), *The German Economy* (New York: Routledge).

Smith, Gordon (1991), "The Resources of the German Chancellor," *West European Politics*, 14 (2) (April).

Sontheimer, Kurt (1988), "The Federal Republic of Germany (1949): Restoring the Rechtstaat," in Vladimir Bogdano (ed.), *Constitutions in Democratic Politics* (Aldershot: Gower).

Tezuka, Kazuaki (1989), *Gaigokujin Rodosha* (Tokyo: Nihon Keizai Shimbunsha).

Upham, Frank (1987), *Law and Social Change in Postwar Japan* (Cambridge, MA: Harvard University Press).

Wehrmann, Martin (1989), *Auswirkungen der Ausländerbeschäftigung auf die Volkswirtschaft der Bundesrepublik in Vergangenheit und Zukunft* (Baden-Baden: Nomos Verlag).

Weidelener, Helmut and Hemberger, Fritza (1993), *Deutsches Staasangehörigkeitsrecht 4*, Auflage. (München: Jehle).

Werner, Jan (1992), *Die Invasion der Armen: Asylanten und Illegale Einwanderer* (Mainz-München: v. Hase & Koehler).

Yoshino, Kosaku (1992), *Cultural Nationalism in Contemporary Japan: a Sociological Inquiry* (New York: Routledge).

Zimmerman, Ekkart and Saalfeld, Thomas, (1993), "Three Waves of West German Right-Wing Extremism," in Peter Merkl and Leonard Weinberg (eds), *Encounters with the Contemporary Radical Right* (Boulder, CO: Westview Press), pp. 50–74.

Young, Brigitte (1995), "The German Political Party System and the Contagion from the Right," in a special issue on the Bundestag elections of 1994 of *German Politics and Society*, 13 (1) (Spring), pp. 62–78.

Newspapers and Periodicals

Aktuell, 42, 20 October 1991; January 1993; June 1993.

Bulletin der Bundesregierung, no. 40, May 18 1993, p. 363.

Das Parlament, 28 May – 4 June 1993, p. 1.

Der Spiegel, no. 36/46, 31 August 1992, pp. 18–32; no. 49/46, 30 November 1992, pp. 18–29.

Frankfurter Rundschau, 27 November 1993.

Frankfurter Allgemeine Zeitung, 27 May 1993, pp. 1, 2, 4; 15 November 1994, p. 2.

Nikkei, 4 July 1992, p. 6.

Part VI
Controlling Migration

12 Japan's Dilemma: Can International Migration be Controlled?

Yasuo Kuwahara

EMERGENCE OF THE ISSUE

About a decade has passed since Japan first experienced a large inflow of immigrant workers. Until the beginning of the 1980s Japan had never considered itself to be a host to immigrants with the exception of the Koreans and Chinese who were brought to Japan as forced laborers before and during the Second World War. Thus the recent influx of immigrant workers from many developing countries in Asia and Latin America has had a sudden and unexpected impact on various aspects of Japanese society.

Above all, the rapid increase in the number of illegal immigrants willing to perform unskilled labor has created many difficult problems for Japanese society, as opposed to the immigration of those qualified as skilled workers or experts and sanctioned under current immigration law. In brief, the Japanese government has adopted a two-sided policy on immigrant workers. Those who want to find jobs in the market for unskilled labor are denied entry, while certain skilled workers and specialists who have abilities not common among the Japanese are permitted to work in Japan.[1] In the last decade, however, maintaining this policy has become increasingly difficult, as the number of illegal immigrant workers has increased sharply despite the introduction, beginning in June 1990, of employer sanctions and other control measures.

The estimated number of foreigners residing illegally in Japan peaked in 1993 at approximately 300 000 and declined only slightly in 1994, despite a severe recession. It appears that demand for foreign labor is becoming sensitive to the business cycle. Opposition to the influx of immigrant workers surfaced in the late 1980s, but the discussion quieted down with the coming of a recession. What factors brought about these changes? How should we interpret them? Can Japan maintain its current immigration policy? What are the alternatives?

The purpose of this paper is to analyze the current situation and investigate the major problems of illegal immigration to Japan, which, unlike legal immigration, has generated many difficult problems. The paper also examines the viability of Japan's current immigration policy in an age of global migration.[2]

ILLEGAL IMMIGRANT WORKERS: WHO ARE THEY?

Here, illegal immigrant workers are defined as individuals employed in Japan in violation of their residence status under the Immigration Control and Refugee Recognition Law ("the Immigration Control Law"). It is impossible to know the exact number of illegal immigrant workers who live in Japan, since they make every effort to conceal themselves, but some estimates are available. The Immigration Bureau of the Ministry of Justice twice a year calculates the number of foreigners overstaying their visas, which can be estimated by correlating immigration and emigration records. These estimates have been published on a regular basis since the summer of 1990. However, these figures should be interpreted as minimum numbers for reasons explained in the following section.

The number of illegal overstayers increased remarkably in recent years. As of July 1990, approximately 106 000 foreigners illegally resided in Japan, having overstayed their visas. The number increased to 216 000 in November 1991, about 279 000 in May 1992, and over 290 000 in November 1992. Because of the severe recession, the number did not increase during the years 1993 and 1994, but nevertheless remains high. The latest figure, as of May 1996, is 284 500 (Immigration Office, March 1994).

Overstayers are mainly from Thailand, Korea, China, the Philippines, Iran, Malaysia, Peru or Taiwan. Bilateral visa agreements have been suspended in some instances to reduce the number of illegal immigrants from particular countries;

	1 July 1990	1 May 1991	1 May 1992	1 May 1993	1 May 1994	1 November 1994	1 May 1995	1 November 1995	1 May 1996
Thailand	11,523	19,093	44,354	55,383	49,992	46,964	44,794	43,014	41,280
South Korea	13,876	25,848	35,687	39,455	43,369	44,916	47,544	49,530	51,580
China	10,039	17,535	25,737	33,312	39,738	39,552	39,511	38,464	39,140
The Philippines	23,805	27,828	31,974	35,392	37,544	38,325	39,763	41,122	41,987
Iran	764	10,915	40,001	28,437	20,757	18,009	16,252	14,638	13,241
Malaysia	7,550	14,413	38,529	30,840	20,313	17,240	14,511	13,460	11,525
Peru	242	487	2,783	9,038	12,918	14,312	15,301	14,693	13,836
Taiwan, ROC	4,775	5,241	6,729	7,457	7,871	7,906	7,974	8,210	8,502
Bangladesh	7,195	7,498	8,103	8,069	7,565	7,295	7,084	6,836	6,500
Pakistan	7,989	7,864	8,001	7,733	6,921	6,517	5,915	5,689	5,294
Myanmar	1,234	2,061	4,704	6,019	6,391	6,335	6,189	6,022	5,885
Other	17,505	21,645	32,290	37,511	40,421	40,721	41,681	42,890	45,536
Male	66,851	106,518	190,966	192,114	180,060	172,516	168,532	164,154	160,836
Female	39,646	53,310	87,896	106,532	113,740	115,576	118,172	120,590	123,664
Total	106,497	159,838	278,892	298,846	293,800	288,092	286,704	284,744	284,500

SOURCE: Ministry of Justice, Immigration Bureau.

for example, the Japanese government has suspended the visa exemption agreement for visitors from Iran since 15 April 1993, resulting in a sharp decline in the number of Iranian immigrants from 1992 to 1993. In June 1993 a similar action was taken for Malaysians, encouraging them to acquire visas before visiting Japan. Also the Japanese Ministry of Justice asked the government of Thailand to cooperate with a "public awareness program" to discourage Thais from traveling to Japan with the intention of working illegally. Due to these measures, the number of entrants from these Asian countries declined substantially in 1993.

Most overstayers are assumed to be working. Among those who were deported by the Immigration Control Bureau in 1993, about 91 percent had been working (Immigration Control Bureau, 1995). Therefore we can justifiably state that the majority of those overstaying their visas in Japan are illegal immigrant workers. However, overstayers amount to only a few of the nearly 4 million foreigners who annually enter Japan as short-stay visitors for the stated purpose of tourism, business or visiting relatives.[3]

No one can say exactly how many of these people worked illegally beyond the scope of their visas during their short stays, nor do we know how much illegal work is being done by students who exceed the hours they are permitted to work. A college-level student with a 4-1-6 status of residence may work part-time without special permission, provided that: the purpose of the part-time job is to provide for tuition, fees or other expenses of living in Japan; he or she does not work more than 20 hours per week; time spent on the job does not

Table 12.2 *Trends of foreign visitors to Japan (millions)*

	1988	1989	1990	1991	1992	1993	1994	1995	1996
New Entrants	196	246	293	324	325	304	309	293	341
Re-entrants	45	52	57	62	68	71	74	80	83
Total	**241**	**298**	**350**	**386**	**393**	**375**	**383**	**373**	**424**

SOURCE: Ministry of Justice, Immigration Bureau.

interfere with studies; and the job is appropriate for a student and in accordance with laws, regulations and public morals. If such a student wishes to work beyond these limitations, he or she must first receive permission. On the other hand, a student of a Japanese language school or other non-collegiate educational institution with a 4-1-16-3 status must obtain permission from the Regional Immigration Bureau to engage in a part-time job, even if the working hours do not exceed 20 hours per week.

Therefore we must conclude that the real number of illegal workers far exceeds the Immigration Control Bureau's official estimate of approximately 284 500 as of 1 May 1996. In addition to illegal immigrant workers, there are various categories of legal immigrant workers in Japan. A summary of these workers is shown in Table 12.3.

Characteristics of Illegal Immigrants

Although it is difficult to know the precise number of illegal immigrant workers, we can estimate the nature of violations committed by examining the numbers of people discovered by various means to be working illegally. In this context, the issues concerning illegal immigrants changed substantially during the 1990s.

In spite of the 1990 revision of the Immigration Control Law, the rate of increase in the numbers of illegal workers apprehended has been remarkable. Most illegal immigrant workers in Japan violate one or more conditions of lawfully permitted entry and thus resemble the US "visa abusers" (Chiswick, 1988: 2). This category includes those who work in violation of their visas, tourists who stay longer than permitted and students who work in violation of their visas.

According to *Statistics on Immigration Control* (Ministry of Justice, 1996), 19 199 foreigners were refused entry to Japan in 1993. This was a 33 percent increase over the previous year's 14 434. Moreover, the number of cases referred to the Immigration Bureau's Special Inquiry Office for detailed review due to dubious purposes of entry in 1993 showed a remarkable increase over the number of cases in the previous year. This indicates that those who would violate the law are becoming more clever and devious. For instance, some represent

Table 12.3 *Foreign workers in Japan (estimate)*

Residence status	Number of foreigners	New entrants in 1995
Legal workers		
Professor	4,149	1,296
Art	230	103
Religious Activities	5,264	1,219
Journalist	442	212
Investor; business manager	4,649	1,021
Legal, accounting services	67	7
Medical services	152	1
Researcher	1,711	870
Education	7,155	2963
Instructor	9,882	3,717
Humanities; international activities	25,070	4,982
Intrafirm transfer	5,901	3,074
Entertainer	15,967	59,833
Skilled labor	7,357	2,210
Sub-total	**87,996**	**81,508**
Students		
College students	60,685	
Pre-college students	34,441	
Estimated number of workers[a]	57,075	
Nikkeijin[b]	150,000	
Illegal overstayers	284,744	
Illegals		
Unqualified activities	(substantial)	
Total	**580,000 (approx.)**	

[a] Estimate based on assumption that 60 percent of students are working.
[b] Estimated by Ministry of Foreign Affairs as of June 1992.
Others: estimated by Ministry of Justice: legal workers as of December 1995, illegal overstayers as of November 1995.

themselves as airline staff or United Nations workers; instances of passport forgery have increased. During the Asian Games at Hiroshima in October 1994, 56 Filipinos neatly dressed in blue blazers landed at Fukuoka Airport and told the immigration officers they were a delegation of volleyball players. However, the officials had a sharp eye for deception and suspected that these Filipinos were awfully short for volleyball players. The would-be immigrants were deported within hours (*Newsweek*, 17 October, 1994, p. 10).

Such violations of the Immigration Control Law are tabulated in Table 12.4. The numbers represent cases of foreign nationals found violating the Immigration Control Law against whom deportation procedures were initiated by local immigration offices. In 1993, for the first time, the number of such cases reached 70 000.

Since Japan is an island country, relatively few foreigners enter surreptitiously, although the number of such incidents is increasing year by year. Most are Chinese hoping to find jobs in Japan. Instances of disguised Chinese or Vietnamese who attempt illegal landings by boat are given great publicity by the news media. These attempts are usually organized and guided by underground Chinese groups operating in China, particularly Fujian province, and also in Japan. Such immigrants who cross the border without immigration officials properly inspecting their documents are called "EWIs" (entry without inspection) in the United States. Obviously it is difficult to know the real number of such immigrants, so the estimates released by the Immigration Control Bureau must be viewed as conservative.

It is reported that a substantial number of overstayers turn themselves in to immigration offices after achieving their financial goals. Having accumulated the amount of savings they targeted, these workers ask the officials to send them home. They usually buy discount air tickets and are returned to their countries of origin. Such cases are included in the figures for violations mentioned above, though these people were not apprehended as the result of any initiative on the part of immigration officers.

The nationalities of immigrant workers apprehended by immigration officers as violators of the Immigration Control Law generally correlate with the estimates of the nationalities of visa overstayers. Although there have been some variations from year to year, Thai nationals account for the largest number, followed by Iranians, Malaysians, South Koreans, Filipinos, Chinese, Bangladeshis, Pakistanis, Taiwanese,

Table 12.4 Violations of immigration control law

	1986	1987	1988	1989	1990	1991	1992	1993	1994	1995
Overstaying visa	9,215	12,792	15,970	19,105	32,647	32,820	63,265	63,905	58,692	49,453
Illegal employment	8,131	11,307	14,314	16,608	29,884	32,908	62,161	64,341	59,352	49,434
Illegal entry	597	542	616	2,349	2,320	1,662	3,459	5,227	5,598	4,663
Unqualified activities	349	372	839	696	751	882	393	306	455	439
Violation of penal order	288	289	280	218	189	192	174	170	176	157
Illegal landing	124	134	149	258	357	347	533	796	697	758
Total	**18,704**	**25,436**	**32,168**	**39,234**	**66,148**	**68,811**	**129,985**	**134,745**	**124,970**	**104,904**

SOURCE: Statistics on Immigration Control (1993).

Burmese and Sri Lankans. Regarding the relatively small number of Chinese violators apprehended, it is said that illegal Chinese workers are difficult to find because they physically resemble Japanese. Men and women of practically all nationalities and a diversity of languages are immigrant workers, which makes it difficult to conduct in-depth research. In 1993 the number of countries of origin for illegal immigrants was 90 as compared to 58 in 1990.

According to statistics on illegal immigrants apprehended and deported, 4783 foreigners were working illegally in Japan in 1984. This figure had risen to over 10 000 in 1987, and to 64 000 in 1993. Most of these illegal workers had overstayed their visas and/or were engaged in work outside the scope of that permitted by their residence status. In 1993 a special investigation team was established at the Tokyo Regional Immigration Bureau to prosecute offenders. This is one reason for the increase in discoveries of Immigration Control Law violations, according to the Bureau.

More recent changes in trends among illegal immigrant workers include the following.

Increasing numbers of illegal group entries
Foreigners hoping to enter Japan illegally avail themselves of every opportunity and are becoming more clever and devious. Above all, the numbers of immigrants who attempt illegal entry in groups have substantially increased. These groups are guided by brokers[4] whose networks extend to major sources and destinations of labor migration, and who often exploit the immigrants atrociously. Among the 64 341 illegal immigrant workers who were deported in 1993, 13 710 indicated that they had received assistance from brokers (Nyukoku Kanrikyoku, 1994).

Longer periods of overstay
Among overstayers, in 1990 about 21.4 percent (approximately 22 800) had spent more than 3 years in Japan, but by 1994, 31.8 percent (approximately 93 400) of overstayers had done so.

In the latter 1980s some journalists and other Japanese insisted that the number of immigrant workers in Japan would not increase very much. They also contended that the length of stay of such persons would be short due to Japan's high cost of living; thus they saw no need to worry about immigrants working. Yet subsequent developments have not met their expectations.

More crime committed by illegal immigrant workers

In addition to these changes, the number of crimes committed by foreigners in Japan has increased sharply. The proportion of serious crimes (similar to felonies) committed by illegal overstayers, of all serious crimes committed by foreigners in Japan, increased from 38.9 percent in 1991 to 52.8 percent in 1993. The number of foreigners arrested for criminal acts in 1993 increased 22.1 percent (and arrests for serious crimes increased 33.0 percent) over 1992; cases of foreigners arrested in association with illegal drugs increased 32.6 percent in the same period. This is quite remarkable because the total number of persons arrested for criminal acts in Japan during the same period increased only 4.5 percent (total arrests for serious crimes increased 10.2 percent), and total arrests associated with drugs increased 3.9 percent (Keisatsucho: Gaikokujin Mondai Taisaku Iinkai – National Police Agency, 1994: 3). This rapid increase in criminal cases involving overstayers has become a serious social problem in Japan, which was formerly a comparatively safe country.

WHY DO THEY COME TO JAPAN?

There are many factors in Japan that attract foreign workers from less developed countries in Asia and other parts of the world. One is the relatively high wage level and standard of living in an economically developed nation. The economic factor was exacerbated by the sharp appreciation of the yen relative to the currencies of other major countries in the 1980s, which raised the value of the wages foreign workers could earn in Japan in terms of their home currencies. The exchange rate in 1975 was about 297 yen per US dollar but dropped below 100 yen in the 1990s. Despite the low wages these workers receive (due partly to their illegal status) and the high cost of living in Japan, people from developing countries are still attracted to working in Japan by the opportunity to make "good money". According to one calculation, the wage difference between China and Japan amounts to a factor of 90 (Zhao and Qian, 1993: 35).

In addition to this international wage differential there is a strong demand within the Japanese economy for cheap foreign labor. In the second half of the 1980s, the supply of local labor continued to shrink in Japan, while the economy experienced new expansion. This forced up wages and other labor-related costs as employers competed to attract scarce workers.

Table 12.5 *Economic indicators (GNP growth and unemployment rates)*

Fiscal year	GNP growth over previous year (real)	Unemployment rate (%)	Exchange rate yen / US$ Interbank rate
1972	9.0	1.3	265.8
1973	4.7	1.3	273.8
1074	0.2	1.5	292.7
1975	4.0	2.0	299.1
1976	4.0	2.0	292.3
1977	4.8	2.1	256.5
1978	5.1	2.2	201.4
1979	5.5	2.0	229.7
1980	3.2	2.1	217.2
1981	3.2	2.2	227.5
1982	3.5	2.5	249.6
1983	3.0	2.7	236.3
1984	4.5	2.7	244.2
1985	4.8	2.6	221.1
1986	2.9	2.8	159.8
1987	4.9	2.8	138.3
1988	6.0	2.4	128.3
1989	4.5	2.2	142.8
1990	5.3	2.1	141.3
1991	3.2	2.1	133.2
1992	0.7	2.2	124.8
1993	0.1	2.6	107.8
1994	0.4	2.9	99.4
1995	2.4	3.2	96.5

SOURCE: Economic Planning Agency (1996), *Keizai Hakusha* [Economic White Paper] (Tokyo: Ministry of Finance, Printing Office).

Pressed by the appreciation of the yen, large Japanese manufacturing companies have moved some labor-intensive operations offshore to less developed countries such as China, Malaysia and Thailand, but this solution is not available to every small and medium-size firm based outside the largest cities. The result is an economic "pull" from Japan for inexpensive foreign workers, with some Japanese believing that foreigners must inevitably satisfy Japan's labor shortage. After 1983, when labor markets in the Middle East began to lose their vitality, increasing number of workers from Asian countries turned their attention to Japan as well as to Taiwan and South Korea as potential job sources.

In addition to these changes, Japanese society is aging. The proportion of the Japanese population aged 65 and over relative to the working-age population (those aged 15–64) is predicted to rise to approximately 22 percent by the year 2025. Significant supply/demand mismatches with respect to age, region and job category developed in the 1980s (Koshiro, 1993).

The values of young Japanese entering the labor market are not the same as in years past. Young people accustomed to a higher standard of living are more attracted to white-collar than blue-collar jobs. A common complaint is that young Japanese do not have the will to work that characterized the postwar generation. Thus there are few takers for so-called "3K" jobs: *kitanai*, *kitsui* and *kiken* – dirty, demanding and dangerous, the English-language "3D" jobs.

Effects of the Recession

The lengthy recession beginning in May 1991 (which continued until October 1993 according to official benchmarks) had a severe impact on the Japanese economy. The labor market is no exception. The unemployment ratio increased, reaching the critical level of 3 percent in July 1994, despite reports of recovery. Yet the inflow of immigrant workers has continued at a high level. With the advent of the recession, all those Japanese who had advocated a wider opening to foreign workers fell silent. The heated 1980s debate over whether to permit increased immigration has subsided.

Despite the recession, the number of illegal immigrants has continued to rise. Many lost their jobs or had difficulties finding work during the recession; in particular, those who came late had great difficulty finding jobs. In the fall of 1990, when the Japanese economy was still in the midst of a boom, first-time immigrants from the Philippines had little difficulty finding jobs in construction or manufacturing with an hourly wage of about 1000 yen (about US $10) and occasionally more. But during the recession starting in the spring of 1991 the labor market rapidly deteriorated and jobs for immigrants decreased substantially. During the recession many immigrant workers moved from large cities to rural areas where they thought they could find jobs among small and medium-size local firms (*Nihon Keizai Shimbun,* evening edition, 8 October 1994).

In this context, attention should be paid to the drawing power of the world's largest cities. Enormous cities are powerful magnets which attract various factors of production such as capital and labor from all over the world. Tokyo, for example, is now the largest city in the world, with a population of about 25 million. Despite the high cost of living due to the recent appreciation of yen and other factors, many companies as well as immigrants have located in Tokyo. Immigrants from practically any country that can be named are working legally as well as illegally in Tokyo and its vicinity. Tokyo's population of legally registered foreigners was about 2.3 percent foreigners as of 1993, and a few wards such as Minato Ward (7.4 percent), Shinjuku Ward (6.6 percent), and Toshima Ward (6.1 percent) have fairly substantial foreign populations (Tokyo-to, 1994: 90). These figures exclude illegals (see Table 12.6).

Push Factors

"Push" factors have also contributed to the increased outflow of workers from less developed Asian countries including China, the Philippines, Pakistan and Bangladesh. With large populations and struggling economies, these countries are experiencing high levels of unemployment or underemployment and wages are low. Naturally the wide differentials in wage and employment rates between these developing

Table 12.6 Population of the world's ten largest cities (millions)

	1990		2000		2005		2010	
1.	Tokyo	25.0	Tokyo	28.0	Tokyo	28.7	Tokyo	28.9
2.	São Paulo	18.1	São Paulo	22.6	São Paulo	24.0	São Paulo	25.0
3.	New York	16.1	Bombay	18.1	Bombay	21.3	Bombay	24.4
4.	Mexico City	15.1	Shanghai	17.4	Shanghai	19.7	Shanghai	21.7
5.	Shanghai	13.4	New York	16.6	Lagos	17.2	Lagos	21.1
6.	Bombay	12.2	Mexico City	16.2	Mexico City	17.1	Mexico City	18.0
7.	Los Angeles	11.5	Beijing	14.4	New York	16.9	Beijing	18.0
8.	Buenos Aires	11.4	Lagos	13.5	Beijing	16.3	Dakka	17.6
9.	Seoul	11.0	Jakarta	13.4	Jakarta	15.4	New York	17.2
10.	Rio de Janeiro	10.9	Los Angeles	13.2	Dakka	14.5	Jakarta	17.2

SOURCE: United Nations, Department of Economic and Social Information and Policy Analysis (1993), *World Urbanization Prospects: The 1992 Revision* (United Nations).

countries and developed ones such as Japan causes labor to flow in the direction of higher wages and ample employment opportunities. Theoretically, at least, the economic forces generating international labor migration should continue to exist until wage and unemployment levels reach an approximate equilibrium.

Many countries in Asia encourage workers to go abroad. The Philippines, Indonesia and Bangladesh, for example, openly encourage temporary emigration. Those who take this path, and particularly those who work overseas illegally, have few rights and their working conditions are often appalling. The recent political conflict between Singapore and the Philippines over the execution of a Filipino maid in Singapore arose from a case of immigrant labor.

JAPAN'S LABOR MARKETS FOR ILLEGAL IMMIGRANTS

The Formation of a Segmented Labor Market

Most illegal laborers enter Japan legally using tourist, student or other types of visas under which they are prohibited from working, though their actual intent is to work, which they do illegally by overstaying or disobeying their visa restrictions. Often they are recruited by agents or brokers operating both in Japan and their native countries, who not only offer travel arrangements but often find job opportunities through their networks.

It is extremely difficult to acquire accurate information on the wages illegal workers receive in Japan because they make every effort to hide themselves. Among the smattering of information available, a recent study on the experiences of Bangladeshi workers in Japan reveals certain aspects of their working conditions. Most Bangladeshi workers are assumed to be illegal because only a few Bangladeshis have been granted permission to work in Japan (NIRA, 1994).[5]

Since the mid-1980s, Japan has emerged as one of the most preferred destinations for Bangladeshi workers, next to the United States and Canada. Compared with Bangladeshi workers who went to the Middle East, those who came to Japan were younger and better educated. This shows that immigrant workers choose their destinations according to their personal attributes such as skills, education and aspirations, and the types of jobs available at the destination.

Desire among Bangladeshis to work in Japan increased due to their knowledge of the availability of jobs and the greater potential for accumulating savings in Japan. Because of an abrupt increase of Bangladeshi workers entering Japan, a temporary suspension of the visa exemption was imposed by Japanese government in March 1989.

According to the survey mentioned above, the average income of Bangladeshis working as laborers in Japan is about 45 percent of that of Japanese workers with similar duties. In fact, when compared to similar workers from other Asian and Latin American countries, Bangladeshi workers earned the least, partly because of their illegal status and partly because of discrimination by employers and other workers. Their average income is, however, more than four times the highest income of civil servants in Bangladesh and about forty times the average income of industrial workers in Bangladesh (NIRA, 1994: 43–4).

In this connection, another study revealed that a certain degree of stratification was gradually emerging among immigrant workers according to characteristics such as nationality, type of work, qualifications, gender, etc. (Inagami *et al.*, 1992: 20–5). Workers from Southeast Asian countries are usually ranked at the bottom of this stratified labor market, since most are illegal. The jobs they take require very little skill, training or experience; most are unskilled or semiskilled and in the "3K" category. The situation of Bangladeshi immigrant workers is typical.

Among immigrant workers there is a fairly wide disparity in wage rates and working conditions. In this context, *Nikkeijin* (descendants of Japanese emigrants) from South American countries usually get better jobs, since they are legally permitted to work in Japan. However, there are subtle differences even among *Nikkeijin* by nationality, generation, experience, etc., and other immigrant workers commonly rank below them. As a result, *Nikkeijin* are coming to dominate certain sectors of the labor market which had been occupied by Japanese nationals.

Illegal Workers: Their Work and Their Lives

Generally, firms that employ illegal workers are small companies in industries such as manufacturing, construction or services. They often depend heavily on these foreigners since few Japanese are interested in doing the work because of inferior working conditions, low social status and other factors.

One reason few Japanese want to work in such companies is that working conditions, particularly wages, are inferior to those elsewhere. During the "bubble economy" era of asset inflation which started around the end of 1986, these small companies found it increasingly difficult to hire Japanese workers, particularly young workers, and faced great difficulties in maintaining the viability of their firms. Some could not secure enough workers; many were unable to pay wages that would attract Japanese workers. For these employers, the sudden influx of immigrant workers was a welcome rainfall after a long drought. For the immigrant workers, on the other hand, wage levels at such companies were quite attractive compared with wages in their home countries, even if they were often discriminated against with respect to Japanese workers and sometimes with respect to other immigrant workers. Thus, demand and supply came together.

The potential for saving money is central to the issue of foreigners immigrating to Japan and is a factor of their income and expenditures. Research on this aspect of immigrant workers is also scarce at this stage. A study on Bangladeshi immigrants reports that savings averaged 33 000 taka (Tk) per month (equivalent to US $943) in 1991, based on an average monthly income of Tk 45 000 ($1350) and monthly expenditures of Tk 13 000 ($390). At this rate of savings, a worker could accumulate Tk 396 000 per year (equivalent to $11 314). Moreover, the average cost of emigrating to Japan of Tk. 78 000 ($2340) could be recouped in about 2.4 months. Bangladeshis working in Japan sent home an average of Tk. 553 000 (equivalent to $15 800) during their stays in Japan (NIRA, 1994).

A survey of *Nikkeijin* workers from South America concluded that many of them had a target of saving between 1 and 3 million yen during their stay in Japan. Savings of 1 million yen (about $10 000) would enable such a worker to purchase a decent house in the home country, while 3 million yen ($30 000) would be enough to buy an upper-class house with a pool. Living standards of most illegal immigrants working as laborers in Japan are very poor compared to those of Japanese and foreigners working legally. In order to avoid being sighted, they try to remain at home during their off-time (Inagami, Kuwahara and KKS, 1993).

Japan's economic dependence on immigrant workers
Although Japan does not have a great deal of experience with immigrant workers, there is little reason to expect that its situation should be any different from that of other countries. Allowing foreign laborers to enter the Japanese work force in any significant numbers would likely establish a continuing dependence on them as an integral part of the economy, regardless of efforts to limit the length of stay of individuals or the number of such workers. In fact, it is apparent that some sectors of the Japanese economy, such as construction and manufacturing, already rely heavily on illegal foreign labor.

It is important to point out that a kind of entrenchment can occur whether labor migration occurs legally or otherwise. As long as there is an essentially unlimited supply of workers overseas who are willing to work in Japan for any wage above what they can earn in their home countries, and as long as brokers and employers can profit by delivering and employing illegal immigrants willing to work for less than the prevailing wages earned by Japanese, there will always be illegal workers attempting to circumvent the system.

Some claims have been made that legalizing the immigration of foreigners willing to work as laborers will reduce the significance of illegal immigration to Japan. This would only be the case if the number of workers admitted were so large as to reduce the pressure from outside Japan's borders. Given the number of potential immigrant laborers in major labor-exporting countries of Asia, it is unlikely that this could take place without causing considerable adverse impact on Japanese workers. For example, China, which is the largest threat to Japan in terms of potential immigrants, has a surplus labor force of more than 100 million people (Zhang, 1993: 108).

EVALUATION OF POLICIES ON ILLEGAL IMMIGRATION

Criteria for Policy Options

Although Japan's immigration policy is sometimes criticized as a backdoor policy, this is more or less true for many developed countries. In Japan, as well as other developed countries, various special interest groups exert influence over the process of policy formation, making it difficult to reach a consensus.

If government wanted to eliminate illegal immigrants, theoretically it would be possible to do so. One way would be to open the border to all who wish to enter, making all immigrants legal. Needless to say, few developed countries could adopt this policy, since they could not tolerate the increased unemployment among their nationals resulting from the unrestricted arrival of immigrant workers.

The other alternative is to close the door tightly and impose strict controls on those attempting illegal entry. Some countries have adopted such a policy and maintain rigorous border controls, while strictly deporting people discovered residing illegally in the country. However, implementation of such a policy is hindered by exorbitant administrative costs and the nuisance caused to legitimate foreign residents, as well as the general reluctance of a democratic society to restrict the free movement of people.

Up to the bursting of the "bubble economy" in the spring of 1991, there was a series of feverish controversies in Japan between those who advocated greater opening and those who opposed admitting immigrant workers. Many of the arguments were unrealistic, despite the loud voices raised. The severe recession which followed has been a cooling-off period, and the boom and subsequent recession have left both sides facing some undeniable facts. In particular, those who advocated that Japan open its borders wider to immigrant workers have become silent after being confronted with aggravated labor market conditions, while many in the opposing camp seem to have accepted the presence of foreign workers. These are very interesting developments to those who observed the heated and often unrealistic arguments a few years ago.

The Japanese government has maintained a policy that accelerated innovation will bring better results than a free influx of foreigners willing to do unskilled labor, resulting in the widespread use of labor-saving machinery in various industries. According to the International Robot Association, 324 895 industrial robots were installed in Japan as of 1991 compared to 44 000 in the United States and 34 140 in Germany. The replacement of labor with capital is clearly progressing. However, some small firms cannot afford to introduce new technologies, and must depend on illegal immigrants for survival. The future of such enterprises is not promising, since many lack the entrepreneurship and business acumen required to meet the challenges of global competition.

The high appreciation of the yen during the past several years has brought about radical changes in investment behavior. Facing global competition, both large and small companies are shifting production to developing countries in Asia such as Malaysia, Thailand and China. They take advantage of international differences in production costs, importing parts and products manufactured in these developing countries. Direct investment abroad by small Japanese firms has greatly increased since 1985. Today, small firms must consider the global market in order to survive.

Through these experiences many Japanese seem to have become more realistic, at least on the surface. The next question must be, What is a realistic Japanese policy for immigration control?

EVALUATION OF THE CURRENT IMMIGRATION CONTROL POLICY

Border Management

In recent years Japanese officials have inspected approximately 4 million foreign nationals seeking entry annually, including re-entrants, a significant increase over the 1970 number of about 700 000. This does not include illegal entrants or individuals apprehended and deported while attempting illegal entry. Because Japan is an island country, most arrivals are inspected at major airports or sea ports.

Relative to continental countries, the number of foreigners crossing the border without proper inspection by immigration officials is low; in 1993, only 796 people making such an attempt were apprehended. Yet the number of foreigners attempting this sort of entry every year has increased steadily over the past decade. Considering the tremendous labor surplus elsewhere in Asia, Japan cannot disregard such activity. It is extremely difficult effectively to control the flood of would-be immigrants and refugees when political upheaval occurs in these neighboring countries.

Japan's Immigration Control Law in principle bars people from entering the country for the purpose of employment unless they have special skills or know-how. Nevertheless, with both demand and supply factors working strongly to encourage foreigners willing to perform unskilled labor to do so in Japan, it is hardly surprising that the country is experiencing a rapidly rising influx of illegal foreign workers.

Border control is the primary responsibility of the Immigration Control Bureau of the Ministry of Justice, whose major responsibilities include detecting and preventing the entry of illegal aliens. It also investigates hiring practices, observes the activities of brokers, interdicts and arrests aliens who have committed serious crimes and, with the cooperation of the police, investigates drug- and alien-smuggling links. At the branch level of the Immigration Bureau, at airports and other locations, there are three stages of inspection: inspection by bureau officials, verbal examination by special examiners, and submission of immigrant objections to the Minister of Justice.

The government has recently introduced various measures in response to the crimes committed by an increasing number of illegal entrants. The measures include increasing the number of special examiners, holding policy meetings to cope with forged passports and visas, introducing the Photo Phone system which quickly verifies documents on a nationwide network, and instituting special weeks of intensified immigration control at major ports. The number of Immigration Control Bureau officers has increased steadily from 1816 in 1990 to 2263 in 1994. In accordance with the rising numbers of illegals to be deported, accommodation facilities have been expanded from a capacity of about 600 to over 661 600 in 1995.

Work-site Enforcement

The various control measures introduced at the borders are of seriously limited effectiveness, since many "covert" immigrants still pass through without being detected. Accordingly, supplemental post-entry measures are needed, including work site enforcement of employer sanctions and labor standards, and introduction of the trainee system.

The Revised Immigration Control Law which came into force on 1 June, 1990 has three main features. First, with the objective of simplifying immigration procedures for highly qualified foreigners with special skills or knowledge, the new law reclassifies the various categories of residence status, making them easier to understand and extending their scope. Second, the new law clarifies the standards for immigration screening and simplifies the red tape involved. Finally, the revised law reaffirms the strict ban on immigration for the purpose of employment by foreigners who cannot obtain a residence status that would permit them to work. This is backed by employer sanctions, which were not prescribed by the old law, to penalize employers and brokers who assist illegal employment by knowingly hiring or recruiting for a fee an alien who is not authorized to be employed in Japan. When this revision was introduced many employers and brokers decided to refrain from hiring illegals.

The Growing Influx of *Nikkeijin*

Employers have sought out *Nikkeijin* workers, who are given legal status and upon whom no restrictions are imposed regarding the types of activities they engage in while resident in Japan. Current law, implemented in May 1990 by a decree of the Minister of Justice, permits newly-arrived *Nikkeijin* to work for up to 3 years in Japan. What might be called "the first generation" of returning *Nikkeijin* "was subject to no employment restriction under the official status of 'return to the homeland'". Under some conditions, similar benefits are provided to second- and third-generation *Nikkeijin*.

Some employers, finding themselves in an acute labor crunch during the era of the bubble economy, ventured as far as Brazil and Peru looking for workers, and immigration of

Nikkeijin increased remarkably, from 54 359 in 1990 to 129 506 in 1993. With the recession since 1992, the rate of increase has declined. *Nikkeijin* arrivals substantially mitigated the labor shortage, since many found jobs as unskilled laborers, while employers who could not afford to employ high-wage *Nikkeijin* workers sought illegal Asian immigrants. These changes, as described in the preceding pages, encouraged the formation of segmented labor markets between immigrant and domestic workers.

Current work-site enforcement mechanisms have proved less effective than anticipated in deterring illegal immigrants, the hiring of unauthorized workers, and unfair immigration-related employment practices, as has been demonstrated by the rise in the estimated number of illegal aliens resident in Japan.

Employer sanctions

Contrary to the expectations of government officials and other observers, employer sanctions have not proved effective. For uncertain reasons, they have not been strictly enforced, and only extreme cases have been exposed. There may be a shortage of immigration inspectors to respond to the rapidly changing situation, as the Ministry of Justice claims, but this half-hearted enforcement has created an ambiguous atmosphere that companies employing illegal immigrants rather welcomed. They are aware of their delicate position: if more legal ways of employing foreigners willing to do unskilled labor – a quota system or permit system – are officially introduced, they are not well prepared to meet qualifications such as the ability to provide acceptable working conditions and housing, nor can they afford to pay the higher wages legal foreign workers demand. Thus the current situation, though quite ambiguous, is in some respects convenient for these companies, who also find it easy to hire and fire illegals.

While some illegal aliens secure employment through the use of fraudulent documents, others are employed in the underground economy by firms that do not check their papers. Japanese employers are not obligated to verify employment eligibility. Many firms that employ illegal immigrant workers violate other labor standards as well; the presence of unauthorized workers may be the very factor that enables those employers to break other labor laws and regulations.

It is questionable whether this ambiguous enforcement of sanction procedures will survive. If there is a further increase of illegal aliens there may be calls for the introduction of a more transparent system such as one based on employment permits. Some of Japan's neighbors, such as Korea and Taiwan, are considering the introduction of employment permit systems in response to labor shortages. Yet it should be noted that the introduction of such a system cannot eliminate the employment of illegal aliens. Since the number of officially acceptable immigrant workers is limited, people unable to get permission to work will continue to infiltrate by subterfuge.

Anti-discrimination measures
The increasing number of illegal immigrant workers and the resulting labor market segmentation between immigrants and Japanese underlie the emergence in Japan of unfair immigration-related employment practices. Some firms indirectly employ illegal immigrants via brokers to avoid employer sanctions; others cannot offer arrangements such as housing and transportation, and depend on brokers, who routinely handle such matters. These firms often have no desire to deal with the legal status of such workers. For their managers, the presence of bodies is sufficient. Illegal immigrants consequently often find themselves victimized by unscrupulous brokers and employers. The Ministry of Justice has established special research teams in Tokyo and Osaka to identify such brokers and employers, yet the numbers of violations have rapidly increased.

Toward more effective control of illegal immigrant workers
The national immigration policy may gain credibility if employer sanctions are enforced more strictly, although employer sanctions alone will not effectively deter unlawful employment practices. Stronger enforcement of labor standards must be seen as a complement to enforcement of employer sanctions and as integral part of the strategy to reduce illegal immigration. Employers who violate one labor standard with impunity are likely to violate others.

The current system of immigration control undoubtedly has many problems. Despite the various measures introduced during the past decade, the influx of illegal immigrant workers has continued to rise, although a slight decline was seen during the recession. The policy of admitting *Nikkeijin* and the establishment of a field-training skills program were unofficially intended to mitigate the rapid increase of illegal immigrant workers; in fact, the arrival of *Nikkeijin* reduced the flow of illegal immigrants to a certain extent since many of them found jobs as unskilled laborers. Otherwise, more illegals would have entered Japan.

The field-training skills program
This was introduced in April 1993. In the initial stage, foreigners interested in this program apply to enter Japan as trainees. Those who complete the first stage of the program, the training course, apply for the second stage, employment. Their skills and performance are evaluated by the Japan Industrial Training Organization (JITCO), a new private organization established to meet the needs of this program. After taking the JITCO examination, eligible trainees can work under the new status of field practice. They usually find jobs requiring semi-skilled labor, and are paid wages rather than trainee allowances. The maximum period of residence in Japan under this program is 2 years, after which they are required to return home.

This program will not effectively reduce the influx of illegal immigrants; it mitigates but cannot stop it. A great deal of thought and effort were applied to bringing this program into existence. Although it is officially characterized as a new means of training and skills transfer, many employers want to utilize it as a way to meet their labor shortage. There is thus a lack of clear correspondence between its purposes and effects. It is also impractical for companies pressed by a shortage of labor; firms suffering from acute labor shortages are mostly small and medium-size enterprises. Many cannot afford the time and resources required for training, and immigrants want to work for immediate wages rather than train for future semi-skilled positions. Both employers and immigrants are asking for a more straightforward way to satisfy their needs.

In an age of globalization there is no single way effectively to reduce the influx of illegal immigrants willing to perform unskilled labor. The Japanese government must manipulate a set of various, often patchy, measures to mitigate the rapid increase of illegals. If the influx of illegal immigrants should expand again once the recession is truly behind us, debate over illegal workers is likely to re-emerge. There will be calls for more direct ways of bringing together immigrant workers and employers, such as an employment permit system or a quota system. Yet there is no assurance that such measures would limit the influx of illegals, since the number of jobs offered through such channels would necessarily be limited.

SEARCHING FOR A REALISTIC PERSPECTIVE

Based on the facts so far accumulated, it can be argued that the current immigration situation in Japan is out of control. To a certain extent, this is an issue related to the costs and benefits of attaining a target level of effective control: financial and manpower expenditures at the Immigration Bureau offices versus mitigation of a shortage of people willing to perform unskilled labor. Some officials think the current level of illegal immigrant workers could be substantially reduced if the immigration control budget is increased, and more controllers and inspectors hired.

The nature of Japan's current immigration policy is far from ideal and much lies in the gray zone. The lack of national consensus makes it difficult to implement a more clearly defined immigration policy. If the number of illegal overstayers should increase substantially, voices will be raised demanding more direct ways of employing immigrants as unskilled laborers rather than expanding the trainee program. Others will call for tighter restrictions against would-be illegal immigrant workers. One of the most likely options for handling this difficult situation may be the strict operation of a "modified" guest-worker program based on an employment permit certificate. However, embarking on such a course will not solve Japan's immigrant worker problem, since their potential number is extremely large. The recent appreciation of the yen has only intensified this aspect of the problem.

Despite the loopholes in the national immigration control system, implementing a "modified" guest-worker program based on an employment permit certificate could increase transparency to some extent. To make this guest worker program compatible with the field training skills program, the latter should be operated as a stand-alone training program rather than as a hybrid of training and employment.

In the end, we need consistency and unity in Japan's immigration policy. Issues concerning immigrant workers are no longer restricted to the dimensions of immigration control and individual establishments, but include regional employment, human rights, housing, education, crime and so forth, which may be called "social dimensions of foreign nationals willing to perform unskilled labor in Japan". Current immigration policy is lagging in its response to these diverse issues. A decision-making system based on consultations among various ministries seems unable to generate an effective response to the challenge, but leaves residents, companies and local administrative bodies burdened with these problems. There is keen awareness of the need for a national administrative organization such as a "Ministry of International Cooperation" which could take responsibility for immigrant workers and their families, and a need for greater effort to achieve consensus on this issue, so vital for Japanese society (Hanami and Kuwahara, 1989:196–7).

NOTES

1. As a basic rule, no foreign national can enter into and stay in Japan unless he or she falls under one of the statuses of residence provided for by Article 4, paragraph 1 of the Immigration Control Law: 16 categories permitting employment and a seventeenth, "specific activities", under which employment may be permitted on an individual basis. These categories do not include permanent residents and their dependents or refugees, who are permitted to engage in any employment. In addition, college students and pre-college students are allowed to work a limited number of hours a week.

2. Although a considerable volume of literature exists on this subject, sources written in English are rather scarce. The following are well-researched and give a good overview: Cornelius (1994); Oka (1994); Shimada (1994); Japan–ASEAN Forum II (1991); and Kuwahara (1991b, 1992). For more details see Hanami and Kuwahara (1989, 1993), Kuwahara (1991), and Rodosho (1991), although in Japanese.

3. The total of foreign visitors including re-entrants was 4 244 529 in 1996, a 13.7 percent increase from the figure for 1995. There are

many reasons for the increase, among them increased tourists due to the reversed appreciation of the yen and improved tourists' image on Japan after the Kansai earthquake. The decrease is anticipated to be a temporary phenomenon and visitor traffic is expected to rise again with Japan's economic recovery.

4. These are called "snake heads," and exploit illegal immigrant workers in various ways (Mo, 1994).

5. The discussion of Bangladeshi immigrants who worked in Japan is based mostly on the NIRA report, which was commissioned by the Bangladesh Institute of Development Studies. See also Hase and Miyake (1993).

REFERENCES

Chiswick, B. R. (1988), *Illegal Aliens: Their Employment and Employers* (Kalamazoo, MI: W. E. Upjohn Institute for Employment Research).

Cornelius, W. A. (1994), "Japan: The Illusion of Immigration Control," in Wayne A. Cornelius, Philip L. Martin, and James F. Hollifield (eds). *Controlling Immigration: A Global Perspectives* (Stanford, CA: Stanford University Press).

Hanami. T. and Kuwahara. Y. (eds), (1989), *Asuno rinjin: gaikokujin rodosha* [Tomorrow's Neighbor: Migrant Workers] (Tokyo: Toyo Keizai Shimpo Sha).

—— (1993), *Anatano rinjin: gaikokujin rodosha* [Your Neighbor: Migrant Workers] (Tokyo: Toyo Keizai Shimpo Sha).

Hase, Y. and Miyake, H. (eds), (1993), *Banguradeshu no kaigai dekasegi rodosha* [Migrant Workers from Bangladesh] (Tokyo: Akashi Shoten).

Immigration Control Bureau (1994), *Number of Illegal Overstayers in Japan* (March); published twice a year.

—— (1995), *Statistics on Immigration Control 1994* (Tokyo: Japan Immigration Association).

Inagami, T., Kuwahara, Y. and Kokumin Kinyukoko Sogo Kenkyujyo (KKS) (1992), *Gaikokujin rodoshao senryokukasuru chushokigyo* [Small and Medium Sized Firms which Strategically Employ Migrant Workers] (Tokyo: Chushokigyo Risati Senta).

Japan–ASEAN Forum II (1991), *International Labour Migration in East Asia*, proceedings of forum held in Tokyo, 26–7 September (Tokyo: The United Nations University).

Keisatsucho: Gaikokujin Mondai Taisaku Iinkai (National Police Agency: Committee for the Problems Committed by Foreigners) (1994), *Rainichi Gaikokujin Mondai Hakusho* [White Paper on the Problems Committed by foreigners Visiting Japan], March.

Koshiro, K. (1993), "Labour Shortage and Employment Policies in Japan," in *International Labour Migration in East Asia*, Japan Asean Forum II (Tokyo: The United Nations University).

Kuwahara, Y. (1991a), *Kokkyoo koeru rodosha* [Workers Moving across National Boundaries] (Tokyo: Iwanami Shoten).

—— (1991b), "Labor Migration and Development in Asia", paper submitted to Second Japan–ASEAN Forum on International Labour Migration in East Asia, Tokyo, United Nations University, 26–7 September 1991.

—— (1992), *To Tie the Untied String: Migrant Workers and Japan's Economic Cooperation*, working paper, World Employment Program (Geneva: International Labour Office).

Ministry of Justice. Immigration Bureau (1994), *Statistics on Immigration Control 1993* (Tokyo: Japan Immigration Association).

Mo, Bangfu (1994), *Snake Head*, in Japanese (Tokyo: Soshisha). *Newsweek* (1994), "Off to Work," 17 October.

Nihon Keizai Shimbun (1994), Evening Edition, 8 October.

NIRA (1994), *Nihon eno dekasegi Banguradeshù rodosha no jittai chosa* [A Survey: Experiences of Bangladesh Workers in Japan], NIRA Research Report no. 930025 (Tokyo: National Institute for Research Advancement).

Nyukoku Kanrikyoku [Immigration Control Bureau] (1994), "Shutunyukoku-kanri-seisakuno genjyoto toumenno kadai" [The current situation of immigration policy and its tasks], Immigration Control Bureau.

—— (1996) "Honpo ni okeru fuho zanryusha su" [An Estimate of the Illegal Overstayers in Japan], *Kokusai Jinryn*, no. 112, September, pp. 18–21.

Oka, Takeshi (1994), *Prying Open the Door: Foreign Workers in Japan* (Washington, DC: Carnegie Endowment for International Peace).

Rodosho, Shokugyo Anteikyoku (1991), *Gaikokujin rodosha mondai no doko to shiten* [Report on the Trend and Viewpoints on Foreign Workers' Issues] (Tokyo: Romugyosei Kenkyujyo).

Shimada, H. (1994), *Japan's "Guest Workers"* (Tokyo: University of Tokyo Press).

Tokyo-to. Kokusai-Seisaku Kondankai (1994), *Tokyo-to Kokusai-seisaku Kondankai Hokokusho* [Report of the Round-table on International Policies of Tokyo Metropolitan Government] (Tokyo: Tokyo-to).

Zhang, K. (1993), "Chugoku no rodoryoku haichi senryaku to rodoryoku idc" [Labor Force Placement Strategies and Labor Mobility in China], In Y. Kuwahara (ed.), *Kokusai rodoryoku ido no furontia* (Frontier of International Labor Migration) (Tokyo: Nihon Rodo Kenkyu Kiko).

Zhao, Hui and Qian, Xiaoying (1993), "Boeki no shiten kara mita rodor-yoku no kokusai ido" [International Labor Mobility as seen from a Trade Perspective], *Nihon Rodo Kenkyu Zasshi*, 35, pp. 32–8.

13 Appearances and Realities: Controlling Illegal Immigration in the United States

Wayne A. Cornelius

The United States in the 1990s is passing through yet another of the recurrent anti-immigrant spasms that have marked its history since 1798, when the Alien and Sedition Acts equated the foreign with immorality and political radicalism.[1] The current pursuit of restrictionist measures is being fueled by a combination of factors: economic frustrations and uncertainties about the future, which are largely the result of many years of stagnant or declining real wages for the average middle- or working-class citizen, and the more recent specter of job loss due to corporate downsizing and foreign competition; the increasingly visible presence of large numbers of ethnically and culturally distinct foreigners in large cities; declining confidence in the country's ability to absorb immigrants and refugees, regardless of their legal status; and inflammatory posturing by opportunistic politicians who see immigration and its fiscal impacts as a "hot-button" issue that can be used to mobilize large numbers of voters.

Most – but certainly not all – of the public hostility and the political fire of the 1990s are being directed at illegal immigrants, particularly Mexicans who enter clandestinely via the southern border, rather than at legal immigrants or the numerous, predominantly *non*-Mexican visa overstayers who enter mostly as tourists. By most estimates, visa overstayers constitute between one-third and one-half of the total stock of unauthorized immigrants in the United States today, but their presence is almost totally ignored by the general public, as well as most elected officials. The reasons for this neglect, which have to do with the political sensitivities and economic disruptions inherent in tougher enforcement of immigration laws within the US interior as contrasted with border enforcement, are quite telling.

Most of the purported remedies for illegal immigration now being implemented or advocated are policy options that have been discussed for many years. Some policy options, such as fines and criminal penalties against employers who knowingly hire illegal immigrants, are already "on the books," but have never been enforced vigorously and uniformly. Others, such as concentrated enforcement operations along the southwestern border with Mexico and the creation of a new employment eligibility verification system, are being attempted seriously for the first time. Thus, the US policy-making process in the 1990s is clearly locked into a "get-tough" mode on immigration control. It remains to be seen, however, if the outcomes of this process will be any more significant than the largely symbolic immigration control measures enacted at the federal and state levels in the United States from the 1940s through the 1980s (see Calavita, 1982, 1992, 1994).

This chapter reviews recent US experiences in applying each of the principal approaches to control of illegal immigration that are theoretically available to the United States, Japan, and other advanced industrialized countries. I also offer some empirically grounded speculations about the potential long-term efficacy as well as the political feasibility and sustainability of each of these policy options.

BORDER ENFORCEMENT

Under growing political pressure to "do something" to reduce the porosity of the United States' southern border, the Clinton Administration in 1993 embarked on a major build-up of Border Patrol resources. Interestingly, this effort was buttressed by the recommendations of a study commissioned by the Office of National Drug Control Policy and conducted by the Sandia National Laboratories, a federal government-supported facility devoted primarily to research for the military. The study recommended that the Border Patrol focus on preventing illegal entries rather than trying to apprehend illegal aliens once they have entered the country, through the installation of multiple physical barriers at the border, use of enhanced electronic surveillance equipment, and other measures to increase the difficulty of illegal entry (Sandia National Laboratories, 1993). The US General Accounting Office went further, arguing that "the key to controlling the illegal entry of aliens is to prevent their initial arrival" in the border area, by deterring would-be migrants from leaving home (General Accounting Office, 1993). In August 1994, the INS (Immigration and Naturalization Service) Commissioner approved a "national strategy" for the Border Patrol that formally adopts the "prevention-through-deterrence" approach. The strategy calls for more agents, lighting, fencing, motion sensors, and other technological barriers along the border, but, more importantly, it would concentrate these augmented resources initially in the five short segments of the southern border with Mexico where most illegals attempt to cross: San Diego–Tijuana, Nogales, Douglas–Agua Prieta, El Paso–Juárez, and Brownsville-Matamoros (see Figure 13.1).

This effort to fortify the "main gates" of illegal entry has focused initially on El Paso. Texas (site of "Operation Hold-the-Line", initiated on 19 September 1993, covering a 20-mile stretch of the border) and San Diego, California (site of "Operation Gatekeeper", begun on 1 October 1994, with most of the new resources deployed along the westernmost, 5-mile, "Imperial Beach" sector of the border). The tactics employed in the two operations differ: The El Paso operation has placed all available agents directly on the border in highly visible, closely-spaced Border Patrol vehicles, to deter people from even trying to enter illegally. Operation Gatekeeper in San Diego has relied on a three-tier deployment of agents, some of them stationed up to 1 mile from the border, who apprehend illegal crossers after they have scaled a 10-foot-high, welded steel fence. "Gatekeeper" uses high technology (infra-red night vision scopes; computerized biometric fingerprint scanning of each apprehended illegal entrant, to detect repeat entrants with criminal records), as well as more traditional hardware (underground, motion-detecting sensors; high-intensity, stadium-type lighting). The new, three-tier apprehension strategy, designed for the Border Patrol by federal

Figure 13.1   *The US–Mexico border region*

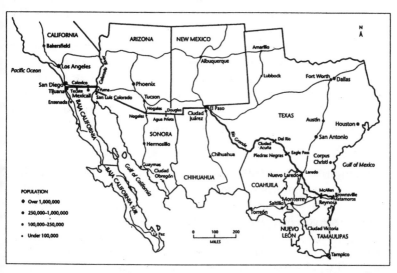

SOURCE: Adapted from Lawrence A. Herzog (1990), *Where North Meets South: Cities, Space, and Politics on the US–Mexico Border* (Austin: CMAS Books, University of Texas at Austin), p. 34.

military planners, is being implemented with the help of hundreds of additional officers brought to the San Diego sector for "Gatekeeper".[2]

Any conclusions about the medium-to-long-term efficacy of these concentrated border enforcement operations would be premature. However, some indications of future outcomes can be gleaned from the results obtained thus far in the El Paso and San Diego sectors, and from the historical record concerning other major shifts in US policy affecting migration flows from Mexico. A careful academic evaluation of the El Paso operation, which was originally code-named "Operation Blockade", found that it had been effective in reducing unauthorized border crossings by certain categories of "locals" (e.g. domestic service workers and street vendors who live in Ciudad Juárez, directly across the border, and would normally commute daily to work in El Paso; juvenile delinquents who crossed the border to commit petty crimes). However, this impact on localized illegal migration for employment or criminal activity has not been matched by a deterrent effect on long-distance migration from the interior of Mexico. To quote the researchers:

> Overall, ... we conclude that the Operation has been more successful in curtailing illegal migration among local crossers than among long-distance migrants. The latter can go around the "line," either with the help of *pasamojados* ["guides" who assist would-be illegal border crossers] or by choosing another entry point along the 1,900 mile border. (Bean *et al.*, 1994: v)

During fiscal year 1994, the first year of Operation Hold-the-Line, apprehensions of illegal entrants in the El Paso sector were down by a remarkable 76 percent, compared, with fiscal 1993. However, in the second and third years of the operation, the trend was reversed: apprehensions crept upward, reaching 38 percent of the pre-Hold-the-Line level by mid-1996. The apparent weakening of the deterrent effect of the El Paso operation, after just one year, led some US government analysts to warn that "Illegal migrants and smugglers are learning to adapt and adjust. Some are learning to go around the line and others to run through it" (US Department of Justice, 1995: 6–7).

The short learning curve of would-be illegal entrants and professional people-smugglers (*coyotes*) observed in El Paso can be seen even more clearly in San Diego. Apprehensions in the San Diego sector had been been dropping for 2 years *before* the initiation of Operation Gatekeeper; in fiscal 1994, they were down 20 percent. This reflects, in part, the large volume of family reunification migration from Mexico that occurred in the early 1990s. Hundreds of thousands of family heads who succeeded in legalizing their own status through the two "amnesty" programs created by the US Immigration and Reform and Control Act (IRCA) of 1986 soon moved their dependents, including those who did not qualify for amnesty, from places of origin in Mexico to the United States. A nationwide Current Population Survey conducted by the US Census Bureau found that, among those Mexican nationals who had migrated to the United States between January 1990 and March 1994, 45 percent were women and children – more than double the proportion of women and children reflected in annual INS apprehension statistics during the 1980s.[3] With immigrant families reunified and living permanently on the US side of the border, shuttle migration declined, and fewer authorized migrants were at risk of being apprehended.[4]

Border Patrol officials reported a 26 percent drop in apprehensions in the San Diego sector during the first 6 weeks of the fiscal year that began 1 October 1994, as compared with the same portion of the previous fiscal year, which they attributed to "Gatekeeper". But most of that decline occurred in the westernmost Imperial Beach subsector where Operation Gatekeeper resources were concentrated, and it was largely offset by a surge in apprehensions in the more isolated areas to the east (see Figure 13.2). Residents of these rural parts of San Diego County were terrified as they encountered, for the first time, large groups of illegal migrants, hiking up mountain trails or trudging for many miles along rural back roads to spots where they can board vans or trucks that transport them north to Los Angeles and other destinations (Huffstutter and Sánchez, 1995).

Figure 13.2 *Results of concentrated border enforcement ("Operation Gatekeeper") in San Diego Sector, fiscal year 1995, by Border Patrol station: percentage change, from 1994 fiscal year (absolute increase in apprehensions in parentheses).*

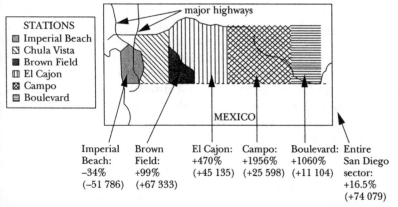

SOURCE: Calculated from statistics compiled by US Immigration and Naturalization Service.

Operation Gatekeeper has clearly succeeded in forcing would-be illegal border crossers into less populated areas where supposedly they can be apprehended more easily. This was a key goal of the Border Patrol planners responsible for "Gatekeeper" as well as "Hold-the-Line" in El Paso. But rerouting the traffic to eastern San Diego County apparently does little to reduce overall entries. When would-be illegal entrants move east, informed by relatives and *coyotes* that conditions for crossing undetected are more favorable there, they continue climbing over, crawling under, or going around the steel border fence. The relatively small Border Patrol contingents in those "easier-to-control" areas have been overwhelmed and the lack of access roads makes apprehensions difficult.

INS interviews with apprehended illegals, conducted while they were still in custody, have found that they recognize the increased difficulty of entry with Operation Gatekeeper in place; but they believe it is still possible to get across and intend to keep trying, whether it takes two tries or ten. Even the new physical hazards to which illegal entrants have been exposed by their long trek through the mountainous terrain east of San Diego (freezing weather in the winter months; high, dehydrating heat in the summer) have not been a sufficient deterrent; dozens of migrants perished from such conditions in 1996–7 (Gross, 1997).

The fees charged by people-smugglers operating in the San Diego sector have been pushed sharply upward by Operation Gatekeeper; for example, a pre-Gatekeeper fee of $300 for assistance in crossing the border and transport to Los Angeles had risen to $500–800 by mid-1996. However, many migrants continue to use their services. Some pay *coyotes* in installments, after becoming employed in the United States; others borrow whatever sum is needed from relatives (often, those who are already based in the United States) and moneylenders in their home communities.

The INS' working hypothesis – the essence of "prevention through deterrence" – is that as the probability of apprehension rises, the number of people "giving up" after their nth apprehension will also rise; but anecdotal evidence suggests that this is not happening on any significant scale. Despite rising frustration, life-threatening and economic hardship, even migrants accompanied by their wives and children who are caught several times are not giving up and returning to their places of origin (Huffstutter and Sánchez, 1995). This pattern of behavior is consistent with a large body of empirical research demonstrating that undocumented Mexican migrants keep trying to enter the US until they are successful (Espenshade, 1994, 1995a, 1995b; Donato, *et al.*, 1992; Kossoudji, 1992).

A key indicator of the potential, long-term effectiveness of concentrated border enforcement operations is what is happening along other, previously less-transited segments of the border. Border Patrol statistics strongly suggest that much of the traffic that heretofore occurred in the El Paso sector has simply been shunted westward to Arizona, where apprehension rates at places like Yuma and Tucson have soared since Operation Hold-the-Line began, and eastward into southern Texas, where apprehensions have been rising sharply in border cities like Del Rio, Laredo, and McAllen. A surge of illegal entries has also occurred in El Centro, California, two hours', drive east of San Diego, clearly in response to Operation Gatekeeper.

What is happening appears to corroborate the so-called "balloon theory" which Border Patrol officers themselves have cited to explain the ephemeral impacts of previous changes in border enforcement tactics. The notion is simply that if the US–Mexico border is squeezed in one section, it will bulge somewhere else. The traditional cat-and-mouse game between Border Patrol agents and illegal entrants continues, but in more spatially dispersed fashion. "Lesser gates" in need of urgent fortification begin to pop up, as information flows quickly back to sending communities in Mexico that it is easier to get through at these points.[5] Professional people-smugglers simply shift their operations to these new areas.

Not surprisingly, the number of apprehensions made by the Border Patrol, borderwide, has continued to rise. Total apprehensions increased by 30 percent in the 1995 fiscal year and 11 percent in fiscal 1996 (reaching 1 549 876 apprehensions – close to the historical record, set in 1986). In the San Diego sector, apprehensions rose by nearly 17 percent in fiscal 1995 (the first year of Operation Gatekeeper) and declined by 8 percent in the following year. Nevertheless, the 487 682 apprehensions made in the San Diego sector in fiscal 1996 were still 34 000 *above* the pre-Operation Gatekeeper level. It is impossible to estimate, with data currently in the public domain, how much of the recent, borderwide increase in apprehensions resulted from the expansion of Border Patrol resources (see below), from higher recidivism rates among a relatively stable (or even declining) pool of clandestine border crossers (see Bustamante, 1995), or from a real increase in attempted entries caused by the collapse of the Mexican economy, following the peso devaluation of December 1994. However, it is clear that concentrating border enforcement resources in most heavily used illegal immigration corridors has failed to stem the tide.

One of the inherent weaknesses of the concentrated border enforcement approach is that new Border Patrol agents cannot be trained, equipped, and transferred quickly enough to plug the new holes in the leaky dike. "Every time *we* do something, *they* do something", laments one INS planner, "and we can't move military-sized battalions!" Indeed, resource constraints, training and supervision requirements make it virtually impossible for the Border Patrol to stay a jump ahead of the migrants and the relatives and *coyotes* who organize and support their movements.[6] As the US General Accounting Office has acknowledged, "Tightening border control in some sectors seems to put added stress on other sectors. This speaks to the need for a comprehensive approach along the entire border" (Ekstrand, 1995: 11).

Determined, economically motivated, long-distance illegal migrants from Mexico have always treated changes in U.S. border enforcement strategy and tactics as additional impediments but not as insurmountable obstacles. For example, the deployment pattern of Border Patrol agents within the San Diego sector has been changed several times over the past 15 years, in an effort to "herd" illegal border crossers into more exposed areas where they could be apprehended more easily. After each of these redeployments, the migration flow simply rechanneled itself, as if a boulder had been tossed into a swiftly flowing stream. If history is any guide, the deterrent effect of concentrated border enforcement operations like those currently in force will prove to be weak and short-lived.

Those who confidently assert that the US border with Mexico is finally being "brought under control" as a result of concentrated enforcement operations should not forget what occurred in the years immediately following enactment of the Immigration Reform and Control Act in 1986. Apprehensions of illegal border crossers in the southern and western regions dropped sharply in the 1987, 1988, and 1989 fiscal years, but began to rise again in fiscal 1990 (beginning in October 1989),[7] as IRCA's sanctions against employers who knowingly hired illegal immigrants proved toothless and would-be illegal entrants regained confidence that they could still find work in the United States. By 1989, 59 percent of illegal migrants who had recently returned to three high-emigration communities in central Mexico, and 71 percent of prospective US-bound migrants from these rural communities (persons who had no previous US work experiences) believed it was still possible to get a job in the United States without papers (Cornelius, 1990b: 233). Various analyses of borderwide INS apprehension statistics in the post-IRCA period found the same decline in the law's deterrent effect that was revealed by community-level surveys in Mexico (Bean *et al.*, 1990: Chs 2,4,6,9; González de la Rocha and Escobar Latapí, 1991; Donato *et al.*, 1992)

Moreover, IRCA had several major, unintended consequences, which may now be repeated as a result of the concentrated border enforcement strategy of the 1990s: it lengthened the average stay of temporary illegal migrants within the United States and increased the propensity of some to become permanent settlers (Cornelius, 1990b). Fearful of not being rehired by their US employers if they returned to Mexico for even a brief visit, some illegals opted to remain permanently and, if married, to bring their immediate relatives to the United States, rather than continue shuttle migration from Mexico. As in Europe, where governments abruptly suspended "guest-worker" recruitment in the aftermath of the Oil Shock of 1973, the psychology of the closing door increased the incidence of permanent settlement as well as family reunification immigration.

Similarly, survey data gathered in 25 Mexican communities during the 1987–92 period indicate that enhancements in the US border enforcement effort (raising the probability of apprehension) *increased* the likelihood that a resident of these communities who had not previously migrated would make a first illegal trip to the United States: "Prospective migrants seem to interpret a crackdown [by the Border Patrol] as evidence of even more stringent policies to follow, and seek to gain entry while they still can" (Massey and Espinosa, 1997). This and other studies of Mexican migration to the US have also found that being apprehended at the border *raises* the likelihood of making another undocumented trip, as a way of offsetting the costs of the previous, failed entry attempt (Kossoudji, 1992). Thus, raising the probability of apprehension through tougher border enforcement has encouraged those not yet in the migratory stream to enter it, while inducing experienced, unauthorized migrants to return to the US as quickly as possible. Why should we expect a fundamentally different outcome from the concentrated border enforcement strategy of the 1990s?

The 1994 INS strategic plan calls for a long-term, phased effort to extend concentrated enforcement operations to encompass the entire southwestern border. The INS has set no specific time-frame for completion of this ambitious plan, nor has it released any specific cost estimates. But even in the event that Congress and the taxpayers could be persuaded to pay the enormous expense of implementing and maintaining El Paso or San Diego-style enforcement operations all along the 2000-mile land border with Mexico, it is doubtful that such a massive (and commercially disruptive) effort would halt illegal entries. Sealing up the land border could be expected to stimulate a bustling maritime human smuggling trade, similar to the traffic in illegal liquor that flourished along the California coast during the 1920s Prohibition era. In the 1990s version, the Mexican state of Baja California Norte would become the principal staging area for unauthorized "boat people" from Mexico and many other Third World countries. In fact, the penultimate phase of the Border Patrol's long-term "strategic plan" anticipates the need to shut off sea approaches in the Pacific Ocean and the Gulf of Mexico. The final phase would consist of ensuring the integrity of the northern border with Canada, including the Great Lakes (Stern, 1994; Ekstrand, 1995: 10).

Whatever the fate of concentrated enforcement operations like those already implemented in El Paso and San Diego, it is highly probable that the federal government, Whether under

Democratic or Republican Party control, will support a continuing build-up of general border enforcement capabilities. Congress has more than doubled the overall INS budget, from $1.4 billion in 1992 to $3.1 billion in fiscal 1997, with most of the new funding earmarked for border enforcement. Both Congress and the Clinton Administration have committed to rapid expansion of the Border Patrol, with a goal of having no fewer than 7000 and perhaps as many as 10 000 agents "on the line" by the end of this decade.

Clearly, there is a broad, bipartisan constituency for major new investments in this approach to immigration control. But most experts believe that border enforcement *per se* cannot possibly staunch the flow of illegal entrants, if immigration law enforcement in the workplace remains at a token level.

REDUCING THE "SOCIAL SERVICES MAGNET"

Illegal immigrants in the United States are already ineligible to receive most types of federal and state-government funded social services, including general welfare assistance. In California, for example, the only exceptions have been tuition-free public education, prenatal care for expectant mothers, emergency room medical care, nursing home care for elderly immigrants,[8] and foster home care for illegal immigrant children who have been abused by their parents or whose parents have died. Until a new federal welfare assistance law was implemental in 1997, immigrant families in which one or both parents are illegally resident could receive Aid to Families with Dependent Children (AFDC), if one or more of the children in such families were born in the United States (and therefore have US citizenship), *and* if the family's total income fell below the official poverty level. Illegals who sought to regularize their status under the 1986 amnesty programs were prohibited from receiving any type of federal aid based on need, for a period of 5 years after their legalization was completed.

Despite the numerous restrictions on provision of public services to illegal immigrants, the perception that they are making extensive use of welfare and virtually all other tax-supported social services is pervasive among the general public.[9] Moreover, it is widely believed that many illegal immigrants are attracted to the United States in the first place by the "social services magnet": the easy availability of tuition-free public education, health care, and welfare benefits not available to them in their home country. Politicians, especially in states heavily impacted by the most recent wave of illegal immigration (see Figure 13.3) have lost no time in exploiting both of these misperceptions.

To date, the most sweeping and politically successful attempt to promote restrictions on access to social services as a tool of immigration control has occurred in California, with the passage of a "citizens' initiative" ballot measure labelled Proposition 187. This draconian measure would, among other things, bar illegal immigrants from receiving all public health services except for emergency room-care and the delivery of babies, make illegal immigrant children ineligible to attend

Figure 13.3 *Distribution of estimated illegal immigrant population in the United States, by state (October 1992)*

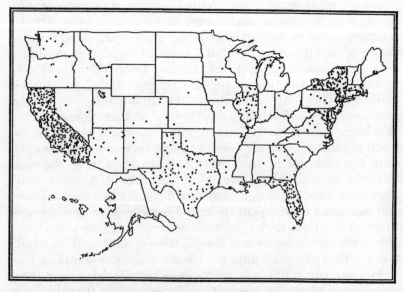

NOTE: Each dot represents 3,500 illegal immigrants residing in the United States. Dots are randomly distributed within each state.
SOURCE: 1993 Statistical Yearbook of the Immigration and Naturalization Service (Washington, DC, September, 1994).

public schools, and compel the schools to report such children *and* their parents to state and federal authorities, if school officials "reasonably suspect" that a student is an illegal alien. Health care administrators and law enforcement personnel would also be required to report suspected illegal immigrants to state and federal authorities.

Proposition 187 was approved by 59 percent of the California electorate on 8 November 1994. Its implementation was immediately blocked by a flurry of challenges in federal courts, with plaintiffs arguing that much of Proposition 187 (particularly the denial of tuition-free public education) is unconstitutional.[10] The measure's key provisions affecting immigrants' access to health, education, and other social services were, in fact, struck down by a federal judge in Los Angeles in November 1995, but most legal experts anticipate several more years of litigation, leading to a final resolution of the issues by the US Supreme Court. Meanwhile, members of Congress have been trying to circumvent the most powerful legal objection that has been used to block implementation of Proposition 187 (e.g., that states cannot usurp the federal government's exclusive power to make immigration policy), by enacting federal legislation to accomplish the same ends. Provisions of both the federal welfare reform law and the immigration control act of 1996 authorize state governments to drastically curtail social services to immigrants, both legals and illegals.

Whatever the outcome of these legal battles, Proposition 187 and similar laws that may be enacted at the state or federal level cannot be expected to deter appreciable numbers of first-time illegal border crossers. Nor will such measures induce illegal immigrants with long, continuous residence and work experience in the United States to return to their places of origin. The reason is simple: the empirical assumptions underlying the Proposition 187 approach are fundamentally flawed. First, the potency of the "social services magnet" has been vastly exaggerated. A large body of field work-based research has shown that there are not nearly enough would-be illegal immigrants for whom the availability of social services (as compared with jobs and family ties with long-time US residents) is a significant incentive for migrating to the United States. Second, there are not enough illegals already settled in the country for whom the denial of tax-supported services would be sufficient cause for voluntary repatriation.

There is no evidence from studies of prospective Mexican migrants to the United States, returned migrants interviewed in their places of origin, nor detained illegal immigrants indicating that appreciable numbers of them have migrated or seek to migrate to certain parts of the United States in order to take advantage of free or better-quality social services. The expected value of welfare benefits that Mexicans might receive in the United States is *negatively* correlated with making a first trip to the US without documents, and the expected values of medical benefits and public education have only weak or statistically insignificant effects on first-time illegal migration (Massey and Espinosa, 1997). In most survey studies conducted in migrants' communities of origin, the proportion of respondents who mention social service availability in the United States, even as a secondary motive for migration, is so small that it is lumped together with several infrequently mentioned reasons, in a residual, "other" response category. The overwhelmingly important motives identified in these studies are invariably: (1) greater availability of jobs; (2) higher relative wages; (3) family ties with the United States (see Cornelius, 1990a; Massey *et al.*, 1994).

The same factors usually determine the selection of a destination within the United States. For example, in a study of Mexican labor-exporting communities in three different states, conducted in 1988–9, I found that 45.1 percent of residents who were considering permanent emigration explained their choice of destination by citing the presence of relatives or friends already living in that place, while 14.6 percent mentioned job opportunities awaiting them there. A similar proportion mentioned the availability of better-paid or steadier employment in the intended destination. These factors together accounted for three-quarters of the choices of migration destinations. All other reasons were mentioned by much smaller proportions of interviewees; again, access to social services was mentioned too infrequently to merit a separate response category (Cornelius, 1990a: 30).

More recent research among prospective and recently returned migrants to the United States, conducted in a rural community deep in the interior of Mexico, reveals how little

Proposition 187, if ever implemented, can be expected to diminish the propensity to migrate. In January 1995, a remarkably high 90 percent of the community's residents knew that Proposition 187 had been approved by California voters in the November 1994 election, and 86 percent could cite specific provisions of the measure. Nevertheless, 77.4 percent said that Prop. 187 would have no effect on their plans to work or live in California.[11] Among those whose most recent migration to the United States had occurred in 1993–4, 82.4 percent said that Prop. 187 would not affect their propensity to migrate; among those who had never migrated to the United States (prospective first-timers), the proportion rose to 85.7 percent. And among the minority who said they would be less likely to go to California because of Prop. 187, many believed, erroneously, that the concentrated border enforcement operation underway in the San Diego sector was part of (actually mandated by) Prop. 187. These would-be migrants were concerned primarily about the increased difficulty and cost of illegal entry – not about being refused public services once they entered California. A few interviewees told us that they planned to bypass California in 1995 and migrate to other states where anti-immigrant hostility is less strong; Prop. 187 would not deter them from trying their luck in other parts of the United States.

In this sending community, we found that the perceived costs of living and working in post-Proposition 187 California vary considerably according to family obligations. Young, unmarried men see little or nothing to be lost, even if implementation of Proposition 187 means that they may be hassled more frequently by immigration authorities and local police. Some parents, however, worry about possible lack of access to medical care and schooling for their children. Virtually no one (exactly one out of 160 respondents) was concerned about the possible denial of welfare benefits or other forms of public assistance; people from communities like this do not migrate to the United States expecting hand-outs from the government. The universally held view in this community of migrants was that economic necessity, not laws and policies in the United States, will determine whether a community resident migrates or not.

Even Alan Nelson and Harold Ezell, the two former top-ranking INS officials who wrote much of Proposition 187, have admitted that the real magnet for illegal migration to the United States is jobs. Proposition 187 addresses the employment incentive only tangentially, by creating state-level penalties for the manufacture or use of fraudulent documents to get a job. Federal penalties for these same offenses have been on the books since the passage of IRCA in 1986; since then, both the manufacture and use of bogus documents for gaining employment have increased enormously.

Is it plausible that punishments of the sort to be meted out under Proposition 187 will cause large numbers of settled, illegal immigrant families to pull up stakes and return to their home countries? If Proposition 187 is upheld in the courts, such families may be forced to pull their children out of the public schools and to pay out-of-pocket for all of the medical care that they receive (which many already do). Some families with multiple wage earners might try to scrape up enough money to enrol their children in private, especially church-run schools. These are sacrifices that most immigrant families who have lived in the United States for five or more years would be prepared to make. The economic sacrifices involved in relocating to someplace in Mexico or another Third World country of origin would be much greater.

This is particularly true for the increasingly large fraction of immigrant families containing members with varying legal statuses: some who are permanent legal residents (many of whom legalized themselves through the amnesty provisions of the IRCA), some who are in the process of gaining legal status via petitioning by US citizen spouses or other close relatives, some who were born in the United States and therefore have US citizenship, and some who remain illegal. Such "mixed" families will face very difficult choices if certain parts of Proposition 187 are upheld in the courts. For example, if the provision denying tuition-free public education is deemed constitutional, young, US-born children would be permitted to remain in school, but their older, foreign-born siblings would be forced to leave school, and their parents, if undocumented, would be reported to the immigration authorities. Some parents, not wanting to risk deportation and being separated from their children, might respond by not enrolling their US-born offspring when they reach school-age (thereby violating another US law), and/or by removing already enrolled children who do not have papers and pushing these children prematurely into the labor market. In other cases, if Proposition 187 were being vigorously enforced, illegal immigrant parents living in the United States without dependents might be deterred from sending for their children, who are often left at home initially, in the care of relatives.

However painful such adaptations may be, returning to the home country is likely to be a viable option for only a small minority of settled illegal immigrants, because their economic base long ago shifted to the United States. They have no assets and no employment prospects in their places of origin; "Go back to *what?*" they ask.[12] Nevertheless, California Governor Pete Wilson and other advocates of the Proposition-187 approach to immigration control continue to promise large numbers of "self-deportations." The Governor's rationale is that "If it's clear to you that you cannot be employed, and that you and your family are ineligible for services, you will self-deport" (quoted in Safire, 1994).

But the available evidence provides little support for the "immiseration" hypothesis (i.e. if government drives down immigrants' living standards sufficiently through social service restrictions, voluntary repatriation will be seen as a desirable option). Moreover, Proposition 187-type legislation does *not* make illegal immigrants unemployable in the United States, and that is the only brand of punishment that would cause large numbers of them to "self-deport". Indeed, as argued in the preceding discussion of border enforcement, any approach to immigration control that does not significantly reduce the availability of employment opportunities for the illegal immigrant population is doomed to failure.

REDUCING EMPLOYER INCENTIVES FOR USING ILLEGAL LABOR

Worksite enforcement is, without doubt, the weakest element of the current US strategy for controlling illegal immigration. This is in sharp contrast to most other industrialized countries, where immigration control, to the extent that it is pursued as a national policy goal, typically takes the form of workplace-based enforcement of labor laws. Much more could be done to reduce the financial incentives that US employers have to use illegal immigrant labor. Both state and federal governments could commit the resources for a systematic, well-staffed crackdown by inspectors on wage and working condition violations in industries known to hire large numbers of illegal foreign workers.

Among the most obvious potential targets for stepped-up worksite enforcement are agriculture and the garment industry. US Labor Secretary Robert Reich announced in November 1994 that a week-long sweep of sweatshops in the southern California had found that 93 percent of the inspected firms had been violating federal labor laws, and up to 40 percent of their workers were undocumented. Even higher levels of dependence on exploited, illegal migrant labor can be found in California's agricultural sector, where the proliferation of independent farm labor contractors (especially since the passage of IRCA) has made it easy for growers to replace "old" immigrant workers (most of them now legalized) with newly arrived illegals who will accept lower wages and substandard working conditions (Krissman, 1996; Rosenberg, 1995).

For more than 20 years, labor standards enforcement has been advocated as one of the potentially most effective options for reducing illegal immigration to the United States. Perhaps more than any other approach, however, it has received little more than lip service from both government officials and conservative advocates of immigration restriction. Enforcement of existing labor and occupational safety laws has been notoriously lax, throughout the most recent wave of Latin American and Asian immigration. The pitifully small allocation of resources by the US federal, state, and county governments to enforcement of labor standards is a highly revealing indicator. In the entire state of California, on an average day in 1994, only sixteen State Labor Commission inspectors were working to enforce the laws pertaining to payment of minimum wages and overtime, coverage by workers' compensation, tax withholding by employers, environmental and other health and safety standards, in tens of thousands of businesses. Los Angeles County has only three such inspectors; San Diego County, one; and Orange County, none (it is "covered" by San Diego's single inspector). Even if federal Department of Labor inspectors are added to these totals, the maximum effort of which they are capable is only symbolic. As of mid-1996, the Labor Department had fewer than 800 labor standards inspectors to police more than 7 million US workplaces – 19 percent fewer inspectors than a decade ago.

Moreover, the number of INS worksite investigators charged with enforcement of the employer sanctions provision of IRCA dropped from 448 in 1989 to 245 in 1994; by 1996 it had risen to only 320. In southern California, which has the nation's largest concentration of illegal immigrant workers, 30–5 INS inspectors were expected to monitor the compliance of nearly 500 000 employers spread over a vast area. Nationally, the number of employers investigated for immigration law violations plummeted from 14 706 in 1989 to 5963 in 1995. The amount collected in fines from employers fell from $6.2 million in 1992 to $4.1 million in 1995. Criminal penalties have been virtually non-existent. In southern California, the first criminal conviction of an employer for violation of the 1986 immigration law was obtained only in 1994; it involved the manager of a small, private health-clinic that serves a predominantly Latino immigrant clientele.

What explains this token level of workplace enforcement? In an era when "improving the regulatory climate" has become the mantra of public officials at all levels, there is little enthusiasm among politicians, particularly Republicans, for increasing government intrusion into the affairs of businesses, especially the small and medium-sized businesses where most illegal immigrants are employed. In 1993, when former California State Assembly Speaker Willie Brown and several other Democratic leaders in the state legislature fleetingly advocated employer asset forfeiture (government seizure of businesses found to be employing illegal immigrants) as an alternative to the denial-of-social-services approach to immigration control being promoted by Governor Wilson and many Republican members of the state legislature, they got no response. An attempt to include a similar asset confiscation provision in the federal immigration control act of 1996 was defeated by vigorous business lobbying, most notably by the American Restaurant Association.

Worksite enforcement by federal authorities checking for violations of the 1986 Immigration Reform and Control Act currently consists of painstaking searches of employer records, to identify employees from whom no proof of legal residence or work eligibility was requested by the employer at the time of hire, and employees who may have presented fraudulent documents. There are severe limits on the efficacy of such paperwork inspections as a tool of immigration control, however. Most importantly, the 1986 law does not require employers to verify the authenticity of the documents presented by job applicants. Employers must only attest, by completing and filing a simple INS "I-9" form, that: (1) they have seen certain documents establishing personal identity and employment eligibility; and (2) the documents presented to them reasonably "appear", on their face, to be genuine and relate to a particular job applicant. Satisfying this minimal requirement gives the employer an "affirmative defense" against any subsequent allegation that he "knowingly" hired an illegal immigrant. Moreover, most of the documents that can be used to prove employment eligibility are easily counterfeited and can be purchased on the street, complete with photographs of the buyer, for a nominal sum. Not surprisingly, the vast majority of employers have found it easy to "comply" with what IRCA requires of them (see Cornelius, 1989; 42–5); and prospective unauthorized employees have found it equally easy to beat the system by acquiring false documents or borrowing genuine documents from friends or relatives (Cornelius, 1990b: 234).

A broad consensus exists among both public officials and academic experts that the employer sanctions mandated by IRCA in 1986 cannot be enforced effectively, regardless of the manpower assigned to the task, without some new type of worker identification system that would preclude the use of fraudulent or fraudulently obtained documents to gain employment. Debate continues as to whether a computerized, "national registry" of eligible workers using existing government databases would suffice, or whether the issuance of a new type of counterfeit-resistant personal identifier – a "national ID card" – to all workers in the country would be necessary to make the system sufficiently secure. The latter course would be much more costly, take much longer to implement, and would provoke stronger political resistance from some quarters.

The "national registry" option was proposed in 1994 by the bipartisan US Commission on Immigration Reform (US Commission, 1994: 54–76). The Commission's proposal, which has been endorsed by the Clinton Administration,[13] involves the creation of a computerized registry that is supposed to include all persons who are legally entitled to work in the United States. It would use data provided by the Social Security Administration (SSA) and the INS. The SSA would supply personal identifiers such as name, Social Security number, date of birth, and mother's maiden name. The INS would provide information on the immigration status of all lawfully admitted immigrants and refugees as well as aliens who have been granted temporary work permits. Employers would access this data base through an automated phone-in system, resembling systems presently used to obtain authorization for credit card purchases, to verify the authenticity of Social Security numbers presented by job applicants. If the information given by an applicant matches what is in the national registry's database, a confirmation number would be transmitted to the employer. Under the Commission's proposal, "this verification number would be kept by the employer and could be used as an affirmative defense if the employer is accused of knowingly hiring an illegal alien" (US Commission, 1994: 61).

Setting aside the usual civil-libertarian objections to such a system, there are a number of practical obstacles that stand in the way of its becoming an effective deterrent to the hiring of illegal immigrants, and to illegal immigration itself. First, the effectiveness of the system will depend on a high level of voluntary compliance by employers. If it proves to be as quick and easy to use as a commercial credit card authorization system, we might expect high levels of compliance. But in the absence of total reissuance of the Social Security card or the establishment of some new kind of national ID card, "employer compliance" with such a system may have no greater practical significance than the 80–90 percent rates of compliance with the paperwork requirements mandated by IRCA since 1986. There is also a high potential for abuse by illegal immigrants seeking to thwart a "national registry"-type system. They can do so easily enough, by obtaining and presenting to the employer a valid Social Security number that has been issued to another person (say, a legally resident relative or friend). Unless the creation of a national employment eligibility registry were to be *combined* with the issuance of a new, much more counterfeit-resistant, photo-ID card to all workers in the country, it is difficult to envisage how it could function as an effective tool of immigration control.

The Commission on Immigration Reform suggests a variety of possible protections against fraud, such as programming the computer system to flag particular Social Security numbers that are being used too often or in too many locations; employers who submitted such numbers for verification would then be informed that the employees hired under this number must "reconfirm" the information in the database. But how will employer and worker behavior subsequent to such a notification be monitored? If the employee cannot demonstrate to his employer that the national registry database contains erroneous information about him, and is discharged, he can simply walk away and seek work elsewhere; he would not be removed from the labor market. Moreover, the availability of an improved system of worker identification would have little effect on the behavior of the numerous employers who *knowingly* hire illegal immigrants, as a matter of preference or economic necessity.

The Commission on Immigration Reform has called for further study of the necessity, feasibility, and cost of reissuing Social Security cards to the entire US population. The Commissioner of Social Security, in recent testimony to Congress, estimated that verifying identities and issuing a new, more secure Social Security, card to everyone would cost $3–6 billion and take 10 years or more. But even if such a Herculean effort were to be made to create and distribute a more secure worker identifier, its security would be no greater than that of the base or "breeder" documents that one would present to obtain the new identification card. Counterfeit versions of all of the documents commonly used to establish an identity in the United States can be purchased readily on the streets for a nominal sum. In addition, the Commission on Immigration Reform reports that more than 7000 local and state registrars throughout the country currently issue certified copies of birth certificates, mostly in response to requests arriving by mail; there is no standardized application form (US Commission, 1994: 74). The potential for fraudulent access is obvious. In short, how does one build an adequate level of document security into an employment eligibility verification system, at all levels? This basic problem must be solved, at reasonable cost, if workplace enforcement is ever to become an effective tool of immigration control in the United States.

Perhaps mindful of some of the practical obstacles to be overcome in establishing a new, nationwide system for verifying employment eligibility, and responsive as ever to its business constituency, the Congress in 1996 declined to approve legislation creating such a system and mandating universal employer participation in it. Instead, it approved only three-year pilot projects to be conducted by the INS in five of the states having the largest concentrations of illegal immigrants. Moreover, employer participation in these pilot projects was made voluntary.

Finally, it must be recognized that the structure of the US economy is changing in ways that may undercut even the most ambitious, brilliantly designed, well-funded program of workplace enforcement. Immigrant labor, of all legal statuses, is increasingly dispersed through the economy, geographically and sectorally. This pool of relatively cheap, flexible, highly motivated, readily available labor is now drawn upon by a broad swath of industries, from "traditional" ones such as agriculture and horticulture, textiles and apparel, shoes, and construction to "non-traditional" employers such as high-tech electronics manufacturing, food processing, hotels, restaurants, fast-food outlets, retail commerce, janitorial services, landscape maintenance, medical and convalescent care, car washes, dry cleaning, domestic service, child care, messenger and package delivery services, and a wide range of other services provided to individuals and businesses in large metropolitan areas (see Cornelius, 1989; Cornelius, 1992: 177–82). In the five US states where an estimated 80 percent of all illegal immigrants now work (California, New York, Texas, Florida, and Illinois), it is difficult to find a single industry of any economic consequence in which illegal immigrant labor is not amply represented, at some level. This secular trend toward sectoral dispersion greatly complicates the targeting of workplace enforcement efforts.

Within many of these industries, a process of "layering" has been underway for some time, in which the most labor-intensive tasks are subcontracted to non-unionized, smaller firms, which are significantly more immigrant-dependent than those above them in the industry hierarchy. These small and medium-sized subcontractors, which also employ the bulk of clandestine foreign workers in Japan (see Mori, 1994: 626–7), typically face intense competition from domestic and even foreign firms and operate on narrow profit margins. Thus, they have powerful incentives to hire the lowest-cost immigrant workers. Increased use of independent labor contractors by firms of all sizes, not only in agriculture but in urban industries such as construction, apparel and building maintenance, is also promoting the employment of such workers. But because of subcontracting arrangements and the services of independent labor contractors, large firms are increasingly insulated from penalties for violations of immigration and labor standards laws. In sum, as labor economist Philip Martin has observed, "the workplace is changing in ways that make enforcement of *all* labor laws, including immigration and minimum wage laws, more difficult" (quoted in McDonnell, 1995: A30).

Yet another complication derives from the fact that clear violations of minimum wage and other labor standards laws tend to be concentrated in only a few industries (especially agriculture and the garment industry), which together do not employ a majority of illegal immigrants in any of the principal receiving states today. Numerous studies based on personal interviews with illegal immigrants themselves have found that the vast majority of them are *not* receiving less than the legal minimum wage (Chiswick, 1988: 98–102; Cornelius, 1989: 40–2). It is more likely for illegal immigrants to receive lower wages for similar work than legal-resident workers, or to be underpaid for overtime work, or (most commonly) to receive few or no non-wage benefits, such as health insurance. But most of these employer policies and practices are not demonstrably illegal, and even vigorous and persistent enforcement of labor standards would probably not reduce the proportion of illegals in the work forces of such firms. Selectively targeting and heavily fining employers who do systematically violate minimum wage and other labor laws might reduce the demand for illegal workers in a few subsectors of the economy. However, eliminating these pockets of hyperexploitation would by no means dry up employment opportunities for illegal immigrants in most large US cities, which now include significant numbers of jobs in businesses owned and operated by immigrants themselves (see Sassen and Smith, 1992; Muller, 1993: 111–60; Light and Bhachu, 1993; Rodriguez, 1993; Guarnizo, 1996).

OTHER INTERNAL ENFORCEMENT MEASURES

Some experts believe that a much more formidable immigration law enforcement apparatus will have to be deployed in the US interior, to supplement what is being done at the border and in the workplace. Internal controls on the geographic movement of individual residents are commonplace in Europe, but alien to the US experience, with the exception of requirements for obtaining a new driver's license within a specified period of time, if one moves to a new state. As even incumbent INS Commissioner Doris Meissner readily acknowledges, her agency's internal enforcement capabilities have been badly neglected over the years. In the 1996 fiscal year, the INS detained and "removed" only 68 000 persons who were apprehended in areas away from the border, and the vast majority of these were "criminal aliens" – those who had committed serious crimes after entering the United States – rather than unauthorized workers. Empirical research suggests that the typical illegal immigrant who is already established in the US has an annual probability of being apprehended of 1–2 percent (Espenshade, 1994: 872).

This situation is partly attributable to the negative public response to internal enforcement efforts. Sporadic INS efforts at rounding up suspected illegal immigrants through neighborhood "sweeps" invariably elicit protests and sometimes even legal challenges from community organizations, immigrants' rights groups, and local elected officials. Immigration control in the abstract, "wholesale" sense, especially by blocking new entries at the border, is one thing: but interior enforcement necessarily must occur at the "retail" level.[14] Rooting out and deporting individual illegal immigrants who are the valued employees, co-workers, neighbors, classmates, fellow church members, and so forth of US citizens provokes hostile reactions.

In the current US climate of declining tolerance for immigrants of any type, it may be possible to bolster internal enforcement activities in ways that might have been politically prohibitive in the past. Recent federal legislation has streamlined deportation procedures to enable the INS to remove "criminal aliens" more expeditiously from the country. The INS has also launched pilot programs in Los Angeles and San Diego countries aimed at deporting "criminal aliens" who have finished serving their time in county jails on the same day that they are released from county custody, by stationing agents at the jails in round-the-clock shifts. While some immigrants' rights activists have warned that such fast-track deportation hearings could deny immigrants due process under the Constitution, these objections have been brushed aside. The INS has also pledged to use its new, computerized fingerprint scanning system, installed for Operation Gatekeeper in San Diego, to identify returning "criminal aliens".

While politically popular, such innovations will do little to reduce the overall stock of illegal immigrants in the United States, only a small minority of whom have ever been apprehended for committing non-immigration-related crimes. This applies particularly to the large fraction (one-third to one-half) of that population consisting of people who entered the country legally on short-term visas, overstayed them, and found regular employment. As in all industrialized countries experiencing significant immigration flows today, such law-abiding visa overstayers are often difficult to detect and are seldom deported (see Cornelius *et al.*, 1994). To the extent that they (and, in many cases, their children) have become integrated socially and economically into the receiving communities, their expulsion is disruptive. It also represents a morally questionable and inefficient use of scarce INS resources for internal enforcement. If the object is to deter new illegal entries, these resources would be far more productive if invested in workplace enforcement operations, despite their inherent limitations.

TURNING ILLEGALS INTO LEGAL TEMPORARY WORKERS: "GUEST-WORKER" PROGRAMS FOR THE 1990s?

Throughout the 1970s and up to the passage of IRCA in 1986, the national debate over illegal immigration was frequently punctuated by calls for new-style, "*bracero*-type" programs that would permit the importation of legal, temporary workers from Mexico and perhaps other key sending countries. The creation of the Special Agricultural Workers (SAW) program, enacted as part of IRCA, was the main response to this clamor, most of which emanated from the agricultural sector.

Today, we are once again hearing calls for some sort of new "guest-worker" program, this time as an "insurance policy" for growers and certain non-agricultural employers against temporary labor shortages that might develop if large numbers of would-be illegal entrants were deterred by California's Proposition 187 and tighter border enforcement. The advocates of a new guest-worker program range from senior Mexican government officials to California Governor Pete Wilson. A recent public opinion poll showed overwhelming (74 percent) approval among the Mexican people for negotiating a labor mobility accord with the United States, as another "side agreement" to accompany the North American Free Trade Agreement (NAFTA).[15]

The United States already has a dozen different federal government programs through which employers can legally employ foreign workers on a temporary basis, in jobs for which US citizen workers are not recruitable. Approximately two-thirds of the 150 000 legal temporary foreign workers admitted in recent years have been highly skilled professionals and entertainers; the remaining one-third (40 000–50 000 per year) have been unskilled workers, the largest contingent of whom were seasonal farm workers admitted under the H-2A visa program. That program has been used mainly by farm owners on the East Coast to import workers from the Caribbean for harvesting of apples and sugar cane. Employer requests for H-2A farm workers have been declining since 1989, partly due to mechanization of the sugar-cane harvest in Florida, but also to the increasing availability of Mexican migrant labor (both legals and illegals) to Eastern growers (Martin, 1995a: 14–15). This expansion of the East Coast farm labor supply reflects the continuing geographic dispersion of Mexican migrants within the United States.

In light of a wealth of historical evidence from both the United States and Western Europe, there is no reason to believe that a new guestworker program could actually be effective in reducing illegal immigration. The US record, especially the "*bracero*" program of contract labor importation that operated from 1942 through 1964, would lead us to expect exactly the opposite. Based on the "*bracero*" program experience, we should anticipate an *increase* in unauthorized entries, by workers who had hoped to find a place in a guest-worker program that would be quickly oversubscribed. Moreover, the stock of illegal workers permanently employed in the country undoubtedly would be expanded, by "guest-workers" who failed to return home at the end of their contract. And once the program is terminated, many of the former "guest-workers" would continue to migrate to the United States, with or without legal documents (see García y Griego, 1983; Liang and Massey, 1989; Calavita, 1992).

Most officials and opinion leaders in the United States tend to dismiss the "guest-worker" program as an idea whose time has come and gone. However, a few prominent politicians and media commentators continue to urge its resurrection, preferably in a modernized, more humane form. And some Japanese immigration experts advocate such a program for their country, if it offers sufficient protections for the foreign workers against employer abuse *and* gives them the opportunity to "build equity" and thereby remain permanently in the work force, if certain conditions are met (Shimada, 1994).

In the US context, the unintended (but entirely predictable) consequences of a new, large-scale guest-worker program – even one that is tailored to specific, labor-short sectors of the economy – would quickly overwhelm its beneficial effects in terms of reducing the illegal component of labor migration from Mexico. In practice, foreign "guests" cannot be neatly confined to specific industries and geographic regions. Employers often encourage them to remain after their initial contracts expire. The bureaucratic and police apparatus necessary to monitor their movements and compliance with the terms of a guest-worker program does not exist in the United States. Thus, the leakage of workers out of a tightly structured guest-worker program into the general labor market becomes inevitable, and many of the participants in such a program will not return to their places of origin, even if they are forced to post "repatriation bonds" in the form of withheld wages, as some US political leaders have been advocating. Certifying the eligibility of employers to participate and monitoring their compliance with the terms of a new guestworker program would also be difficult, since "governments at all levels have lost their ability to understand what is going on in immigrant-dominated labor markets; the quality of official wage and employment data collected in these labor markets is declining".[16]

Finally, the feasibility of winning Congressional approval for a large-scale guest-worker program in the current opinion climate, favoring much less immigration of all types, is highly questionable. An attempt to include a 500 000-per-year guest-worker program for agriculture in the 1996 federal immigration bill failed, even though it had been endorsed by the House Agriculture Committee. Despite aggressive lobbying in Congress by agricultural interests,[17] the only viable political constituency for this policy option appears to be in Mexico and possibly other labor-exporting countries – not in the United States.

THE DEVELOPMENTAL APPROACH TO IMMIGRATION CONTROL

Using augmented trade and direct foreign investment in sending countries to create "stay-at-home" alternatives to unauthorized emigration is an approach to immigration control that has been widely debated in the United States. Reliance upon trade and investment was the principal recommendation of the blue-ribbon Commission for the Study of International Migration and Cooperative Economic Development, which issued its final report in July 1990 (Commission for the Study of International Migration, 1990). It was also a rationale used frequently by proponents of the North American Free Trade Agreement (NAFTA), approved by Congress in 1993.[18]

Specialists on the economic development of Mexico and other key sending countries have questioned the feasibility and efficacy of this approach to reducing emigration, on technical grounds (see below). However, the crucial issue in evaluating the political realism of the "developmental option" concerns the time frame for results. Expert estimates of the amount of time required for trade-led development in labor-exporting countries like Mexico to significantly diminish incentives for migration range widely, from 10–15 years (Cornelius and Martin, 1993) to several generations (Commission on the Study of International Migration, 1990: 35). Certain domestic policy shifts in the sending countries (e.g. to promote more labor-intensive development, more spatially dispersed industrialization, and a more egalitarian income distribution) theoretically could shorten this period (see Martin, 1995b: 62). What is indisputable is that the trade-and-investment route cannot possibly serve as a "quick fix" to the contemporary illegal immigration problem.

The short-run, net effect of combining neo-liberal economic restructuring with trade liberalization in Mexico is likely to be more emigration from rural Mexico (whether internal or international) than would otherwise have occurred (Acevedo and Espenshade, 1992; Cornelius and Martin, 1993). Government policy in recent years has emphasized the need to boost agricultural production by reorganizing *ejido* parcels (the small, poorly capitalized plots of land doled out since 1917 through Mexico's agrarian reform program) into larger, supposedly more efficient units of production – not to create additional small peasant producers. Indeed, government technocrats hope to sharply reduce the proportion of the nation's population employed in agriculture over the next 10 years or so (Martin, 1995a: 52). As an inducement to greater efficiency and recapitalization of land within the *ejido* sector, the Constitution was amended in 1992 to permit (but not compel) the rental or sale of *ejido* plots to private farmers and investor groups. Early indications are that this historic change in the rural land tenure system will not cause a mass exodus of the current generation of mostly middle-aged or older *ejidatarios*, but the next generation is much more disposed to privatize the land they will inherit and emigrate (Cornelius and Myhre, 1997). Furthermore, the flood of relatively cheap, processed food imports made possible by NAFTA has driven down producer prices sharply in Mexico's small-scale agricultural sector. Thus, trade liberalization will have a more immediate, stimulative effect on migration from rural Mexico to the United States than changes in the government's agricultural policies.

Since the Mexican government has yet to articulate an active, comprehensive labor market policy that explains how the millions of workers who will leave agriculture over the next two decades will be absorbed into productive, non-agricultural employment, we must assume that it is depending on a revitalized, export-oriented industrial sector, as well as continued access to labor markets in the United States, to accommodate this displaced labor. However, the large Mexican firms most deeply involved in the post-NAFTA export boom are precisely those that are continuing to *shed* labor, in order to increase their competitive advantage in the United States and other world markets. Big, internationally oriented corporations are also the least likely to be making investments in labor-intensive microenterprises (potential suppliers of inputs for larger firms) situated in the predominantly rural regions where "push" factors are strongest. According to one survey, only about 12 percent of Mexico's small and medium-sized businesses – those where most of the employment-creation potential resides – export anything.[19] Moreover, there are still large sectors of the Mexican economy (agriculture, textiles, shoes, etc.) in which additional, large employment losses resulting from trade liberalization can be anticipated during the remainder of 1990s and beyond.

For all these reasons, the employment base in Mexican regions having high emigration potential (owing to historical, demographic, and environmental reasons) is likely to remain quite inadequate during a period of macroeconomic restructuring and high labor-force growth (Cornelius, 1995).[20] Improving the Mexico-based employment prospects of workers still living in these regions (especially highly migration-prone young people) would require a more active, well-targeted program of government interventions, including aggressive efforts to channel direct foreign investment into regions and communities that have the highest degree of emigration pressure, expanding access to credit for micro- and small-scale enterprises, and investing more in vocational education and government-subsidized job training in private, non-local enterprises (see Abella and Lönnroth, 1995: 27–35). With the Mexican government currently preoccupied with macroeconomic stabilization to cope with the disastrous consequences of the mega-devaluation of the peso in December 1994, it is unlikely that microeconomic intervention strategies will get significant attention in the foreseeable future.

In short, the trade-and-investment approach can be considered a realistic option only if US politicians and the general public are prepared to accept the lack of a short-term payoff – or even a temporary increase in unauthorized emigration, resulting from economic dislocations – in return for a reversal of the trend toward higher illegal immigration at some later point. But there is no evidence that either US political leaders or their constituents are willing to wait that long for effective control of illegal immigration.

CONCLUSION

It should be apparent from the preceding review of policy options and their track records to date that there is among them no obvious panacea, no "quick fix" to the US immigration control problem, especially as it pertains to the century-old labor flow from Mexico. As Barry Chiswick has accurately observed, no single policy approach will do the job, but a "basket of approaches" is more likely to succeed.[21] Even in the most optimistic scenario, however, the combined effects of various government interventions will probably fall short of what the US public in the mid-1990s seems to demand.

Based on the results to date of the new US strategy of "fortifying the main gates" (i.e. concentrated border enforcement operations like those in El Paso and San Diego), and given the low probability that this strategy can be extended far enough and sustained long enough to create a durable, borderwide deterrent to illegal entry from Mexico, a strategy of internal controls focusing on workplace enforcement would be more effective in the medium-to-long term. Moreover, to the extent that enhanced enforcement of labor standards benefits *all* workers employed in industries where these standards are chronically violated, US citizens as well as permanent legal resident aliens can benefit from such a strategy.

It is by no means clear, however, that US immigration authorities possess either the tools or the broad public tolerance that would be necessary to significantly strengthen internal enforcement efforts against illegal immigrants. As in other liberal democratic states, US policy-makers are trapped in a web of constraints, perhaps able to initiate policy changes but incapable of marshalling the resources and public resolve to implement them effectively. But without tough, efficient internal controls, rigorously and uniformly applied, the effort to build a Fortress America by strengthening border control alone almost certainly will fail. One way or another, large numbers of illegal immigrants will continue to get into the country, and an increasingly high proportion of them will stay.

Labor economist George Borjas (1990) has argued that the overwhelming focus in the US immigration debate on deterring illegal entries is misplaced. A more cost-effective approach to shaping future immigration flows to the United States, he contends, would be to concentrate on "reforming" the criteria for admitting legal immigrants – specifically, by reducing the proportion of visas allocated to relatives of US citizens without regard to occupational skills, and giving priority to workers with special educational, skill, and language qualifications. There was some movement toward a more skills-based immigration policy in the Immigration Act of 1990, which altered several elements of the US system for legal immigration (see Calavita, 1994:74–6), but not nearly enough, in the view of critics of non-skill-based immigration such as Borjas. While we can anticipate further legislative attempts to shift the ratio of skilled to unskilled workers within legal immigration flows, it seems unlikely that more tinkering with the rules for legal immigration will suffice to assuage public opinion, especially in California and the four or five other principal destination states for illegal immigrants.

It cannot be overemphasized that in this area of policy-making, the Law of Unintended Consequences remains quite strong. The historical record in the United States and most other industrialized labor-importing countries is littered with the wreckage of failed experiments in immigration control – policy changes that appeared to work reasonably well at first but had little staying power, or which had long-term consequences exactly the opposite of the initial, intended changes.[22] In most of these countries, the political impulse remains strong to respond to special interest pressures and foreign policy concerns by weakening potentially more effective control measures through legislative compromises and administrative actions, before the measures can even be implemented. Most importantly, there are still too many employers – businesses as well as individual citizens – in today's labor-importing industrial democracies for whom immigrants are a preferred labor source, irrespective of their legal status.

For all these reasons, *any* policy option now being touted in the United States as both a politically realistic and efficacious instrument for controlling illegal immigration, especially from Mexico, must be greeted with a strong dose of skepticism. Such claims require us to assume that the policy option being promoted is sufficiently powerful to counteract – and not be overwhelmed by – the fundamental market forces, demographic pressures, and transborder family networks that drive most illegal migration to the United States today. The self-sustaining nature of this migratory movement has been demonstrated by ethnographic and survey-based research in numerous sending communities in Mexico and other principal source countries for illegal migration to the United States. Previous migration experience, both within one's family and in the community of origin generally, has become one of the most important factors prompting new decisions to migrate to the United States. As networks of family members and friends are consolidated in specific US destinations, the costs of migration are lowered and the expected economic returns of each new trip rise (Massey *et al.*, 1987: 139–71; Delechat, 1994). Social network-mediated migration further consolidates the "culture of out-migration" that has developed over several generations in labor-exporting communities and renders border controls increasingly useless (Cornelius, 1991: 111–13; Massey and Espinosa, 1997).

Nevertheless, immigration policy-makers in the United States must continue to operate on the assumption that viable, cost-effective options for the control of illegal immigration still exist. Such options "must" accomplish the impossible: yield significant short-term reductions in the stock and flow of illegal immigrants, permanently change the dynamics of US-bound unauthorized migration (especially from Mexico), and sharply reduce the utilization of illegal immigrant labour in the US economy.

Policy-makers undoubtedly will push ahead, notwithstanding the poor prospects of achieving the impossible, because they must create at least the image – if not the reality – of state control over immigration flows. Whatever concessions it may make to special interests that benefit from continued access to clandestine low-wage labor, the state, as an autonomous corporate entity concerned with its own preservation, has an independent interest in pursuing policies that can convince the general public that the government has not "lost control of our borders", a basic element of national sovereignty (see Portes, 1983; García y Griego, 1992). In the past, this has usually taken the form of taking administrative actions and passing legislation that have been, at best, only weakly and sporadically enforced (Calavita, 1982, 1992, 1994). Successive US administrations, whether Republican or Democratic, persist in this area "because what threatens them is an electorate that believes that government is not effectively controlling immigration. One should therefore expect them at least to maintain appearances, whether or not they deal effectively with the realities."[23] In trying to anticipate the evolution of US efforts to control illegal immigration in the remainder of the 1990s and beyond, the past is, indeed, the most helpful prologue.

NOTES

1. The classic history of American nativism is Higham (1963); see also Calavita (1984). Turn-of-the century hostility toward European immigrants of certain religions and nationalities (e.g. Catholics in general; Germans, Irish, and immigrants from southern and eastern Europe) is well documented in Fuchs (1990: 7–75). An excellent account of anti-Mexican nativism can be found in Reisler (1976: 127–97).
2. By mid-1996, the Border Patrol contingent in the San Diego sector had grown to 1740 agents – a nearly 70 percent increase over the pre-Operation-Gatekeeper level.
3. Another point of historical reference is the data collected by El Colegio de la Frontera Norte through brief interviews conducted

every weekend with would-be illegal border crossers who congregate in preferred crossing areas in the Tijuana area. Among those interviewed in 1986, 1987, and 1988, the proportion of migrants who were women varied between one-fifth and one-third of the total flow. The representation of women in the flow entering via Tijuana was higher than elsewhere along the border, due in part to proximity to California's expansive labor markets for women in the domestic service and garment industries (Bustamante, 1990: 216). For an ethnographic study of the increasing participation of women in Mexican migration to the United States, see Hondagneu-Sotelo (1994).

4.   Evidence corroborating this important change in the pattern of Mexican migration to the United States in the post-IRCA era was found by the author during recent fieldwork in a traditionally high-emigration rural community in west-central Mexico, which has been under study since 1975. It was discovered that between January 1989 and January 1995, at least 36 entire families had emigrated permanently to the United States, leaving no relatives behind. These missing families represented 18 percent of the random sample of 200 households in which interviewing was last conducted in the community. Key informants also reported a sharp drop off in cash remittances flowing into the community from US-based migrants, far fewer return visits by US-based emigrants for recreation, and a near-halt to construction of vacation homes by "*norteños*" (former shuttle migrants who are now buying houses in the United States, as their principal residence).

5.   Information levels about the concentrated border enforcement operations in El Paso and San Diego are quite high in the areas of heaviest labor emigration to the United States. For example, among a random sample of residents of a rural community in the Mexican state of Jalisco who were interviewed in early January 1995, 81 percent were aware of Operation Hold-the-Line and/or Operation Gatekeeper. A similarly high proportion thought that it was now more difficult to enter the United States illegally. Yet 71 percent of recent migrants to the United States (those who had worked there for some period of time since January 1990) planned to return in 1995. Moreover, there was no statistically significant difference in propensity to migrate to the United States between those who were knowledgeable about the concentrated border enforcement operations and those who were not (unpublished field research conducted by the author, January 1995).

6.   Planning has begun to assemble a reserve force of highly mobile, well-trained Border Patrol agents to cope with the constant rechanneling of the illegal migrant flow, but this "rapid mobile deployment force" is still years from becoming a reality.

7.   Unpublished INS tabulations of apprehension data, controlling for the number of Border Patrol agents on duty and the number of hours that they spend in direct border enforcement activities ("linewatch hours"), show that the number of apprehensions per 1000 linewatch hours was 394 in fiscal 1986 (the year of IRCA's enactment). The same

figure had fallen to 214 by fiscal 1989, but rose to 262 in fiscal 1990 and 298 in fiscal 1991. In the following two fiscal years, linewatch apprehensions declined somewhat, but a decline of this magnitude could be explained largely by the low rate of job creation in the recessionary US economy, especially in hard-hit California.

8. This is a public service rarely used by immigrants, for cultural reasons. In San Diego County, for example, only one illegal immigrant was receiving long-term convalescent care during 1994, according to County officials.

9. In fact, the available evidence shows that the heaviest users of social services among immigrants in the United States are legally admitted, political refugees, most of them from Southeast Asia and Cuba. For example, in Dade County, Florida (the Miami metropolitan area), more than 100 000 immigrants currently receive some form of cash assistance from the government. By far the largest proportion of these recipients are elderly Cuban refugees who arrived in the 1960s and now collect Supplemental Social Security Income (SSI) from the federal government. Extraordinarily high rates of general welfare dependence have also been encountered among the Indochinese refugee population in southern California (Haines, 1989: 35–6, 160–3). See also Fix and Passel (1994: 58).

10. In 1982, in the case of Plyer v. Doe, the US Supreme Court declared that public school districts in Texas (and, by implication, all other states) were obligated by the equal protection clause of the US Constitution to provide tuition-free education to all children who are physical *residents* of their districts, regardless of their immigration status. The proponents of Proposition 187 deliberately sought to provoke litigation that could lead the Supreme Court to reverse its decision in Player v. Doe.

11. In English translation, the specific question asked was: "Now that there is the Proposition 187 in California, is it less likely that you will go to work or to live permanently in that state, or does it have no effect on your intentions?" The in-home interviews were conducted with 160 randomly-selected residents of the community, which has a total population of about 3000 inhabitants.

12. See, for example, the testimony of immigrants quoted in McDonnell (1994: Al, A20–2). The shift from a temporary to a long-staying or permanent Mexican immigrant population in the United States, consisting increasingly of nuclear family units that no longer try to maintain an economic foothold in both Mexico and the United States, was well underway by the 1970s and accelerated during the 1980s. See Cornelius (1992: 175–7).

13. The President's proposed "Immigration Enforcement Improvements Act of 1995" authorized an "Employment Verification Pilot Program to conduct tests of various methods of verifying work authorization status, including using the Social Security Administration and INS databases."

14. I am indebted to David Martin (School of Law, University of Virginia) for suggesting the use of this terminology.

15. National telephone survey conducted 11–14 November 1994, by MORI de México. The poll was conducted in 55 localities, with 529 respondents; the margin of sampling error was plus or minus 4.3 percentage points. The two extant "side agreements" to NAFTA deal with environmental issues and certain labor protections. The transborder mobility of labor was explicitly excluded from the negotiations leading to the main NAFTA treaty, at the request of the United States Government.

16. Philip L. Martin, personal communication.

17. For a description of the specific "guest-worker" proposal being pushed by the agricultural lobby, see: "Guest Workers?," *Rural Migration News* (Department of Agricultural Economics, University of California-Davis), vol. 1, no. 2 (May 1995), pp. 8–9.

18. For a summary and critique of the migration-related arguments used by both proponents and opponents of NAFTA, see Cornelius and Martin (1993). For an analysis of the trade/migration relationship focusing on agriculture, see Martin (1993).

19. Calculated from the survey data presented in Ruiz Durán and Zubirán Schadtler (1992: 158).

20. Most econometric forecasts for Mexico predict that NAFTA will yield a net increase of about 300 000 jobs over the next 10 years or so. However, this will occur during a period in which approximately 1 million new jobs are needed *each year*, just to accommodate the new job-seekers entering the Mexican labor market, let alone to reduce accumulated unemployment and underemployment.

21. Comment at the US–Japan Workshop on Immigration, Refugee, and Citizenship Policies, Massachusetts Institute of Technology, Cambridge, MA, 1–2 December 1994.

22. For examples from nine industrialized countries, see the case studies included in Cornelius, *et al.* (1994).

23. Michael Teitelbaum, comment at the US–Japan Workshop on Immigration, Refugee, and Citizenship Policies, Massachusetts Institute of Technology, Cambridge, MA, 1–2 December 1994.

REFERENCES

Abella, M. I. and Lönnroth, K. J. (1995), "Orderly International Migration of Workers and Incentives to Stay: Options for Emigration Countries," *International Migration Papers*, no. 5 (Geneva, Switzerland: Employment Department, International Labour Office).

Acevedo, Dolores, and Espenshade, Thomas J. (1992) "Implication of a North American Free Trade Agreement for Mexican Migration to the United States", *Population and Development Review.* 18 (4), pp. 729–44.

Bean, Frank, Barry Edmonston, and Jeffrey Passel (eds) (1990) *Undocumented Migration to the United States: IRCA and the Experience of the 1980* (Washington, DC: Urban Institute Press).

Bean, Frank, R. Chanove, R. G. Cushing, R. de la Garza, G. Freeman, C. W. Haynes, and D. Spener, (1994), *Illegal Mexican Migration and the United States/Mexico Border: The Effects of Operation Hold-the-Line on El Paso/Juárez* (Austin, TX: Population Research Center, University of Texas-Austin).

Borjas, George J. (1990), *Friends or Strangers: The Impact of Immigrants on the U.S. Economy* (New York: Basic Books).

Bustamante, Jorge A. (1990), "Undocumented Migration from Mexico to the United States: Preliminary Findings of the Zapata Canyon Project," in Frank D. Bean, Barry Edmonston and Jeffrey S. Passel (eds), *Undocumented Migration ·to the United States: IRCA and the Experience of the 1980s* (Washington, DC: Urban Institute Press), pp. 211–26.

—— (1995), "Immigration from Mexico and the Devaluation of the Peso: The Unveilling of a Myth," paper presented at the International Congress of the Latin American Studies Association, Washington, DC, 29 September.

Calavita, Kitty (1982), *California's Employer Sanctions: The Case of the Disappearing Law* (La Jolla, CA: Center for US–Mexican Studies, University of California-San Diego), Research Report No. 39.

—— (1984), *U.S. Immigration Law and the Control of Labor, 1820–1924* (New York: Academic Press).

—— (1992), *Inside the State: The Bracero Program, Immigration, and the I.N.S.* (New York and London: Routledge).

—— (1994), "U.S. Immigration and Policy Responses: The Limits of Legislation," in Wayne A. Cornelius, Philips L. Martin and James F. Hollifield (eds), *Controlling Immigration: A Global Perspective* (Stanford, CA: Stanford University Press), pp. 55–82.

Chiswick, Barry R. (1988), *Illegal Aliens: Their Employment and Employers* (Kalamazoo, MI: W. E. Upjohn Institute for Employment Research).

Commission for the Study of International Migration and Cooperative Economic Development (1990), *Unauthorized Migration: An Economic Development Response* (Washington, DC).

Cornelius, Wayne A. (1989), "The U.S. Demand for Mexican Labor," in Wayne A. Cornelius and Jorge A. Bustamante (eds), *Mexican Migration to the United States: Origins, Consequences, and Policy Options* (La Jolla, CA: Center for US–Mexican Studies, University of California-San Diego).

—— (1990a), *Mexican Labor Migration to the United States*, Final Report to the Commission for the Study of International Migration and Cooperative Economic Development (Washington, DC).

—— (1990b), "Impacts of the 1986 U.S. Immigration Law on Emigration from Rural Mexican Sending Communities," in Frank D. Bean, Barry Edmonston and Jeffrey S. Passel (eds), *Undocumented Migration to the United States: IRCA and the Experience of the 1980s* (Washington, DC: Urban Institute Press), pp. 227–49.

—— (1991), "Labor Migration to the United States: Development Outcomes and Alternatives in Mexican Sending Communities," in Sergio Díaz-Briquets and Sidney Weintraub (eds), *Regional and Sectoral Development in Mexico as Alternatives to Migration* (Boulder, CO: Westview Press), pp. 89–31.

—— (1992), "From Sojourners to Settlers: The Changing Profile of Mexican Immigration to the United States," in Jorge A. Bustamante, Clark

W. Reynolds and Raúl A. Hinojosa Ojeda (eds), *U.S.–Mexico Relations: Labor Market Interdependence* (Stanford, CA: Stanford University Press), pp. 155–95.

—— (1995), "Designing Social Policy for Mexico's Liberalized Economy: From Social Services and Infrastructure to Job Creation," in Riordan Roett (ed.), *The Challenges of Institutional Reform in Mexico* (Boulder, CO: Lynne Rienner).

—— and Martin, Philip L. (1993), "The Uncertain Connection: Free Trade and Rural Mexican Migration to the United States," *International Migration Review*, 27 (3), pp. 484–512.

—— and Myhre, David (eds) (1997), *The Transformation of Rural Mexico: Reforming the Ejido Sector* (La Jolla, CA: Center for US–Mexican Studies, University of California-San Diego).

—— Martin, Philips L. and Hollifield, James F. (eds.) (1994), *Controlling Immigration: A Global Perspective* (Stanford, CA: Stanford University Press).

Delechat, Corinne (1994), "Household Labor Supply and Migration Decisions: The Case of Mexican Labor Migration," Unpublished paper, Georgetown University, October.

Donato, K. M., Durand, Jorge and Massey, Douglas S. (1992), "Stemming the Tide? – Assessing the Deterrent Effects of the Immigration Reform and Control Act," *Demography*, 29 (2), pp. 139–57.

Ekstrand, Laurie E. (1995), *Border Control: Revised Strategy Is Showing Some Positive Results*, testimony before the Subcommittee on Immigration and Claims, Committee on the Judiciary, US House of Representatives (Washington, DC.: United States General Accounting Office), Report GAO/T-GGD-95–92, 10 March.

Espenshade, Thomas J. (1994), "Does the Threat of Border Apprehension Deter Undocumented US Immigration?", *Population and Development Review*, 20 (4), pp. 871–92.

—— (1995a), "Using INS Border Apprehension Data to Measure the Flow of Undocumented Migrants Crossing the US–Mexico Frontier," *International Migration Review*, 29(2), pp. 545–65.

—— (1995b), "Migrant Cohort Size, Enforcement Effort, and the Apprehension of Undocumented Aliens," *Population Research and Policy Review*, 14, pp. 145–72.

Fix, Michael, and Passel, Jeffrey S. (1994), *Immigration and Immigrants: Setting the Record Straight* (Washington, DC: The Urban Institute).

Fuchs, Lawrence H. (1990), *The American Kaleidoscope: Race, Ethnicity, and the Civic Culture* (Hanover, NH: University Press of New England and Wesleyan University Press).

García y Griego, Manuel (1983), "The Importation of Mexican Contract Laborers to the United States, 1942–1964: Antecedents, Operation, and Legacy," in Peter G. Brown and Henry Shue (eds), *The Border That Joins: Mexican Migrants and U.S. Responsibility* (Totowa, NJ: Rowman & Littlefield), pp. 49–98.

—— (1992), "Policymaking at the Apex: International Migration, State Autonomy, and Societal Constraints," in Jorge A. Bustamante, Clark

W. Reynolds and Raúl A. Hinojosa Ojeda (eds), *US–Mexico Relations: Labor Market Interdependence* (Stanford, CA: Stanford University Press), pp. 75–110.

General Accounting Office (1993), *Immigration Enforcement: Problems in Controlling the Flow of Illegal Aliens*, testimony before the Subcommittee on Immigration, Committee on the Judiciary, US House of Representatives (Washington, DC: United States General Accounting Office), Report GAO/T-GGD-93–39, 30 June.

González de la Rocha, Mercedes and Escobar Latapí, Agustín, (1991), "The Impact of IRCA on the Migration Patterns of a Community in Los Altos, Jalisco, Mexico," in Sergio Diaz-Briquets and Sidney Weintraub (eds), *The Effects of Receiving Country Policies on Migration Flows* (Boulder, CO: Westview Press), pp. 205–31.

Gross, Gregory (1997), "The Mountain Route is Treacherous Journey," *The San Diego Union-Tribune*, 24 January.

Guarnizo, Luis E. (1996) "The Mexican Ethnic Economy in Los Angeles; Capitalist Accumulation, Class Restructuring, and the Transnationalization of Migration," unpublished paper, Dept. of Human and Community Development, University of California-Davis, Davis, CA.

Haines, David W. (ed.) (1989), *Refugees as Immigrants: Cambodians, Laotians, and Vietnamese in America* (Totowa, NJ: Rowman & Littlefield).

Higham, John (1963), *Strangers in the Land: Patterns of American Nativism, 1860–1925* (New York: Atheneum).

Hondagneu-Sotelo, Pierrette (1994), *Gendered Transitions: Mexican Experiences of Immigration* (Berkeley, CA: University of California Press).

Huffstutter, P. J. and 'Sánchez, Leonel (1995), "Borderline Hýsteria," *San Diego Union-Tribune*, 21 May.

Kossoudji, Sherrie A. (1992), "Playing Cat and Mouse at the US–Mexican Border," *Demography*, 29 (2), pp. 159–80.

Krissman, Fred (1996), "The Role of Farm Labor Contractors in California's Agricultural Labor Market, 1964–92," PhD dissertation, University of California-Santa Barbara.

Liang, Zai, and Massey, Douglas S. (1989), "The Long-term Consequences of a Temporary Worker Program: The U.S. Bracero Experience," *Population Research and Policy Review*, 8 (3), pp. 199–226.

Light, Ivan and Bhachu, Parminder (eds) (1993), *Immigration and Entrepreneurship: Culture, Capital, and Ethnic Networks* (New Brunswick, NJ: Transaction).

McDonnell, Patrick J. (1994), "Complex Family Ties Tangle Simple Premise of Prop. 187," *The Los Angeles Times*, 20 November.

—— (1995), "INS to Get Tough with Employers", *The Los Angeles Times*, 7 May.

Martin, Philip L. (1993), *Trade and Migration: NAFTA and Agriculture* (Washington, DC: Institute for International Economics), Policy Analyses in International Economics, No. 38.

—— (1995a), "Guest Worker Policies: An International Survey," unpublished paper, Department of Agricultural Economics, University of California-Davis.

—— (1995b), "Mexican–US Migration: Policies and Economic Impacts," *Challenge: The Magazine of Economic Affairs*, 38 (2), pp. 56–62.

Massey, Douglas S., Rafael Alarcón, Jorge Durand, and Humberto González (1987), *Return to Aztlán: The Social Process of International Migration from Western Mexico* (Berkeley, CA: University of California Press).

—— (1994), "International Migration Theory: The North American Case," *Population and Development Review*, 20 (4), pp. 699–751.

Massey, Douglas S., and Espinosa, Kristin E. (1997), "What's Driving Mexico–US Migration? A Theoretical, Empirical, and Policy Analysis," *American Journal of Sociology*, 102 (no. 4) pp. 939–99.

Meissner, Doris (1995), "Statement of Commissioner Doris Meissner, Immigration and Naturalization Service, before the House Judiciary Committee, Subcommittee on Immigration and Claims," Hearing on Border Control, Washington, DC, 10 March.

Mori, Hiromi (1994), "Migrant Workers and Labor Market Segmentation in Japan," *Asian and Pacific Migration Journal*, 3 (4), pp. 619–38.

Muller, Thomas (1993), *Immigrants and the American City* (New York: New York University Press).

Portes, Alejandro (1983), "Of Borders and States: A Skeptical Note on the Legislative Control of Immigration," in Wayne A. Cornelius and Ricardo Anzaldúa Montoya (eds), *America's New Immigration Law: Origins, Rationales, and Potential Consequences* (La Jolla, CA: Center for US–Mexican Studies, University of California-San Diego), pp. 17–30.

Reisler, Mark (1976), *By the Sweat of Their Brow: Mexican Immigrant Labor in the United States, 1900–1940* (Westport, CT: Greenwood Press).

Rodríguez, Néstor P. (1993), "Economic Restructuring and Latino Growth in Houston," in Joan Moore and Raquel Pinderhughes (eds), *In the Barrios: Latinos and the Underclass Debate* (New York: Russell Sage Foundation), pp. 101–27.

Rosenberg, Howard R. (1995), "IRCA and Labor Contracting in California," in Philip L. Martin *et al.* (eds), *Immigration Reform and US Agriculture* (Oakland, CA: Division of Agriculture and Natural Resources, University of California), Publication 3358, pp. 269–93.

Ruiz Durán, Clemente, and Schadtler, Carlos Zubirán (1992), *Cambios en la estructura industrial y el papel de las micro, pequeñas y medianas empresas en México* (México, DF: Nacional Financiera).

Safire, William (1994), "Self-Deportation?," *The New York Times*, 21 November.

Sandia National Laboratories (1993), *Systematic Analysis of the Southwest Border* (Sandia, New Mexico).

Sassen, Saskia, and Smith, Robert C. (1992), "Post-industrial Growth and Economic Reorganization: Their Impact on Immigrant Employment," in Jorge A. Bustamante, Clark W. Reynolds and Raúl A. Hinojosa Ojeda (eds), *US–Mexico Relations: Labor Market Interdependence* (Stanford, CA: Stanford University Press), pp. 372–93.

Shimada, Haruo (1994), *Japan's "Guestworkers": Issues and Public Policies* (Tokyo: University of Tokyo Press, distributed by Columbia University Press).

Stern, Marcus (1994), "U.S. Draws New Border Strategy," *The San Diego Union-Tribune*, 9 December.

United States Commission on Immigration Reform (1994), *U.S. Immigration Policy: Restoring Credibility*, Washington, DC, September.

United States Department of Justice, Immigration and Naturalization Service (1995), "Status of Border Enforcement Evaluation: Preliminary Report," 7 March.

Part VII
Refugee and Asylum Policies

14 Japan's Responses to Refugees and Political Asylum Seekers

Isami Takeda

INTRODUCTION

The end of the Cold War generated enormous changes and political instability worldwide, caused new mass movements of people, and increased the number of political asylum seekers in all the advanced countries except Japan. Japan is still free from serious political/social problems caused by the mass movements of people in Europe and Africa, but will be no exception in the near future, first because of possible political–economic crises in China (including Hong Kong and Taiwan), North Korea and Russia, and, second, because of an increase in independent political asylum seekers from the developing countries.

During the Cold War, Japan did not experience the problem of political asylum seekers, except for the case of Indo-Chinese refugees. Among the OECD countries, Japan has experienced the fewest migration and political asylum problems, and the total number of political asylum seekers accepted is relatively low, because Japan has traditionally been a sending, not a receiving country, and because of its non-political international policy since the end of the Second World War. Since the Japanese decision-making system and its bureaucratic mechanism concerning political asylum problems were developed in the Cold War framework, the Japanese official response has been restrained, as the government carefully avoided a political decision that would influence Japan's foreign relations. This general avoidance of political commitments in international affairs is part of the post-war Japanese decision-making style.

Unlike the United States, Canada and Australia, Japan is one of the few advanced countries that have no tradition of immigration. Japan became one of the traditional countries of emigration in 1868; except for the Korean and Chinese workers imported in the 1930s and during the Second World War, it had no policy governing immigrants. Japanese attitudes to both immigrants and political asylum seekers are conservative, and the asylum problem has continued to be low-profile.

It is important to note that the advanced countries with refugee policies are traditionally the countries of immigration. The United States, Canada and Australia started their nation-building by taking in huge numbers of overseas immigrants. For them, immigration policy and refugee policy often overlap. Japan has neither an immigration policy nor a refugee policy, but its own pattern of responses to political asylum seekers and refugees; as political asylum and refugee problems emerge as a new, unavoidable international problem for Japan, it must reform its old-fashioned decision-making system into a new system with new political thinking. The Cold War is over, and Japan must overcome the Cold War mentality to cope with current international political problems. (Regarding an international framework of the new refugee problem, see Loeschier and Monahan.

The purpose of this chapter is first to analyze statistical data showing the Japanese experience of accepting political asylum seekers and refugees; second to examine the Japanese government's position regarding asylee and refugee problems and why for decades Japan has accepted a limited number of asylees; third, to trace the Japanese attitudes to and perception of the refugee issue through public opinion surveys; and finally, to point out briefly the bureacratic constraints on refugee issues. The terms political asylum-seeker and refugee will be used interchangeably.

REFUGEES AND ASYLUM-SEEKERS IN JAPAN

In 1981, Japan became a signatory to the United Nations 1951 Convention and its 1967 Protocol Relating to the Status of Refugees, and a new law, the Immigration Control and Refugee Recognition Act, dealing with refugees and asylum seekers, came into force in 1982. From 1982 to May 1995,

1141 people have applied for asylum in Japan and 208 applicants have been recognized as refugees. Six hundred-fifty applicants' claims were rejected, 185 applications were withdrawn and 100 are still pending or in process. The Japanese government (in this case the Ministry of Justice) provides no information as to the nationality of the applicants whose claims were accepted or rejected, explaining that it is the duty of the government to protect the privacy of asylum seekers. According to a survery conducted by Amnesty International, "1156 of the cases accepted were of Vietnamese, and ... the remainder included 23 Iranians, nine Afghans and three Burmese refugees" (Amnesty International, 1993: 58).

In addition to these asylum seekers, Japan has accepted 8679 Indo-Chinese refugees as permanent settlers in Japan, while the United States has accepted 819 909 Indochinese, Canada 136 888, Australia 136 623, France 95 660, the United Kingdom 19 932, Germany 19 425, and New Zealand 10 523 (UNHCR, 31 December 1995).

Table 14.1 shows the number of applications for refugee recognition from 1982 to 1995. It is interesting to note that refugee applications after the Tiananmen incident of 1989 in Beijing did not show sharp increase. It is reported that about 60 000 Chinese students and trainees were in Japan from 1989 to 1990, but surprisingly, few of them applied for refugee recognition to the Justice Ministry. There were only 82 applications in the 2 years from 1989 to 1990. It is possible to argue that many Chinese students were discouraged from applying for refugee recognition in Japan, but there are no statistics available to prove it. According to contemporary sinologists, the Chinese chose to go to a third country such as the United States or Taiwan, to stay in Japan, or to return to China. The dissidents had two choices: either to go to the United States or to stay in Japan. In the latter case, most of them were finally granted "Long Term Resident" visas which allowed them to stay and work in Japan as long as they wish.

TWO KINDS OF REFUGEES

There are two kinds of refugees in the Japanese decision-making system: Indo-Chinese refugees, in particular Vietnamese, and other refugees and political asylum seekers. The Japanese bureaucratic system treats the Vietnamese very differently from the others. For them, there is a well-established bureaucratic mechanism and settlement procedures under an inter-departmental committee of a cabinet office. The Japanese commitment to Indo-Chinese refugees started on 12 May 1975 when nine Vietnamese boat people, rescued by a US ship, landed in Japan. Just after the fall of Saigon on 30 April 1975, thousands of Vietnamese left South Vietnam for the United States and the neighbouring countries. Over 2 years later, facing a continuous flow of refugees from Vietnam, the Japanese government decided on 20 September 1977 to establish an inter-departmental committee dealing with the problem. The committee consists of members of five ministries directly and constantly involved in the Indo-Chinese refugees: the Ministries of Foreign Affairs, Justice, Labor, Education, and Welfare; and seven other ministries involved in the issues: Police, Local Government, Finance, Transportation, Construction, International Trade and Industry, and Agriculture.

The number of Vietnamese refugees in Japan reached 833 in December 1977. Since then, Japan has repeatedly expanded the number of Indochinese refugees it would accept, from 500 in 1979, to 1000 in 1980, to 3000 in 1981, to 5000 in 1983, and finally to 10 000 in 1985. From 1977 onwards, a series of decisions made by the government on the refugee quota and settlement procedure has reflected a policy of gradualism and incrementalism.

In the settlement process, the government works closely with the UNHCR (United Nations High Commissioner for Refugees) and non-government organizations such as the Japanese Red Cross, Caritas Japan and Rissho Kosei-Kai, the last two being religious organizations.

As far as the non-Indo-Chinese refugee and political asylum seeker is concerned, the Ministry of Justice plays a major role in determining individual cases of refugee status recognition, from a legal point of view. It is the Ministry of Justice that makes every decision concerning refugee recognition, while other ministries, such as the Foreign Affairs Ministry, do not get directly involved in the decision-making process.

Among the 49 067 officials of the Justice Ministry (Headquarters), the Immigration Bureau has 163 officials, only five of whom are in the Refugee Recognition Section and directly involved in examining the materials relevant to refugee recognition, supplied to them by Regional Immigration Bureaus in eight cities. The Regional Immigration Bureau has 1939 officials, 38 of whom are refugee examiners who can interview political asylum seekers and refugees. They are mainly responsible for determining the refugees' status. Other ministries, such as the Foreign Affairs Ministry, can help only by providing information to the Immigration Bureau requested by the Justice Ministry. Therefore, a total of only 43 officials are entitled to examine and judge refugee recognition cases in Japan. This exemplifies the low level of this issue's policy importance in the Japanese bureaucratic system.

For the Japanese government, the recognition of refugee status is mainly a legal, not a political matter. Nor did the Japanese government regard the refugee issue as important to Japanese foreign policy. It was not necessary for Japan to express independent political judgment on international affairs under the post-war US–Japan alliance system; while Japan was a good diplomatic and alliance partner for the United States, it was reluctant to be involved in the international refugee crisis. The 1990s, however, have seen a new Japanese commitment to international refugee crises in two areas: (1) its positive assistance to the UNHCR, whose head, Sadako Ogata, is Japanese, and (2) its sending Japan's self-defense forces to the peace-keeping operations that led to a partial solution of refugee problems in Cambodia. These two efforts being outside the scope of this chapter, however, they will not be analyzed here.

THE COLD WAR: JAPAN AS A STOPOVER/TRANSIT PORT TO THE UNITED STATES

During the Cold War period, the United States used migration as an instrument of its foreign and security policy, basing its response to refugees and political asylum-seekers upon political and strategic considerations. The post-war history of US refugee policies clearly reveals that political and strategic concerns have been of great significance in its attitudes to refugee and political asylum issues. The United States has accepted a huge number of refugees, political asylum seekers and immigrants from various parts of the world, perceiving this to be vital to its security interests.

The East–West confrontation from the late 1940s to the late 1980s caused a continuous flow of East Europeans into the United States, making a powerful symbolic statement about the legitimacy of US foreign policy and its national goals. The same policy was also applied to Cuban refugees under communist rule. For example, "the arrival in Florida of one-tenth of Cuba's population before 1980 (800 000 refugees) was viewed as concrete evidence of the bankruptcy of communism and the superiority of the free-enterprise system" (Loescher, 1992: 34). For the United States, refugees were a challenge to the sending states of the communist regimes, and they became instruments of US foreign and security policies. For a number of refugees and political asylum seekers, the United States was the final destination of their long journey from the communist regimes, while Japan was a place of transit, stopover and a gateway to the United States from communist regimes such as the former Soviet Union, China and Vietnam.

The following two examples of defection from the communist regimes to the Western block via Japan, before and after 1981, when Japan signed the 1951 Convention and the 1967 Protocol, demonstrate Japan's method of handling requests for asylum. The first case was the defection of a Soviet Mig-25 fighter pilot to the United States in 1976, the second the defection first to the United States, but finally to West Germany, of a member of the Chinese Embassy staff in Tokyo in 1989, just after the Tiananmen incident in Beijing.

The Mig-25 Fighter Pilot's Case

On 6 September 1976, Japan saw the unexpected arrival of a Soviet MiG-25 jet fighter from Siberia. Just after landing at Hakodate Airport, in Hokkaido, the Soviet fighter pilot, Viktor Ivanovich Belenko, was arrested by local police and detained at the Hakodate Police Headquarters, where he had his first interview with Japanese officials. He left Japan for the United States as a political asylum seeker on 9 September, and was only in Japan for 4 days.[1]

According to a statement of the National Police Headquarters in Tokyo on 7 September, Belenko said "There is no freedom in the Soviet life and the situation is just like the imperial Tsar days. For a long time, I have been thinking of going to America, a country of freedom. I thought that I should go to Japan, because I can achieve my purpose of going to America via Japan" (*Asahi Shimbun*, Evening Edition, 7 December 1976; *Yomiuri Shimbun*, Evening Edition, 7 September 1976).

Belenko had planned for 2 years to seek political asylum in the United States. The Japanese Ministry of Foreign Affairs confirmed on 7 September that Belenko had a strong desire to go to the United States as a political asylum seeker, and started diplomatic negotiations to see how the United States would respond to his request. That same day, the United States said it would grant him political asylum, which also made available to US security information on the supersonic MiG-25 jet fighter and the Soviet air defense system. On the evening of 7 September, Belenko moved to Tokyo under police protection; he left for the United States on 9 September (*Asahi Shimbun*, 7 and 8 December 1976).

Legal records show that Belenko was arrested and charged with six crimes: illegal entry, carrying weapons, possession of gunpowder, threatening by firing pistol shots, low-altitude flying, and using an airstrip without official permission. With this list of crimes, Belenko was taken into custody and the Hakodate Police Headquarters brought charges against him according to the regular legal procedure. On 8 September, the Japanese government started the deportation procedure, and subsequently Belenko was deported to the United States (*Asahi Shimbum*, 10 September 1976; *Yomiuri Shimbun*, 8 September 1976).

The Belenko defection was the thirteenth case, and Belenko the fifteenth Soviet defector, to use Japan as a transit and stopover to the United States (*Yomiuri Shimbun*, 7 September 1976). It is important to note that Japan was not in a position to make any decision on recognising political asylum in this case.

The Chinese Embassy Staff Member's Case

Just after the Tiananmen incident on 4 June 1989, a number of Chinese students and diplomats in Western countries protested against the Beijing government and sought political asylum. Among the Western countries, the United States moved swiftly to open the door for these Chinese dissidents and asylum seekers, while its embassy in Beijing played an important role in protecting dissident astrophysicist Fang Lizhi and his wife, Li Shuxian, both of whom took refuge there.[2]

For a number of Chinese, the United States was a symbol of freedom and their final future destination. A 27-year-old woman on the Chinese Embassy staff in Tokyo was no exception. After informing the US Embassy staff of her defection plan on the evening of 13 June, she came to the Japanese Foreign Ministry on 14 June and requested Japan's assistance with her plan to defect to the United States. In an official press conference on 16 June in Tokyo, Foreign Minister Mitsuzuka said that she strongly wished to go to a third country and that the Japanese government had started consultation with the countries she had mentioned (*Yomiuri Shimbun*, 21 June 1989; *Asahi Shimbun*, Evening Edition, 16 June 1989).

Her first option was the United States, which declined to accept her; her other alternatives were Australia and Canada. The Japanese Foreign Ministry started a series of talks with these countries, but they were unsuccessful. The United States rejected her request and suggested that Japan accept her. It was fortunate for Japan that West Germany showed its willingness to accept her. Since her husband, a Chinese diplomat in East Germany, had already sought political asylum in West Germany, Bonn was prepared to meet her request. On 28 July, she left Japan for West Germany (*Yomiuri Shimbun*, 29 July 1989).

Japan found itself in a difficult position in this case. The first problem was that the United States had changed its general practice and decided not to accept her as a political asylum seeker. The second problem was a possible deterioration of Sino-Japanese relations if Japan had decided to accept her as a defector. A Japanese government official said that since Japan had already been accepting political asylum seekers, it should not reject Chinese defectors, or it would be isolated in international society. At the same time, a Foreign Ministry official confirmed that Japan would deal with individual asylum cases independently if asylum-seekers want to go to a third country via Japan. In this context, the *Yomiuri Shimbun* made a penetrating comment that the political asylum referred to by the government official was meant to be political asylum to a third country, not to Japan (*Yomiuri Shimbun*, 13 June 1989). Japan seemed to take it for granted that the third country would always come to assist Japan in solving political asylum cases, and that Japan might be simply a transit or stopover point to the third country.

These two examples demonstrate clearly how Japan was functioning as a stopover for political asylum seekers to the Western bloc, mainly the United States, during the Cold War period. Facing political asylum seekers from communist regimes, Japan's basic response was first to protect them under its police and immigration offices, second to hold hearings and investigations by Japanese government officials, third to confirm the final destination of the asylum seeker, fourth to contact the Embassy of the final destination and to take them there, and finally to escort them to airport.

Japan was viewed as a gateway, transit port, and stopover to the United States by a number of political asylum seekers, who rarely gave Japan as their final destination. Through this historical experience, Japan was freed from judging, recognizing or evaluating the refugee status of applicants.

THE NON-POLITICAL DECISION: DE FACTO REFUGEES AS LONG-TERM RESIDENTS

Although the number of political asylum seekers and refugees accepted by Japan is small, as shown in Table 14.1, Japan has actually officially accepted them not as refugees under Japanese law, but as long-term residents given "special permission to stay in Japan" by the Justice Minister under Article 50 of the Immigration Control and Refugee Recognition Act, under which they can stay in Japan as long as they wish.

A 1983 North Korean defector to Japan is an example. On 30 October 1983, Min Hong, a 20-year-old North Korean soldier, stowed away on a Japanese freighter off the coast of North Korea. He was found on the way to Japan and arrested by a local police authority at the port of Shimonoseki. When he was arrested, the initial judgement of the Immigration

440

Table 14.1 Number of applications for refugee recognition[a]

	Total number of applications	Accepted	Rejected	Withdrawn	In process
1982	530	67	40	59	364
1983	44	63	177	23	145
1984	62	31	114	18	44
1985	29	10	28	7	28
1986	54	3	5	5	69
1987	48	6	35	11	65
1988	47	12	62	7	31
1989	50	2	23	7	49
1990	32	2	31	4	44
1991	42	1	13	5	67
1992	68	3	41	2	89
1993	50	6	33	16	84

Table 14.1 (*Continued*)

	Total number of applications	Accepted	Rejected	Withdrawn	In process
1994	73	1	41	9	106
1995 (January–May)	12	1	7	10	100
Total	**1,141**	**208**	**650**	**183**	**1,285**

^a Statistics are available only from 1982, after Japan signed the UN Convention Relating to the Status of Refugees and the Protocol Relating to the Status of Refugees.

Source: Immigration Bureau, Ministry of Justice, 31 May 1995.

Bureau of the Justice Ministry was that this might be a simple illegal entry case, and that he should be deported to North Korea according to standard procedures. But because he started strongly protesting that he was a political asylum seeker and requested the Japanese government to protect him, the Immigration Bureau interviewed him in mid-November (*Asahi Shimbun*, 17 and 18 December 1983; *Yomiuri Shimbun*, Evening Edition, 14, 17 and 19 November 1983 and Evening Edition 17 December 1983; *Nikkei Shimbun*, 18 December 1983).

According to the newspaper articles, the Immigration Bureau had a series of interviews with Min Hong to confirm his request for political asylum, but the Justice Ministry did not reach its final decision of either deportation or protection, since he did not clearly name a country for his final destination. Generally speaking, the Japanese government expected to hear from a political asylum seeker the name of the third country, for example the United States, but this man offered none. Commenting on the general practice of political asylum cases in Japan, the *Yomiuri Shimbun* said, "The Japanese government does not have a policy of accepting asylum seekers. The government's position is, first to confirm the North Korean's request, and second to arrange a transfer of the defector to the third country where he wants to go" (*Yomiuri Shimbun*, Evening Edition, 14 November 1983; Evening Edition, 17 December 1983).

The final decision by the Japanese government was a typical example of the administrative procedures regarding "refugee recognition": The Japanese government, through the Justice Ministry, refused to recognise or accept him officially as a political asylum seeker and refugee, and began legal deportation procedures, since he had entered Japan illegally. Upon completion of the proceedings the Justice Minister gave the suspect special permission to stay in Japan under Article 50 (Special Cases of Decision of the Minister of Justice) under the Immigration Control and Refugee Recognition Act, followed by "Long-Term Resident" status, which made it possible for him to stay in Japan as long as he wished.

This is the Japanese way of accepting a political asylum seeker or refugee. Since the Japanese government had no policy framework for the acceptance of political asylees and refugees and did not regard them as a foreign policy tool, there was no official consensus on receiving them. This is a by-product of Japan's post-war tradition of avoiding a political commitment to international affairs.

After the Second World War, Japan consistently avoided making political decisions on international affairs and pursued a non-political course in international society. Japan was a good follower and partner of the United States, obtaining its security environment under the US–Japan security pact. The Japanese people, free from political and strategic thinking about international affairs, devoted their efforts to achieving high economic growth, and the government avoided a political decision on whether Japan should accept political asylum-seekers and refugees. When the government faced a political decision on political asylum cases, it always sought the best solution for Japan, refusing them admission as political

Table 14.2 *Number of deportees granted special permission to stay*

	1986	1987	1988	1989	1990	1991
Total number	618	450	477	432	438	393
Birthplace						
South Korea/North Korea	550	387	391	324	325	304
China	43	35	45	45	43	26
Others	25	28	41	63	70	63
Cause of deportation						
Illegal entry/illegal landing	166	101	105	74	85	61
Illegal overstay	165	124	134	137	146	178
Criminal offense	287	225	238	221	207	154

NOTE: Most of the Koreans are not *de facto* refugees, since they have already obtained permanent resident status in Japan. As far as the birthplace category is concerned, the *de facto* refugee cases are mainly from China and countries listed as "Others". In the classification of causes for deportation, *de facto* refugee cases are mainly illegal entry/landing and illegal overstay.

SOURCE: Justice Ministry, Immigration Bureau (1993), *Immigration Control*, 1992 edn (Tokyo: Government Printing Office), p. 117. This report is published every 3 years.

asylum-seekers or refugees, but accepting them legally as long-term residents of Japan.

This mechanism gives the government a kind of insurance policy on each long-term resident, as a deportation order could be issued in case of accident or crime. If an asylum-seeker were to be formally accepted as a refugee, he would have a chance to obtain permanent resident status and eventually to be naturalized in Japan; when he is accepted as a long-term resident, he must renew his "Long Term Resident" status either every 6 months, every year or every 3 years, and faces difficulties being naturalized in Japan. Generally, he is entitled to 1-year "Long Term Resident" status, and has to renew it every year with fingerprint proof of identity. After several years, the Justice Ministry may give him 3-year status after investigating his daily life.

Under this administrative and legal practice of the Justice Ministry, a number of *de facto* political asylees and refugees have been permitted to stay in Japan as "Long Term Residents." This approach was recently applied to eleven Burmese who requested Japanese recognition of their status as refugees. Although the Justice Ministry officially rejected their request for refugee recognition on 17 November 1994, it was reported to have expressed unofficially to a group of lawyers that "the Ministry would not take any action such as deportation which would endanger the Burmese life" (*Asahi Shimbun,* Evening Edition 17 November 1994). The Justice Ministry's reported issuance of "Long Term Resident" status to these Burmese made them *de facto* refugees in Japan. This method was also applied to the dissident Chinese students who expressed a strong desire to stay in Japan after the Tiananmen incident.

JAPANESE PERCEPTIONS AND THE OPINION POLLS

The Prime Minister's Office regularly conducts a public opinion poll on major policy issues facing the Japanese government, and publishes a monthly journal entitled "*Yoron-chosa*" (Public Opinion). From 1980 to 1995 there were twelve such surveys relating to Japanese perceptions of and attitudes toward refugees and foreign laborers, five on refugees, and seven on foreign laborers.

On the Indo-Chinese refugee issue, the first poll was conducted in May 1980 when Japan faced many boat people from Vietnam and was preparing for the Venice Summit which discuss this problem. The second survey, the only major and detailed poll, was undertaken in 1982, when Japan accepted a number of Indo-Chinese refugees and became a signatory to the 1951 UN Convention and the 1967 Protocol. The third survey in 1991, the fourth in 1993 and the fifth in 1994 were questionnaires concerning Japanese diplomacy and international cooperation, when participation in the peacekeeping operation in Cambodia became a major topic of discussion in Japan.

The findings from the 1980 survey clearly show Japanese basic attitudes toward refugee issues in Asia (*Yoron-chosa,* November 1980). Under the question, "What should Japan do about refugees, for example Indochinese refugees in the Asian region", 36 percent of 2400 respondents answered that Japan should strengthen its bilateral assistance (for example, food assistance) to Asian countries being troubled by an influx of refugees, and 33 percent said that Japan should offer financial asssitance to international institutions giving aid to refugees. Thus a total of 69 percent of those responding selected financial assistance as a major policy option for Japan. On the other hand, only 21 percent favored direct aid to the refugees: 18 percent of these said that Japan should send its medical teams to a refugee-receiving country, and only 3 percent said that Japan should receive these refugees as settlers. Of those remaining 9 percent did not answer and 1 percent requested other alternatives. From this survey, it is quite clear that the majority of Japanese preferred both bilateral financial assistance for the refugee-receiving countries in Asia and multilateral financial assistance for the international institutions, to direct aid such as sending Japan's medical team or receiving refugees from Asia.

Japan's conservative attitudes to refugees was further confirmed by a questionnaire relating to an intake quota of Indo-Chinese refugees. Only 23 percent of the respondents answered that Japan should increase its intake quota; 39 percent favored keeping the present intake quota; and 11 percent felt that Japan should not accept refugees. When this opinion poll was conducted, from May 29 to June 4 1980, the intake quota of Indo-Chinese refugees was 500, and in September it was increased to 1000. For the Japanese government to announce a refugee quota was unprecedented. Although the numbers were negligible from the standpoint of the United States and other Western countries, it is important to note that Japan had opened its heavy door, however slightly, to foreigners. Since then, Japan has been experiencing a gradual increase in the number of Asian refugees and laborers.

One positive attitude toward the refugees was found in responses to the question: To what extent are you prepared to cooperate if a temporary reception center for the Indochinese boat people were to be constructed in your neighborhood? This was based upon the assumption that the boat people would stay only temporarily at this center before being accepted by third coutries. To this conditional questionnaire, 57 percent responded affirmatively, and only 14 percent negatively.

The conservative nature of Japanese attitudes toward refugees was also shown by a 1982 survey on Indo-Chinese refugees, which also revealed that Japanese had begun having some positive concerns about this issue (*Yoron-chosa*, December 1982). Of 2310 respondents, 19 percent had no interest, while 76 percent answered that they were interested in the Indo-Chinese refugee problem, and of these 21 percent showed a great interest and 55 percent mild interest.

For a questionnaire as to whether Japan should help Indo-Chinese refugees, 74 percent agreed and 8 percent disagreed. Those who agreed were asked if they favored an individual level of commitment, not a governmental level of refugee assistance. The majority of respondents (70 percent) agreed to supplying materials, but the minority chose either financial contributions, donations (32 percent) or voluntary activity (30 percent). (This survey allowed multiple answers.) This result indicates that the majority declined to provide direct financial and physical commitment, behavior that may be understood as part of the general Japanese character.

In June 1982 a poll asked: To what extent should Japan expand its intake quota in the future" While 7 percent of the respondents wanted a substantial increase of the refugee quota, 43 percent shared the middle-of-the-road opinion that Japan should increase it "to a certain extent". Combining these responses, 50 percent answered positively, which indicates a change in Japanese attitudes to the refugee issue compared with the 1980 survey. But the remaining 29 percent (673 respondents) still opposed further increase of the quota, arguing mainly that Japan is small and overpopulated.

The respondents who answered positively did so on the basis that Japan ranked the lowest among the advanced countries that received a large number of Indo-Chinese refugees. The survey presented a clear statistical chart showing how the United States, Canada, France, Australia, West Germany and the UK had accepted thousands of refugees, and the respondents might have been impressed by the contrast with Japan. There may be various ways to interpret the results: first, the number of positive responses might have increased even further had the respondents fully recognised Japan's low level of refugee intake compared to the other advanced countries, which would mean that the Japanese were still conservative and not so serious about this issue; or the number of positive responses might have decreased if this statistical chart of Japan's poor showing had not been provided. With these reservations in mind, it is still possible to state that the Japanese attitudes toward Indo-Chinese refugees had gradually become positive compared with the 1980 opinion poll.

Although the 1982 survey shows that the Japanese still maintained their conservative attitudes to the acceptance of Indo-Chinese refugees, in April 1982 the Japanese government increased its intake quota to 3000 and in November 1983 to 5000. In July 1985, the government announced that the expanded quota for Indo-Chinese refugees would be 10 000.

More contradictory were responses to questions regarding the construction of refugee reception facilities. To the question: how would you respond to a proposal to construct a facility for Indochinese refugees?, 19 percent answered positively – "as much as possible", and 58 percent answered ambivalently that they would "welcome warmly, but were not prepared to cooperate with it," and 12 percent were opposed to it. This questionnaire was slightly different from the 1980 survey as to whether the refugee reception facility would be temporary or permanent. Since the 1982 survey referred to the permanent nature of the refugee reception center, the majority of the respondents showed their ambivalent and cautious attitudes in their answers. The responses to the two different types of questions suggests that the Japanese would be inclined to accept a temporary refugee reception center, but not a permanent facility.

The main findings from these surveys are: the Japanese main priority is to help refugees overseas through foreign assistance programs such as bilateral and multilateral aid through financial contributions and donations of first-aid materials; the level of individual commitment may be limited to providing rescue materials to refugees; Japanese acceptance of refugees may be the last resort; and finally, the basic nature of the Japanese attitude toward refugees is conservative and restrained. In Honma's phrase, "a deep-rooted insularity" appears to condition the Japanese ambivalent attitude toward refugees (Honma, 1990: 122).

CONCLUSION

While the United States has shown "calculated kindness" in welcoming refugees and political asylum seekers as its foreign policy and strategy tool, refugees and asylum seekers form no part of Japan's broad policy framework. While the United States accepts them as members of the US citizenry, Japan tends to regard them only as "Long Term Residents," not as citizens of Japanese society.

During the Cold War, Japan regarded itself as a transit port or gateway to the United States for political asylum seekers, and had no refugee policy at all. When it faced asylum seekers and refugees who requested Japan's protection, the Japanese government generally accepted them as *de facto* refugees under the status of "Long Term Resident", after a *pro forma* legal prosecution.

The main reason to accept the *de facto* refugees is humanitarian. When Japan found it had no way to solve political asylum cases through its diplomatic channels, it finally proceeded quietly to receive the political asylum seekers as *de facto* refugees, based upon humanitarian considerations. As shown in the public opinion surveys, Japanese conservative attitudes towards refugees have not challenged the Japanese government to develop a refugee policy, since the general public preferrs assisting the refugees overseas through assistance to the governments that accept the refugees directly.

The Justice Ministry makes each decision on the status of political asylum seekers, and it is notable that only 43 officials are engaged in determining the refugee status of applicants from all over the world. Under budgetary constraints, it is difficult for the Justice Ministry to increase the number of officials responsible for refugee issues and to provide them with overseas training. There is no area/country expert on refugee issues, no budget allocation for overseas research trips, and no systematic training for these officials in international institutions. It is under these conditions that the Justice Ministry must take responsibility for the international dimensions of the problem of political asylum seekers and refugees.

APPENDIX: DIVISION OF FUNCTIONS AMONG BUREAUS

1. Cabinet
    Administrative coordination among ministries and agencies regarding Indo-Chinese refugees.
2. Ministry of Foreign Affairs:
    (1) collects information;
    (2) manages FWEAP (Foundation for the Welfare and Education of the Asian People) (Headquarters: Tokyo);
      Himeji Resettlement Promotion Center (Hyogo Prefecture),
      Yamato Resettlement Promotion Center (Kanagawa Prefecture),
      International Refugee Assistance Center (Tokyo);
    (3) Handles Communications to UNHCR.
3. Ministry of Justice:
    (1) recognition of refugee status, inspection, screening;
    (2) manages Omura Reception Center for Refugees,
4. Ministry of Education:
    Japanese language training.
5. Ministry of Labor:
    (1) employment promotion (requests small and medium-sized companies to employ refugees);
    (2) vocational training;
    (3) accomodation and housing.
6. Ministry of Welfare:
    (1) medical service to refugee reception and assistance centers;
    (2) financial support to Japan Red Cross.

NOTES

1.   For the impact of the MiG-25 incident on Japan's defense system and its relations with the Soviet Union, see Susumu Awanohara, "Jet-lag Snarls Tokyo's links with Moscow", *Far Eastern Economic Review*, 17 September 1976; "Japan Changes direction," ibid., 1 October 1976; "Dogfight over Moscow's MiG", ibid., 8 October 1976. The government started the deportation procedure, and subsequently Belenko was deported to the United States (*Asahi Shimbun*, 10 September 1976; *Yomiuri Shimbun*, 8 September 1976).
2.   Regarding the Tiananmen incident and Chinese politics, see Robert Delfs, "Tiananmen Massacre," *Far Eastern Economic Review*, 15 June 1989; Simon Leys, "When the 'Dummies' talk back," ibid., R. Delfs, "Repression and Reprisal," ibid., 22 June; "Angling for Influence," ibid., 21 December 1989.

REFERENCES

Amnesty International (1993), *Japan: Inadequate Protection for Refugees and Asylum-Seekers* (Tokyo: Nihon Hyoron-sha).

Homusho Daijin-kanbo Shiho-housei Chosabu-hen [Justice Ministry, Judicial System and Research Department, Minister's Secretariat.] (1994), *Dai 33 Shutsu-Nyukoku Kanri-tokei Nenpo*, Annual Report of Statistics on Legal Migrants.

Homusho Nyukoku Kanri-kyoku-hen [Justice Ministry, Immigration Bureau] (1980), *Shutsu-Nyukoku-kanri no Kaiko to Tenbou* [Immigration Control: Restrospect and Perspective].

——— (1993), *Heisei 4-nenban Shutsu-Nyukoku Kanri* [Immigration Control, 1992 edition] Tokyo: Government Printing Office).

——— (1994), *Shutsu-Nyukoku Kanri Gaikokujin Toroku: Jitsumu Roppo* [Immigration Control, Alien Registration: Migration Law and Practice] (Tokyo: Nihon Kajo Shuppan).

Honma, Hiroshi, (1990), *Nanmin Mondai towa Nanika* [What is the Refugee Problem?] (Tokyo: Iwanami Shoten).

International Migration, vol. xxxi (2/3) (1993).

Kato, Takashi and T. Miyajima (1993), *Nanmin* [Refugees] (Tokyo: Tokyo University Press).

Kawashima, Yoshio (1987), "Minimum Standards concerning Refugee Determination" (in Japanese language), *Osaka Law Review*, no. 141/142.

——— (1990), "The Revision of the Immigration Control Act and Some Problems" (in Japanese language), *Osaka Law Review*, no. 153/154.

——— (1991), "Indo-Chinese Refugees: Present Situation and Perspective" (in Japanese language), *Osaka Law Review*, no. 160/161.

——— (1993), "Law and Practice in the Protection of Refugees in Japan: In light of Amnesty International's Report" (in Japanese language), *Osaka Law Review*, no. 168/169.

Loescher, Gil (1992), *Refugee Movements and International Security*, Adelphi Papers 268 (London: The International Institute for Strategic Studies).

Loescher, Gil and Monahan Laila, (1990), *Refugees and International Relations* (Oxford: Clarendon Press).

Naikaku Kanbo Indosina Nanmin Taisaku Renraku-chosei-kaigi Jimukyoku [Cabinet Secretary, Inter-departmental committee on Indochinese Refugees] (1995), *Indosina Nanmin no Genjo to Wagakuni no Taio* [Indochinese Refugees: Present Condition and Japan's Response].

Sakanaka, Hidenori and Saito Toshio (1994), *Shutsu-Nyukoku Kanri oyobi Nanmin–Ninteiho: Chikujo Kaisetsu* [Immigration Control and Refugee Recognition Act: Commentary] (Tokyo: Nihon Kajo Shuppan).

UNHCR (1993), *The State of the World's Refugees 1993: The Challenge of Protection* (London: Penguin Books).

—— (1995), *The State of the World's Refugees 1995: In Search of Solutions* (Oxford: Oxford University Press, 1995).

Yamagami, Susumu (1990), *Nanmin Mondai no Genjo to Kadai* [Refugee Problems: Present Situation and Perspective] (Tokyo: Nihon Kajo Shuppan).

15 US Responses to Refugees and Asylum Seekers

Michael S. Teitelbaum

United States policies toward refugees and/or asylum-seekers[1] need to be understood in the context of US policies toward international migration in general, and with an understanding of the political structures and processes that led to these positions.

A COUNTRY OF IMMIGRATION

First, the United States is one of the few "traditional countries of immigration," joined by Canada, Australia, New Zealand, Israel, perhaps France – and not many others. This longstanding tradition goes back to Colonial times beginning in the seventeenth century, when the British colonies in North America began as small settlements, struggling to attract settlers and welcoming those fleeing persecution in Europe. The Puritans were only the most fabled among these groups of what now might be considered "refugees," which also included French Huguenots (and later French Acadians who became the Cajuns of Louisiana), Anabaptist sects and Jews from Central Europe, Catholics from Great Britain, and groups embracing diverse political opinions viewed as threatening by monarchist states. Later and much larger migration movements included both the manifestly forced migrants of the African slave trade, and more-or-less voluntary migrants seeking economic opportunity or escaping famine in Ireland, England, Sweden, Germany and elsewhere. Current US policies toward refugee and asylum movements cannot be comprehended without a clear understanding of this long history of international migration. It is an important component of what can only be described as a profound public ambivalence about interna-

452

tional migration which has bedeviled the US policy process for decades (Keely, 1979; Teitebaum, 1992: 208–25).

AMBIVALENCE

Put briefly, Americans generally hold a negative view of large-scale immigrations as an aggregate phenomenon, but (unlike citizens of many other industrialized countries) express generally positive views about individual refugees and their families. Indeed, the attractiveness of the United States for international migrants is often described as a vote of confidence in the country, and immigrants are often celebrated as economic or intellectual success stories and as concrete human reflections of the longstanding tradition of refuge offered by the United States. At the same time, policies admitting large numbers of such refugees have long been viewed with great skepticism, and American public opinion has become more negative in recent years.

DISCONNECTS AND DISJUNCTIONS

The *leitmotif* of ambivalence surrounding US policy toward international migration is complicated and exacerbated by several longstanding disjunctions "disconnects" that underlie the framing and implementation of such policies: between elite and mass opinion; between focused interest groups and the broad public; between federal and state/local levels of government; and between migration policy on the one hand and foreign policy and trade policy on the other.

Elite and mass opinion diverge greatly on the subject of immigration, and have done so consistently for decades. In general, elite opinion is far more positive about the admission of large numbers of immigrants and refugees. One scholar, herself a supporter of increased migrant admissions, summarized four decades of public opinion polls up to 1987 as follows:

Briefly, all of the data ... indicated that most Americans say they would like to decrease the number of immigrants and refugees permitted to enter the United States. If public opinion polls dictated US immigration policy, much of the restrictionist legislation of the 1920s would have remained in place, and refugee programs would probably have never been enacted. (Simon, 1987: 50)

Only very recently has there appeared to be some convergence between mass and elite opinion, most notably in the main destination state for international migrants, California.

Interest Group versus Public Opinion

Questions regarding immigration and refugee policy have been posed in national public opinion polls since the end of the Second World War. One compilation of findings from 1946 to 1990 is presented in Table 15.1. Generally speaking, only a small minority (less than 10 percent in all years except 1953) indicated support for the "more/increase" choice, while substantial pluralities or majorities (ranging from 33 to 66 percent) supported "fewer/decrease." Yet in 1965, 1986 and 1990 legal admissions were increased substantially by Congressional action, and in 1980 refugee admissions were similarly liberalized (see discussion below). At least two explanations may be offered for this apparent anomaly.

First, while public opinion has long been strongly negative concerning increased admissions in the aggregate, it is more ambivalent at the more individual level; meanwhile more favorable views are held by political and economic elites.

Second, as discussed below, it is the US Congress that has long claimed primacy in policy-making on immigration and refugee matters, a claim to which the executive and judicial branches have generally acquiesced. The Congress, in turn, is strongly responsive to the views expressed by well-organized and financed interest groups, of which there are many surrounding the issues of international migration. Indeed, it is not uncommon for such groups to draft proposed legislation themselves to be introduced and promoted by their supporters in the Congress.

Taken together, the ambivalence and perhaps shallowness of an apparently quite negative public opinion, the more positive views of elites, and the activism and political efficacy of concerned interest groups, has produced what would

Table 15.1 *Distribution of responses about the number of immigrants that should be permitted to enter (%)*

Choices	1946[a]	1953	1965	1977	1981	1982	1986	1988	1990[b]
More/increase	5	13	8	7	5	4	7	6	9
Same/present level	32	37	39	37	22	23	35	34	29
Fewer/decrease	37 [14][c]	39	33	42	65	66	49	53	48
No opinion/ don't know	12	11	20	14	8	7	9	7	14

[a] In 1946, the question was phrased: "Should we permit more persons from Europe to come to this country each year than we did before the war, should we keep the number about the same, or should we reduce the number?" In the subsequent polls the question was usually phrased: "Should immigration be kept at its present level, increased, or decreased?"

[b] In 1990, the question was phrased: "Is it your impression that the current immigration laws allow too many immigrants, too few immigrants, or about the right number of immigrants into this country each year?"

[c] "None" was offered as a choice of response only in 1946, and 14 percent selected that choice.

SOURCE: Roper Center (Storrs, CT: University of Connecticut Press, 1991), cited in Rita J. Simon and Susan H. Alexander, *The Ambivalent Welcome: Print Media, Public Opinion and Immigration* (Westport, CT: Praeger, 1993), p. 41.

otherwise appear to be a consistent policy tilt in directions quite opposite from those reportedly desired by the electorate.[2]

Federal versus State/Local Levels of Government

US policies on international migration are made at the federal level; indeed, the Supreme Court has formally ruled that states *may not* pass any laws that are inconsistent with federal policy in this domain. At the same time, high percentages of international migrants settle in only a few states and in few areas within them. Hence the policy making is national, while the principal effects – both positive and negative – are felt concretely at quite local levels.

It has now become routine in American political discourse for state and local officials to complain that they are being unfairly required to absorb the costs of federal immigration and refugee policies. Most recently, several state governors have filed civil suits against the federal government, seeking multi-billion-dollar reimbursement for the costs their states allegedly incur as a result of illegal immigration. It is only fair to note, however, that state and local officials from areas with heavy migrant concentrations typically fail to acknowledge that the federal policies they criticize often have been supported, and even spearheaded, by their own federal representatives to the US Senate and House of Representatives.

Foreign policy and trade policy in relation to migration

Until the last few years, little attention was paid to international migration consequences in the framing of US foreign policies and trade policies. Instead, the resettlement of large numbers of "refugees" (defined before 1980 as those fleeing communism – see below) was supported by the US foreign policy establishment as a means to discredit communist regimes, or alternatively as a moral obligation following failure of anti-communist interventions such as those in Cuba and Vietnam (Loescher and Scanlan, 1986).

This view began to change in the 1980s, and now is very much in flux. The dangers of the policy were demonstrated by the so-called Mariel Boatlift of 1980, in which the regime of Fidel Castro facilitated the migration to Florida by boat of more than 125 000 Cubans within a few months. A minority of these Cuban migrants turned out to be violent criminals released from jail for the purpose, as well as persons with serious physical and psychiatric illnesses. In response, the US government declared that it would never again allow such an encouraged mass exodus from Cuba to occur. Subsequently, US foreign policy began to encourage opponents of the Polish communist government to stay in Poland and continue their resistance, reversing the previous posture that would have welcomed their flight as refugees from communism.

Over the past few years, US policy in this sphere has changed dramatically. During the summer of 1994, the Clinton administration reversed nearly three decades of official policy that provided automatic admission to any Cubans who could arrange to depart from their island nation. The precipitating events were the announcement by the Castro government that it would no longer prevent irregular departures by boat or raft, followed promptly by rapid increases in the numbers departing in this manner. The Clinton administration announced that Cubans leaving irregularly would no longer be admitted to the United States, and entered into urgent diplomatic negotiations with the Castro government to reverse its policies about deterring such departures. An interim agreement embraced an undertaking by the Cuban government to restrain further disorderly departures, along with a US government undertaking to admit more than 20 000 Cuban immigrants per year through a more or less regular process.

In May 1995, the US government announced further that it would begin to return to Cuba any additional irregular departures unless credible claims could be made to political asylum, thereby in effect reversing some 30 years of practice by which all Cubans were admitted automatically as putative refugees from communist persecution. The Cuban government asserted the hope that this migration agreement might serve as a basis for additional easing of tension between the United States and Cuba, a possible future development that was energetically denounced by Cuban–American political activists based in Miami. During the same period, mass outflows from Haiti, coupled with domestic political pressures, led to a long-deferred use of American military power to dislodge the military government that had deposed the elected government of Jean-Bertrand Aristide.

The transformation now appears to be complete. Until the 1980s, framers of US foreign policy paid little attention to migration consequences, and indeed welcomed many large-scale flows as serving US foreign policy interests. By 1995, there was not only no such encouragement being offered, but in some regions US foreign policy was itself being framed with the principal goal of preventing large flows of irregular migrants.

Past US trade policies have also been adopted with little reference to their likely migration impacts. The "sugar program" of the US government, driven by domestic politics to protect a small number of US sugar producers, has had the effect of sharply reducing agricultural employment in several countries producing large numbers of legal and illegal immigrants to the United States – the Dominican Republic and the Philippines in particular.[3] Regional trade preferences intended to stabilize the economies of Central American and Caribbean nations (the Caribbean Basin Initiative) systematically excluded labor-intensive products such as garments and shoes, in deference to US domestic interest groups.

More recently, trade initiatives such as the North American Trade Agreement (NAFTA) have been promoted as effective means to reduced illegal migration from Mexico. However, it is well known that such effects are likely to occur only after the passage of several decades, during which the effect of NAFTA may be to increase the potential for such migration (Martin 1993).

THE POLICY-MAKING PROCESS

US policies regarding immigration and refugee issues are made in at least three, and perhaps four, different ways.

First is the route of "executive" initiative, the way in which most liberal democracies frame government policies. The government of the day (the President, Premier, Prime Minister) proposes changes in legislation or practice, and the parliament debates and then accepts or rejects such proposals. Such executive initiative does occur in implementation of US immigration and refugee policy, though in recent years US presidents have rarely proposed legislative changes. Presidents may, however, issue Executive Orders that, within the framework of existing legislation, make important changes in the manner of implementation. Presidents also have authority to admit international migrants outside of the regular system on the basis of what is termed the Attorney General's "parole" authority, though the exercise of such authority has long been criticized as excessive by Congress. There are, of course, those elements of foreign policy that have migration implications, for which primacy resides in the Executive. Finally, there is initiative of a clearly administrative character, in which the Executive Branch interprets and administers the laws regarding issuance of visas, admission of visa holders, management of borders and ports of entry, and handling of asylum applications. Actions by the Executive that fail to implement effective regulation over entries and departures by non-citizens represent a form of negative policy making. Even at this directly administrative level, there is considerable diversity of practice, since the Immigration and Naturalization Service accords considerable autonomy to its Regional Directors and Chief Border Patrol Officers.

The second policy-making route is directly legislative. As noted elsewhere, this has been the principal source of immigration and refugee policy making for decades. The US legislative process is a highly complex and convoluted one, about which numerous lengthy treatises have been written. For our purposes here, suffice it to say that there are two Subcommittees of the Judiciary Committees of the Senate and the House of Representatives that hold jurisdiction for most immigration and refugee legislation. The memberships of these Subcommittees are to some degree self-selected, and hence often include politicians with strong personal or constituency interests in the issues involved. These two Subcommittees initiate legislation and review legislative proposals offered by others. If agreement is reached at the Subcommittee level, it is forwarded to the full Judiciary Committee for consideration, where amendments can be offered and adopted. If, as amended, there is agreement at the full Committee level, the bill usually (though not necessarily) goes to the floor of the full House of Representatives or Senate for debate, amendment and final vote. In many cases quite different bills are passed by the two houses. This, in turn, requires the appointment of a Conference Committee, a special joint committee appointed by both houses which seeks to iron out the differences between the two bills. The Conference Committee process has been a critical one during past changes in immigration and refugee law, though it is little understood outside of Washington. Should the Conference Committee report out a compromise bill, this Conference product must then be approved again by both houses. If it is, it is forwarded to the President for signature. The President may sign or veto the bill; a veto can in turn be overruled by a two-thirds majority of both houses.

Finally, there is role of the judiciary, the Federal court system, which has the Constitutional right to review lawsuits challenging legislation, Executive orders, administrative practice, etc. and declare these to be unconstitutional and hence null and void. The role of the federal judiciary has expanded dramatically since the triumph of the civil rights movement during the 1960s. Some critics allege that Federal judges now *make* law rather than merely interpret it, while others believe the courts have been forces for constructive change and protection of rights when these were blocked by political forces.

There is possibly a fourth way in which policy is made, driven by the highly federal nature of the US governmental system. State and local governments can themselves adopt policies with impacts upon the effectiveness of enforcement of immigration and refugee laws. These range from state and local policies regarding provision of access to benefits, to willingness or unwillingness to allow state and local law enforcement officials to cooperate with Federal immigration officials, to affirmative rejection by local governments of national policies regarding immigration and refugees. The last of these occurred with the adoption of so-called Sanctuary Resolutions by, for example, the City Council of San Francisco, which during the 1980s declared the territory of the city to be "sanctuary" for heavily unlawful migrants from Central America.

Finally, it is important to recognize that in US immigration and refugee policy, the Law of the Unintended Consequence applies with particular force. Many of the policies adopted by

Congress in this domain have produced outcomes very different from those intended. There are many reasons for this now-common experience, among them the fact that there is hugely excessive demand for access to the United States by non-citizens, relative to the categories and numbers made available for such entry by policy makers. However, the dominance of Congressional initiative and action on international migration is one explanation for the repeated experience of unintended consequences. The Congress is by its very nature a non-contemplative, non-analytic body. It lacks both the time and the staff resources to assess plausible but unwanted outcomes of its initiatives. Even if it could undertake such analyses, some political actors would prefer that the full implications of their proposals be left murky. Moreover, the legislative process is itself inherently unpredictable. Even a carefully analyzed bill can be unceremoniously amended during floor debate, and at this stage there is little opportunity to step back and assess the possible implications of such amendments.[4]

LEGAL PROVISIONS

The basic US law relating to international migration is the Immigration and Nationality Act (INA) of 1952, as amended most prominently in 1965, 1980, 1986 and 1990. Of these major amendments, only the 1980 Refugee Act focused mainly upon refugees and asylum seekers, while the others focused upon legal and illegal immigration.

The main purpose of the 1980 Refugee Act was to regularize the handling of proactive refugee resettlement from third countries. The impetus for this legislation derived from concern in the Congress about the ad hoc manner in which refugees from Vietnam had been handled by the President. In addition, the Act reflected longstanding criticism about the narrow definition of "refugee" embodied in then-current law, dominated by Cold War criteria, which required that applicants for refugee status be from communist countries or from certain regions of the Middle East.

The new definition adopted under the 1980 Refugee Act closely followed that embodied in the 1951 UN Refugee

Convention and its 1967 Protocol, to which the United States had acceded in 1968:

> Any person who is outside of any country of such person's nationality ... and who is unable or unwilling to return to, and is unable or unwilling to avail himself or herself of the protection of, that country because of persecution on account of race, religion, nationality, membership in a particular social group, or political opinion. (Immigration and Nationality Act, Section 207)

In practice, however, little actually changed. The choice of which refugees would be affirmatively resettled from abroad remained discretionary ("of special humanitarian interest to the United States"), and while the numbers resettled were large, they were tiny compared with the multiple millions who might qualify. Empirically, admissions continued to follow the pre-1980 pattern, with heavy preferences accorded those from communist countries. This continuing pattern may be attributed in part to continuing Cold War commitments, and in part to collective senses of guilt and responsibility following the failed US intervention in Vietnam during the 1960s and 1970s. In particular, State Department officials with deep personal involvement in Vietnam policies were among those strongly advocating generous admissions from that country. In the appraisal of one of the chronicles of this period, human rights groups and Cold Warriors together formed a powerful coalition supporting large refugee admissions (Loescher and Scanlan, 1996: Ch. 1).

In addition, earlier passage of the Cuban Adjustment Act of 1966[5] provided specific national preference for Cuban migrants. As implemented until 1994, any Cuban able to depart the island was admitted expeditiously, provided with special financial assistance unavailable to others, and allowed to adjust his/her status to that of permanent resident after the passage of 1 year. It took nearly three decades before these practices were changed, as described above.

In the context of 1980 reform of refugee policy, nearly all informed observers agree that the closely related issue of *asylum* was handled unsatisfactorily by the Congress. According to the late Staff Director of the Senate Subcommittee on Immigration and Refugee Policy, asylum was dealt with only as "an after-thought" to the Refugee Act of 1980, the major emphasis of which was US admission and resettlement of refugees from third countries. Asylum was perceived to apply only to a few cases each year of foreign residents (students, visitors, etc.) unable to return home due to political changes while resident in the United States. Since there was no real information as to the numbers involved, Congressional staff did a quick count of the annual numbers of adjustments made administratively for cases such as these (which had averaged about 2500 per year), and doubled the number to allow for increases over time. What was not appreciated was that the shift to a worldwide definition of "refugee" had greatly expanded the numbers of asylum-claimants who were able to depart their countries and travel to the United States to claim asylum, and that there would be a dramatic increase in the numbers seeking to do so.[6]

CONGRESSIONAL PRIMACY

Any comparison of US refugee/asylum policy with that of Japan must be informed by an understanding of the unique structure of the US government mandated by its constitution. Unlike the parliamentary systems prevailing in Japan and most other liberal democracies, the American government embodies a distinctive doctrine of "separation of powers" among three co-equal branches – the Executive (the President and administrative departments); the legislative (Congress); and the judicial. Over the past several decades, this structure has had important impacts upon the process and substance of US refugee and asylum policy.

Whereas primacy for foreign policy is accorded to the Executive Branch, the Congress has long asserted primacy regarding the admission of immigrants and refugees. Indeed, Congressional passage of the Refugee Act of 1980 was itself in part an expression of frustration with the extra-legal refugee admissions practices followed by successive presidents during the 1950s, 1960s and 1970s. Of particular concern to Congressional critics was the repeated invocation of the President's "parole" authority as a means to admit large groups of refugees outside the boundaries of applicable law.

464 Temporary Workers or Future Citizens?

This parole authority was based upon an obscure provision of the 1952 Immigration and Nationality Act, providing that the Attorney-General may:

> allow aliens to physically enter the United States (but not obtain any of the legal benefits of formal admission) "temporarily under such conditions as he may prescribe for emergent reasons or for reasons deemed strictly in the public interest." The legislative history of that provision made it clear that it was intended to serve very narrow objectives, and was designed to address such cases as those involving "an alien who requires immediate medical attention before there has been an opportunity for an immigration officer to inspect him [or situations] where it is strictly in the public interest to have an inadmissible alien present in the United States, such as, for instance, a witness or for purposes of prosecution."[7]

The use of parole authority for purposes of mass admission of refugees began in 1956, with invocation of this authority by President Eisenhower to admit some 32 000 Hungarians following Soviet suppression of the Hungarian uprising that same year. Subsequently, parole authority was invoked to admit large numbers of refugees from Cambodia, Cuba, Haiti, Laos and the USSR, and smaller numbers from Argentina and Chile.

The Refugee Act of 1980 explicitly abolished the use of parole authority to admit large numbers of refugees, and established a specific numerical provision for such admissions, with a "normal flow" anticipated to be 50 000 per year. It also provided a formal role for Congress in determining both the numbers and the allocations of refugee slots, via a requirement that the President consult with Congress on an annual basis on these issues.

As a political institution, Congress has been exquisitely sensitive to ethnic politics. For decades many members of the US Congress have seen themselves principally as ethnic politicians elected from constituencies that are heavily made up of one or two ethnic groups. Moreover, in recent decades the allocation of government-controlled benefits according to ethnicity has been increasingly legitimized by "affirmative action" criteria and notions of "group rights". As but one legislative example, the Voting Rights Act now requires that the boundaries of Congressional districts be set to assure that certain under-represented minority groups would be able to elect a specified number of Representatives from their ethnic group. (On the Executive branch side, the Clinton administration has guided its appointments to governmental positions by what are called the "EGG" criteria, standing for numerical proportionality among Ethnicity, Gender and Geography.) Or, in the words of an old Chicago political saying, "All politics is ethnic."

The sensitivity of the Congress to ethnic politics has made it especially receptive to ethnic lobbying regarding immigration and refugee policies, and some organized ethnic lobbies have defined immigration and refugee issues as central to their political agendas. Among the most successful ethnic lobbies in this sphere have been Cubans, Jews, Irish and Salvadorans. Cuban–American lobby groups have successfully protected the 1966 Cuban Adjustment Act from repeal, and until recently had been able to assure that any Cuban able to leave Cuba could gain legal and permanent entry to the United States. Jewish–American lobby groups strongly supported passage of the Jackson–Vanek Amendment to the Trade Act, which precluded Most Favored Nation treatment for the USSR until it allowed free departure of its citizens; once free departure became possible, the same groups were able to gain legislative support for continued admission of Jews from the former Soviet Union according to modified criteria. Irish–American lobby groups took advantage of the fact that between 1988 and 1990 two Irish–American politicians served as chairmen of the Immigration Subcommittees in both the House and the Senate. Irish ethnic concerns drove much of the revision of US immigration law that culminated in the Immigration Act of 1990, which provided a special set of "diversity" visas for Irish migrants already in the United States unlawfully or otherwise unable to qualify. Salvadoran lobby groups and their supporters have succeeded in establishing a succession of semi-permanent legal statuses for large numbers of Salvadorans who entered the United States unlawfully during the 1980s.

JUDICIAL

The third co-equal branch of the US government, the judiciary, has hardly been idle when it comes to the framing and implementation of immigration and refugee policy. Federal courts can intervene only in cases brought before them by litigants. The model for litigation about immigration and refugee issues was forged over the past half century by the successes achieved by groups such as the Legal Defense Fund of the National Association for the Advancement of Coloured People (NAACP). The triumph of the civil rights movement during the 1960s was achieved not only by direct action such as sit-ins and Freedom Rides, but by concerted and effective use of litigation in federal courts. This strategy was adopted following decades of failure by the political organs of the executive and legislative branches to prohibit racial segregation in the South. In effect, the civil rights movement trailblazed the strategy of political action via judicial litigation, a strategy subsequently emulated by many other political and ethnic groups.

In the sphere of immigration and refugee policy, advocates for immigrant and refugee rights in general, and for particular immigrant and refugee groups, have filed energetic legal challenges to federal and state/local laws and policies they find disagreeable. Among the most active such groups are the Mexican American Legal Defense and Education Fund (MALDEF); the Haitian Refugee Center; and the Immigration Project of the American Civil Liberties Union (ACLU). They have found ready financial support for such activities from committed philanthropic sources, including a few large foundations.

In response to such legal challenges, federal courts have intervened to mandate new procedures and to reverse legislation and administrative actions taken by the federal executive branch and by state and local governments. Such judicial decisions have transformed the handling of asylum claims; the treatment of aliens in custody; and access by illegal aliens to free public education[8] and other government services.

In many cases, key rulings have centered less on substance than on process, a result often puzzling to non-American observers who see convictions of self-confessed felons overturned on procedural grounds. Here it must be understood that "due process" is a central canon of American constitutional jurists and lawyers, in a way less commonly seen among their professional colleagues in other liberal democracies.

NUMERICAL OUTCOMES

Table 15.2 presents a tabulation of the numbers of refugees formally admitted between 1982 and 1995, by nationality. As may be seen, the overall numbers have been rising over this period, with the most recent years' admissions dominated by flows from the former Soviet Union and Vietnam.

Figure 15.1 summarizes the numbers of asylum cases filed between 1980 and 1994. Such claims have risen sharply beginning in the late 1980s, while completed adjudications have lagged, resulting in a 1995 estimated backlog of over 420 000 cases (covering perhaps 500 000–600 000 persons).

PERVERSE OUTCOMES

US Dilemmas with Temporary Safe Haven

It is undeniable that in recent years large numbers of desperate people have been deserving of temporary protection that requires safe haven outside their own countries, while combatants in civil wars contend violently, or while other forces make life temporarily unbearable. For a variety of reasons, mostly self-inflicted, the United States has proved itself incapable of providing safe haven that is genuinely temporary; this incapacity has produced the perverse outcome of a widespread reluctance to admit any such persons at all.

Among the reasons are: experience with the Temporary Protected Status (TPS) provisions of the 1990 Immigration Act, which gave Salvadorans illegally in the United States a lawful status guaranteed by its sponsors to be temporary but which has subsequently been repeatedly extended despite the end of civil war in El Salvador; judicial interventions to prevent return of asylum seekers whose claims were unsuccessful despite repeated appeals; and the inability of internal controls and deportation procedures to assure departure even of those judged by the courts to be lawfully deportable.

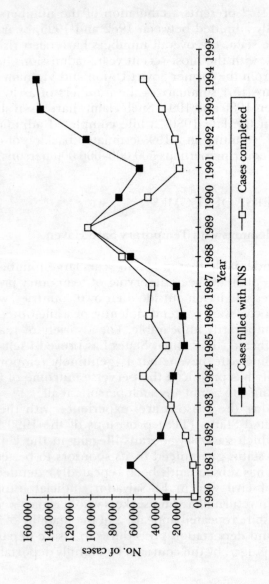

Figure 15.1 *Asylum cases filed with INS*

Table 15.2 *Refugees admitted to the United States by nationality, 1982–95*

	1982	1983	1984	1985	1986	1987	1988
East Asia	**73,822**	**39,408***	**51,960**	**49,970**	**45,454**	**40,112**	**35,015**
Burmese	0	0	0	0	0	0	0
Chinese	0	0	0	0	0	0	0
Khmer	20,234	13,115	19,851	19,087	9,789	1,538	2,805
Lao: Highlanders	2,600	738	2,753	1,944	3,668	8,307	10,388
Lao: Lowlanders	6,837	2,096	4,538	3,472	9,201	7,257	4,168
Vietnamese**	49,851	25,487	24,818	25,457	22,796	23,008	17,654
Near East/S. Asia	**6,389**	**5,465**	**5,246**	**5,994**	**5,998**	**10,107**	**8,415**
Afghans	4,800	2,926	2,128	2,234	2,535	3,220	2,211
Iranians	0	947	2,917	3,492	3,148	6,681	6,167
Iraqis	2,032	1,583	195	284	307	202	37
Libyans	0	0	0	0	0	2	0
Syrians	37	9	8	4	5	0	0
Other	0	0	0	0	3	2	0
USSR and E. Europe	**13,536**	**13,492**	**11,000**	**9,900**	**9,500**	**12,300**	**28,239**
Soviets/Former Soviets	2,758	1,409	715	840	787	3,684	20,421
Albanians	14	70	45	45	84	48	72
Bosnians	–	–	–	–	–	–	–
Bulgarians	122	140	127	130	173	114	140
Czechs	738	1,335	853	981	1,589	1,072	672
Hungarians	386	662	549	530	754	669	784

Table 15.2 *(Continued)*

	1982	1983	1984	1985	1986	1987	1988
USSR and E. Europe							
Poles	6,647	5,668	4,331	3,145	3,735	3,626	3,345
Romanians	2,871	4,003	4,371	4,513	2,373	3,075	2,801
Yugoslavs	4	5	8	6	4	2	4
Other	0	0	0	0	1	0	0
Africa							
Angolans	3,326	2,648	2,747	1,953	1,315	1,994	1,586
Angolans	120	10	81	75	3	40	13
Ethiopians	3,186	2,604	2,533	1,788	1,268	1,831	1,456
Liberians	0	0	n/a	0	n/a	0	0
Mozambicans	3	11	26	7	1	7	13
Namibians	1	2	22	12	5	3	3
Rwandans	0	0	n/a	0	n/a	1	0
Sierra Leone	0	0	n/a	0	n/a	0	0
Somalis	0	0	n/a	0	n/a	1	4
South Africans	6	9	14	29	12	70	42
Sudanese	0	0	n/a	0	n/a	0	0
Togo	0	0	2	8	12	0	0
Ugandans	0	0	35	12	4	24	31
Zairians	10	11	33	22	10	7	10
Other	0	1	33	22	10	10	16

Table 15.2 *(Continued)*

	1982	1983	1984	1985	1986	1987	1988
Latin America	**602**	**668**	**160**	**138**	**173**	**315**	**2,497**
Cubans	600	668	67	135	173	273	2,273
Haitians	0	0	0	0	0	0	0
Nicaraguans	0	0	0	3	0	36	209
Salvadorans	0	0	93	0	0	6	15
Others	2	2	0	0	0	0	0
Total	**97,355**	**61,681**	**71,113**	**68,045**	**62,440**	**64,828**	**75,754**

* Excludes 2028 of those listed below who were admitted to the United States under non-refugee status.

** Total combines Vietnamese arrivals from first asylum camps and through the Orderly Departure Program.

*** Private Sector Initiative admissions not included: 1988: 733 Cubans, 1988: 1512 Cubans, 33 Iranians; 1990: 3003 Cubans, 6 Vietnamese, 1991: 1524 Cubans, 1992: 882 Cubans, 1993: 251 Cubans.

SOURCE: Bureau of Population, Refugees, and Migration, US Department State, compiled by the US Committee for Refugees.

Table 15.2 (*Continued*)

	1989	1990	1991	1992	1993	1994	1995	Cumulative 1982–95
East Asia	45,680	51,611	53,486	51,848	49,858	43,581	36,926	668,431*
Burmese	0	3	14	55	94	75	36	277
Chinese	5	52	4	1	0	0	0	62
Khmer	1,916	2,166	38	141	22	8	1	90,720
Lao: Highlanders	8,476	5,207	6,369	6,833	6,471	6,253	3,658	73,935
Lao: Lowlanders	3,956	3,564	2,881	482	226	19	17	48,714
Vietnamese**	31,327	40,619***	44,180	44,336	42,775	37,228	33,214	456,751
Near East/S. Asia	**6,980**	**4,991**	**5,359**	**6,844**	**7,000**	**5,861**	**4,464**	**88,093**
Afghans	1,716	1,594	1,480	1,452	1,233	21	4	27,054
Iranians	5,147***	3,329	2,692	1,948	1,181	851	978	39,459
Iraqis	114	67	842	3,442	4,605	4,984	3,482	22,156
Libyans	1	1	344	1	0	3	0	352
Syrians	1	0	1	0	1	0	0	64
Other	1	0	0	0	0	2	0	8
USSR and E. Europe	**48,501**	**56,912**	**45,516**	**64,184**	**51,278**	**50,947**	**45,703**	**461,098**
Soviets/Former Soviets	39,553	50,716	38,661	61,298	48,527	43,470	35,716	348,463
Albanians	47	98	1,383	1,108	458	171	51	3,675
Bosnians	–	–	–	0	1,887	7,197	9,870	16,954
Bulgarians	111	332	585	126	34	5	3	2,142
Czechs	925	345	158	18	3	5	3	2,142
Hungarians	1,075	274	7	1	0	1	0	6,692

Table 15.2 *(Continued)*

	1989	1990	1991	1992	1993	1994	1995	Cumulative 1982–95
USSR and E. Europe								
Poles	3,607	1,491	290	134	54	31	39	36,349
Romanians	3,182	3,650	4,452	1,499	215	67	24	37,098
Yugoslavs	1	6	0	0	0	0	0	40
Other	0	0	0	0	0	0	0	1
Africa	1,922	3,494	4,424	5,491	6,968	5,556	4,779	48,508
Angolans	18	59	21	4	0	6	1	451
Ethiopians	1,767	3,229	3,948	2,972	2,765	328	239	29,914
Liberians	0	3	1	637	961	610	52	2,284
Mozambicans	4	3	12	8	0	1	0	96
Namibians	0	0	0	0	0	0	0	48
Rwandans	0	0	2	333	7	31	88	132
Sierra Leone	0	0	0	0	0	0	48	48
Somalis	44	25	192	1,570	2,753	3,555	2,506	10,850
South Africans	20	34	19	15	8	0	0	278
Sudanese	0	7	24	113	244	1,220	1,705	3,313
Togo	0	0	0	0	0	0	25	25
Ugandans	40	27	125	93	24	2	10	398
Zairians	18	79	73	76	198	92	85	712
Other	11	28	7	0	8	11	20	177

Table 15.2 *(Continued)*

	1989	1990	1991	1992	1993	1994	1995	Cumulative 1982–95
Latin America	**2,605**	**2,309**	**2,237**	**2,924**	**4,126**	**5,437**	**7,618**	**32,808**
Cubans	2,271***	1,750***	2,144***	2,867***	2,814***	2,670	8,133	24,835
Haitians	0	0	0	54	1,307	3,766	1,485	5,512
Nicaraguans	323	532	87	1	1	1	0	1,193
Salvadorans	11	22	6	2	1	0	0	150
Others	0	5	0	0	3	0	0	12
Total	105,688	119,317	111,022	131,291	119,231	112,582	99,490	1,299,937

Based upon these experiences, US policy makers in the Clinton administration and in the Congress have concluded that if the United States is to offer safe haven that is genuinely temporary, it must be off-shore: in Guantanamo naval base, Cuba; in Jamaican territorial waters; in Panama; etc. Although various immigrant rights and civil liberties groups have challenged these policies in Federal courts, they have so far been rebuffed by judgments that rights available within US territory do not apply outside – thereby lending judicial endorsement to the policy makers' conviction that truly temporary safe haven can be achieved only outside the territory of the United States.

US Financial Commitments to Refugees and Asylees

The processes by which US governments at federal, state and local levels provide financial support for refugees and asylees have also produced perverse outcomes. Any US funds to assist in the protection of the current 23 million refugees (and perhaps 30 million internally displaced persons) who are located outside the United States must be formally authorized and appropriated by Congress and disbursed by the Department of State. Such funds are therefore necessarily limited by the political process and the very real constraints of the federal budget.

Meanwhile, much of the funds used to assist the far smaller numbers of refugees and asylees within the boundaries of the United States are provided as "entitlements", meaning that whatever amounts are necessary will be provided for those who meet the criteria of economic need. Precise numbers are not available, but it seems certain that far more is being spent on fewer than one million refugees and asylees within the United States than on the 20–50 million who find themselves in similar circumstances outside US borders.

(In this the United States is hardly unique, as can be demonstrated by a simple stark example: Germany has been spending far more each year on the "entitlements" embodied in its in-country asylum system than all the world's countries have been willing to provide to the United Nations High Commissioner for Refugees, charged with providing protection to 20–50 million refugees and those in refugee-like situations.)

CONCLUSIONS

US responses to refugees and asylum seekers have been characterized by the generosity and openness of a traditional country of immigration and refuge, and by the ambivalence of an industrial country experiencing very large and rising influxes of migrants from third world countries. As a result, American policy is far from coherent.

The framing of US policies relevant to refugees and asylum is further complicated by numerous disjunctures in public opinion and in official policy. These arise in part from the complex and cross-cutting political structures of the Constitutional separation of powers and the Federal system and they are exacerbated by a high level of interest group politics.

The results have often been perverse: an incapacity to admit persons who are not refugees but in genuine need of temporary safe haven, and a disproportionate allocation of financial resources to a tiny minority of the world's refugees.

NOTES

1. There are real confusions surrounding the use of the words "refugee" and "asylum." In everyday American usage, anyone fleeing almost anything can be termed a refugee, e.g. "refugees from the floods in Missouri," or "refugees from the cutthroat world of business." However, in legal terms, American usage of "refugee" follows the internationally agreed definition, as indicated on p. 462 of this paper, while an "asylum seeker" is distinguished from a "refugee" solely by location. The refugee is outside his/her own country but not in the United States, while an "asylum seeker" is within or at the US borders. This distinction has produced some significant incentives for those unable to gain admission as refugees to travel to the United States and often to seek to enter illegally in order to claim asylum. For a fuller discussion, see Teitelbaum (1984: 74–86).
2. For a fuller discussion, see Teitelbaum (1992: 208–25).
3. See discussion in US Commission for the Study of International Migration and Cooperative Economic Development (1990).
4. For a fuller discussion, see Teitelbaum (1992: 208–25).
5. Passed 2 November 1966, United States Statutes-at-Large, vol. 80, p. 1161 (1966).
6. Jerry Tinker, personal communication, April 1984.

7. Loescher and Scanlon, *Calculated Kindness*, quoting Section 1182(d)(5), Title 8, United States Code; and House Report No. 1365, 82nd Congress, 2nd Session (1952) reprinted in 1952 US Code Congressional and Administrative News (St Paul MN: West Publishing, 1952), Vol. 2, p. 1706.

8. The 1982 Supreme Court case known as Plyler *v.* Doe declared unconstitutional a Texas state law limiting access by illegal alien children to free public education. This decision is still reverberating, most recently in the California ballot initiative known as Proposition 187, passed by a 59 to 41 percent majority, which excludes such children from publicly funded schools in California. Both proponents and opponents of this proposition agree that it will have to be resolved by the Supreme Court; a Federal Court has already imposed a temporary stay upon its implementation.

REFERENCES

Keely, Charles B. (1979), *U.S. Immigration: A Policy Analysis* (New York: The Population Council).

Loescher, Gil and Scanlan, John A. (1986), *Calculated Kindness: Refugees and America's-Half-Open Door, 1945–Present* (New York: Free Press).

Martin, Philip L. (1993), *Trade and Migration: NAFTA and Agriculture* (Washington, DC: Institute for International Economics).

Simon, Rita J. (1987), "Immigration and American Attitudes," *Public Opinion*, July/August, pp. 47–50.

Teitelbaum, Michael S. (1984), "Political asylum in theory and practice," *The Public Interest*, No. 76 (Summer), pp. 74–86.

—— (1992), "Advocacy, Ambivalence, Ambiguity: Immigration Policy and Prospects in the United States," *Proceedings of the American Philosophical Society*, 136 (2), pp. 208–25.

US Commission for the Study of International Migration and Cooperative Economic Development (1990), *Unauthorized Migration: An Economic Development Response*, Report (Washington, DC: Government Printing Office).

Index

478